Writing through Boyhood in the Long Eighteenth Century

Writing through Boyhood in the Long Eighteenth Century

Age, Gender, and Work

CHANTEL LAVOIE

NEWARK

Library of Congress Cataloging-in-Publication Data
Names: Lavoie, Chantel M., 1970- author.
Title: Writing through boyhood in the long eighteenth century : age, gender, and work / Chantel Lavoie.
Description: Newark : University of Delaware Press, 2024. | Includes bibliographical references and index.
Identifiers: LCCN 2023011178 | ISBN 9781644533192 (paperback) | ISBN 9781644533208 (hardback) | ISBN 9781644533215 (epub) | ISBN 9781644533222 (pdf)
Subjects: LCSH: Boys in literature. | English literature—18th century—History and criticism. | Literature and society—Great Britain—History—18th century.
Classification: LCC PR448.B69 L38 2024 | DDC 809.9338341—dc23/eng/20230706
LC record available at https://lccn.loc.gov/2023011178

A British Cataloging-in-Publication record for this book is available from the British Library.

Copyright © 2024 by Chantel Lavoie

All rights reserved

No part of this book may be reproduced or utilized in any form or by any means, electronic or mechanical, or by any information storage and retrieval system, without written permission from the publisher. Please contact University of Delaware Press, 200A Morris Library, 181 S. College Ave., Newark, DE 19717. The only exception to this prohibition is "fair use" as defined by U.S. copyright law.

References to internet websites (URLs) were accurate at the time of writing. Neither the author nor University of Delaware Press is responsible for URLs that may have expired or changed since the manuscript was prepared.

♾ The paper used in this publication meets the requirements of the American National Standard for Information Sciences—Permanence of Paper for Printed Library Materials, ANSI Z39.48-1992.

udpress.udel.edu

Distributed worldwide by Rutgers University Press

For Jack and Aaron
because of whom, and in spite of whom, this book was written

Boyhood: The state of being a boy; the part of life in which we are boys. This is perhaps an arbitrary word.
　　　　　—*Samuel Johnson,* A Dictionary of the English Language *(1773)*

Contents

Acknowledgments xi

Introduction: Time for Boys 1

1 The Boy in Breeches: Laurence Sterne's *Tristram Shandy* (1759–1767) Growing into Gender 16

2 The Boy in School: Ellenor Fenn's Rhetorical Tools in *School Dialogues, for Boys* (1783) 32

3 The Boy in the Machine: Pierre Jaquet-Droz's Automaton, the Writer (1774) 63

4 The Boy in the Chimney: Sweeps' Apprentices, Suffering Bodies, and Jonathan Swift 84

5 The Boy in the Gallows: Crime, Punishment, Broadsheets, Afterlives 104

6 The Boy in the Printing Press: Printer's Devils and Upward Mobility 126

Conclusion 146

Notes 151
Bibliography 197
Index 221

Acknowledgments

I am grateful for the generous reading, thoughtful feedback, and unstinting friendship of Sarah Winters, Nicholas von Maltzahn, Linda Morra, Kathryn Ready, Erika Behrisch, Susan Glover, Carol Percy, Jenny McKenney, and tom pynn.

My thanks go to colleagues at the Royal Military College of Canada, now and over the years—especially Huw Osborne, Irwin Streight, Steve Lukits, Helen Lu, Andy Belyea, Sarah Johnson, Michael Hurley, Marion McKeown, Laura Robinson, Heather Evans, Brandon Alakas, Jim Denford, Marc LaViolette, Jane Boulden, and Doug Delaney. The Canadian Defence Academy Research Programme awarded me grants that supported this research, the university provided teaching opportunities that enriched it, and the librarians at RMC as well as at the British Library, the Bodleian, and the Fisher Rare Book Library in Toronto gave me the wonderful help that only real live librarians can give. My mother Judy Lavoie flew across Canada to look after my own young boys while I travelled for much of this research. Merci, maman.

Scholars and friends in the Canadian Society for Eighteenth-Century Studies have long nurtured my interest in this period. They have taught me, listened to these chapters as conference papers in fledgling form, and asked trenchant questions. For such camaraderie I thank especially Eric Miller, Isobel Grundy, Leslie Ritchie, Isabelle Tremblay, Maria Zytaruk, Craig Patterson, Shelley King, Alison Conway, Heather Ladd, and Betty Schellenberg. I am also grateful to Julia Oestreich at University of Delaware Press, the anonymous readers who offered feedback on the manuscript, Katie Hunt, Linda Morra (again) for work on formatting, and Kevin Berland for the index.

I remain grateful to April London for sensibility, to David Carlson for print, to Frans de Bruyn for Pope, and to John Baird—whose capacious mind contains everything from *The Boyhood of Raleigh* to Cosmo Kramer's struggles with undergarments and hot tubs.

Finally, I thank my students, friends, brother, and sons—for boyhood.

Introduction

TIME FOR BOYS

In an essay he contributed to the *Philosophical Transactions of the Royal Society* of 1710, Dr. John Arbuthnot tabulated the previous eighty-two years of London christening records to prove that more males than females were born annually in the city and, presumably, beyond English shores. Such a disparity was fortunate, he argued, because "the external accidents to which males are subject (who must seek their food with danger) do make a great havock of them, and that . . . loss exceeds far that of the other sex, occasioned by dangers incident to it, as experience convinces us. To repair that loss, provident Nature, by the disposal of its wise creator, brings forth more males than females."[1] Arbuthnot's conclusion about gendered premature death is a comment on boyhood along with manhood. The argument is curious, given that all children in seventeenth- and eighteenth-century London were susceptible to illness and physical danger, and the poor were also subject to the ravages of hunger. Indeed, girls were more likely to suffer death from certain kinds of causes than boys, among these being infanticide and domestic violence, a discrepancy that remains globally today.[2] Whereas factors less providential could explain Arbuthnot's findings—including that male children might not have been born in greater numbers but merely more often christened for reasons of patrimony—the doctor's wording is telling: accidents, violence, and "great havock" create "loss" among males. In Arbuthnot's argument, males are subject to peril because they "seek their food with danger"; in other words, they strive, they move, they range from home for sustenance and livelihood. And this can shorten their lives.

This book examines how boyhood, as a subset of both childhood and masculinity, was written about in England in the long eighteenth century in texts that variously describe, prescribe, construct, and, in some cases, erase a boy. Given the dominance of maleness and manhood in every aspect of this society, it behooves us to look at how boyhood was then understood as a preparation for an adulthood that was determined in so powerful a nation. Too often boys' history is merely elided in men's history. It is contiguous to that history, but it is not the same thing. Boys—in effect, men under construction—were in eighteenth- and nineteenth-century

England a basic element in the manufacturing of the powerful public sphere, even as they were limited by their youth and either constricted or enabled by class. In lacking adult privilege, boys could be and were a subjected demographic, although some were more subjected than others. Comprehensive and varied studies of childhood have brought us closer to an understanding of youth through the early and late modern periods. These include wide-ranging books like Hugh Cunningham's *Children and Childhood in Western Society since 1500* (1995), Colin Heywood's *A History of Childhood: Children and Childhood in the West from Medieval to Modern Times* (2001), Anja Müller's *Fashioning Childhood in the Eighteenth Century: Age and Identity* (2006), Anthony Fletcher's *Gender, Sex, and Subordination in England, 1500–1800* (1995) as well as *Growing Up in England: The Experience of Childhood, 1600–1914* (2008), and Jane Humphries's *Childhood and Child Labour in the British Industrial Revolution* (2010).[3] These studies of course address gender and gender differences (often with familiar laments that girls had little or no access to education, and immeasurably fewer opportunities than boys overall).

At the same time, the emerging field of masculinity studies has given us new insights into individual lives as well as patriarchy, with important studies such as Elizabeth E. Foyster's *Manhood in Early Modern England: Honour, Sex and Marriage* (1999), Alexandra Shepherd's *Meanings of Manhood in Early Modern England* (2003), and Ruth Mazo Karras's *From Boys to Men: Formations of Masculinity in Late Medieval Europe* (2003). Another study, with a specific class focus over a long period, is Henry French and Mark Rothery's *Man's Estate: Landed Gentry Masculinities, 1660–1900* (2012). With all of this excellent work, boyhood itself nonetheless remains underexplored. Usually, a few pages here and there, or a chapter, of a longer work on masculinity is dedicated specifically to boys, with the greater concern being manhood. An important exception is Kenneth Kidd's *Making American Boys: Boyology and the Feral Tale* (2004), with a focus on the late nineteenth and early twentieth centuries in the United States.[4]

My arguments here are rooted in how boyhood is formulated in literary texts, where such formulations come from, and where they come into play within larger English culture from roughly 1700 to 1830. Work by literary scholars like Matthew Grenby in *The Child Reader, 1700–1840* (2011), Jackie Horne in *History and the Construction of the Child in Early British Children's Literature* (2011), and Andrew O'Malley in *Literary Cultures and Eighteenth-Century Childhoods* (2018) has helped scholars appreciate pedagogical, conduct, and entertaining books aimed at children, especially in the eighteenth century. In examining a variety of genres in *Writing through Boyhood*, I bring historical sources to bear to unpack assumptions that underpin the representations of boyhood in eighteenth-century novels, poetry, essays, and broadside accounts, as well as one automaton, some of which qualify as children's literature or entertainment, although many were for adults. Boys also appear in what we now call crossover genres, serving multiple readerships. As such, fictional constructions of boys targeted a wide swathe of readers (and sometimes spectators or listeners who could not read), combining the descriptive and the prescriptive. For example, texts aimed at schoolboys offered exemplary lives and cautionary tales, whereas others—like one sensationalistic story about a twelve-year-old boy condemned to death—were exclusively the latter.[5] At the same time, both kinds of texts aimed at selling themselves and at selling a particular vision of boyhood along with suggestions for how best to revise boys: improve them. The result here is a collection of representations of boyhood that touch on not only age and gender but also issues of class, labor, and time.

Defining Boyhood: When and What Is a Boy?

Time is an essential consideration of childhood, even as the early modern period does not readily admit a definition of childhood. Whereas early modernity emphasized the labor of children, the Enlightenment argued that childhood should be a time of sanctuary, competing priorities that influenced expectations of children and age parameters for work. Following early modern medical writers and practitioners, Hannah Newton's work on the sick child uses the common parameters for childhood of birth to the onset of puberty at fourteen or fifteen in her work on early modern children's sickness and health.[6] However, writing about other parts of life, Dianne Payne observes that "eighteenth-century men and women had a flexible, indeterminate concept of age and maturity of a 'child,' and this classification included 24 year-old apprentices as well as three year-old infants."[7] At the same time, in the eighteenth century a boy qualified as a child under the law until age fourteen, whereas girls were defined more variably—until age ten or twelve.[8]

Although we tend to think about childhood, even now, as a stage of life determined by one's age, this impression is problematized by those of different ages being subject to different rights and responsibilities from one context to another. For example, whether one can leave school, be tried as an adult in court, consent to sexual activity, drive a motor vehicle, drink alcohol, or join the military is dependent upon their age.[9] Cognitive science, moreover, has put forward evidence to suggest that since the brain is not fully developed until a person reaches the age of twenty-five, it is only at that point that adulthood begins—meaning that a person has then acquired the judgment to think through potential consequences of their actions.[10] Uncertainty about when and how the transformation from boy to man occurs informed even Samuel Johnson's *Dictionary of the English Language*, in which, by the 1773 edition, the definition of "boyhood" took on a qualifier: "This is perhaps an arbitrary word." This addition shows that Johnson had mulled over just what constituted boyhood, and therefore a boy, since his first, shorter definition some twenty years earlier: "The state of being a boy; the part of life in which we are boys." The addition does not clarify so much as it signals dissatisfaction with any definition. One of Johnson's definitions for the word "boy" alone is clearer (and in keeping with Hannah Newton's findings): "One in the state of adolescence; older than an infant, yet not arrived at puberty or manhood."[11] The definition provides a predictable age range; however, it also implies that a male infant is *not* a boy and either equates puberty with manhood or indicates that one or the other ends childhood.[12] At the same time, the definition does indicate that boyhood as a period of time and the boy as a person are both fleeting. Boyhood is therefore a time of transforming, unraveling, and undergoing dissolution. It is, in being, also being grown out of, the child having "not yet arrived at puberty or manhood." Ideally, then, a boy childhood disappears into that particularly revered, nonchildish thing—manhood.

"Fleeting" describes not just boyhood but childhood itself. However, the "child" has long been, and tends still unfortunately to be, normalized as male. Further, the eighteenth-century child was "often defined by context—labour practices such as the apprenticeship system, legal trials, or pedagogic manuals."[13] Given the contexts cited here, "child" again usually meant "boy" since both apprenticeship and legal trials (particularly criminal trials and convictions) had far more to do with males than females. Pedagogic manuals, moreover—notably the groundbreaking texts by John Locke and Jean-Jacques Rousseau on how best to educate children, earlier and later in the period—tended to gender the child as male. As different as Locke's *Essay on Human Understanding* (1690) and Rousseau's *Émile* (1762) were with respect to learning and discipline, both were essentially about boys.[14]

Does manhood come at a certain age, as Saint Paul would have it, when the boy "puts away childish things"? When he leaves school? When he begins to work for money, whether this is at six, sixteen, or twenty-six? Given how few boys were schooled, and how uneven schooling was, over the long eighteenth century, this qualifier splits the male population again. Even when boyhood begins might be construed as arbitrary: does the boy come into being at birth—in effect, when he is born with a phallus—or only when the infant is taken from a baby's frock and put into breeches, the sartorial sign that a child is a boy? More appropriate than Johnson's boy "in the state of adolescence," therefore, seems to be the boy's inexactness and Johnson's definition—acknowledging boyhood as "perhaps an arbitrary word," relating to "the part of life in which we are boys." The word "perhaps" can also be interpreted as touching on other issues of liminality, such as social status (even as Johnson makes clear that his audience for the *Dictionary* is male and learned, like himself, his readers were all at one point boys).

Something of this ambiguity with respect to not only age but also status appears in Samuel Johnson's third and final definition of "boy," which is idiomatic: "A word of contempt for young men, as noting their immaturity."[15] Whereas this gloss is an insult denoting the "immaturity" of young men, "boy" as "a word of contempt" might also be directed at non-young men, in that "boy" was a word that conveyed inferior socioeconomic standing or class. In fact, Eric Tribunella points out that "boy" was a pejorative for a servant or slave long before it became a common word for a male child.[16] The word continued to be used into the twentieth century as a way to denigrate men of color—particularly Black men. In this case, "boy" became an identity that a male could never grow out of. So, then, the word is a cage rather than a stage.

Historians are rightly wary of imposing twentieth-century abstract nouns on the past. For example, Elizabeth Foyster uses "manhood" in her work on the early modern period because "masculinity" was not a term employed before the mid-eighteenth century. This linguistic lacuna has interesting implications for boys.

Alexandra Shepherd notes that in the period, "apart from gender, age was the most directly acknowledged difference to inform constructions of normative manhood," yet we have seen that the age that determined manhood (and therefore delimited boyhood) was not universally agreed upon. Indeed, Shepherd's research into *Meanings of Manhood in Early Modern England* demonstrates by the plurality of her title that "full manhood" relied upon much more than age: "Besides being a qualitative set of attributes, manhood was approached in advice literature as a distinct stage in the life cycle. . . . Parenting manuals, father-son advice, sermons, and tracts on ageing approached manhood as an ideal to which young men should aspire and from which old men would decay. Manhood was thereby portrayed as the golden mean of existence, although it was also deemed a fleeting phase. Theoretically limited to a mere ten or twenty years of the life cycle it was, as a consequence, restricted to a minority of men at any one time."[17] As such, those entitled to full manhood occupy a narrower field, as manhood was itself fleeting, truncated, and uncertain. As a result, boyhood occupied a wide field indeed, with shifting, sometimes wobbly, parameters.

So, age is one problem we confront in talking about boys. Another is gender. Johnson dealt with gender simply enough in his very first definition of "boy": "A male child; not a girl."[18] This gloss combines gender and age through what the boy is, a child, and what he is not, a girl. However, talking about gender has become considerably more complicated since 1755. It is now widely understood that masculinity and femininity are constructs within a fluidity that is gender, no longer binary—an idea espoused by scholars like Judith Butler, who has argued that gender is largely performed.[19] While I use components of Butler's work where it suits my purpose, I understand that her theories are troubled especially by arguments put forth by materialist feminists like Susan Bordo and Martha Nussbaum, whose work on gender is urgent and political, focused on historical and current abuse as determined by—and carried out against—female bodies.[20]

More broadly, the ideological and scientific movement that approaches gender as fluid and that invites individuals to identify with one gender, with two, or with neither has brought a sea change to how we talk about such markers as boyhood. Anja Müller points out that "a middle way that straddles the thin line between radical constructivism and historical essentialism is hard to find."[21] To be clear, for the purposes of this book, I am employing the notion that boyhood is biological and constructed because it is treated as both in writing of the long eighteenth century. This historical position does not address those who identified as a gender other than the one biologically indicated at birth. Although it was understood that boys had "female attributes," which time and training would be expected to minimize,[22] few would have conceived of the option of identifying as "other."

Diverse voices across the long eighteenth century advanced their own theories about and uses for boys: what it meant to be born as a boy, raised as a boy, and educated as a boy, and how the boy might be useful or threatening, depending on all of the former conditions. In *Writing through Boyhood* I confine myself to the use of boys and some of the work performed by them in the long eighteenth century and how this work defined them. In using the term "boy" for the child biologically gendered male, while keeping in mind ongoing debates about gender identity, I bring the work of current gender historians to bear in close readings of texts that speak to the wider eighteenth-century perspective on boyhood, with the understanding that historical boyhood is an area of human identity for which habits, tendencies, characteristics, and dangers have been considered as readily identifiable and enduring (if evolving) over centuries. Included among the related clichés and stereotypes about boys are paradoxes: they are energetic and lazy,[23] violent and vulnerable, full of potential or potentially doomed. I strive in these chapters to study boys in a way that unites looking at boyhood as a construct and enquiring into the social reality of boys in the past, about whom we have written (and are writing) a long and winding story.

Interrogating and unpacking what has been taken as a given and showing that the category of "boy" was complex and far from monolithic, *Writing through Boyhood* complements the feminist work that has been done in thinking through the category of "woman" in the period and enriches the understanding of gender politics during the eighteenth century overall. In drawing attention to new ways of uncovering women's agency in history, Joy Damousi joins those who warn against the failure to see "masculinity and men as gendered constructions" and argues that it is necessary to "appreciate that the public sphere is defined by such considerations."[24] Judith Kegan Gardiner's *Masculinity Studies and Feminist Theory* (2002) demonstrates the importance of the relationship between the disciplines in her title. Like Gardiner, Michael Kimmel specifically strives to "make masculinity visible" since "when we study men, we study them as political leaders, military heroes, scientists, writers, artists. Men, themselves, are invisible *as men*."[25] Kimmel sees such lacunae as especially related to the often unmentioned (because reified) relationship between masculinities and violence. Issues of masculinity are therefore not separate from, but essential to, feminism. As regards early modernity, if Foyster is right that "childhood and youth were essential periods of a man's life for acquiring reason and strength, and learning how to exercise self-control and control over women," then the importance of understanding early and late-modern boyhood cannot be underestimated.[26]

Whereas in so many discussions of masculinity it is related to agency and power, here I investigate the nexus of masculinity and youth to see where this relationship holds up and where it falls apart in the long eighteenth century. As noted above masculinity studies—historical, psychological, literary, and feminist—has undergone a related surge in interest.[27] James Kim delineates some of the complexities one encounters in this field, reflecting "complex historical developments—not just in bourgeois social ascendancy and the installation of regimes of heteronormativity, but also in discourses of British nationalism ... and in the equally gradual and uneven shift from a Galenic, single-body model of the sexes to an essentialist, two-body model."[28] Further, work by diverse scholars has gone far to show how essential histories of masculinity, particularly formations of masculinity, are to understanding patriarchy itself, which, as Stephen Orgel argues, is "primarily concerned with the management of the class structure."[29] Again, it is worth understanding where boy children have fit into such management, including how they have been managed. Kim hearkens back to Natalie Zemon Davis's assertion in 1976 that historians "should not be working on the subjected sex any more than an historian of class can focus entirely on peasants."[30] This book looks at the subject of boys who were themselves sometimes privileged, and sometimes peasants, in a period when writing about children (like print itself) was undergoing tremendous growth. They were not the "subjected sex," but they were certainly still subjected to men.

Boy as Tool

Act in such a way that you treat humanity, whether in your own person or in the person of another, always at the same time as an end and never simply as a means.
—Immanuel Kant, Grounding for the Metaphysics of Morals (1785)

Familial letters written to and about boys through the eighteenth and nineteenth centuries "reveal the close link between work, industry and masculinity, the way that work defined masculinity."[31] I suggest that masculinity combined with youth encourages us to consider the historical construct of boy as a type of *tool*: a child put to use doing multiple tasks including acts of construction, maintenance, reparation, and destruction—experiences in which the boy himself participated and to which he was susceptible. Worth noting is that "tool" was also a term used for "a wretch who acts at the command of another" and for the blade of a knife, or a knife itself.[32] The first definition the *Oxford English Dictionary* (*OED*) offers for "tool" effectively equates the word with instrument: "Anything used in the manner of a tool; a thing (concrete or abstract) with which some operation is performed; a means of effecting something; an instrument."[33] However, we do not always use the words "tool" and "instrument" interchangeably, and certainly not when talking about people and what they do. Tools are wielded by others; they are objects without agency. So too are instruments. However, the latter are conceived of as having an intrinsic value and beauty that tools do not. To liken any human to a tool is, therefore, derogatory because we have the option of using the word "instrument" instead.

In Pope's "Epistle to Arbuthnot" (1735), the poet uses the word "tool" as an insult, not as a means of building something but rather as a sign of human failure—in this case, a conduit for a sort of mindless zeal. By contrast, the speaker characterizes himself as

> Not Fortune's worshipper, nor Fashion's fool,
> Lucre's madman, nor Ambition's tool,
> Not proud, nor servile; be one Poet's praise
> That, if he pleas'd, he pleas'd by manly ways.[34]

The rhyme of "fool" and "tool" was common and, as here, regularly aligned rather than contrasted the two nouns. It is clear from the above that it is not "manly" to be a tool. Swift had brought to the word the same kind of derision in a 1711 pamphlet to "set right" those who "affect to make use of that word tool, when they have a mind to be shrewd and satirical." As Swift explains it, "A tool, and an instrument, in the metaphorical sense, differ thus: the former is an engine in the hands of knaves; the latter in those of wise and honest men." Swift continued to refer to "the greatest ministers" of government as "instruments in the hands of princes, and so are princes themselves in the hands of God."[35] One who acts as an instrument, then, might be noble, even fulfilling a sacred duty. However, one who functions as a tool never could be.[36]

Whereas one does not encounter a boy described as a "tool" in the eighteenth century more often than one might a man (see below), one does find depictions throughout the period of boys being used, and for a wide variety of reasons. To this end, this book considers texts that reveal a deep interest in boys as doing things—moving their developing bodies into breeches, starting school, reading and writing, sweeping chimneys, setting type—in ways that both reify their boyhood and move them toward becoming nonboys. In the case of most, that transformation meant growing into manhood, ideally beyond being used by others through mastery of whatever skills their trade or education required of them. In the case of the chimney sweeps discussed later in the book, however, their transformation often meant not growing at all but rather dying in boyhood, either from the dangers of the work itself or from the wages of crime.

In order to better understand the variability of the boy-as-tool in the eighteenth and nineteenth centuries, a useful way of thinking about him is to draw upon the notional "space" that Paula Backscheider associates with woman: "available as fetish, trophy, trope, and symbol, woman can stand for whatever is needed."[37] A tool is not a space, of course; the former has material presence, heft, whereas the latter describes absence. Nevertheless, in combining the privilege of masculinity with lack—of experience, of agency, of authority—so too can "boy" "stand for whatever is needed." He is a stand-in, a representative of the child, the male, the target for education (academic and moral), the nation's future, the next generation of landowner, or employer, or peer, because the men currently in power will decline and expire and women are less often in these positions. At other times, in different situations and narratives, the boy is the most destitute laborer, the butt of pranks, the youngest apprentice, the criminal element, the victim of violence—fetish, trophy, trope, and symbol.

In addition to capturing the mechanization of male children through work like rote learning, chimney sweeping, and rolling ink on the letterpress, the metaphor of the tool is a valuable one with respect to broader ways in which males are depicted in contrast to females.[38] Much critical work has addressed the extent to which girls and women of certain classes were—in the eighteenth century, in particular—represented as ornamental. Kant was not alone in believing that "women have a strong inborn feeling for all that is beautiful, elegant, and decorated. Even in childhood they like to be dressed up and take pleasure when they are adorned."[39] The discourse of these "inborn" feelings, leading to a pretty, insipid uselessness, drove proto-feminists like Mary Astell and Mary Wollstonecraft to bitter complaint, as when the former asked her fellow women, "how can you be content to be in the world like tulips in a garden, to make a fine show, and be good for nothing?"[40] Issuing a backhanded compliment, Alexander Pope would later conclude that women are indeed "variegated tulips" (which Jonathan Swift infamously added are "sprung from dung").[41] Pope's sylph, Ariel, speaks with affectionate dismissal disguised as reverence in "The Rape of the Lock": "With varying vanities from every part / They shift the moving toyshop of their heart."[42] The "moving toyshop" portrays woman as automaton; there is color, movement, and beauty here, but not real, useful life. While we are accustomed to unpacking such objectification of women (and, by association, girls), their bodies, and their hearts, scholars of boyhood should consider William Morris's advice in the nineteenth century regarding aesthetics and worth: "Have nothing in your house that you do not know to be useful, or believe to be beautiful."[43] In contrast to females, who were aestheticized via tropes, boys were chiefly judged according to whether they were useful. This is not to say that the majority of girls and women did not work, nor to say that girls and women were not used—including, needless to say, for procreation and child-rearing. Indeed, one of the chief "uses" of women was to bear boys who would become men. The adult male gaze and attendant objectification of women were part of that use cycle.

Working against the enduring tropes we see perpetuated by Pope and others, Laura Mulvey argued that "woman . . . stands in patriarchal culture as signifier for the male other, bound by a symbolic order in which man can live out his phantasies and obsessions through linguistic command by imposing them on the silent image of woman still tied to her place as bearer of meaning, not maker of meaning."[44] *Writing through Boyhood* comes up against boys as "phantasies and obsessions" in representations of the symbolic order of the long eighteenth century in Britain. At the same time, it considers how the largely silent image of the boy signifies "the male other" in a particular way. This way entailed the action and movement associated with boys and men, versus the appearance associated with girls and women. More specifically, however, boys were depicted as tools—of education, of cultural and commercial expansion, of regenerative seed, and/or of menial work that denied them agency in a different way.

I depart from the ornamental focus in literature about females in order to delve into the emphases on the usefulness of and uses for the young male and to show that this grand narrative of action, too, is problematic. Equally problematic is the tradition behind John Berger's observation on gendered expectations: "Men act and women appear."[45] Already a loaded term in relation to class and ways of working or performing, to "act" as boys rather than as men makes "act" a very different verb and certainly lessens the agency we assume comes with action, even though we know that a great deal of human action is predicated upon desperation. The men to whom Berger refers act to assert themselves and to make things happen in the world. In the eighteenth century, some boys acted for assertive, agentive reasons. Most did not.

This book looks at the privileged as well as the desperate: those boys with the expectation of becoming men with agency, and those who were doomed to remain tools. Part of my argument for employing the trope of the tool in order to talk about boys hinges on a crucial point about childhood that Aparna Gollapudi identifies in Locke's political, rather than pedagogical, writings (for whom, again, the child was formulated as male). Locke's *Two Treatises of Government* (1689) lead in the eighteenth century to "interdependence of property and personhood," owning of one's self and one's labor. Gollapudi reads the novels of Daniel Defoe to show how "the liminality of children ... and their persistent reduction to an economic function indicate how the child was excluded from full personhood in a culture in which Lockean liberty and property became crucial natural rights.... Thus, in Locke's discourse of natural rights, the child—neither proprietor nor property—becomes an entity with only nebulous selfhood who occupies the margins of legitimate market relations allowed to adults."[46] With this in mind, I argue that, whether their immediate employment was to learn to read and write, to rid chimney flues of calcified and carcinogenic soot, or to run errands and mix tubs of printer's ink, boys were ciphers. They were of little value until proven useful, without individuality until distinguished by rising up through the ranks of manhood, or falling—often to death—while still a boy. Obviously, therefore, class can never be divorced from the very word "boy," nor from "contempt" for the boy, as in Johnson's third definition. Eric Tribunella posits that "boyhood has ... always constituted a kind of problem. To be a boy means to be a flawed, inchoate, or incomplete man, and boyhood involves the fundamental paradox between the privileges of maleness and the subaltern of youth, class or race."[47] Each of the categories of the son or servant or even slave, of the male whose manhood is incomplete, contrasts with the privilege inherent in having a combination of the right gender, the right age, the right race, and the right class.

Thinking about boys as tools is especially appropriate for interrogating their place in the eighteenth century, a period of intense cultural concentration and expansion, when museums and libraries and gardens and cabinets of curiosities reflected questions about what the earth yielded and what might be made out of its materials. Behind these questions were others, bolstered by colonialism, regarding what might be made by and, in certain ways, out of the earth's people. With respect to practical objects, this interest in making is of particular concern in Denis Diderot's grand taxonomic project, *L'Encyclopédie* (1751–1772). Diderot believed "it would be desirable for the government to authorize people to go into the factories and shops, to see the craftsmen at their work, to question them, to draw the tools, the machines, and even the premises."[48] Scholars studying the laboring classes have illustrated the importance that encyclopedic endeavors placed on the trades, in part because fewer people were able to make and mend objects in an increasingly specialized and commercialized Europe.[49]

Records of labor and blueprints for how to make things were also attributable to a new sense of posterity and an odd interplay of self-reliance and commerce, at which point the ultimate boy book, *Robinson Crusoe*, is usually invoked. Indeed, as Seth Lerer notes of Defoe into the nineteenth century, "Central to the popularity of Crusoe is play: the use of tools, the world of things behind the novel. A good part of that world emerged from the Lockean landscape of impressions and particulars."[50] However, Peter Walmsley draws our attention to the fact that scholarship "has focused almost exclusively on one side of the nexus of production—on commodities in the market rather than on the bodies that made them."[51] Although I do not address manufacturing (factory or cottage) work in *Writing through Boyhood*, the lacuna Walmsley points out is in part why boys' bodies play a key role here: while the title of each chapter refers to the metaphorical significance of the boy "in" something—breeches to signal manhood; school; an automaton in the form of a boy; the chimney sweep trade; prison; the printing press—each is also about the boy's body both physically in a given space and conceptually in the public imagination.[52]

What of boys? And in whose hands are they? Bill Brown's argument about our relationship to things, for which "identity depends less on authorized value and function, more on recognition and use,"[53] describes an association not that far from the historical relationship between society and boys. Scholars have paid attention to how "it" narratives of the long eighteenth century reveal both conspicuous consumption and commodification of people.[54] Ways in which the personhood of a boy was forfeited for use, and indeed how some boys were used up, sacrificed for others as means to an end, also lead me to address boys as usefully abject (another word commonly associated with females). The Bible abounds with the sacrifice of boys: to prove a patriarch's devotion to God (and so Abraham binds his son), to prevent the rising up of an army against a pharaoh (the infant boy slaves are killed). These typologies were deeply entrenched in most eighteenth-century readers' understanding of the world. Boys are a particular kind of currency, both valuable and expendable—valuable because of gender, expendable because of youth. As such, a boy's story might run the gamut from trivial to tragic.

One enduring multivolume work, Joseph Moxon's *Mechanick Exercises; or, The Doctrine of Handy-works* (1677–1783), employs rhetoric that at once humbles and elevates the human body in stating "it is Rational to think, that the Mechanicks began with Man, he being the only Creature that Nature has imposed most Necessity upon to use it, endow'd with greatest Reason to contrive it, and adapted with properest Members (as Instruments) to perform it."[55] Whereas Moxon means prehensile fingers and opposable thumbs here, society as a construct also has been made up of those in power, allowed to exercise their reason, and others—"properest Members (as Instruments)"—to carry out the work. The latter have been the laboring classes and, within the male world, boys. Boys' bodies are important in *Writing through Boyhood* in their provision of a partial response in this book to what John Stephens identifies as the inadequate attention paid to how "patriarchal ideology structured representations of male bodies and behaviours."[56] Thinking about such representations in combination with ideas about gender performance, Susan Bordo asks, "If the body is treated as pure text, subversive, destabilizing elements can be emphasized and freedom and self-determination celebrated; but one is left wondering, is there a body in this text?"[57] Together with a consideration of how labor contributed to the various losses "occasioned by dangers incident to" the male sex of which John Arbuthnot wrote, I show how not all male bodies have been represented as being equal or treated that way in fact.

These are some of the issues I consider in this book, as I explore how boys in eighteenth- and early nineteenth-century England were perceived with respect to their utility, their value, and their cost. That being said, the book is not a study of labor laws or apprenticeship practices, nor do I mine all that has been written on eighteenth-century pedagogy for schoolboys, male juvenile delinquency, or the success of some boys in the printing press, from lowly "devil" to master printer. Rather, I offer case studies that explore how boyhood was constructed in different creative spaces that reflected boys' lived experience. Subjected to a variety of tasks, expectations, and objectifications, boys—real, imagined, or a bit of both—were tools in supporting and maintaining the constructs (and edifices) of civil society, commerce, and empire. In books of poetry and dialogues about or for boys, activist writing on behalf of the most destitute among them, complaints about beggars and thieves, and biographies of criminals or of successful entrepreneurs, boys can be read as objects that either contributed to or undermined the civilization their elders were in the midst of shaping.

Cleaning, or building, or growing things, or preparing through education to contribute to his family by taking on or beginning a family business, and carrying on a family name, a boy in the long eighteenth century was first and foremost useful. Then again, he could be a dangerous tool, susceptible to bad influence and injurious to others, belonging to the demographic most associated with mischief, from lively and energetic to thieving and even murderous. All of these functions, productive or detrimental, depended—like boyhood itself—on the combined presence of that vulnerable, potent tool, "the male generative organ,"[58] and that other vulnerable, potent thing, youth.

Writing through Boyhood simultaneously comprehends two kinds of structure. The first loosely follows a boy's chronological life, from birth to either death or manhood. The second divides the book into three sections: (1) privilege, (2) penury and punishment, and, at the end, (3) progress. In the first, the imaginary boy's life begins with being breeched and moves to him going away to school, learning to get along with others, to read and write, and to know his duty, and then entering into the workforce as a graduation into adulthood. This fictional boy represents those who were privileged in the eighteenth century. The middle section of the book addresses working boys, the most destitute and hopeless who began work far too young, even at a time when child labor was the norm. Chimney sweeps' apprentices, for instance, were without education, most were without prospects and without health. Many of these desperate boys, particularly the criminalized boy in the penultimate chapter, did not live to manhood. These depictions of boyhood in the center of the book speak to the penury and punishment of boys. The final, more historical and hopeful, chapter is about older apprentices who worked in the print industry, and there we find progress, as these apprentices were generally more privileged and healthier than most boy apprentices and more likely to become successful men—and to become men at all.

The first chapter here is about the point at which a boy went from wearing a frock or "petticoats" to breeches and, in a sense, became a boy. "In the eighteenth century," Dianne Payne notes, "upper and middle-class children increasingly enjoyed a period of 'childhood,' typified by long-term schooling, distinctive dress, toys and children's literature, but children in the poor communities were unlikely to experience this distinct phase."[59] The "distinctive dress" of boyhood involved sartorial transition, the timing of which was most contingent upon class, in terms of either when the boy went to school (for which he had to be in breeches) or when he entered the workforce. In this light, I consider breeches in Laurence Sterne's *Tristram Shandy* (1759–1767), particularly for the boy Tristram, although breeches are an issue for both generations of his family. Again, the penis is a tool that must be mastered by the boy (in toilet training to move on from wearing nappies, for instance), which in turn conflates nature and artifice. Confined to males and a frequent cause of discomfort, this organ with which the boy is born could prove (pro)creative, dangerously destructive, or both. The function of the boy qua boy here is biological, yet Sterne's novel hints at how complex that biology is and what social and cultural implications are entangled in the ritual of breeching because of it. As this chapter considers a ritual associated with beginning life as a boy, the discussion of Sterne begins our discussion of boyhood.

From breeching to school-going, the next chapter moves to a reading of Ellenor Fenn's *School Dialogues, for Boys* (1783), the first schoolboy story in English.[60] In Fenn's book, six-year-old Sprightly has just arrived at the homosocial world of a boarding school, where he encounters challenges to the values instilled in him at home, especially by his mother. While his fellow pupils, good and bad, and his schoolmasters are male, Fenn calls these characters her "puppets" and her "phantoms." They are tropes, rhetorical tools serving to legitimize and empower her, even as she warns the schoolboy reader about the pitfalls and snares that await him. I consider both the warnings Fenn gives the boy reader and those she gives that boy's mother, veiled as some of these are, along with the usefulness of the figure of the schoolboy to the woman writer.

Boyhood in the third chapter appears in a discussion of a remarkable automaton built circa 1774. The Writer (*L'écrivain*) was a machine in the form of a boy, the purpose of which was to impress audiences and enrich its inventor, Swiss watchmaker Pierre Jaquet-Droz. The automaton functioned both as a spectacle and as an advertisement for pocket watches and other clockwork. The little "Writer" also embodied the idealized European boyhood of a class meant to read, write, and lead, and simultaneously embodied the precept that "children should be seen and not heard." The imaginary boyhood of the machine would have conveyed a great deal to spectators who watched the exotic miniature boy use inkstand and quill pen, his eyes seeming to scan the parchment. How eighteenth-century proponents of their time as one of enlightenment fetishized some boyhood is evident in both the youth and the gender with which this machine was vested—the garments and flesh of privilege.

From material perfection to fleshly abjection, the fourth chapter shifts focus to the impoverished chimney sweep's apprentice who was associated with the waste he hauled out of homes, then later in the period became the subject of pseudo-abolitionist activism. Given the labor conditions imposed upon indigent "climbing boys," I take a fresh look at Swift's satiric essay *Meditation upon a Broomstick* (1703) by applying it to the condition of the boy whose labor conflates the child with the tools of his trade. Together with his other writings, Swift's essay about "mortal man," worn down and ultimately "rendered into kindling," offers a way into understanding the conspicuous ambivalence with which these boys were depicted across a range of literary genres, including William Blake's depiction of them as "Little Black Boy[s]." As such, I also consider the deployment of racialized discourses later in the era to provide another illustration of intersecting systems of oppression regarding boyhood.

The boy in the fifth chapter is a twelve-year-old criminal, formerly at Newgate Prison and since condemned to the gallows.[61] His story appeared in an early nineteenth-century broadside publication (likely with an earlier provenance), linking gender and age with labor and violence in the "Dreadful Life and Confession of a Boy." As Arbuthnot hints in warning about the "havock" to which males "(who must seek their food with danger)" were exposed, boys were both more likely to commit crimes than girls and more likely to receive severe punishment, including whipping, transportation, and execution. As a result, official and more informal reports about criminal activity, as well as laws themselves, reflected attitudes toward poor boys and apprentices that assumed them to be both criminally inclined and likely to reoffend. This threat to society is exemplified in the young boy we see in the broadside, who begins as a chimney sweep, falls into bad company, and becomes a tool of hardened criminals—a familiar trope, as is his death at the end of a rope. As a reminder of state authority and a tool of the sensational press, this boy's short life and death are deadly useful.

The boy at the end of the book is another who is caught up in the world of ink, paper, and the press. This is a less literary, more historical chapter, and it moves well into the transatlantic nineteenth century to explore a happier apprenticeship story—that of the "printer's devil." Although boys who ran errands and carried out other menial tasks at the printing press were, like chimney sweeps, also besmeared and sullied by their work, the success stories of men who began as "printer's devils" reinforce the relationship inferred between machinery, masculinity, and, in this case, progress for boys. Not surprisingly, surplus "boy labor" in different countries led to widespread complaints about yet another "boy problem" in this business, with male laborers resentful of cheaper, untrained workers in the press. With all the ambivalence implied in the moniker, the young "printer's devil" nevertheless had the potential to rise in a trade that relied upon and promoted literacy. The press also offered some hope that, however stained he was by ink, this boy could master the tools of his trade, rather than being merely a tool himself.

Together, these chapters on breeching, education, writing, dangerous manual labor, criminality, and, finally, work in the printing press that offered real opportunity for advancement explore boyhood in all its variability in the long eighteenth century. The representations of boys in literature, art, medical texts, the law, and the press all commented on the livelihood of young males as well as their lives, each echoing Arbuthnot's observation that "external accidents to which males are subject (who must seek their food with danger) do make a great havock of them,"[62] while at the same time cautioning that boys themselves, if not sufficiently managed and constrained, were apt to "make a great havock" in the world. Such accounts of boys argue that the fates not only of individual children but also of England and its empire were determined by age, gender, and work.

CHAPTER 1

The Boy in Breeches

LAURENCE STERNE'S *TRISTRAM SHANDY* (1759–1767)
GROWING INTO GENDER

Tool 2 (b) A bodily organ; spec. *the male generative organ (or* pl. *organs).*
—Oxford English Dictionary

Regardless of biological gender, babies and toddlers wore frocks in the eighteenth century—that is, clothing longer than the body and reaching below the feet. In an era when clothing was comparatively more costly than now, when a male infant was put into breeches might occur at any time from the age of three but could happen much later, as a frock provided room for physical growth and so could be worn longer.[1] Completion of toilet training being a significant consideration, the responsibility for the shift in clothing tended to rest with the child's mother. Whether and when a boy began work—which for poorer children was earlier than seven—or began school, which was usually around that age, largely determined the decision to breech.

Yet the move into breeches signaled a great deal more than physical development. It also signaled boyhood that had previously been rendered ambiguous by the child's frock (or skirts); it appeared to *turn* the child into a boy, thereby indicating new performative demands of him. Every boy, regardless of class, was therefore put into breeches as an indicator of both age and gender. The rite that Anthony Fletcher calls "symbolic of the first step on the road to manhood" calls attention to bodily difference, particularly to the regenerative function of the phallus, the boy's tool, and the metonymic possibilities of the boy himself as reduced to the phallus.[2]

The transformative power of breeches as well as their potential to conceal and to reveal are preoccupations evident in Laurence Sterne's *Life and Opinions of Tristram Shandy, Gentleman* (1759), a novel wherein this garment causes no end of confusion.[3] Paterfamilias Walter Shandy is unable to speak his son's name at the boy's christening because he, Walter, cannot get his breeches on in time (229). The nature of Tristram's Uncle Toby's wound to the groin is hidden by his breeches, then his wooing of the Widow Wadman is hindered by his trying to fit into old breeches (and again when his brother Walter has an antaphrodisiac, "camphorated cerecloth," sewn into Toby's new breeches to prevent intimacy with the widow [360]). Mrs. Shandy does not accompany her family on the grand tour ostensibly because she is knitting Tristram's father a "pair of large worsted breeches" (411). Then there is the character named in only one anecdote who suffers when a roasted chestnut falls "perpendicularly into that particular aperture of Phutatorius's breeches, for which, to the shame and indelicacy of our language be it spoke, there is no chaste word throughout all *Johnson's Dictionary*" (256).[4] Tristram's own breeches are an endless source of past and present shame as he writes the purported autobiography. His father, when addressing his brother on courtship, advises, Polonius-like, "Let not thy breeches be too tight, or hang too loose about thy thighs, like the trunk-hose of our ancestors.—A just medium prevents all conclusions" (477). Evidently, "the apparel oft proclaims the man"—as Polonius did in fact advise Laertes. Both Walter's and Polonius's statements are loaded with implications about wealth and thrift, character and care, and, in a more fundamental way, maleness and masculinity.

Historians have examined the ritual of breeching for good reason. Here, I consider the gendered practice in order to interrogate debates about how boys in the eighteenth century (like Tristram) were taken out of frocks or "nursery skirts" and put into breeches and about why this ritual for constructing gender through clothing matters. Looking at the eighteenth-century discourse about breeching outside of Sterne's text alongside current scholarship reveals that—despite how unusual the Shandy family is—their preoccupation with the boy's breeches is not as singular as one might think. It is because of such practices that Philippe Ariès identifies a boy as "the first specialized child."[5]

Whereas much research has been done on breeches and breeching among historians of clothing as well as by critics of early modern portraiture and theater, less critical engagement has been brought to bear on the practice of breeching in eighteenth-century literature. Cynthia Wall's significant reading of the role that clothing plays in constructing identity in novels such as *Pamela* and *Clarissa* focuses for the most part on women.[6] Similarly, the wearing of breeches tends to be considered more in terms of women's parts in the theater (as with Patricia Fara's book on science, *Pandora's Breeches*);[7] therefore, we often talk about the wearing of breeches as transgressive.[8] We are doubtless invited to do so: a search for the word "breeches" on Eighteenth-Century Collections Online (ECCO) yields myriad references to women.[9] Yet breeches were first and foremost important to the lives of the males who wore them.[10] Variously metonymic, the word (and the garment) "breeches," so often signaling a man as opposed to a woman, also stands for a boy as opposed to an infant or a toddler.[11] Breeching, a rite of passage inevitable for every boy, was an irrevocable ritual that demonstrated—and thereby enacted—the signs of approaching both adulthood and masculinity.

Referring to an "anxiety" of masculinity in the early modern period, Mark Breitenberg asserts that the problem of gender performance is "more acute in a culture where performance and theatricality are built into everyday life": "Paradoxically, apparel and language—both mutable and manipulable semiotic systems—are often the media in which 'natural' differences are supposed to find accurate representation."[12] While Breitenberg is referring to cross-dressing in the Restoration, Terry Castle points out that "the eighteenth century perceived a deep correspondence" between clothing and language: "Not only was language the 'dress' of thought—that lucid covering in which the mind decorously clothed its ideas—but clothing was itself a kind of discourse. . . . It reinscribed a person's sex, rank, age, occupation—all the distinctive features of the self."[13] The quadrumvirate "sex, rank, age, occupation" signaled a person's value as well as their function in society. Sterne's novel testifies to, even as it mourns, the powerful social valence of clothing because it is far-reaching. Although it is to a jerkin that Sterne overtly refers when Tristram asserts "a man cannot dress, but his ideas get cloath'd at the same time" (506), we see that breeches are the most common and problematic garment in that novel—as they no doubt were in reality. Putting a boy into breeches called forth disparate responses involving celebration and lament, for the taking on of one role was the leaving off of another. Unlike the role-play of masquerade, however, breeching was for life.

Such finality is evident in the protracted and ineffectual discussion between Tristram's mother and father about putting their hitherto frocked adolescent son into breeches. His parents' tortured conversation not only testifies to a fascinating morass of individual and collective Shandean eccentricities but also speaks to larger debates about child-rearing. They are worried about the conclusiveness of the decision, about its irrevocable nature.

Mr. Shandy does not even propose the act directly; instead, he says to his wife, "We should begin to think, Mrs. Shandy, of putting this boy into breeches":

> We should do so,—said my mother.—We defer it, my dear, quoth my father, shamefully.—
> I think we do, Mr. Shandy,—said my mother.
> —Not but the child looks extremely well, said my father, in his vests and tunicks.—
> —He does look very well in them,—replied my mother.—
> —And for that reason it would be almost a sin, added my father, to take him out of 'em.—
> —It would so, said my mother:—But indeed he is growing a very tall lad,—rejoin'd my father. (351)

While the wording "almost a sin" undoubtedly refutes original sin, this is not dwelt upon. Instead, there follow hints to which the reader has grown accustomed about the ambiguity of who sired this tall lad, with Mr. Shandy venturing to say, "I am very short myself." (The question of paternity hovers in the air with Mrs. Shandy's "I cannot conceive, for my life.") Ambivalence about the sartorial project itself dominates, with Mr. Shandy fretting,

> —When he gets these breeches made . . . he'll look like a beast in 'em.
> He will be very aukward in them at first, replied my mother.
> —And 'twill be lucky, if that's the worst on't, added my father.

> It will be very lucky, answered my mother.
> I suppose, replied my father,—making some pause first—he'll be exactly like other people's children.—
> Exactly, said my mother.—
> —Though I should be sorry for that, added my father: and so the debate stopped again. (352)

As noted, this debate occurs when Tristram is older than he should be (another recurring theme in the novel) and contains much that is unsaid, including unease about what others think of the damage done to Tristram's penis at the age of five by the infamous fallen window, although he claims he "did not lose two drops of blood by it" (287).[14]

In his quest for the perfect breeches for his son, Walter consults an ancient Roman text by the philosopher Albertus Rubenus, *De Re Vestiaria Veterum*, and there unsurprisingly finds no reference to breeches whatsoever—a reminder of the modernity of this invention and evolving conventions, and therefore a reminder of the absurdity of modern life.[15] Walter decides, eventually, after exhaustive worry about materials and closures, to order "with hooks and eyes" the "breeches to be made" (355). It is particularly curious, and not a little telling, that Walter fears his son will look "like a beast" in his breeches. This phrase suggests that not even Tristram's breeches can uphold the distinction, encompassed by clothing, between civilized and uncivilized life. Further, the breeches seem no mere marker of identity but a creator thereof. As such they are fraught with difficulties.[16]

Jonathan Lamb sees Walter's "hopeless symbolism of putting his damaged child into breeches" as following upon his "impatience with the accidental ambiguity of the conception."[17] Both the sign of putting the child into breeches and the anxiety about conception have to do with a phallus, and so signal more universal concerns about the male body.[18] Whereas Tristram is an unreliable narrator, and his family is eminently odd, medical treatises of the eighteenth century, as well as other types of texts directed at adults, lend gravitas to what might otherwise be read as merely Shandean eccentricity. In one such polemic, *On Clothing* (1797), Manchester printer George Nicholson expresses doubts about "the future secretion of the seed" of small boys constrained by breeches. "Every avenue of the beneficent air to the testicles is shut up," Nicholson laments, when

> a boy must be hardly three years old but he must be a man, he must wear breeches. In his frock the boy was easy, and free to jump and gambol at his pleasure; in his breeches he is, 1. Pent up and shackled, and by way of compensation his mind is stuffed with opinion and folly. He bears the burden of his breeches without a murmur, because he is taught to believe his breeches fine, honourable, and manly, 2. During the first and second year the boy can neither button nor unbutton his breeches, and he is continually in a sad condition, 3. To make water he must pull and strain his *little pipe* to get clear of his breeches, for a year and more he is unable to perform this operation himself, children, maids, and valets, lend their assistance in pulling and playing with his private parts.[19]

This sounds fairly serious as well as provoking. Linking the garment also to "ruptures" (hernias or perhaps burst bladders), Nicholson pleads, "Away then with the breeches of children!"[20] The garment that at first "he can neither button nor unbutton" seems like a machine the small boy lacks manual dexterity to operate. Added to this, the "little pipe" he must "get clear of his breeches" is a tool, the function of which is paradoxically compromised by the trappings of *sartorial* boyhood. Further, the sardonic "compensation" of seemingly unsuitable education that Nicholson derides as "opinion and folly" suggests other—and premature—manipulation of the boy's *mind*. Last, others "pulling and playing with his private parts" might confuse the child, put him at risk of sexual interference, possibly influence his future conduct with his own and others' private parts, and, by implication, endanger his soul.

Children's Literature

In contrast to Nicholson's warnings, allusions to breeching in literature written for children and directed at boys themselves were predominantly positive. As Donelle R. Ruwe points out, poems for children "invariably" associated going into breeches with "a boy's advancement into greater learning and maturity."[21] In Anna Laetitia Barbauld's dialogic *Lessons for Children, from Two to Three Years Old* "written for a particular child" (1778–1779),[22] the speaker asks little Charles a question about clothing that receives an answer appropriate to his age: "What has Charles got to keep him warm? / Charles has got a frock and warm petticoats."[23] Following this answer is a catalogue of what other creatures have to keep them warm—sheep have wool, birds have feathers—followed by the shelters of some—wolves have their dens, bees have their hives—after which the speaker asks Charles,

> Can you climb a tree?
> No.
> But you must learn then.
> As soon as you have breeches you must learn to climb trees.
> Ask puss to teach you; she can climb.[24]

The adult speaker then transitions to an admonishment of the cat, arguing that "Puss" should not kill birds and lamenting at the sight of "two or three feathers on the ground all bloody. Poor sparrow."[25] Clearly, the boy in breeches has the capacity to climb like Puss, but with new freedom comes new responsibility to be less like an animal.

Charles and Mary Lamb make a similar argument in the celebratory poem—attributed to Charles—titled "Going into Breeches."[26] Now that "the childish season is gone," the speaker explains, "little Philip" may rejoice, for he has eschewed

> Sashes, frocks, to those that need 'em—
> Philip's limbs have got their freedom—

> He can run, or he can ride,
> And do twenty things beside,
> Which his petticoats forbad:
> Is he not a happy lad?[27]

This statement of apparent fact contains imperatives, too, whereby, as Ruwe argues, "the unity of the nursery is broken by gender differentiations of culture":[28]

> Now he's under other banners,
> He must leave his former manners;
> Bid adieu to female games,
> And forget their very names,
> Puss-in-corners, hide-and-seek,
> Sports for girls and punies weak![29]

That the boy is "under other banners" is a military image, bringing in loyalty to one side (team, country, gender) as opposed to another. We might read the forgetting of the "very names" of games that are fit only for "girls and punies" as deeply unfortunate, if not surprising; it is as though celebrating new possibilities and privileges cannot occur without scorning those who are excluded from them.

> Instead of being bound within that effeminate sphere, little Philip can now
> Show his skill and strength at Cricket,
> Mark his distance, pitch his wicket,
> Run about in winter's snow
> Till his cheeks and fingers glow,
> Climb a tree, or scale a wall,
> Without any fear to fall.[30]

Breeches allow the boy liberty to enjoy himself more—to move about and to prove himself. As in Barbauld's poem, this boy can now climb. Should he fall while climbing, however, further expectations arise:

> If he get a hurt or bruise,
> To complain he must refuse
> Though the anguish and the smart
> Go unto his little heart.
> He must have his courage ready,
> Keep his voice and visage steady,
> Brace his eye-balls stiff as drum,
> That a tear may never come,
> And his grief must only speak
> From the colour in his cheek.
> This and more he must endure,
> Hero he in miniature!

> This and more must now be done
> Now the breeches are put on.[31]

With the privilege of climbing that the poem describes come both fearlessness and the duty not to cry. Yet the tree climbing itself, a boyish activity, will not carry on into manhood. The not crying, however, must be a permanent part of his life. He seems to owe this to the breeches. Boyhood then is concomitant with manhood such that the time of the boy's life itself is telescoped, the boy himself insistently temporary and in a state of flux. Arguably, in more fully becoming a boy he both picks up childish things (like climbing) and puts away childish things (like weeping), hence becoming a little man.

This act of becoming is already present in the poem's opening, where now with "manly breeches on" the boy rehearses stages of manhood while he—touchingly—experiences rational pride as yet untainted by sin:

> Officer on gay parade,
> Red-coat in his first cockade,
> Bridegroom in his wedding trim,
> Birthday beau surpassing him,
> Never did with conscious gait
> Strut about in half the state,
> Or the pride (yet free from sin)
> Of my little Manikin:
> Never was there pride, or bliss,
> Half so rational as his.[32]

And so breeches mark a beginning, when the boy ("manikin" here used as little man) steps over a threshold to many new experiences. Even as reflections on boyhood celebrate that state of male life, they emphasize its transitory nature. Moreover, the soldierly description of the no longer frocked boy being like an "officer on gay parade, / Red-coat in his first cockade" imposes the implication of a uniform onto the breeches, the boy owing loyalty to the powers that command him. As such, he becomes at once more independent, and more obliged to obey those powers: a tool perhaps of the state. Yet another common use of the word "boy" is "a junior military rank in various forces; a person of this rank."[33] Indeed, John Locke had emphasized the importance of military readiness in his advice about child-rearing: "a Gentleman, in any age, ought to be so bred as to be fitted to bear arms and be a soldier."[34] The boy in Lamb's "Going into Breeches" is approaching the age of reason; however, the phrase "yet free from sin" shows the short duration of this stage of life in real time, for innocence will be lost.

As noted above, Eric Tribunella argues "boyhood has always constituted a kind of problem. To be a boy means to be a flawed, inchoate, or incomplete man."[35] In significant ways, boys are liminal. Moreover, we can see the multifarious problem of *boy* indicated even in those three definitions provided by Samuel Johnson in the *Dictionary*.

Boy. n.s. [bub. Germ. the etymology is not agreed on.]
1. A male child; not a girl.
2. One in the state of adolescence; older than an infant, yet not arrived at puberty or manhood.
3. A word of contempt for young men, as noting their immaturity.[36]

Whereas patriarchy determines preference for "boy" over "girl," the word "boy" still implies "contempt" determined by "immaturity." This is because patriarchy privileges man over boy; it is therefore more important for a boy to become a man than for a girl to become a woman (the word "girl" Johnson does not define at all). Although girls' frocks, fripperies, and undergarments did change as they grew older—and much is deservedly made of the impact of corseting in(ter)ventions and the female body—girls were not breeched.[37] For boys, breeching was a more visible sartorial sign of crossing a threshold, a split from the recent babyish past.

Breeches mark a before and an after, a then and a now (as with Charles Lamb's last line: "Now the breeches are put on!"). Yet, as I have noted, not all boys were breeched at the same age, which might contribute to how symbolic the change becomes in discourses about reaching maturity. In advising against indulging young children, Locke drew the same kind of firm distinction regarding apparel and all that it implied: "For he that hath been us'd to have his will in every thing, as long as he was in coats, why should we think it strange, that he should desire it, and contend for it still, when he is in breeches?"[38] Sterne, who also engages with Locke's *Essay Concerning Human Understanding* throughout *Tristram Shandy*, wonders how we came by "—the ideas of time and space—or how we came by those ideas,—or of what stuff they were made,—or whether they were born with us,—or whether we pick'd them up afterwards as we went along,—or whether we did it in frocks,—or not till we had got into breeches" (150). Here the wearing of breeches as opposed to frocks implies manhood itself; frocks, boyhood.

Proud papa Samuel Taylor Coleridge spoke in the same vein as his friend Charles Lamb, with and about joy regarding breeching as a rite of passage, in a letter about his son to Robert Southey: "Hartley was breeched last Sunday—& looks far better than in his petticoats. He ran to & fro in a sort of dance to the Jingle of the Load of Money, that had been put in his breeches pockets; but he did [not] roll & tumble over and over in his old joyous way—No! it was an eager & solemn gladness, as if he felt it to be an awful aera [sic] in his Life. O bless him! bless him! bless him!"[39] There is solemnity in this paternal expression of love, where we see again a new, in some ways constricted attitude toward play (although the "sort of dance" is charming). It is also fascinating that part of this change of behavior is due to the boy having coins in his pocket. A similar yet more necessary reason for gratitude about pockets in breeches comes about in Daniel Defoe's 1722 novel, *Colonel Jack*, when the indigent pocket-picking child narrator finds a pair of breeches and can thereby hide his ill-gotten gains from others: "I Was but a Boy 'tis true, but I thought myself a Man now I had got a Pocket to put my Money in."[40] Breeches, literally as well as figuratively, constitute a great divide.

Ambivalent Breeching

Despite the note of celebration in Coleridge's letter, we cannot forget that ambivalence characterizes references to putting a boy into breeches, evoking the discomfort that Nicholson in his medical treatise alluded to with "ruptures" and "distempers." Earlier in the century Irish poet Mary Barber put words of unequivocal complaint in the mouth of her eldest son in "At His First Putting on Breeches." Possibly related to becoming a schoolboy, since it catalogues the sartorial indignities to which the growing boy is introduced, the poem begins by setting the wishes of boys against those of their mothers:

> WHAT is it our Mammas bewitches,
> To plague us little Boys with Breeches?
> To Tyrant Custom we must yield,
> Whilst vanquish'd Reason flies the field.[41]

Breeches are the beginning of a whole wardrobe of discomforts for this boy. The speaker also complains of shoes, hatbands, cravats, and other unnatural contrivances, due to "Custom . . . The only Monarch All obey."[42] That "Reason flies the field" in Barber's poem, just as the boy has presumably reached the age of school and the age commonly referred to as the age of reason—seven years old—is poignant. When we consider that another poem by Barber written on behalf of her son is a fearful one about his schoolmaster "bringing in the rod," it is worth recalling that "to breech" had also long been synonymous with "to whip."[43]

The fear of complicated "tightness"—determined somewhat by changing fashions in breeches themselves—counters the argument that breeches bring freedom and troubles the kind of binary of privilege described by Donelle Ruwe: "Both boys and girls are given new clothes as they outgrow the nursery, but only boys are allowed to move beyond skirts into the greater freedom of breeches."[44] But this greater freedom was evidently vexed. I have noted that breeches on women are seen as transgressive, representing at least in theory playfulness, or fetishism, or freedom—as creating spaces within and between gender expectations. It is both paradoxical and reasonable that frocks on little boys allow for playfulness and freedom as well, as suggested in Barber's son's complaint about the tight shoes and cravats that the big boy puts on in symbolically casting aside his littler self.

Appeals to avoid breeches—like that put in the mouth of Barber's son—suggest a longing to prolong babyhood, as frocks underscore an expectation of more protection—and surveillance—by the adult world for anyone not (or not yet) in breeches. Elsewhere, the choice to linger within a frocked life for boys invites other anxious responses, which configure the frock chiefly as a symbol of the relationship between boys and women. In Sterne's novel, for instance, not long before the Shandys' discussion about breeching, Tristram's father had opined, "'Tis high time . . . to take this young creature out of these women's hands, and put him into those of a private governor" (332). Ruth Mazo Karras notes, "In some cultures, when a man thinks of being a man, he thinks of not being womanish; in others, however, he may think first of not being childish."[45] In the culture addressed here, as Anthony Fletcher notes, "a key issue for the parents of boys was achieving an upbringing that guarded against effeminacy, slippage, that is, into the weakness, softness, and delicacy of womankind."[46] Walter's disquiet about his son indicates that distance from both women and childish things must occur in order for his son to become a man; at the same time, the neuter/neutral value of the word "creature" gestures toward his son being not entirely human (perhaps yet more of a beast).

That this life change for males was seen at least in part as a dilemma is also evident in visual culture. Portraits of unbreeched boys, often in lace and sashes with long curls, frequently include objects meant to codify the child's maleness, such as whips, toy soldiers, and toy guns—toys that are also tools, and signify the anatomical "tool" under the breeches. As with the gendering of Latin nouns (such as *corpus*), young children were usually viewed as gender neutral: until, that is, they underwent their respective dress-related rites of passage. The sartorial aspect of gender, like hair length, was for children somewhat fluid, yet the props in the paintings serve to solidify masculinity.[47]

Anatomical masculinity is also defended by those who write against prematurely putting boys into breeches, as Nicholson's angst in *On Clothing* testifies ("Away then with the breeches of children!"). Voicing a similar concern, one William Blakey complained of "the fashion in great cities" of getting boys into breeches "even before some can walk." Calling attention to the "healthier men" of Scotland, Blakey argues, "Boys should be kept as long as possible in petticoats; by which their legs and thighs will grow as nature intended."[48] Such polemics contrast the natural and the urban by advocating for the unfettered body, reflecting further on Sterne's delineation of "True Shandeism," which "opens the heart and lungs, and ... forces the blood and other vital fluids of the body to run freely thro' its channels, and makes the wheel of life run long and chearfully round" (270).[49] Basic comfort, privacy, and regeneration were at stake: these are no small matters. If the body can be seen as a living machine, as natural philosophers had argued from early in the seventeenth century (a concept I revisit in chapter three), then the body of a boy had specific parts, anatomical tools that defined his maleness and determined—together with his class—his function.[50]

In *Tristram Shandy*, a novel that Elizabeth W. Harries identifies as "a world centered on men and their reactions to the fundamental dilemmas of being male,"[51] there are problems that precede the association between breeches and sexuality—first, being born male, specifically a son, at all; next, Tristram's family experiences a failure of primogeniture (he is the spare to the lost heir when his brother Bobby dies in London); finally, there is clearly the dilemma we have seen of putting the boy into the two-pronged garment in the first place.

Also at stake is a symbolic reading of breeching—in *Tristram Shandy* and elsewhere—that extends beyond comfort, mobility, and privacy and, to some extent, beyond gender, even unto death. Julie Park contends that "the novel as a literary form appeared to embody and turn into an object the experience of life" at the same time that human identity became increasingly "susceptible to becoming embodied in inanimate objects."[52] Park's application of object theory to the fiction of this period can enrich our reading of Sterne-as-Tristram telling his reader that we are "men cloathed with bodies, and governed by our imaginations" (290).[53] Arguably, breeches offer a sartorial equivalent of the body itself in this way—causing both pain and laughter. Sterne's grown narrator is insistently preoccupied, indeed almost obsessed, with his own breeches—how revealing they are of his poverty, how vulnerable their paltry state demonstrates him to be: "I beseech thee!—behold these breeches! They are all I have in the world" (521).[54] Indeed, unease about mutability and mortality throughout the novel is conveyed by mention of breeches. Brian Michael Norton notes that Sterne "employs sartorial metaphors to illustrate his characters' never-ending struggles to shield themselves from external evils."[55] A preoccupation with seeming trivialities of clothing alongside life and death is part of Tristram's awareness of the fragile body as the soul's clothing.

Clothing as metaphor—not just for the ideas we have but for the very bodies we wear—is an insistent one in writings of the period. Of the discourse about early modern midwifery, for instance, Robert A. Erickson observes, "God, the first sewer and knitter-up of the skin, flesh and bones of the clothes-creature man, is the original of the midwife with her scissors and thread for tying off the umbilicus, and he it is who takes this creature out of the womb-belly."[56] Further, "the child is sewn in the womb . . . but as he moves towards the birth he must break out of this original clothing. He is like a small hero breaking his chains, overcoming the bonds and restrictive or oppressive forces of his womb-world to make for himself a breathing space, a new life, though one in which he will be far more vulnerable."[57] Such birth imagery is suggestive of the infant's struggle to break the "ligaments, reins, and coats in which it is involved," as Erickson points out in his study of Sterne and midwifery authors such as James Wolveridge.[58] I argue that breeches—that garment that is literally sewn to cover the (boy's) body—reenacts embryonic development and birth itself. Birth was terribly dangerous to child and to mother, often proving fatal to both. The flattening of Tristram's nose by forceps is a reminder that he got off lucky.[59] As Erickson observes in regard to the embryonic human in *Tristram Shandy*, Sterne "play[s] with the imagery of miniatures as emblems of mortality."[60] By going into breeches, the small hero again breaks free of his little frock as from the amniotic sac, to take longer strides toward manhood, and to move inevitably closer to death. Sterne knew as well as Samuel Beckett, that humans "give birth astride of a grave."[61] This darker way of reading the freedom that comes with breeches recalls Thomas Gray's "Ode on a Distant Prospect of Eton College."[62] It is only in breeches, after all, that Gray's schoolboys can "chase the rolling circle's speed, / Or urge the flying ball."[63] Pursued by mortality,

> Still as they run they look behind,
> They hear a voice in every wind,
> And snatch a fearful joy.[64]

The seriousness and the silliness of discussions about breeches in the period suggest that breeches allow the male child to "snatch a fearful joy." So, as with Lamb's just-breeched boy "yet free from sin," unbreeched boys might be still (as Seneca called barbarians) "men fresh from the gods."[65]

Furthermore, breeches themselves split, divide, fork the body—again, much as with fetal development (and the mandrake root). Consider John Dunton's 1691 *Voyage round the World*, with his account of being "in my Mother's Belly,—just Rambled out of nothing, or next to't, nothing like what I am now, into the little live thing, hardly as big as a Nit. I should tell you, as the virtuosi do, that I was shaped at first like a Todpole, and that I remember very well, when my tail Rambled off, and a pair of little Legs sprung out in the room on't."[66] Like the splitting embryonic body Dunton describes, breeches lend themselves to all kinds of jokes.[67] And how could it be otherwise, with the object and the word "breech," given that Johnson's definition of it includes both "the garment worn by men over the lower part of the body" and "the hinder part of the body" itself?[68] Norton points out that Sterne gives the man who suffers from the hot chestnut in his breeches the name Phutatorius, meaning "'copulator' or 'fastener,' and his anecdote joins these outer frames of masculine distress."[69] All of which is of a piece with Walter Shandy's assertion that "every thing in this world . . . is big with jest, and has wit in it, and instruction too,—if we can but find it out" (314). Similarly, much is made of the comical and complicated off-stage birth of Tristram, and of Mrs. Shandy being delivered of the jest that is Tristram. As the well-named and untrustworthy Dr. Slop wants the birth to occur in the breech orientation, we can also identify the preoccupation in Sterne's text with an act of nature that breeching a boy would mimic, for both kinds of breeching force a reconsideration of what is natural and what is not. Gail Kern Paster points out that birth is always an off-stage event in early modern drama: "Birth, like all events of the lower bodily stratum, has a larger part to play in the history of shame than in the history of representation."[70] Paster's phrase "events of the lower bodily stratum" can apply to breeching as well as birthing, and hence the shame inherent in the practice, whatever the representations in painted breeching portraits and, later, in breeching photographs. Look at this boy, they say. Look at his lower body, his hinder parts.

Sterne's novel, which surely reflects the culture that surrounded it, also contorts and disfigures that culture into unrecognizable shapes and patterns. Clothing itself has the power to "contort and disfigure . . . into unrecognizable shapes and patterns."[71] It is a power that has been studied more in relation to women's clothing, women's shapes and patterns and contortions and disfigurements. I began this look at one beginning of boyhood with the reminder that we should consider breeches more fully in terms of how they were constructed as a sign of progress in boys' lives, rather than merely in terms of transgressive representations of women "wearing the breeches." Breeches were clearly transformative, even as putting a boy into them was a normative act. They clothe and construct the boy in order for him to function as adults wish, and as he begins to be a man. They cover and contain—and simultaneously reveal the presence of—that "tool . . . the male regenerative organ."[72]

Shortly before the death of Tristram Shandy's elder brother, and the notorious circumcision-by-window incident, comes Sterne's famous echoing of sentiment about books in Robert Burton's *Anatomy of Melancholy* (1621). Tristram asks, "Shall we for ever make new books, as apothecaries make new mixtures, by pouring only out of one vessel into another? Are we forever to be twisting, and untwisting the same rope?" (275). Taken together, these Shandean moments are often read as phallic conceits in the service of contemplating regeneration—as Erickson, again, argues, "making new books out of old ones would seem to be a trope for making new human beings out of old ones."[73] Yet we should also imagine a little boy himself "poured out of one vessel into another" when he is taken out of petticoats and put into breeches. Proud, embarrassed, tough, vulnerable, different from what he was and yet the same, he is recontextualized, reimagined, and reshaped—because of the tool between his legs. Whether a text encourages boys to embrace this new phase of life or warns adults against haste in the practice, the fiction, poetry, jests, and medical essays of the long eighteenth century suggest that putting a boy into breeches twists and untwists him to fit into the world of men.

Figure 1.1. Francesco Bartolozzi (1728–1815), *Mr. Philip Yorke* (1788), print after Joshua Reynolds (1723–1792). Yale Center for British Art, Paul Mellon Fund.

Figure 1.2. John Singleton Copley (1738–1815), *Richard Heber* (1782). Yale Center for British Art, Paul Mellon Collection, B1981.25.745.

Figure 1.3. Breeches, red, wool, American (1761). Brooklyn Museum Costume Collection at the Metropolitan Museum of Art, Gift of the Brooklyn Museum, 2009; Gift of Idalia Hare, 1926. Accession Number 2009.300.2982a, b. Used with permission.

CHAPTER 2

The Boy in School

ELLENOR FENN'S RHETORICAL TOOLS IN *SCHOOL DIALOGUES, FOR BOYS* (1783)

Tool 3 (a) A person used by another for his own ends; one who is, or allows himself to be, made a mere instrument for some purpose; a cat's-paw.
—Oxford English Dictionary

He maintained, that a boy at school was the happiest of human beings. I supported a different opinion, from which I have never yet varied, that a man is happier; and I enlarged upon the anxiety and sufferings which are endured at school.
—James Boswell, The Life of Samuel Johnson

In spite of the boy's freedom to play and climb trees, once he moved from frock coats to breeches he took a step closer to other sorts of confinement. If he was privileged so as not to be obliged to start earning his living, this confinement usually took the form of school.[1] Boy qua boy, conceptualized as an "inchoate or incomplete man," requires maturation and completion, in one way or another to become other.[2] School is a step toward such completion. Books written to educate boys, even when largely about developing habits of good conduct, focused on the future—with both the earth-bound goal of thriving in the world after school and the religious reminder of life after death. Such was arguably the primary focus of children's literature at its beginnings, indicated by such texts as John Bunyan's *The Pilgrim's Progress* (1678) and the 1690 *New England Primer*. The latter's lesson about the letter A is "In Adam's fall / We sinned all" and, for B, "Thy life to mend, This Book attend," accompanied by a miniature drawing of the Bible. Books written to educate parents about educating their boys focus on the life to come along with how the boy will turn out in this life. These were frequently the same books. The primer, of which a reported two million copies were sold in the eighteenth century, teaches the letter F thus: "The idle Fool / Is whipt at school."

School for Boys

The eighteenth-century English boy's options depended upon his class. Children in agrarian households, for example, tended to have little if any formal education, and well into the nineteenth century the poor relied on cheap dame schools.[3] Privileged families continued a tradition of sending sons away as day scholars or as boarders at a paid grammar school (also called private school), which served the seven to eleven age group. Only in 1870 would compulsory education be introduced nationally in Britain, and then just for children from five to eleven years old.[4] That being said, the eighteenth century witnessed the rising middle class send far more boys to school, with schools for children of dissenting families and charity establishments called Blue Coat schools taking in ever greater numbers of children across England.[5] Grammar schools, originally exclusive to instruction in Latin,[6] retained an emphasis on the classics (Johnson's *Dictionary* [1755] defined a grammar school as "a school in which the learned languages are grammatically taught") but expanded to include other subjects like English, arithmetic, and sometimes French.

The boy going to grammar school crossed a threshold into being that new creature: a schoolboy. Again, as with going into breeches, the liminal experience differentiated him from his former self. It also set him apart from those who were not in school, although, as will be seen, entering the workforce could and did complicate such distinctions of growth and manhood. For some, school lasted only until the boy began a life of work as an apprentice to a tradesman, or returned home to work with his father, which could be at fourteen, eleven, or younger. If higher born, the boy might enter a public school, such as Eton or Westminster, around the age of eleven to thirteen. After this usually came university in order to take up an elevated profession (medicine, for example, or law, these particularly for a son not benefitted by primogeniture) or to earn his (inherited) leisure and match his power with knowledge prior to embarking on the grand tour, privileged education completed by exploration of distant lands.

The boy in grammar school upon whom I focus here was the brainchild of prolific children's author Ellenor Fenn (1743–1813). Published in 1783 "By a Lady," her two-volume *School Dialogues, for Boys. Being an Attempt to Convey Instruction Insensibly to Their Tender Minds, and Instill the Love of Virtue* was one of no fewer than six books Fenn saw published within a year, all under pseudonyms.[7] Fenn has received attention from scholars such as David Stoker, Carol Percy, Karlijn Navest, Andrea Immel and Rebecca Davies, with focus on her (largely pseudonymous) bibliography, innovative approach to education, grammar books, spelling blocks, and adoption of the role of maternal educator. *School Dialogues*, the first schoolboy book, has not itself been much considered in terms of the gendered subjects and intended readership of the book.[8] It is a school story, but more importantly, it is a way of constructing the schoolboy in part by addressing his mother along with him.

Inspired by writings on behalf of even younger children by Anna Laetitia Barbauld, Fenn was one of many women who were, as Lissa Paul says, "engaged in the kinds of maternal teaching practices directed towards encouraging children to become thinking and knowing adults." At the same time, Andrea Immel is right to point out, "Before Fenn, few educators paid much attention to children before they attained the age of reason and began formal schooling: Fenn is one of the first to focus on the particular needs of this age group and to make the case for engaged adults like mothers talking, playing, and exploring with small children as a way of integrating learning fully with everyday life."[9] This preschool audience we see most fully in Fenn's popular *Cobwebs to Catch Flies; or, Dialogues in Short Sentences Adapted to Children From the Age of Three to Eight Years* (1783). Fenn's *School Dialogues, for Boys*, for school-age males, was published later the same year but written prior to *Cobwebs*. Because *School Dialogues* is about a little boy just arriving at grammar school, the format allows Fenn to comment not only on schoolboy conduct but also on the education boys received at home before coming into their new milieu.

Set at an unnamed boarding school, *School Dialogues* is a conduct book of vignettes composed, its author tells us, of "Prattle" in order to convey "instruction in the vehicle... most agreeable" to her young readers.[10] Patricia Demers numbers Fenn among the "Rational Moralists" publishing in the second half of the century who were strongly influenced by Locke.[11] Fenn's subtitle about communicating "instruction insensibly" shows she is aware of and in agreement with Locke's advice that "none of the things [children] are to learn, should ever be made a burthen to them, or impos'd on them as a task."[12] As such, Fenn claims to offer "two grains of Moral, hidden in two bushels of prattle" (1:xxiii). The little boy named Sprightly who is just arriving at his new school in Fenn's book is six and a half years old.

In thirty dialogues ranging mostly from five to twelve pages, Sprightly and his schoolfellows are discovered in the classroom, in the schoolyard, and on outings. The new boy endears himself early to all the good characters, works hard at his lessons, and is guided by the Head Boy, Sensible, in choosing boys with whom to form friendships. Sprightly ages one year over the course of the book, armed with the lessons of scholarly perseverance, kindness, and piety that his parents have instilled in their son. These qualities are tested, as Fenn makes clear they must be, in vocabulary aimed at such boys themselves. The conclusion of the *School Dialogues* celebrates Sprightly being named one of the three best scholars of his year. In this, "the first time there have been three claimants," Sprightly tries to withdraw his claim to the award because he has "enjoyed such superior advantages" and had "such incitements to goodness" (2:123). Both he and his best friend, Gentle, promote Supple (a boy who had fallen in with bad friends and been expelled from his last school before coming to this one) "as a reward for the struggle he has undergone" (2:124). All three boys are crowned with laurels, as one schoolmaster in an aside declares them "glorious boys!" In order to reach this high point, Sprightly's home life evidently gave him a firm foundation on which to build. The cornerstone of that foundation, we learn, has been Sprightly's mother, who equipped the boy to learn in a new environment by teaching him well in his first one. Implicitly, Fenn's book is like Rousseau's *Émile*, aimed at adults who teach children; unlike Rousseau, Fenn employs the institution of the boys' school to teach both.

School as Away (Tempering the Tools)

Sensible:
Do you remember coming to school?
Frisk:
Yes; I cried all night . . .
Sprightly:
And do you cry often now?
Frisk:
No, no; I am as merry as the day—(1:33–34)

Young Sprightly, the boy going into a grammar school, is the boy going away from home. Fenn would later choose a boarding school as the setting for another book, *School Occurrences: Supposed to Have Arisen among a Set of Young Ladies* (1790), as well as other books for girls. Her construction of the figure of the schoolboy evinces many of the same techniques as these other texts; however, significant differences shaped boys' education and boys' futures, made for a different understanding of the male child's experience. Jackie Horne notes that the next stage of most grammar school boys' education—public school—was notoriously difficult: "Public schools for boys before the nineteenth century, primarily populated by sons of the landed classes, were famous for their harsh or indifferent teaching, their uncomfortable and often immoral living conditions, and their tolerance of bullying."[13] Well through the nineteenth century (and the twentieth), such infamy continued to be reflected in books like Maria Edgeworth's *Frank: A Sequel* (1822), which "depict[s] public schools as places where innocent boys learn to be roughed up into experienced men."[14] Kristin Olsen notes that despite widespread ambivalence about these institutions, "wealthy parents sent their sons to such schools in increasing numbers, mostly because of social connection that could be made in youth and exploited later in life. By 1800, 70 percent of English peers had attended Eton, Westminster, Winchester, or Harrow."[15] The majority of these sons would have previously attended grammar schools at a distance from their homes.

Joseph Bristow has called Thomas Hughes's wildly successful mid-nineteenth-century novel set at Rugby, *Tom Brown's Schooldays* (1857), "the first story that places a special value on education away from home" for the boy.[16] Whereas this can be said of Hughes's private school story as a novel, some seventy years earlier Fenn's vignette collection in *School Dialogues* did just this for grammar education away from home. Fenn does not emphasize the manliness of boys, as Hughes did, and her principal focus is the importance of preparing little boys for the challenges they will face at school, but her text—which amounts to a short story cycle—certainly places special value on the boy's "education away from home."

The value of such education lies largely in its very distance—to test the boy's mettle, and at the same time to temper it. Mark Rothery and Henry French have collected epistolary evidence that reveals how "the separation of young boys from home and family during their schooling was not merely an incidental consequence of the boarding system. Rather, it was a crucial aspect of the process, meant to wean boys from their dependence on their parents, particularly mothers, and to toughen and develop character in preparation for the rigours and responsibilities of adult life."[17] One Elizabeth Warriner, for example, wrote to her son George upon his leaving for school with combined fondness and resolve: "I could not feel quite comfortable after parting from you, as I know your heart went with us, but bless you, you behaved like a man . . . poor Sophie's tears flowed afresh, but my dear love we know it is all for your good, both for your health & for the improvement of your mind, as you know there is many things you are yet deficient in, so I hope & trust in a few days, you will find yourself quite reconciled & comfortable."[18] In Fenn's *School Dialogues* our first sight of Sprightly at his new school finds the six-year-old crying when he speaks of home and family. The Head Boy, reassuringly named Sensible, takes Sprightly under his wing, and advises they change the subject, not talking about family until the new scholar is able to "speak of home without tears" (1:32).[19] Another boy, Mildmay, later admonishes the (again) homesick Sprightly, "*Why* did you leave your parents?—*why*, because it was proper for you to be placed at school" (2:25). Stoicism and self-mastery were necessary qualities for a boy to exercise in becoming a man; and becoming a man—as Fenn iterates throughout the *Dialogues*—is the very point of boyhood, even as the specific needs of childhood must be understood to educate the boy. Our boy Sprightly must grasp the necessity of his new distance from home, drying his eyes as he states, "I know I ought to be content where my parents choose to place me" (1:35). Both the homesickness and the construction of the sentence "I know I ought" empathize with and encourage the child reader: the boy is not yet content, but it is his duty to be content.

The intended audience is explicit in Fenn's book: the dialogues about boys are aimed at boy readers, even though, as Elizabeth Segel notes, "in the few books intended for children published before the eighteenth century, no distinction seems to have been made between male and female readers." Segel points out this lack of gender distinction was because "both the Puritan aim of saving the child's soul and the characteristic eighteenth-century aim of developing good character seemed to require no distinction between girl-child and boy-child." However, "early school stories were an exception. Because boarding schools were for boys or girls, not both, books with school settings were aimed at one sex or another."[20] As Fenn's title makes explicit, the gender of its intended audience, the youth of the boys also receives attention throughout: the text is printed in large font with wide margins, easy for boys to read or have read to them prior to going to school.[21]

The book's subtitle also emphasizes that these schoolboys are quite young by indicating the "*attempt to convey instruction insensibly to their tender minds.*" Below, I consider the dialogic ways in which these tender minds are instructed through Sprightly, his friends, and his adversaries. I then examine how boys—as readers and as characters—are employed as rhetorical tools in educating and empowering their mothers, while enhancing the authority of the woman writer. The idea of a double or dual readership of children's books has been explored by many scholars.[22] As Jacqueline Rose points out in her study of that famous boy-shaped character, J. M. Barrie's Peter Pan, "There is, in one sense, no body of literature which rests so openly on an acknowledged difference, a rupture almost, between writer and addressee. Children's fiction sets up the child as an outsider to its own process, and then aims, unashamedly, to take the child in."[23] While Barbara Wall identifies women writers in the second half of the nineteenth century like Mary Louisa Molesworth, Louisa May Alcott, and Anna Sewell as being "comfortable and confident in the familiar role of talking intimately to children,"[24] decades or even a century earlier Ellenor Fenn comfortably addressed a readership that was clearly intended as dual—the children about and to whom she wrote, and the mothers of those children. How *School Dialogues, for Boys* constructs its boys and takes in its boy readers involves relationships between them and, as we shall see, between boys and women.

Dedication

Fenn's dedication of *School Dialogues* to her nephew, William, is worth quoting in full:

To Master W ****** F****

Did you ever read of a people who obliged their slaves to drink to excess; and then exposed them to their children, in order to deter *them* from the vice of drunkenness, by shewing it in all its deformity?

I have created a set of Puppets, to whom I impute such faults as may suit my purposes; and this with a design similar to that of the people to whom I alluded,

"Vice, to be hated, needs but to be seen."

On the other hand, I have raised phantoms, on whom I have bestowed what degree of perfection I think proper; to serve as examples to you.

May they influence your conduct!

May God preserve you blameless amidst a crooked and perverse generation—prays,

My Dear,

Your sincerely affectionate Friend,

****** ****

The real boy to whom Fenn dedicated her book, William Frere (1775–1836), was seven years old when the book was published.[25] Fenn and her husband adopted William, the son of her brother, around 1779, and she might herself have read to him the story of the "slaves" obliged to "drink to excess," to which she refers. The anecdote is one taken from Plutarch, who records that the Spartans treated their helots—publicly owned slaves—in this way, "to show the young men what a thing drunkenness was."[26] Plutarch's works are alluded to throughout *School Dialogues*. For instance, a boy named Goodwill quotes aphoristically, "'Brothers should be like the fingers upon a hand, each assisting the other.'—I believe it is in *Plutarch's Morals*" (1:135). Here Fenn demonstrates her understanding of the schoolboys' curriculum from early to late education: Plutarch's *Morals* and his *Lives of the Noble Greeks and Romans* (commonly called *Parallel Lives* or *Plutarch's Lives*), along with translations of other Greek as well as Roman texts were staples of the English schoolboy, most coming to English through French translations.[27]

While these translations made Plutarch accessible to a wider audience, including women, scholars like Coppélia Kahn emphasize the extent to which "'Roman' virtue" was "almost synonymous with masculinity in the early modern period."[28] "Rome is familiar to the school-boy and the statesman," wrote Edward Gibbon, who knew of what he spoke.[29] Not only curricula but also familial correspondence bear this out. Some ten years after Fenn's *Dialogues*, a Master Woolcombe wrote to his younger brother that to know "the histories of ancient Greece & Rome is so indispensable in a Man of a liberal education that we cannot too soon acquire it."[30] Sir Thomas Dyke Acland wrote more specifically to his son Thomas at Harrow, "Let me recommend you to search out *Plutarch's Lives*, particularly with respect to Spartan heroes who you may remember were trained by public education... those parts at least which relate to public virtues as generosity, disinterestedness, courage, patriotism, enlarged friendship, & wisdom & prudence in public concerns."[31] Thus in *School Dialogues* by beginning with an authoritative text that the boys were already taught (or which younger boys were to encounter) Fenn sets up her schoolboy characters as the author's slaves, making real boys—her schoolboy readers—the Roman children who will learn from cautionary tales of excess. Both the puppet and the phantom boys that inhabit the dialogues are schoolboys, held up as exemplars and cautionary figures, respectively, like the subjects of Plutarch's biographies, to mold readers into good citizens and men.

In addition to referencing Plutarch, Fenn's dedication—and project in *School Dialogues*—resonates with the final volume of Samuel Richardson's *Pamela* (1742). The heroine, now in her "exalted state" (married with children), describes "nursery tales and stories" with which she entertains her children: "My method is to give characters of persons I have known in one part or another of my life, in feigned names, whose conduct may serve for imitation or warning to my dear attentive Miss; and sometimes I give instances of good boys and naughty boys for the sake of my Billy and my Davers; and they are continually coming about me, 'Dear Madam, a pretty story,' now cries Miss: 'and dear mamma, tell me of good boys, and of naughty boys,' cries Billy."[32] Pamela's young listeners' gendered responses are unsurprising. Fenn's *School Dialogues* is a book to please little Billy: it gives boy readers boys "for imitation or warning." Moreover, both in the person of schoolboy Sprightly's first teacher, his mother, and in Fenn's own authorial persona, *School Dialogues* also creates "dear mammas." The opportunity of reading these dialogues offers what Pamela provides to Billy: good boys and naughty boys.

The Dialogues

Fenn was to produce several dialogue collections for children and thought a lot about the value of this genre, insightfully explaining in this book for boys that "dialogue keeps awake that attention which flags even in a speech beyond a few lines" and asserting that "remarks come with double weight from those who are of their own age" (1:xxix). John Marshall, Fenn's publisher, specialized in producing the dialogue format, which, as Andrew O'Malley points out, "invites the participation of children and turns principle and precept into lived experiences, albeit heavily mediated and scripted. It allows the children to draw conclusions themselves and contributes to supervisory pedagogy's ideal operation, in which children imagine they are learning by themselves."[33] Such a pedagogical method might work on both younger and older children, those read to and those who can read themselves. Ideally, Fenn's readers will not know they are being instructed, so enjoyable is the vehicle that conveys the instruction "insensibly" (title page).

While all children benefit from the dialogue genre—as she makes plain in her books for girls—here in her boys' book Fenn's introductory matter (dedication, "To the Reader," and then a preface) indicates that boys especially require (or at least it is optimal that they learn through) a measure of subterfuge. Samuel F. Pickering Jr. quotes the *Critical Review* response to Fenn's *School Dialogues*: "The scheme of conveying instruction, by the conversation [*sic*] of boys is in a great measure new.... and perhaps more commodiously insinuated than in any other."[34] Like other such books, *School Dialogues* resembles a printed play, with virtue names of the PERSONS listed at the beginning: Mr. Aweful, Mr. Wiseman, and Mr. Sage are masters at the school, and the names of twenty-two boys too are reminiscent of the personages in parabolic and enduring texts like *The Pilgrim's Progress*. Head Boy Sensible is matched with Worthy, the Second Boy, who together look after the others: Mildmay and Goodwill, down to Spiteful, Sly, and Wilful. Our six-and-a-half-year-old hero, Sprightly, must learn the ways—seemingly of the world—through the other pupils, by conversing with them and choosing to be or not to be like each of them.

Of course, the schoolmasters play their part in guiding the new pupil as well. In Dialogue VI, commencing "A Library. Mr. STEADY is seen sitting at a table, writing. SPRIGHTLY stands by him," Sprightly is tasked with reading a handwritten parish registry from 1602 about a boy of good disposition who died at the age of seven (a footnote lets us know this was in fact written in 1782) (1:79). The boy in the registry is a paragon by the name of Jeremy Baldock who "had learned his Accidence, and a great part of the Grammar Rules" (1:80). Kind, thoughtful, and pious, Jeremy had also learned how to die. In sickness he prayed, "O Lord, send me health, or else take me out of this miserable world," and then resigned himself to the death he knew was coming (1:81). Here Fenn carries on a centuries-old tradition in which, as J. H. Plumb notes, "nothing was regarded as more edifying than the death of a model child."[35] The hagiographic combination of scholarly application and piety is efficient, and the lesson stays with Sprightly throughout the course of his first school year.

Upon reading Jeremy Baldock's miniature spiritual biography, Sprightly says, "I wish I were like him," taking some comfort in having at least, like Jeremy, applied himself to his studies. Yet he is warned against boasting even this much by

Mr. Steady: "I am told that you are a docile child; that is what I value you for: that is the disposition which will make you be beloved both by God and man" (1:82). The lesson about docility aimed at the boy is significant, as it contrasts with Robert Shoemaker's observation, "Not only did boys and girls learn different skills, but schooling exacerbated personality differences. While boys' grammar schools and public schools encouraged self-control, endurance, striving, and athletic prowess, girls were taught to combat vanity and pride."[36] Fenn's model boys' school, however, offers numerous lessons in combatting vanity and pride among its schoolboys—and little in the way of athletic prowess. Good habits and character are more important than measurable academic accomplishment as well, although the latter does follow upon the former.

The example of Jeremy Baldock is of a piece with the evangelical mission behind much of the conduct literature of the late eighteenth century. In *Dialogues*, the boys not only discuss family, duty, and lessons but also on occasion refer to scripture. In a letter to the schoolboys from a master who is ill, the latter asks, "What is all the learning which they can acquire, without the knowledge of God?" (2:115). This evokes Mark 8:36: "For what shall it profit a man, if he shall gain the whole world, and lose his own soul?"[37] Education itself being a way to grow closer to God comes through in Fenn's work, as Sprightly is a little Christian scholar.[38] We have not yet arrived at the later nineteenth-century ideal of muscular Christianity; certainly, Fenn has no concerns about a decline in manliness in emphasizing that the best boys are mild-mannered and generous. When Sprightly and his dearest friend assert that neither wants preferment over the other, one Mr. Brown bursts out: "Amiable children! love each other, and be good; love each other, and be happy" (2:39).

In tandem with building up moral fortitude in the boy, Fenn's recognition of the difficulty of learning is itself important, as is her recognition of the need to build up the fortitude necessary to learn. Decades earlier, publisher John Newbery had capitalized on Locke's advice about helping children learn through games and toys, producing all sorts of texts to encourage children to take an interest in their letters. In the iconic *Little Pretty Pocket-Book* (1744), a "Letter to Sir" gives an account of "a little Boy who learned his Book to that surprising Degree, that his Master could scarce teach him fast enough," who ends up riding in "a Coach and Six," for "learning is a most excellent thing and easy to be acquired too, when little Boys set themselves about it."[39] Fenn's *Dialogues* demonstrate the excellence—and the necessity—of learning; she does not, however, as Newbery did, pretend learning is "easy," nor does she promise a coach and six to the boy who applies himself in school. Rather, she offers dialogues that convey realistic anxieties, such as a lament about not being as "quick" or having as great a capacity for learning as another scholar: "I am discouraged that my memory is so bad," one boy reveals, to which his friend replies, "Exercise will strengthen it" (2:82).

Thus, the *Dialogues* promote values that Rothery and French through their work in archival correspondence identify as "pillars" of boys' education in the long eighteenth century, including "self-mastery, the control of the emotions and of the purse, of manners and behavior befitting a gentleman, truth and trustworthiness, stoicism, hard work through rational learning, and independence of mind."[40] Self-mastery is most evident in the *Dialogues* through moments of temptation that the boys—especially Sprightly—undergo, from the temptation of sloth to the temptation to think well of oneself because one *has* applied oneself. Here is the via media indeed. Other themes mentioned by Rothery and French of which there is ample evidence in the *Dialogues* include "control of the purse," which appears in Dialogue XXV: "The Account-Book," when a boy named Supple, a shilling deficient on his account, is "ashamed to say" he "let it to Frank Careless." Although this is a "fault that arose from good humour," Master Sage admonishes Supple with the reminder that one of the boy's own father's injunctions is (as Polonius advised Laertes) "never to lend or borrow money" (2:96–97).

The last in the list of ideal masculine behavior noted by Rothery and French, "independence of mind," is always a somewhat paradoxical aim to set for children, applying in Fenn's book only to resisting those other pupils who would lead one astray, not to defying authority at the school or at home (recall Sprightly is praised for his docility). Sensible tells his young charges that "a wise man said, 'the first thing necessary for a boy to learn, at going to school, is to be able to say, NO, with a firm and manly assurance'" (1:50). Such a moment occurs for Sprightly when appealed to by Supple. Unprepared to recite his lesson, Supple begs our protagonist to help him cheat: "Dear Sprightly, whisper me when I am at a loss." Sprightly resists: "Say you are not ready; that will be honest; and study as hard as you can" (2:86). Again, such independence is desirable only in relation to other boys like this would-be-cheater and against the pack mentality of boys who would and do cause mischief at the school. For instance, the theme of Plutarch's drunken servants is echoed when some of Fenn's puppet schoolboys, including the too-tractable boy named Meek, enter a tavern and drink alcohol. Sprightly is not present in this scene, a dialogue titled "The Timid Criminal." Young Meek regrets having been led astray, but, reprimanded for his timorousness by Master Sage, he is warned, "If you do not conquer that false modesty, you will go on all your life sinning without inclination; and repenting without amendment.—You must exert resolution to do what *you know is right*" (2:60). Remorse felt and expressed without future action is useless. Such scenarios call for the boy to put into practice the precepts of the catechism he would have learned before starting school and been called on to repeat regularly.[41]

The Puppets and the Phantoms

Fenn's dedication to *School Dialogues* quotes without attribution the line "vice, to be hated, needs but to be seen." The statement on its own conveys the importance of learning from the unlikeable "puppets" the author has created, and it seems fairly straightforward as a maxim. Worth noting, however, is that "vice, to be hated, needs but to be seen" is a truncation of a more cynical passage from Pope's *Essay on Man*:

> Vice is a monster of so frightful mien,
> As to be hated needs but to be seen;
> Yet seen too oft, familiar with her face,
> We first endure, then pity, then embrace.[42]

Vice familiar, endured, pitied, and eventually embraced is vice embodied, and it is this that the bad boys in *School Dialogues* represent, including those who permit themselves through weakness to be the tools of other boys (like Meek entering the tavern).

Matthew Grenby observes that "even some of the very earliest school stories" including Fenn's *School Occurrences* (about girls) "offer a perfect opportunity to depict children learning to balance their sense of self and of community, to mature by integrating themselves into society."[43] The "puppets" or bad boys in Fenn's schoolboy story are both prone to disobedience and inclined to incite the same in others. The threat of such incitement is not taken lightly, and Sprightly comes forewarned: "My papa told me my conduct would depend upon the companions of my leisure hours" (1:53). Even so, when other boys have been reprimanded for wrongdoing, Sprightly admits, "I should have done as ill, if I had not had such a friend as Sensible." When asked why he was tempted to transgress, Sprightly is candid: "I thought it was manly to copy after older boys" (1:53).[44] He does not see the paradox of it being "manly to copy . . . boys," because it is enough that they are "older," but he shows himself to be developing perspicacity by copying the exemplary older boy Sensible.

Schoolboys were widely characterized as ungrateful for and resentful of their education: in the second of seven stages of man that Shakespeare describes in *As You Like It*, the child goes from mewling infant to

> whining school-boy with his satchel,
> And shining morning-face, creeping like snail
> Unwillingly to school.[45]

The very term "schoolboy" is frequently a pejorative in this period, indicating ignorance rather than learning, along with lack of resolve, as in Henry Fielding's *Tom Jones* (1749), where Squire Allworthy complains to his sister, "I have more occasion of patience, to be used like an overgrown schoolboy, as I am by you."[46] The complaint conflates the very state of being a schoolboy with being used by another. It is not usually women who are the source of concern about a schoolboy being "used," however; it is more often other males—young or old. In her essay "On National Education" (1792) from *A Vindication of the Rights of Woman*, Mary Wollstonecraft states the problem not only of being influenced by the wrong boy but of being subjected to him, for "in great schools, what can be more prejudicial to the moral character than the system of tyranny and abject slavery which is established amongst the boys . . . ?"[47] A comprehension of such possible manipulation or exploitation of the schoolboy in Fenn's text explains her focus on the serious business of learning correct conduct. It is a seriousness underscored by the wish that closes her dedication to the real-life boy, her nephew: "God preserve you blameless amidst a crooked and perverse generation."[48] Generation here refers both to the present age (which is always a corrupt one) and also to the "generation" that always consists of boys—youth. Not in Fenn, therefore, do we find much sympathy for what Eric Tribunella identifies in children's literature as a wink at "the morally and socially subversive high jinks of boyhood," although we do get "the sense of boyhood as a time of constraint and confinement."[49] Fenn acknowledges the human frailty of Sprightly as our hero, yet for the most part, while the "puppets" in Fenn's book are morally and socially subversive, her "phantoms" are practically perfect.

Despite the simplicity of good and bad boy characters performing good and bad acts, *School Dialogues* operates on a level of sophistication balancing parental awareness with boyish innocence and possible gullibility. Mr. Quondam, a former pupil at the school, admits to the headmaster, "I should tremble to expose a child to the contagion of a school, where one wicked boy may root out every virtue, which a careful parent has been labouring to plan" (2:104). It is no accident that the list of persons at the front of the book contains more bad boys (Haughty, Taunt, Sly . . .) than good (Sensible, Worthy, Gentle . . .). Fenn did the same in her books for girls. Acquaintance with a variety of faults and persons is inevitable; friendship, by contrast, is a choice not to be taken lightly. The following exchange with Sensible is a common one for Sprightly and indicates the role that guidance from an older boy can play: "Sensible: I intreat you to be very cautious with whom you are intimate. / Sprightly: Indeed I wish to be so, pray advise me" (1:46). Habits of befriending begin here at school, when the boy is missing home and seeking relationships to stand in for those intimacies of family life. Shortly after this encounter, another boy, Worthy, tells Sprightly, "You are come amongst a great many strangers" (1:58). The vulnerability of the boy's position in light of those who would influence him calls for discernment—a discernment not that different from what he will need in a few years when he is even further from home—and now is the time to develop it.

The Head Boy asserts that "most boys may be won by gentleness," but of course gentleness is not what most boys will be limited to encountering at school (1:100). Indeed, William Godwin believed that "all education is despotism." Godwin nevertheless admitted that "a boy, educated apart from boys, is a sort of unripened hermit."[50] John Tosh identifies values believed to be instilled by public schools, where "learning to stand on one's feet, to rub shoulders with all sorts, to have the guts to stand out against the crowd—these qualities were integral to manliness, and they were not likely to be acquired at home."[51] Understanding the need (or, at least, the inevitability) of rubbing shoulders with all sorts, Fenn's work reflects the same concerns about acquaintances voiced by real parents to their sons, for example in a letter from Juliana Buxton to her thirteen-year-old son at Harrow: "Remember my dearest John all the admonitions we gave you & do not let the number of Boys & the bad examples of some of them make you forget them . . . & you will find it my dear of infinite consequence with whom you form your friendships as young people are often led into many scrapes and much mischief by making hasty friendships."[52] Such anxiety permeates writings about school, both in terms of how much the boy will apply himself to his work and in terms of whether he will learn to judge the characters of others rightly and prove himself worthy of his parents' considerable investment of money and time.

Evidence of pitfalls awaiting boys comes in *School Dialogues* with the story of Supple. This new scholar "was a charming boy" when he began at his former school but was subsequently expelled and now has arrived at Sprightly's school. The explanation for this turn of events is that "he met with many very idle companions at Lington." To this observation about the other (fictional) establishment, Master Sage replies, "They are to be met with in all schools" (2:173).

The counsel Fenn gives for the benefit of six-year-olds in her cautionary dialogues was anticipated by Mary Astell in *Some Reflections upon Marriage* (1700) regarding older, but still gullible, males in the company of their peers:

> A young Gentleman . . . should by degrees be inform'd of the Vice in Fashion, and warn'd of the Application and Design of those who will make it their Business to corrupt him, shou'd be told the Arts they use and the Trains they lay, be prepar'd to be Shock'd by some and caress'd by others; warn'd who are like to oppose, who to mislead, who to undermine, and who to serve him. He shou'd be instructed how to know and distinguish them, where he shou'd let them see, and when dissemble the Knowledge of them and their Aims and Workings.[53]

That Astell brings this up in light of her critique of the tyranny and machinations practiced by men and women in the institution of marriage shows the roots of both in youth—especially masculine youth.

Every "young gentleman" (like every old gentleman) was once a boy, and Fenn does not let her readers forget this. For example, one former pupil, Tom Wayward, is recalled in a discussion between two adults thus: "What a disagreeable wretch he was! . . . And is; and will be;—such as the boy was, such is the man" (2:105). An interesting point about the transformation a boy must undergo—and how many fail to do so as a result of poor education—appears in the first example of *Boyhood* Johnson provided in his 1755 definition. This from Swift, who opined in "An Essay on Modern Education" that the poorly educated gentleman remains a child, "in every Article as fully accomplished at Eight Years old, as at eight and twenty; Age adding only to the Growth of his Person and his Vices; *so that if you should look at him in his Boyhood, through the magnifying End of a Perspective, and, in his Manhood, through the other, it would be impossible to spy any difference; the same Airs, the same Strut,* the same Cock of his Hat, and Posture of his Sword."[54] Sound education, by contrast, turns the boy into a proper man. Sensible thereby bucks up a discouraged Sprightly by urging him to reflect upon the fellowship of generations: "Consider, my dear boy, that the most learned man in England was only a little child, and ignorant as you are, and probably thought the first rudiments as difficult as you do" (1:97). While the example of Tom Wayward who will ever remain "a disagreeable wretch" cautions the reader along with Sprightly, mention of "the most learned man in England" consoles.

Rods and Sugar-Plums

When Sprightly meets Wilful, a boy who must be disciplined at school to counteract the effect of having been spoiled at home, our narrator notes ominously, "Children who are improperly indulged, must occasionally be as improperly corrected. Rods and sugar-plums meet in the same house" (2:n91). It is an interesting methodology for achieving the via media when faced with a recalcitrant child, resonating with the specific diction of Locke's advice:

> Beating them and all other sorts of slavish and corporal punishment are not the discipline fit to be used in the education of those who would have wise, good, and ingenious men; and therefore very rarely to be applied, and that only on great occasions, and cases of extremity. On the other side, to flatter children by rewards of things that are pleasant to them, is carefully to be avoided. He that will give to his son apples, or sugar-plums, or what else of this kind he is most delighted with, to make him learn his book, does but authorize his love of pleasure, and cocker up that dangerous propensity which ought to by all means subdue and stifle him.[55]

Fenn's picture of "rods and sugar-plums [that] meet in the same house" reflects the unfortunate spoiling of the son Locke warns against.[56] Although Locke does not state it explicitly, Fenn does: flattery and bribery lead to corporal punishment sooner, or later, or both.

In Locke's opinion, there is but "one fault, for which . . . children should be beaten, and that is, obstinacy or rebellion."[57] In Fenn's book, even as we hear about obstinacy in the upbringing of some boys, those parental errors set the stage for rebellious rumblings at school. A former scholar, now a father, laments, "What unhappy creatures are spoiled children when they come to school!" to which one of the masters adds with a heartfelt intimation of deterioration and contagion, "They are unhappy at home, but when they mix with other boys!" (2:105). We see not only obstinacy in *School Dialogues* but also attempts at planting seeds of rebellion in discussions among the grammar school boys about the public scandals of real-life public school riots. This begins with one of the pupils receiving a letter containing "an account of the riot at Harrow"—one of the seven leading public schools (which would be the next stage of Sprightly's education). Evidence is not hard to come by that "conditions at the great public schools in this period were very rough. Discipline was harsh; yet the boys were apt to be truculent" and riots were the result.[58]

Sprightly's school is a model of fairness, and the principal lesson behind talk of riots in this dialogue is that "a becoming spirit is shewn by resisting all persuasions to a breach of duty" (2:110). Still, troublemaking little Pert desires to "make a riot here," prompting a debate between those who think it would be great fun, and those who oppose it and find themselves accused of sermonizing (2:106). Sprightly recounts what Mr. Bright has told him about the riot at Eton that occurred "whilst he was there" (this would have been the riot of 1768; Bright is not identified among the *School Dialogues*' list of persons). This dialogue concludes with a comment about rebellious boys who "little think what opinion rational people form of them" (2:113). One might argue, however, that as children who have yet to develop reason themselves, rebellious boys have minimal interest in what "rational people" think, and this is the problem. Teresa Michals points out of this period that "generally ... those who wanted to widen the franchise of knowledge in England or to start a revolution in American argued that education turns children into adults by developing their reason, and that these reasonable adults turn tyrannies into republics."[59] In Fenn's schoolboy story, however, reason belongs to the boys who pose no threat of revolution, and school is not a republic. The most sincere words spoken on this topic are those of our little cypher, Sprightly. When asked what he would do if there were to be a riot at the school, he answers tentatively and humbly, "I dare not be confident that I should act as I ought to do" (2:108). This is a surprising statement considering Sprightly's goodness, which makes it a powerful one for the boy reader smugly confident about his own conduct in hypothetical situations. Fenn has also set up Sprightly's self-doubt with his having previously admitted to thinking it "manly to copy after older boys" when he first arrived at school (1:53).

Although at times we might indeed feel, like Pert, that there is too much "sermonizing" in the conversation of the exemplary boys (and the dialogues themselves are certainly stilted), Fenn shows the role that childhood discussions can play as rehearsals for greater hazards and temptations to come. Naughty boys who jostle against the good ones—irritating, tempting, and exasperating—show the value of her fictive "puppets."

Worlds Little and Big

In her preface to *School Dialogues*, Fenn explains that one cannot adhere to the advice of Horace (by which time the expression was associated with Pope) to "keep your piece nine years" in a project such as the one she was writing for children, "still less by her who writes more immediately for a particular Boy, who is on the point of emerging from her wing into that LITTLE WORLD, a SCHOOL" (1:ix).[60] This idea of the little world runs through the book, near the end of which one master explains to a visitor, "A school, madam, is a little world; the members of the community are not what we *wish*; we must make the best that we *can* of them" (2:135). The discourse about worlds—that there were essentially three of them the boy would encounter (that of his family, that of his school, and that of manhood) was an entrenched mode of speaking about masculine development. Mavis Reimer identifies the metaphor as "also a figure borrowed from allegory. While the repeated use of the metaphor sometimes makes it appear to be little more than a commonplace, there is a residual power in the figure. It is a figure that asserts that a school is a complete and circumscribed system, but at the same time a figure that implies the correspondence of the school system to 'world' systems on other scales and levels."[61]

In the 1801 book *Juvenile Philosophy*, by Richard Corbould and Samuel Springsguth, a mother spells out for her son the demands he is to face, and the reasons for doing so:

> You are yet a child, a spoiled child, as it is called:—you must very soon go to school, which is not only a place for the education of youth in different kinds of learning, but a school is a little world, which prepares you to act with more firmness when you appear in the real world. In a school, if you shew any little fretful airs, your schoolmates will correct you more effectively than your masters. You will there, in some degree, learn to subdue your passions, improve your manners, endure some hardship and prepare you the better to meet those buffets, which you will certainly find when you arrive at manhood, and have dealings in the world.[62]

Here again the mother's love encompasses her willingness to send the boy away from that love, that he might "meet those buffets" that are beyond her purview as his first teacher. In *School Dialogues*, our boy Sprightly is just entering that second, larger, "little world," and he does indeed learn more from his schoolmates than from his masters.

Sophia Woodley observes that the debate between public and private education in the long eighteenth century involved serious questions such as "Did school teach virtue or vice? Did children flourish under authority or liberty? Were children naturally good, or did they need to be taught goodness? In viewing schools as microcosms of society as a whole, both radical and evangelical writers placed their opposition to public education within the context of their criticisms of society as it was currently constituted."[63] Fenn, no radical, writes about school in a measured, judicious, and cautionary way. The little world of the school is, as such, somewhat heterotopic, for it is not as safe and predictable as Sprightly's home, yet it is necessary he experience this sometimes disturbing other place. Fenn was a rational moralist, and the *Dialogues* are also, as we have seen, somewhat evangelical: head boy Sensible recommends for Sprightly's further reading Saint Paul and is emphatic in his response to Sprightly's wonder at some children's wickedness: "O, my dear, do you forget that we are naturally prone to evil?" (1:72, 75). The little world of the school is important for testing and teaching not only to prepare boys for the larger world of men but for the still larger world to be met with after the terrestrial, because "we Christians are as certain, as if we could see Heaven with our eyes, that all good people are happy" (1:72).

It is clearly important that the boy has one instructive, safe "little world" at home before he ventures into that larger world of the school, onward and upward until he arrives at manhood and has dealings in "the world." So, while Rebecca Davies is right to point out that in this period "when understood as a feminine concern, education implied domestic education rather than a publicly defined system of schooling,"[64] Fenn's school story argues the boy's success in the publicly defined system is deeply rooted in his domestic education. This rootedness is evident in the observation made by one of his masters: "Sprightly is acquainted with several naughty boys, yet Sprightly remains good" (2:66). In fact, a faultless little child named Gentle becomes Sprightly's closest friend, even going home with him for a holiday, and they bond "like brothers." The love between good boys is a touching thing in Fenn's book. Sprightly encounters it because he earns it, and he values it because he has grown up in a loving household.

Trifles and Mothers

The correlation between the familial world and the scholarly is highlighted in the *Dialogues*, as when Sprightly compliments Gentle for keeping his linen neat. The reply is telling: "I always consider whether my drawers are in such order as my mamma would approve, if she saw them." Sprightly vows to follow suit, "and make it a rule to do as I know [my mamma] would have me, even in those seeming trifles" (1:111). Given research into the wider early modern period that evinces the belief in "a parent's duty, and that of the individual himself when he reached adulthood, to ensure that his female attributes were kept in abeyance,"[65] this incident with the linen suggests a couple of things. First, Fenn is saying it is not only acceptable but ideal for a boy to be like his mother in some ways. Second, Sprightly's phrase "seeming trifles" is important to Fenn's project—again and again the phrase is raised to indicate that good habits—like bad—are not trifles. When Sprightly's mother visits the school, she tells the master, Mr. Wiseman, directly that "to a *parent* nothing is a *trifle*" (2:44). This precept is particularly relevant to mothers in the book. Prior to Fenn's work, "Augustan conduct literature ... perceived mothers as uniquely suited, indeed obligated, to be their children's first teachers and constant companions."[66] Carol Percy points out "Fenn's method [of educating children along with mothers] not only acknowledges but exploits the temporal and spatial constraints of the so-called 'private' sphere in which women's agency extends to running the household and raising an uncontrollably growing brood of children. Privately educating children is a source of pride or anxiety; a mother of a male child in particular might eventually indirectly influence the public, or be harshly judged by them."[67] Good mothers in texts written for children (whatever gender their author) were earnest in their duty to prepare their children for school, the masters, and, most of all, the other children they would encounter in the world of school itself—where all such individual worlds and personalities meet.

The good boys at the school in Fenn's book experienced living up to their duties well before leaving home. The bad boys learned something different at home, with unreasonable behavior and unlikeable characters being the result. At the beginning of Fenn's second volume, schoolboy Wilful is told that when he was brought to the school, the servant who accompanied him "said he was glad to get rid" of the boy and, further, "that even your mamma could not bear you any longer at home" (2:10). This is a serious indictment, compounded by the fact that Wilful's younger brother at home is cut from the same cloth. Fenn's book thereby offers cautionary tales through which parents—mothers especially—are meant to learn about duty too. The "puppets" (unlikeable boys) provide cautionary tales for mothers as much as for sons.

Fenn does not shy from making very clear that, like boys themselves, some mothers are better than others, and a negligent mother, or one who lacks seriousness, has a dire effect on her boy. While Sprightly is on holiday at home, his sister reads to him an anecdote in which a mother threatens her son: "She said to the eldest boy, 'now your brother is coming home; and if you be not very good, I shall love him best.'" Sprightly's response, "How contrary to my mamma's management!," is surely didacticism aimed at all mammas. What follows this anecdote is a passage from Richardson's *Sir Charles Grandison*, the translation of a sonnet beginning, "See a fond mother, encircled by her children . . ." (2:53). Part of Richardson's texts, and Fenn's message, is that a good mother is like Providence itself: whether such a mother "smiles or frowns, 'tis all in tender love." She is therefore never capricious, but rather a mistress of the via media.

The solemnity of the mother's duty in her son's early years is brought home to both generations in the final pages of the second volume of dialogues.[68] When one of the masters, Sage, explains to a visiting mother that "for the heinous offence of telling a falsehood, a tongue cut in red cloth is worn;—for the still more atrocious crime, a malicious lie, a black tongue," the lady responds, "Proper, doubtless; but it would break the heart of a mother, for her son to deserve them" (2:136). While planting the seeds of fear of both public punishment and guilt itself in the boy reader, the implication is also that the mother who has not done her utmost to prevent such offences deserves the heartbreak.[69] Indeed, boys like Wilful, "an ill-managed child" before turning up at school, appear to have little chance of recovering from their formative years under parental mismanagement (2:91). One Tom Idle's discontent with school fare is laid at his mother's door: "The fault was Mrs. Idle's—not the boy's." The result of maternal overindulgence is far-reaching and bleak: Tom, we learn, "will probably never be happy" (1:38).[70] Thankfully, Sprightly's parents are gratified to learn on a visit that "he is the same engaging child as he was at home" (1:42). Sprightly's uprightness and goodness are largely attributed to his mother's influence: she plainly states, "Of the progress which my little boy makes in his learning, it is Mr. Sprightly's province to enquire; his temper and morals are more immediately my department" (2:43). Women are not fit for the scholarly world, evidently. Anthony Fletcher notes that for centuries "male intellectual powers . . . were seen as superior to women's and therein lay the boy's potential, it was believed, to exercise the command and authority over others which his patriarchal role demanded."[71] There is no reason to suppose that Fenn was not among those who shared this belief. At the same time, the point is made throughout the *Dialogues* that temper, morality, and assiduity *are* the most important things in a boy's life and upon these his future chiefly depends.[72]

As we saw in the previous chapter about the ritual of breeching, too close or too lasting an association between mother and son could still be considered suspicious—threatening to impede the boy on his journey into manhood. Critics who work on nineteenth-century boy stories tend to agree with Elizabeth Segel that "the boy's book was, above all, an escape from domesticity and from the female domination of that world."[73] The threat of the feminine problematized gender expectations, and this was more of a danger if a mother was herself inadequately educated. The specter of a mother neither knowledgeable enough to teach nor wise enough to let go resulted in aligning the mother with old wives' tales and servants rather than exalting her position. Michèle Cohen notes, "Throughout the eighteenth century, parents, particularly mothers, had been blamed for interfering with their children's education—especially their sons."[74] In the *Dialogues*, however, little Sprightly's mother can be accused of no such meddling, remaining in her province of shaping the boy's temper and morals (2:41, 43). Fenn's schoolboy book, as homosocial as the little world is, does not itself evince the seeds of the kind of escape "from the female domination" of the domestic world that Segel identifies elsewhere. Rather, female guidance especially provides the boy with the tools he needs to negotiate the nondomestic world where he will take his place.

Boys' Books: Time Well Spent

I never saw a little dog or cat learn to read. But little boys can learn. If you do not learn, Charles, you are not good for half so much as Puss. You had better be drowned.
—Anna Laetitia Barbauld, Lessons for Children *(1778–1779)*

Contrary to the "beast" Walter Shandy feared his son Tristram would resemble once in breeches, elsewhere, as in Barbauld's lesson above, it is the unlearned boy who is compared to a beast. For example, in a 1774 book for spelling, reading, and orthography, *The School Boy's Sure Guide*, author John Scott stated, "Youth, left to themselves, without any instruction, will remain almost as ignorant as the beasts of the field; but by a liberal education, they may become useful members of society, and an ornament to the nation."[75] Such a distinction between beast-like youth and those rendered both useful *and* ornamental profits the family and England. Scott uses "ornament" here in the sense of one who "enhances or adds distinction to his or her sphere, time, etc." In the same vein, John Newbery advised "would you have a *Wise* Son, teach him to reason early. Let him read, and make him understand what he reads."[76] In *School Dialogues* the act of reading, both assigned and for personal pleasure, is itself like friendship in that reading involves reasoning. The books that have informed the young pupils prior to their arrival at school have played a part in their formation (and are further evidence of parental responsibility).

Sprightly's new friend Gentle lists among his possessions a book of fables, a history of birds and beasts, a history of England, and "a small Roman History." (The last of these might refer to a schoolboy edition of *Plutarch's Lives*.) Both Sprightly and Gentle have also read *Robinson Crusoe*, a "prototypically boys' book" whose influence on children's literature Andrew O'Malley has shown to be considerable yet also vexed:[77] "eighteenth-century pedagogues regarded Crusoe as admirably independent, yet the children whom they would have become like him had paradoxically to be dissuaded from aspiring to an independence that threatened parental authority and in turn social order."[78] We have seen opprobrium directed at real school riots in *School Dialogues* and know that Sprightly is praised most highly for his docility. Perhaps most significant is that Sprightly and Gentle are familiar with Defoe's original, rather than the numerous chapbook versions aimed at plebian readers that O'Malley notes "emphasized and prized (certainly above the novel's spiritual considerations) its seafaring and adventure aspects."[79] It is not adventure but rather adherence to parents' wishes (which Crusoe regrets his failure to practice) that makes the good boys in *School Dialogues* good. Head Boy Sensible tells his young charges, "Obedience to parents is the first duty," to which Pert answers back, "We have no parents here." Yet what they do have here at school are the masters, ushers, and older boys like Sensible himself—"those who are appointed by your parents to act as their deputies" (2:91). Fenn does acknowledge in the words of the head boy, "A child is naturally inclined to prefer *sport* to *study*." However, the docile child—the child with a happy future—"gives up his inclination to the commands of his teachers" (1:106).

One of the most notable aspects of *Robinson Crusoe* is the protagonist's keeping of various kinds of accounts, along with efforts to keep track of time in days, weeks, seasons, and years. For the schoolboy, reading a book—or reading, memorizing, and repeating (and, ideally, mastering) one's lessons from it—is also one way of measuring the time spent at school. The sense of time as fleeting and therefore not to be wasted is introduced in the very first pages of *School Dialogues*, and it is introduced as something that books specifically grapple with: "I could not delay [publication] forever," says Fenn in her preface, because "the boys, for whom they are primarily designed, would be grown up to men" (1:xvii).[80] As the author has been hastened, so are her puppets and phantoms in the dialogues: a comically touching moment arises when schoolboy Supple, far behind in his studies, laments, "I can not learn so fast as I could when I was eight years old." The nostalgia intensifies a few lines further on when he wails, "O! that I could recall time!" (2:84). As amusing as this is, it also serves as a reminder—similar, I think, to that signaled by the occasional precision of the boys' ages: Sprightly is six and a half; Jeremy Baldock (whose story of early death so impresses Sprightly) was seven years and a quarter when he died in 1602. The boy who has lived long enough to become a schoolboy has no guarantee he will grow to manhood—a lesson Rousseau emphasized in *Émile*: "Of the children born, half, at most, grow to adolescence; and it is probable that your pupil will not reach the age of manhood."[81]

However, Fenn's message is not that of Rousseau, who urged the gathering of rosebuds as a response to the uncertainty of a child's life. Rather, Sprightly and other laudable boys in *School Dialogues* are akin to the child speaker we find in Isaac Watts's enduringly popular 1715 poem "Against Idleness and Mischief":

> In books, or work, or healthful play
> Let my first years be past,
> That I may give for every day
> Some good account at last.[82]

Deborah Simonton argues that even as "children's value shifted" as regards how parents invested in their future, "enlightenment society was often concerned there was not enough work for children."[83] At the end of the book when Supple is rewarded along with Sprightly and Gentle, it is lovely to see that Supple—who had left his first school in disgrace—has redeemed himself by hard work and cultivating friendships. Not being able to "recall time" to when he was eight years old and felt it slipping away from him, Supple has nevertheless made up for lost time.

In addition to *Crusoe*, other works recommended in the *Dialogues* include *Spectator #56*, the "Fable of Marraton and Yaratilda," which Fenn in a footnote advises her reader to acquire. The tale tells of an indigenous visionary in the Americas who saw the place his spirit would go after death. From reading the fable Sprightly experiences consolation in his own religious tradition: "that there is a place of happiness prepared for us" (1:71). The *Spectator* piece ends with Marraton catching sight also of "several Molten Seas of Gold, in which were plunged the Souls of barbarous Europeans, who put to the Sword so many Thousands of poor Indians for the sake of that precious Metal."[84] In this way Fenn's narrator offers interpretation of texts that schoolboys might have come across as well as recommendations of those they have not. As with references to Plutarch, she demonstrates both her own knowledge and her authority in doing so.

The précis of "Marraton and Yaratilda" also makes a point about cruelty, another theme frequently directed toward boys. "Pray, Master Savage," the good-hearted Sprightly admonishes a cruel schoolfellow early on, "a goose can feel pain as well as a boy" (1:45).[85] Such sensibility (or more specifically in the case with the goose, empathy) is another important difference between the good and the naughty boy. While in this last instance it is Savage throwing stones that calls forth Sprightly's protest, it is often Sprightly's responses to what he has read that reveals his kind and receptive disposition. Hence Sprightly's continual recollections of little Jeremy Baldock become a touchstone: "What would *Baldock* have done, when *Pert* called out, 'I think your book is very dull?'" Sprightly wonders, hoping to improve his own patience (1:101). Contemplating a boy he admires in a book he has read, Sprightly is better able to cope with a real boy criticizing the book he is reading. What he has read becomes a tool to deal with adversity.

A book-related disappointment encountered by some of the boys arriving at the school is that they have new grammars to deal with—those books containing the first principles of grammar. When Supple, who arrives later than Sprightly despite being older, finds this to be the case, he feels sorry for himself, and others commiserate:

> SPRIGHTLY: It is hard upon Supple that he used a different grammar at Lington.
> TAUNT: He did not learn much in it.
> CAREFUL: But what he has learned is of no use here.
> SENSIBLE: You are greatly mistaken; but if it were not of use, you should not discourage him.—(2:85)

Supple is distraught, feeling "like a great overgrown dunce, surrounded by little boys!" He soon learns, however, that Sprightly was in a similar position when he arrived. "The grammar used here is different from that which my mamma taught me.... I was disappointed," Sprightly admits, but, upon encountering this setback, he studied hard and raised himself to a higher class (2:88–89).

This is an interesting exchange, reflecting what must have been a common dilemma for children arriving at school: one critic in 1764 asked, "How many *complete* English Grammars on *new* plans, have we already had, or been threatened with?"[86] Although none of the grammars under dispute in *School Dialogues* is named, given the fact that Fenn herself would go on to write both *The Mother's Grammar* and *The Child's Grammar* in 1798, we know she had a strong interest in the subject.[87] It is also noteworthy that the discussion about grammars leads to Sprightly's only near-scuffle, related to an alignment of the maternal educator and grammar. When Pert says, "All *his* (pointing to Sprightly) mamma's time was thrown away, and she thought herself so clever," the little boy takes offence:

SPRIGHTLY [interrupting him]: Whatever liberties you take with me, I will not allow such freedom of speech about my mamma.
PERT: Will you fight me?
SPRIGHTLY: If—
SENSIBLE: Do not answer him—Mrs. Sprightly's time was well spent; he had acquired a habit of studying, he had improved his memory, he had learned to consider the allotted task as a duty. (2:90)

Habits of learning are more important than what one learns—a point about effort made repeatedly in the boys' book. Furthermore, given what Percy identifies as "grammar's centrality to separating the sexes," especially in fiction, young Sprightly's willingness to defend his mother is laudable in more than one way—as a son who loves his mother and as a male defending a female on educational grounds (even as his docile character is reinforced by his being dissuaded from fighting).

The association between mother and son through grammar, and the need for the son to adapt to a new grammar beyond that mother's ken, is intriguing, particularly since any standardization of language rules is in some way political. Janet Sorenson argues that Samuel Johnson's "*Dictionary* makes English alien even to many of its 'native' speakers, and in this sense the position of colonial subjects and of national, provincial, female, and labour-class subjects would be aligned."[88] Similarly, according to Sorenson, "Many earlier grammarians celebrated English, yet urged its improvement in accordance with the rules of a universal grammar, thereby effacing, in a sense, the particularity of the vernacular."[89] In Fenn's own grammar books (aimed at boys and girls alike)[90] she would do the same—as any grammar must inevitably deal with rules—however there too mothers are honored as teachers. In the dialogue noted above, grammar is a bridge unifying mothers and their sons, not a branch of learning that divides them.

Percy argues that in addition to correct grammar being a means to social mobility, "As a metonymy of education, grammar is both an impediment to and an instrument of sexual connection: by shaping gender, grammar entails separation as well as the possibility of communication."[91] Mrs. Sprightly and her son have enjoyed the latter—communication (and one might say, too, communion) through grammar. They have both, mother and son, done their duty. As a result, they have not only the natural bond inherent in their relationship but also a cultural one, created with books. *School Dialogues, for Boys* is clearly intended to do the same.

Authorial Persona(e)

Although both were brought out anonymously, *School Dialogues, for Boys* evidences a desire to build on the reputation Fenn began with her recently published reading primer *Cobwebs to Catch Flies*. Prior to the conversations in the *Dialogues*, and following the dedication to her nephew, Fenn included a playful preface evidently directed at the mothers of boys. This preface contains richly associative metaphors that force us to consider Fenn's self-positioning as an author:

> I am a person behind a curtain attempting to fly a kite. If it soar to the skies, I may venture to come forward; should it fall to the ground, I can remain in concealment. I am an old woman in a mask, personating youth. I am a Parthian, shooting my arrows at random, scarce daring to look where they fall. I am a woman exposing my child in a basket, and keeping aloof till it is received. I am an ostrich—I have laid my egg—perhaps for the sun to cherish—perhaps for the passenger to crush. (1:xxi)

Classical Greek tales, biblical allusion, and natural philosophy all come into this theatrical self-identification. Whereas the docile child may be the ideal, the female author is not marked by docility. And as much as the riddles suggest flight from confrontation (the "Parthian arrow" refers to that arrow shot at one's enemy while retreating) playing with the idea of fearfulness on the part of the narrator, authorial pride still frolics with humility. A footnote here informs us, "To those who know that this is not the Writer's first publication, it may be necessary to say that it was designed to be so" (xii). There are other hints about that first publication in the preface, where she calls herself "a spider—I have long spun in a corner, and now venture to fix my web in a more conspicuous situation" (xxi). Given the popularity of *Cobwebs to Catch Flies* the year before, the authorship of *School Dialogues* is an open secret.[92] After identifying herself thus as the spider in a corner, she refers to herself as the very topic about which—and the reader for whom—she writes: "I am a school-boy—I have placed my exercise upon the desk—from a retired corner I observe its success" (1:xxi). This author-as-schoolboy moment echoes nicely at the end of the second volume when Sprightly is rewarded for academic and social success—one of the three "glorious boys!" awarded the laurels—as a result of having cultivated the right qualities again and finally linking the woman behind the text to the boy in the text.

The ostrich having laid her egg "perhaps for the sun to cherish—perhaps for the passenger to crush" in the preface is one of the instances in which, while making clear she is not a mother, Fenn impersonates the mother and, in so doing, her other target audience. We see her here as joining ranks with those women who produced

"Georgian maternal pedagogy," which Mitzi Myers identifies as "linking private and public spheres." This pedagogy "insists on the communal consequences of domestic instruction" with the aim "always to empower the living mother as teacher."[93] After all, a year after *School Dialogues, for Boys* Fenn would specify in the dedication to *The Female Guardian*, "*by the* Public *the writers means Mothers.*" Two years after that, in *The Rational Dame*, she asserted, "Under the inspection of a judicious mother . . . what might—what might not be done."[94] The possibilities of this phrasing are endless—an assertion that mirrors the possibilities of self-identifying in her prefaces to *School Dialogues* (kite-flyer, arrow-shooter, ostrich), where she might also have been revisiting the idea of cards with pictures that accompany her subsequent grammars and can be seen on the learning blocks in her *Set of Toys* (ca. 1780).[95]

Shifting away from listing metaphors in the preface to *School Dialogues*, Fenn's tone turns didactic: "I am—but I will be serious—you may suppose me a person interested in the conduct of children, and consequently desirous of conveying instruction in the vehicle which I believe to be most agreeable to them" (xxii). Having just played with her own role-playing, she now anticipates readers wondering about the woman in the mask:

> I will resume my cheerful vein—and imagine my readers to exclaim—
> "Who can this be?"
> "Mrs.___? Or Mrs. ___? Or Miss___?"
> I answer, what imports my name? I am romping behind the scenes, but do not choose to appear on the stage.
> I am
> ANY BODY!
> Or, I am
> NOBODY! (1:xxv–xxvi)

Whereas it seems to conflate the child reader who enjoys a good brain teaser and the adult reader who might actually think along these lines—"Mrs.___? Or Mrs. ___?"—this playful, riddling kind of introducing is self-consciously literary. The question "what imports my name?" echoes *Romeo and Juliet*. A nonapology for "appear[ing] in a negligent garb—who would not come forth in any dress to do good?" is again evocative of the stage (xvii). This sets the reader up for the dialogues as theatrical vignettes but is itself far from cautionary in tone. It seems that, just as "rods and sugar-plums" meet in the houses of naughty schoolboys, in Fenn's dialogue conduct book the rods are in some measure the dialogues aimed at the boys, the sugar-plum is the preface for the maternal reader or, like Fenn herself, the play-mother or female guardian: another semi-rhetorical figure apart from the boys she creates.

Leading her maternal reader into the text Fenn imagines that woman thinking "I can write better," to which the narrator playfully responds, "Probably you *can*—but *will* you?—have you *leisure*?—If you *have*, and *will* write, will you *print* for those who have *not*?" (xix). She accomplishes a great deal with these rhetorical questions. In addition to pragmatism she supplies the requisite modesty: "Probably you can"; the challenge: "but will you?"; the acknowledgment of a mother's busy life along with a kind of goad: "have you leisure?" And then comes the seemingly philanthropic question: "will you print for those who have not?" This printing, then, is on behalf of those maternal teachers without the leisure to start from scratch.

School Dialogues stands as evidence that "women have historically been understood as 'maternal' whether or not they are biologically mothers."[96] This understanding is one Fenn plays with repeatedly. In the dedication to *Rational Sports* a year after *School Dialogues*, her authorial persona voices a fear "of Strangers! who will say this Preface is a pompous Introduction of my readers to— NOTHING!" The Speaker then compliments the "REAL MOTHER" to whom she dedicates that text, thereby signaling again that she is herself not real, but *some sort* of mother nevertheless—what we might call a play-mother.[97] This idée fixe is worked through with miscellaneous tropes to create such peers. So, in *The Art of Teaching in Sport* (1785) Fenn would explain, "I view a mother as mistress of the revels among her little people."[98] Carol Percy, again, has drawn attention to the extent to which Fenn claimed to tailor her books to the "vivacious" young mother, and the preface to *School Dialogues* shows the play-mother reveling among her little people—her puppets, her phantom boys—as well.[99]

Beverly Lyon Clark—who acknowledges that *School Dialogues* is "probably the earliest boys' school story told by a woman"—is not especially impressed by the book, complaining that "Fenn could allow [fantasy] only in her Prefaces—the site, usually, of greater grounding of our world outside the fiction."[100] She has a point. Whereas naughty and nice boys in the book are one-dimensional, at the same time our hero is Sprightly—a virtue name, as Carol Percy points out, usually associated with women.[101] The name also conveys a potential for change not reflected in the morally loaded names of the other scholars (Worthy, Goodwill, Wilful, Flippant . . .). However, there is a tension to be read therein, for Sprightly does not, in comparison to his docility, seem notably vivacious or lively, but rather timorous and serious. Indeed, the mysterious "lady behind a curtain" who reveals in the preface that she conceals herself in corners proves more sprightly than any of her characters.

Yet in the preface to the *School Dialogues* Fenn uses that adjective full of promise to connect the reading mother to the reading boy: "Such a mother will rejoice to meet with a few pages sprightly enough to engage the attention of her darling son to those maxims which it is her constant aim to fulfill" (1:xiv). In doing so, she pays homage to the relationship already there, speaking to "You, whose hearts throb incessantly with anxiety for your offspring" (1:xv). Wayne C. Booth posited, "The author makes his readers. . . . If he make them well—that is, makes them see what they have never experienced altogether—he finds his reward in the peers he has created."[102] Such a peer group is what Fenn interestingly both creates and sets herself apart from as their teacher. Further, as Fenn's play-mother identifies herself as "Anybody" and "Nobody" in her preface—a cypher—she has something in common with her main character, because Sprightly is everybody.

Rhetorical Tools

Fenn wrote more books for girls than for boys, but most were for both. *School Dialogues, for Boys*, a gift for and inspired by her nephew, is also clearly (albeit indirectly) about and for women. Boys were not unfrequently used as rhetorical tools to achieve female education since, as Wollstonecraft asked, "how should a woman void of reflection be capable of educating her children?"[103] It went unquestioned by the majority of readers that boys were the children whose education mattered most (which is not to say Wollstonecraft thought this). While it is undeniable that, as Susan Staves argues, "the exclusion of women from the schools that provide rigorous classical literary education and from the universities did provide considerable protection for the male monopoly of literary prestige,"[104] the learned mother troubles this monopoly as she teaches the boy: even as she distances herself from prestige, she imparts cultural capital to the next generation of those who will benefit from an education prohibited to her.

I have noted Fenn's place among those at the end of the eighteenth century who wrote books for children that were also very much aimed at women, intellectuals who, as Mitzi Myers describes them, "in their capacity as surrogate mothers" testified "to maternal and pedagogical power."[105] Taylor Walle, too, notes that Fenn's writing is characteristic of two key trends of the period: "the increasing visibility of the female author and the emergence of the mother-teacher."[106] The bluestocking circles largely responsible for and responsive to such movements as Sunday school campaigns (as well as antislavery poetry that emphasized childhood and motherhood in appeals for abolition) are critically situated here, including women like Anna Laetitia Barbauld, Sarah Trimmer, Dorothy Kilner, Hannah More, and Maria Edgeworth.[107] The preoccupations Fenn shares with these writers have been much discussed, yet here in *School Dialogues, for Boys* the mother is elided in the space of the boy's school and the educators—young and old—he meets with there, in ways that empower them both.

I am cautious in the claim I make here for a relationship between women's writing and writing for boys; as Perry Nodelman noted as far back as 1988, some scholars "insist on a significant connection between femininity and children's literature in general," which places limitations on the genre (and all genders).[108] Nodelman takes exception to what he sees as going too far in the argument that "to be a female writer is to be conscious of the freakishness of the very act of writing (much is made of traditional images of pen as penis and blank paper as the female body), so that feminine writing is very much a response to a male-dominated world."[109] While I am interested in the phallic symbolism of the pen in relation to boyhood (see the following chapter), I have been more interested in interrogating the tabula rasa not of the paper, nor the woman's body, but of the boy. If much "feminine writing" is a response to patriarchy (and it would be hard to argue otherwise), what are we to make of the figure of the boy in such responses? How is the schoolboy in particular, with his intersection of gender, age, and education, made to function as a trope, a rhetorical tool for the woman who writes him?

The figure of the schoolboy dominates eighteenth-century depictions of boyhood, albeit not usually as the sweet little boy Fenn creates in Sprightly.[110] In examining the ambiguous position of such a boy, Kristina Straub notes, "He is not a man and therefore is subjected to the domination of them. On the other hand, he presumably will be a man and is, furthermore, engaged in the education process that is the conduit to masculine authority, particularly literary authority, in the eighteenth century. His very figure configures masculinity as contingent and relational, however achievable, and it is not surprising to see him crop up in *ad hominem* arguments about literary authority."[111] Straub, who observes, "The trope of the schoolboy threads through a range of eighteenth-century discourses, connoting a subjected position in a homosocial, sometimes homoerotic economy of power," pays special attention to Colley Cibber and Alexander Pope, whose *Dunciad* "taps into the sexual ambivalence implicit in the trope of the schoolboy to turn it into a sign for an abject, despised masculinity."[112] In stark contrast, what Fenn does with young, nonsexual Sprightly is bring that "conduit to masculine authority" into the service of her feminine literary authority. Sprightly is a schoolboy, but he is no sign of abject, despised masculinity. He is a sign of involved, treasured maternity.

As such, *School Dialogues*, and the relationship between boys and women therein, makes the new schoolboy into something like the "space" Paula Backscheider identifies in the depiction of women: "available as fetish, trophy, trope, and symbol, woman can stand for whatever is needed."[113] In combining the privilege of masculinity with lack—of experience, of agency, of authority—so too can *boy*, again, be a space, and "can stand for whatever is needed" when a woman takes up the pen. Among other effects, to write about schoolboys, who will "one day be men," is an oblique way of commenting on desirable qualities in men themselves (*School Dialogues*, 1:67).

What I am saying is that the oft-troped schoolboy, a figure that lends itself to rhetoric about masculine privilege concomitant with the pitfalls of youth, also lends itself to Fenn's messaging along with shaping her own identity. "Rhetoric," Terry Eagleton reminds us, "the received form of critical analysis all the way from ancient society to the eighteenth century... was not worried about whether its objects of enquiry were speaking or writing, poetry or philosophy, fiction or historiography: its horizon was nothing less than the field of discursive practices in society as a whole, and its particular interest lay in grasping such practices of power and performance."[114] Fenn shows herself in *School Dialogues* to be keenly aware of herself as a rhetorical writer—"given to using rhetorical figures and patterns."[115] Furthermore, as with the reference to Plutarch in the *Dedication*, she demonstrates her own familiarity with curricular aspects of the boy's education, even as she prepares him for them.[116] Again, the depreciative possibilities of rhetoric are played with in her own reference to puppets and phantoms. Consider these eighteenth-century explanations of rhetoric: "The rhetorical author makes use of his tropes and figures, which are his high and low runners, to cheat us" (1721); "To a Rhetorical Writer these calamities presented an easy opportunity to dress up a train of horrible phantoms, to affright his Readers" (1792).[117] Such "high and low runners" and "train of ... phantoms" are precisely what Fenn claims to have created in the *School Dialogues*.

Similar rhetoric characterizes introductory pieces to her numerous books (she wrote twenty-seven in total).[118] For instance, in the dedication to *School Occurrences: Supposed to Have Arisen among a Set of Young Ladies* (1782–1783) Fenn's pseudonymous Mrs. Teachwell begins, "I have read of a country where the courtiers admonished the king indirectly what he *ought to be*, by returning thanks that he was such, for instance that he was wise and virtuous."[119] She had hit on a formula. Like the enforced drunkenness of slaves from Plutarch, this lesson in encomium shows off the author's education even as she simplifies it to explain her aims. But I also think the analogy of the courtiers and the king *is* decidedly different from the slaves made to drink and the young men who observe them in *Plutarch's Lives*. We find in her book for boys the more daring and serious analogy of the Spartan slaves for what the author is doing—due perhaps to her readers being boys who will "grow up to be men." *School Dialogues* participates in the complex mission that Percy identifies in Fenn's grammar books. The latter demonstrate, Percy argues, the "high social value of grammar and the maternal educator; idealized for her 'civilizing' influence, especially on men."[120] *School Dialogues* also argues for the high social value of its own genre.

Fenn's claim that in her fictional schoolboys she has "created a set of Puppets, to whom I impute such faults as may suit my purposes" references another performative genre. Julie Park argues "a poetics of puppetry in eighteenth-century England informed not just the textual productions of narrative, but also the ability for narrative to reconstruct the human subject as a character to create and manipulate across the page."[121] At the same time it is worth recalling, as Park notes, that it was only at the very end of the century that puppets were "relegated to the sphere of children." For Park, the "culture's persistent attachment to the theme indicates a more complex and submerged evaluation of ... issues of agency, self-awareness, and mastery over one's world."[122] The term "puppet" thereby has richer possibilities than those we invest it with now (although both then as now the word has negative connotations, as with the varied ways of defining a "tool," and people being either). The implications of the word "puppet" were well understood by Fenn as rhetorical writer, including "a person who impersonates another; an actor, *esp.* an inferior one. *Obs., as well as* 3. *derogatory*. A person, esp. a woman, whose (esp. gaudy) dress or manner is thought to suggest a lack of substance or individuality."[123] These definitions suggest not only a distancing between the author and her characters in Fenn's preface but also a proximity—between women and boys for, like her characters, the author too is puppet-like: the "Lady" claims to appear "on the stage" in "negligent garb" and "wearing a mask" in her preface. Because of her hints to mothers here, along with her dedication to a real schoolboy in her life, together with lessons in the dialogues themselves, the "Reader" she addresses must be both the schoolboy of the title and that schoolboy's mother. The schoolboy is thereby a tool for female authorial empowerment, and the author's work is an educational tool whereby the boy can enhance and advance his own education.

Fruits of Labor

The lady who visits the school at the end of the book exclaims over the victory of Sprightly and his fellow prize-winning students, "What do you suppose the mothers of such boys must feel?" The schoolmaster who stands beside her answers, "More than they can express, or I conceive" (2:138). Here the reader is very much the maternal one, and there are no boys who speak in the exchange. The unintended humor of this final line (since only mothers can conceive) nevertheless recalls us to the mothers of boys good and bad and to the lessons the book conveys to parents: either negligence or overindulgence can ruin a boy.

But there is another way of reading those final words of the book—"More than they can express, or I conceive"—for they remind the reading mother of the preface, where the author imagines that reader thinking "I can write better," before playfully responding, "probably you *can*—but *will* you?—have you *leisure*?—If you *have*, and *will* write, will you *print* for those who have *not*?" (1:xix). Most mothers were (as many still are) without much leisure time in which to educate their children. Consider again Richardson's *Pamela*: once her virtue has been rewarded with marriage and family, the heroine laments, "But what mother can take too much pains to cultivate the minds of her children?—If . . . it were not for these frequent lyings-in!"[124] Conceiving of children is an obstacle to cultivating their minds, due to the constraints of time and energy. In Fenn's book, to conceive a child places a woman in the position of first educator—Sprightly's mother has done well in her province—yet conception (gestational) and further education are in opposition ("more than they can express, or I can conceive").

I began this reading of the schoolboy, as Fenn began her book, with reference to Plutarch's Spartans: "a people who obliged their slaves to drink to excess." Among other renowned aspects of Spartan civilization is this anecdote from Plutarch's *Morals*: "Being asked by a woman from Attica, 'Why is it that you Spartan women are the only women that lord it over your men,' [the Spartan mother] said, 'Because we are the only women that are mothers of men.'"[125] The context for this boast is that these are the mothers of warriors, willing (even eager) to let their sons enter into battle and die for their nation. There are no such sacrifices demanded of the pupils in *School Dialogues*, nor of their mothers. Yet, when our boy Sprightly's mother visits the school, even as she expresses fondness for her "sweet child," she tells the master, "I wish not to hear *flattery*, but *truth*" (2:44, 40). Mrs. Sprightly betrays the depths of her anxieties with "tears of joy" when she learns that, while he is improving, her son has not otherwise altered: "I find he is the same engaging child as he was at home" (2:42). Fondness is tempered by integrity and exactness, because adulthood—and the afterlife—is serious. "The Lady" narrator posing in the prefatory material of *School Dialogues*—the play-mother—claims among her riddles "I am an ostrich—I have laid my egg—perhaps for the sun to cherish—perhaps for the passenger to crush" (1:xxi). Again, this metaphor plays with maternity and distance. The egg—the book and the boy—is also under threat, awaiting an uncertain future. As such, the egg is a sign that the author's head was not in the sand about the world of boys and men.

In thinking about the place of the schoolboy in the long eighteenth century (as with that of other boys), it is worth quoting Thomas A. King's crucial—and sobering—point that in the early modern era "children, servants, apprentices, students, some adult men, slaves, and women were all property of some other men."[126] Given this fact about power and imbalance, another mask Fenn mentions, which again assumes responsibility in terms of the book-as-child, is the one I find most striking. This is the authorial persona figured as the mother of Moses, and her book as that infant son: "I am a woman exposing my child in a basket, and keeping aloof till it is received" (1:xx).[127] This mask once more conflates book and baby, and in a text aimed at the boy going off to school, the analogy suggests both fear and its reassurance at the sight of that basket drifting away. The myth this evokes is that of a future leader whose mother let him go, and who grew up to free enslaved people, not to be one himself or to enslave others.

From our vantage point we might wish for more pointed lessons, and more straightforward warnings about what the boy leaving the nest could meet with at school—is it only laziness, boastfulness, and cruelty to birds that he has to fear from the next world of the public school?[128] After all, Fenn closes her dedication to her nephew with the prayer that he be preserved "amidst a crooked and perverse generation."[129] Yet the primary intended reader here is like Sprightly—very young. Further, there *are* certainly codifications in these prefatory materials—and the dialogues—which would have been understood on a number of levels by adult readers about the "contagion of bad example" and "the poison of pernicious counsel" to which the author alludes in borrowing from Plutarch. And the "slaves obliged to drink to excess"? There is flesh and blood in that short phrase, as we know that at some stage, at some school, the inexperienced boy could be at risk of becoming another boy's puppet, or another boy's slave. Locke had warned against "that sheepish softness which often enervates those who are bred like fondlings at home ... for fear lest such a yielding temper should be too susceptible of vicious impressions, and expose the novice too easily to be corrupted."[130] In a text where, among other masks, the author claims "I am a school-boy—I have placed my exercise upon the desk—From a retired corner I observe its success," there is empathy. At the same time the boy in school and his education are tools employed by the woman writer in staking a claim to authority.

Figure 2.1. Anonymous, late eighteenth-century educational picture board from the school of Zlatá Koruna (near Český Krumlov). A school interior. Public domain.

CHAPTER 3

The Boy in the Machine

PIERRE JAQUET-DROZ'S AUTOMATON, THE WRITER (1774)

Tool. n.f. 1. Any instrument of manual operation
—Samuel Johnson, A Dictionary of the
English Language

I have noted that the small boy going into breeches was often described as a "manikin" or little man. In my second chapter, I considered the character of a young schoolboy as a rhetorical tool created to educate real boys and their mothers. The boy I look at in this chapter came into being in the eighteenth century not as a boy at all, although he is a manikin—this time in the sense of being "a small representation or statue of a human figure."[1] More than a statue, however, he—or it—is a machine, one constructed visually and symbolically as a boy. Its creator named the automaton Charles, but more often the machine was referred to as *L'écrivain*—the Writer. A mechanical wonder that wielded a quill pen and brought fame and wealth to his inventor, *L'écrivain* again embodies ideas about boyhood as the means to an end and, in using his own writing tool, serves as a youthful, gendered medium of Enlightenment ideas and ideals.

THE SPECTACLE MÉCANIQUE

Mary Hilton notes that, accompanying the rise of the eighteenth-century middle class along with progressive theories about educating the young, there was a marked rise in the availability and importance of "family entertainment," including, as the century progressed, "trips to lectures, museums, zoos, puppet shows, circuses, panoramas, automata and exhibitions of curiosities. Meanwhile many of the new boys' schools offered instruction in mathematics, experimental philosophy and the use of globes, a sign that middle-class parents were anxious for their sons to understand natural and moral philosophy, natural history and technology as well as classical languages and manners."[2] With this plethora of educational exhibits in mind, we might envision those Londoners and visitors to London who could afford and would choose to spend five shillings on an hour's amusement in late 1775 or early 1776, traveling in droves to witness a wonder of their accomplished and cosmopolitan age. This was a mechanical exhibit by the celebrated Swiss horologist Pierre Jaquet-Droz, his son Henri-Louis, and his partner Jean-Frédéric Leschot.[3] Among the four wonders then on display at the fashionable Great Room in Covent Garden was a mechanical landscape of the Swiss countryside called *la grotte*: a tabletop tableau with a Swiss mountain as background, before which a pavilion flanked by topiary gardens and statuettes in the foreground along with miniature shepherd and shepherdess, sheep, dogs and cows, all moving in their spheres revealed the picturesque wedded to the mechanical.[4]

Accompanying *la grotte* was a trio of small-scale human automata constructed between 1768 and 1774. Measuring from seventy-five centimeters (twenty-eight inches) in height, these three were to voyage across Europe and Asia for a decade, displayed even before royalty and emperors. The celebrated performing dolls or, as they were more commonly referred to, "androids" included a boy called the Draughtsman, who sketched four different images on paper, a girl called the Musician, who played five tunes on a miniature harpsichord, and another boy, the Writer (sometimes known as the Scribe), who wrote words with a quill pen. Partly carved in wood, the automata also had parts fashioned from tin and copper, porcelain, wood, papier-mâché, and gems. Now housed at the Musée d'art et d'histoire (Neuchâtel) in Switzerland, the three automated children function still.

The first of the three to be built, the Writer is the most complex of Jaquet-Droz's creations, its function testified to in a prospectus for the exhibit:

> A figure representing a child of two years of age, seated on a stool, and writing at a desk. This figure dips its pen in the ink, shakes out what is superfluous, and writes distinctly and correctly whatever the company think proper to dictate, without any person's touching it. It places the initial letters with propriety, and leaves a suitable space between the words it writes. When it has finished a line it passes on to the next, always observing the proper distance between the lines: while it writes, its eyes are fixed on its work, but as soon as it has finished a letter and words, it casts a look at the copy, seeming to imitate it. The time of viewing is from 12 to 1, from 1 to 2, from 2 to 3, and in the evening from 7 to 8, and from 9 to 10.
>
> Mr. Jaquet-Droz, the inventor, will attend till 11 at night, in order to accommodate those ladies and gentlemen that may chuse to see this exhibition after 10 o'clock.
>
> ADMITTANCE, FIVE SHILLINGS
> To be continued every day, (Sundays and Thursdays excepted)

With nearly six thousand parts, the Writer contains at his core a stack of forty replaceable interior *cams*: disks with variously shaped edges "read" by devices that translate their grooves and circular movements into the up and down motion of the hand and quill.[5] The cams allow the machine to write up to forty characters over a space of four lines.[6] The remarkable machine can be programmed to write any words, letter by letter, dipping his pen into ink between finishing one line and beginning the next, although the boast that he can be "dictated to" is not true—whoever had programmed him would have spoken the words already calibrated into the mechanical system. With clicks and whirs, the metal panel fitted into the desk on which he writes moves to his left upon completion of each letter, which creates the illusion that the hand travels right across the page. His head too turns as he writes, and his eyes shift and seem to follow the labor of his hand in a way that has often been described as eerie and uncanny. In velvet breeches and coat, he is an immaculate, well-dressed, seemingly aristocratic male child seated on a Louis-XV-style stool at a small mahogany writing table. Designed along with his brethren to impress royalty and the aristocracy, sell tickets to the *spectacle mécanique*, as well as sell clocks and watches to anyone who could afford Jaquet-Droz's prices, the Writer was mechanical achievement and advertisement combined. The automaton promoted the craftsmanship and ingenuity of men who created—as is the case with a clock—a whole that was greater than the sum of its parts.

The Boy Machine

This representation of a child "of two years of age" has been discussed in terms of the era that produced it, the mechanical genius that went into it, and the success it brought its inventor. Praised as one of the world's oldest working automatons, along with Jaquet-Droz's other groundbreaking inventions, it comes up in numerous studies, including Jessica Riskin's *Genesis Redux: Essays in the History and Philosophy of Artificial Life* (2007), Adelheid Voskuhl's *Androids in the Enlightenment: Mechanics, Artisans, and Cultures of the Self* (2013), and Kara Reilly's *Automata and Mimesis on the Stage of Theatre History* (2011).[7] However, the machine has not hitherto been considered in terms of boyhood. Little Charles not only wields a tool but is a tool of a particular ideology and culture. He is a gendered artifact that speaks to the place of boys within discourses about education, class, and wealth.

As Alex Wetmore points out, the human body was frequently referred to in the long eighteenth century as the "human machine"; mechanistic language was increasingly employed to talk about all life as machine arts themselves developed.[8] Even at the mid-seventeenth century, Thomas Hobbes had argued, "For seeing life is but a motion of limbs, the beginning whereof is in some principal part within; why may we not say, that all automata (engines that move themselves by springs and wheels as doth a watch) have an artificial life?"[9] By 1748, in *L'Homme Machine*, the atheist Julien Offray de La Mettrie had made this relationship quite plain: "The human body is a machine which winds its own springs: it is the living image of perpetual motion. Food nourishes what a fever heats and excites."[10] Art not only imitates life; the reverse is true. As the unnatural (or contrived) machine mimics nature, so too nature seems to mimic the machine.

The implications of this metaphor went deep and at times resulted in forceful resistance to the inverted conclusion about machinery made by humans as itself approaching life. For one thing, where did this leave God? For another, what was the special value of humans (where was the soul?). Understandably, contemporary reactions to Jaquet-Droz's creations—which Minsoo Kang identifies as marking the "climax ... of the automaton craze"—were, as befits a craze, mixed.[11] One English observer of the Jaquet-Droz spectacle wrote that, although "these are certainly wonderful inventions, and seem to carry the powers of mechanics to a high pitch, but still they are mere toys, and an unworthy waste of great genius: it is Swift making riddles."[12] Similarly, another spectator, William Coxe, author of *Observations on the Present State of Denmark, Russia, and Switzerland*, tempered his admiration for Jaquet-Droz's "mechanical genius" by commenting that "the opening of a brilliant flower, the whistling of a bird, or the various motions of an automaton, are at best but the tricks of art, which, like the problems of calculation, serve to amuse without conveying either use or instruction."[13] Such dismissals are not mere dismissals of foreign accomplishment, being of a piece with the varied reactions to James Cox's museum we encounter in Frances Burney's 1778 novel *Evelina*, wherein Burney allows her heroine "but little pleasure," given that the spectacle of the golden pineapple and attendant machinery "is a mere show, though a wonderful one."[14] As at other moments in Burney's novel, we are meant to discern (and agree with) Evelina's taste. Skepticism is a response to wonder when that wonder is seen as inappropriate.[15]

Despite cynical dismissals of the automata and in part because of them, historians in various disciplines have identified a great deal of instruction in "tricks of art" like Jaquet-Droz's Writer: Marcia Pointon notes, "Cultural historians have linked androids and puppets, recognizing in both a modern paradigm of the problem of human freedom." At the same time, "historians of science ... have identified the eighteenth- and nineteenth-century enthusiasm for automata as an example of the popularization of modish materialist philosophies, and as a stage toward reasoning machines or, as we now know them, calculators."[16] Historical experiments toward artificial intelligence have become more, not less, relevant to the concerns of our own age: in the BBC documentary *Mechanical Marvels: Clockwork Dreams* (2013) Simon Schaffer says of the Writer, "This beautiful boy is the distant ancestor to the modern, programmable computer."[17]

Schaffer notes that Jaquet-Droz achieved with the Writer "a *true* automaton."[18] Perhaps Schaffer's use of the adjective "true" also points to that line that is currently undergoing copious discussion—the line between "thing" and "life" (or between "It" and "Self") represented in automata, as in studies by Julie Park, Ileana Baird, Christina Ionescu, and others who, following in the footsteps of Bill Brown (and before him Immanuel Kant and Martin Heidegger), invite us to think more seriously about things and our relationship with them. According to Brown, "We begin to confront the thingness of objects when they stop working for us ... when their flow within the circuits of production and distribution, consumption and exhibition, has been arrested, however momentarily. The story of objects asserting themselves as things, then, is the story of a changed relationship to the human subject and thus the story of how the thing really names less an object than a particular subject-object relation."[19] With automata, the accurate function of the object increases its resemblance to humans along with its degree of uncanniness. Via nomenclature, the Writer is identified with its function—to write—yet its subject-object relation is also determined as a visual spectacle by embodying a certain kind of person, in age and gender, and this is what I explore here.

Tellingly, Schaffer's admiration for "the distant ancestor to the modern, programmable computer" begins with aesthetic, gendered praise for "this beautiful boy." Critics who study the history of automata identify links between responsiveness to mechanized ingenuity and fine feeling, quality of character, and gender in the era that produced them.[20] It is not surprising that gender comes into play with the study of mechanical people most of all. Timothy Kaufman-Osborn argues that "matters of technology and gender are never unrelated in experience, and any argument that presupposes their isolatability is sure to grasp the political import of neither."[21] Voskuhl fixes her reading about automata and gender on the female harpsichord player Jaquet-Droz produced, while Terry Castle links automata and the importance of the uncanny in the eighteenth century to women in *The Female Thermometer*.[22] M. Norton Wise observes, "Android automata of the eighteenth century were about equally male and female, while those of the nineteenth century were mostly female."[23] This is an interesting shift, which leads Wise to question, "What was the significance of [automata's] female or otherwise exotic nature" in relation to the science of that century?[24] Park, too, sees mechanizing tendencies of the late eighteenth century (their appearance in novels in particular) as finding a corollary in women—women's bodies and women's behavior—since "consumer society propelled female subjects into a perpetual and nongenerative state of wishing for trinkets and apparel."[25] I have already noted Alexander Pope's wink at the "moving Toyshop" of young women's hearts in "The Rape of the Lock." In contrast to studies of feminized objects and the objectified feminine, Alex Wetmore argues that much fiction of the period demonstrates a particular mechanized (or automatic) response by men of feeling—as with Yorick's anguish over the caged singing bird in Laurence Sterne's *A Sentimental Journey* and Matthew Bramble's "automatic" production of tears upon encountering now-decrepit friends at Bath in Tobias Smollett's *Humphry Clinker*.[26]

Jaquet-Droz's Writer bears witness to a relationship between technology and gender in which the animated thing is not simply a human body but a boy body, and embodiment of an ideal construction of boyhood. Further, the very thingness of that body is what makes the Writer ideal. Wise calls automata "a reservoir of embodied meanings."[27] What is the meaning of the boyhood embodied in the Writer? His representational gender was not, I believe, accidental, because form and function—boyhood and penmanship—combine in telling ways in the machine.

First, it is worth pointing out that (like his brother draughtsman) the Writer is a particularly little boy—the youth of whom is emphasized not only by scale but also by his face, and his babyish chubby calves and bare feet, which dangle above the rose parquet floor. One prospectus advertising the exhibit specifies that the Writer is "2 years old."[28] Although Marcia Pointon calls it "unimportant that a two-year old could scarcely be credited with the mastery of the draughtsman or the scribe," I disagree.[29] The youth of the Writer is important because it makes the thing a wonder even as a boy. He looks both too young and too little to write. It is not merely, as Pointon states, "that it would be an unusual two-year-old with the motor skills to perform [careful, well-formed] writing like this."[30] Rather, no two-year-old could manage it. Indeed, as we saw in looking at boys' clothing, a toddler would not yet have been breeched—as this one is—the average boy going into breeches between the ages of three and five, and many doing so later, around six or seven. The Writer is therefore precocious in every way—both as an extraordinary machine and as a boy prodigy producing "beautiful, elegant, and fluid writing."[31] Seth Lerer points out, "Among schoolmasters, tutors, and philosophers, a student's handwriting remained a key to moral character."[32] Being brought to life not as the mechanized food-digesting duck that had earned the French genius, Jacques de Vaucanson, his fame, nor as the musical swan or clockwork chariot in James Cox's museum,[33] but instead as a boy smaller and younger than the youngest schoolboy would have been, the Writer is not merely a writing machine: he is a boy machine, performing idealized boyhood. He is uncanny because of his realistic appearance, and unrealistic because of his size and apparent age.

Seen thus, the Writer represents what Kara Reilly identifies as "the eighteenth-century ideal of a precocious child intellectual, a voracious reader who might capably function as a secretary to a gentleman."[34] The boyhood of the android (and his evident class) is therefore important because he represents the demographic of the European population who were taught to read and write far more than any other—boys from trade or merchant families or the upper classes. I started this consideration of the mechanical spectacle by saying that only those who could afford the high price of admission took in the spectacle, but of course, as always, there must have been those who paid without quite being able to afford it—who did without other items that week or that month, who aspired to more and perhaps wanted their own children to rise on the social scale. As such, the automaton is not merely a mechanical spectacle—or curiosity.[35] He is a striking representation of different kinds of achievement. There is therefore an argument to be made for aspiration—that of the merchant and middling classes, and what they might have seen in the little automaton as boy, writing.

As evidence of scientific achievement and writer combined, the machine is also a tool of empire.[36] Aileen Douglas asserts, "A child's ability to produce a decent writing specimen was seen as the most tangible manifestation of his or her education, a sign of the growth of a civilized Protestant interest."[37] The Englishman George Bickham's *The Universal Penman* (1734[?]–1741) equates skill in writing with manly success, accompanied by nationalistic fervor in his beautiful calligraphical "Advice to Young Gentlemen":

> Ye British Youths, our Ages' Hope & Care
> You whom the next may polish, or impair
> Learn by the Pen those Talents to insure
> That fix ev'n Fortune's, & from Want secure
> You with a dash in time may drain a Mine,
> And deal the Fate of Empires in a Line.[38]

In the other column on the same page Bickham's "Advice to Young Ladies" likens handling the pen to needlework, since "All shou'd be fair that Beauteous Woman frames."[39] This feminized sentiment is purely aesthetic, while young gentlemen are plainly taught to anticipate the wielding of power. (An implicit contrast hovers between the platitude "a stitch in time saves nine" and what we find written here for boys: "a dash in time may drain a Mine.") In *The Universal Penman* writing itself becomes a miniaturizing act: what else might we call the ability to "deal the Fate of Empires in a Line"? The pen is the boy's tool, as is the line of words he produces with it, and both are tools of empire.

The Quill Pen

Jaquet-Droz's writer combines aesthetic pleasure and the impression of usefulness because the way in which he seems to work does produce something—the written word—while other automata might *seem* to hammer or saw away in their entertaining miniature world without actually producing anything. Whereas the Writer's clockwork brother, the Draughtsman, is an equally small boy who produced drawings, writing was considered a more advanced sign of progress than drawing—for an individual, certainly, but also for a nation and a civilization.[40] With reference to the wide publicizing of the Jaquet-Droz automata specifically, Voskuhl reminds us that "the rapid increase in the production and consumption of print media is often noted as one of the characteristics—and even the causes—of the emergence of a specifically Enlightened literary and political public in late eighteenth-century continental Europe."[41] Moreover, although formed "by hand," the letters written by *L'écrivain* are in some ways still like print, for his words are programmed, set like type, and his mechanical writing was reproduced everywhere he went, moving across Europe with his person. Prior to London, he had been with his brethren to Geneva and Versailles; later he would travel farther afield.

The writing automaton is therefore an invention demonstrating the written word, one of humankind's greatest inventions. As Mark Rothery and Henry French note, by the late eighteenth century "*all* groups in society believed in the value of letter writing as a means for their children to get on in the world." This is evidenced by the proliferation of manuals of instruction in "composition, grammar, and even the correct methods of folding and sealing a letter."[42] The automatic Writer is more valuable than his fellow automatons, then, because writing is the action he performs.

As a very young boy, the Writer can therefore be interpreted as the embodiment of a lesson to devote steady application to that particular task. The prospectus for the exhibition contains noteworthy details, such that the "figure . . . places the initial letters with propriety, and leaves a suitable space between the words it writes. When it has finished a line it passes on to the next, always observing the proper distance between the lines."[43] Propriety, suitable, observing, proper distance—such words smack not only of praise but also of pedagogy. As he writes, the movements of the boy are regular, yet individual letters take slightly different amounts of time to form. His hand is steady, his body is still. What is programmed into the machine gives the impression of having been practiced.

In the *Essay Concerning Human Understanding,* Locke advised, "As it is in the body, so it is in the mind; practice makes it what it is, and most even of those excellencies, what are looked on as natural endowments will be found, when examined more narrowly, to be the product of exercise, and to be raised to that pitch, only by repeated actions."[44] Although Locke was referring to the human mind and human behavior, steady repetition evokes mechanics—particularly, by the later eighteenth century, clockwork mechanics. Zakiya Hanafi points out threads of anxiety in the early modern era over automata: "If matter moves of its own accord, it presents a threat of breakdown, of collapsed boundaries, not only in the realm of natural forces—hence the association with demons and necromancy—but especially as a figure for the stability of the social order."[45] I argue, however, that the Jaquet-Droz automata and especially the Writer reinforce certain boundaries, and even reify the social order. Indeed, as Simon Schaffer states, it was order above all that early automation represented. It was the orderly development of the medieval city-state, such as Bern, Switzerland, that first drove the development of automation, where "regularity and order" through clockwork in a space increasingly distant from nature "taught their citizens lessons in morality and virtue" to keep them "well-behaved" and "obedient."[46]

"Clockwork imagery," Park has argued, defines "a moral standard" of human behavior in a number of texts of the long eighteenth century; it is such imagery, she points out, for example, that "fuels Hester Chapone's lecture on procrastination in *Letters on the Improvement on the Mind,*" when Chapone urges youthful readers "to acquire habits of constancy and steadiness."[47] Recall that little Sprightly's headmaster in Ellenor Fenn's *School Dialogues* is named Mr. Steady. The writing automaton's *steadiness* is highlighted by Jaquet-Droz in the prospectus, where the "figure representing a child of two" is also characterized as "it": "While it writes, its eyes are fixed on its work, but as soon as it has finished a letter and words, it casts a look at the copy, seeming to imitate it." This claim—"it writes"—deconstructs itself. As the eyes are only artificially "fixed," it cannot in fact cast "a look," and the truth is in the qualified "seeming" of the mimetic action. Given the unnatural and nonhuman writing machine, "it" is instrument, yet "he" holds, and imitates what humans do, with another instrument (or tool).[48] The Writer is boy as work of art, as both the mirror and—because of the writing the machine produces—the lamp.

Imitation

The Writer made visible any words he was programmed to put to paper, in lower or uppercase letters or a combination thereof.[49] It is significant that the performance includes the boy appearing to learn: as he "copies" a sentence from a specimen of penmanship on the desk, so his eyes seem to move between his own work and the example set out for him. As such, he is a simulation of a child imitating. The duality of the automaton's mimicry anticipates the spectator's enjoyment of that very imitation for, as M. H. Abrams notes, "the historical genesis of art is traced to the natural human instinct for imitating, and the natural tendency to find pleasure in *seeing* imitations."[50] Writing was not, however, an activity in which *all* humans engaged—even as adults. Most peasants and women were taught to sign their names (and only their names) without being able to read at all. At the same time, while many people who learned basic reading were not taught to write, the Writer—whose range appears unlimited—curiously writes without reading, although he seems to do both. Schaffer says the machine "reverse engineer[s] the very act of writing." He merely generates text—"seems to imitate it"—encodes without decoding.

As Marjorie Swann reminds us, "A writer is not necessarily an author."[51] This is strikingly true of the boy automaton. His function was not so much to write as to demonstrate that he was writing. As such, of particular interest to the Jaquet-Droz enterprise is the via media of the aesthetically appealing, cherub-faced boy that embodies the very relationship between wealth and learning—in his own apparent affluence, and in the financial demands made of those who would watch him demonstrating conspicuous "learning." For Simon Schaffer, Pierre Jaquet-Droz's larger "aim was . . . to mechanize reason, and automate passions."[52] In light of this eminently defensible reading of the horologist's work, I suggest that referring to the Writer as the Scribe, as do some critics, is inadequate. His inventors themselves named him *L'écrivain*, not *le Scribe*. He is not merely moveable type—he intimates reason as he imitates it, with his moving eyes. Douglas says that in the "look cast at the copy . . . the android suggests . . . the mental space of human beings, where learning occurs and where consciousness and intelligence reside."[53] Questions about literacy, and indeed learning, are raised by the Writer even as he troubles ways in which we consider Enlightenment ideals about education, age, and gender, including when a boy reached the age of reason (which Locke set at seven—again, he did not specify for a girl). As I have suggested, the machine also represents the civilizing power—and impact—of literacy itself, particularly on the heirs of the future: educated European boys.[54]

In the decade prior to Jaquet-Droz's exhibit, Jean-Jacques Rousseau's *Émile* (1762) was predicated on the philosophe's belief that "everything degenerates in the hands of man."[55] Rousseau's novel "so scandalized his native city of Geneva, as well as his adopted country, France, that Rousseau was banished from both. The Sorbonne condemned it; sales were forbidden; and copies were burned in the public squares of Geneva and Paris."[56] Whereas it was Book IV, arguing for "natural religion," that most damned the book, also offensive to many was Rousseau's critique of the written word—and, as Demers notes, "of civilization in general."[57] Considering the thrust of Rousseau's arguments, the Swiss-"born" little Writer, Charles, stands in sharp contrast to Émile, who was not taught to read and write until the age of twenty.[58] The Writer, a mechanized prodigy, reflects the kind of glory that Alexander Pope was fishing for in claiming that he himself had "lisp'd in numbers, for the numbers came," so innate was verse to him as a boy.[59] Whereas Pope is claiming natural genius, however, the automaton embodies artificial genius housed in a natural-seeming body. Little Charles is meant to appear as one of those boys who would become men—elite men whom "literacy marked ... out from the men of the lower orders."[60] Naturally, the automaton had no genuine "academic accomplishments, including literacy, numeracy and deeper forms of knowledge, of classical history and literature," which were "part of the social and gender status of elite men."[61] Nevertheless, he was an intriguing likeness of a boy who might one day achieve such status. He is a manikin: a little man, in whose hands nothing degenerates.

Foreign and Familiar

The mechanical "dolls" were privileged foreigners in England, welcome (if, sometimes, like other foreigners, mocked) and the programmable *écrivain* was multilingual. As a representation (if not quite a representative) of educated wealthy males, the Writer even might be said already to have been on the grand tour undertaken by high-born young men following university.[62] It has been claimed that the automata were shown "in every court in Europe."[63] As an international import himself, the mechanical boy also portrayed exoticism and the foreign, although he looks much like any well-fed, well-dressed little English boy. At the same time, the Writer—expensive, complicated, serious—was not child's play.

Along with other luxuries, Susan Stewart might well be commenting on the Jaquet-Droz exhibit when she states, about the growth of cabinets of curiosities in the period, "The collection's space must move between the public and the private, between display and hiding."[64] Pierre Jaquet-Droz achieved this spatial liminality by making his collection's availability temporary in each city to which he journeyed, but also through payment to gaze upon that collection. Whereas when the automata were first displayed in his hometown of Chaux-de-Fonds, Switzerland, in 1774 "writers of the day reported that people flocked from all over the country to see such extraordinary works of whimsy and technical skill,"[65] the prices charged abroad reflected the distance traveled and what that new market would bear: "When Jaquet-Droz brought his machines to Paris, he made sure that only the extremely wealthy could see them, by charging ludicrously inflated prices and then proclaiming that no servant would be allowed in to see the show."[66]

As noted above, attendance at the London exhibit cost five shillings.[67] The average laborer in London in 1776 earned about two shillings for a day's work. To put this into context with other entertainment available at this time, we have only to compare J. H. Plumb's observation that in "April 1773 families of Leeds were regaled by Mr. Manuel of Turin with his display of automata which, as well as having an Indian lady in her chariot moving around the table at ten miles an hour, also contained the 'Grand Turk, in Seraglio dress, who walks about the table smoking his pipe in a surprising manner.' ... The prices were cheap enough," Plumb reports, "1s. front seats, 6d. back, and servants at 4d."[68] Three years later, Jaquet-Droz was charging London (not Leeds) prices, but that does not entirely account for the difference, nor does location account for the prohibition of servants at his exhibit: drawing the right people in was also about keeping the wrong people out. Further, the three child-like machines, in dress and in activity, did not represent servants, but rather children who would be served.

As the eighteenth and nineteenth centuries "mark the heyday of the automaton," Stewart notes, "they [also] mark the mechanization of labour."[69] Yet the earnings of those who engaged in physical labor disallowed taking in the wonders of the *spectacle mécanique*. Unlike the purchase of an object, the large cabinet of curiosities that was the Jaquet-Droz exhibit included the price of being a spectator in the moment, of setting eyes upon the lifelike "dolls," as well as the price paid for a memory of having seen them. The wealthiest might then decide to purchase a watch or a snuffbox graced by a singing bird, but the main attractions could not be carried away. Pointon observes, "Like [James] Cox, Jaquet-Droz drew on the work of artists to create an environment for an exhibition of mechanical toys that would be consonant with aristocratic expectations and high art."[70] As such, privileging of high over low (both art and class), educated over uneducated, and male over female are encompassed in the Writer's story.

The early history of automation not only addresses binaries like privilege and poverty but also speaks to the power of ruling classes over the ruled. Gillen D'Arcy Wood interprets the Jaquet-Droz automata as having "defined virtuosity in both its historical senses—as a luxury exhibit, and a mechanical mode of performance." More to the point, the automata were, to those mistrustful of both, "emblems of a new toxic proximity between writing and mechanical virtuosity."[71] Class tension would come to play a part in the history of automata, particularly as the industry moved from public clockwork displays designed to keep medieval cities harmonious to emblems of absolute exclusivity.[72] Indeed, as Simon Shaffer and Julia Douthwaite both demonstrate, in France automation provided a language for fomenting revolution against the ancien régime. While Kara Reilly notes "automata modelled after Marie Antoinette and soldiers trained like automata, demonstrate the importance of automata as ideal aristocrats in eighteenth-century Europe,"[73] the same discourse, pushed to the extreme, held that the king and all aristocrats were nothing but automata—the former with a crown—who in and of themselves accomplished nothing. Pamphlets in France would appear arguing that "while it was easy to be an automaton, like the king, it was very hard to build one, like the artisans."[74] Given new ways of looking at machines, and at humans as machines, it is perhaps not surprising that the discourse of enlightened mechanization would be turned against those who would wield it.

The revolution that would manifest in working toy guillotines in addition to the full-sized machines was still in the future, however. In February 1775 Jaquet-Droz—whose fame and profits were becoming international—had demonstrated his creations before Marie Antoinette and the Dauphin, with the Draughtsman drawing a picture of both royals. Jaquet-Droz's exquisite and pristine Writer is no representative of the majority of boys from those classes who, being used as means to an end, would rise up to use mechanical tools against the aristocrats who saw them that way.

Instead, for those in the mid-1770s who partook of the exclusive spectacle in London, the Writer dipping his quill into ink was not only a symbol of human achievement in clockwork but a complicated articulation of order beyond even that of a clock with its numbers. The automaton, described in his maker's own words as "about two years old," was not a terrible toddler; rather, he was a perfectly behaved boy—sitting still, keeping his eyes on his work, predictably reproducing the letters he had been programmed (as if taught) to form. No mischief was forthcoming from this boy. He was thus foreign and familiar in another way, not just as machine, but also as boy. Much is made in the advertisement of how silent the ingenious, well-oiled mechanism was. The advertisement quoted above boasts, "The Automaton . . . writes distinctly and correctly . . . without anyone touching it either directly or indirectly." If we think about the boy writing without physical contact between human and android (or adult and boy) we might also recollect John Locke's exhortation to avoid corporal punishment—"the rod, the usual lazy and short way of chastisement . . . the only instrument of government that tutors generally know, or even think of."[75] This extraordinary mechanical little boy obeys, always keeping a look of earnest concentration on his cherubic face. Insofar as idle hands may be the devil's playground, the industrious moving toy is silent and obedient, seen and not heard.[76] As such, the Writer stands not only for what our highly automated age has inherited from Enlightenment technology but also for an inheritance in terms of model boyhood.

Miniaturization

Jaquet-Droz's boy wonder is worth exploring with reference to other artistic representations of male children, and within that domain the specifics of miniaturization that he also exemplified. Melinda Alliker Rabb identifies a profound interest in "the idea of the small" from the mid-seventeenth century onward, an idea that, she observes, "like the idea of carnivalization, also taps into some fundamental emotions, although its manifestation is not primarily in terms of human bodies and bodily functions but rather in terms of created objects."[77] In humanoid automatons, however, the idea of the small is manifest in terms of both human bodies *and* created objects. Rabb identifies numerous "theories of small scale representation" that "intersect with history. Miniatures are symptomatic of a society seeking ways, through indirection and displacement, to deal with problems of the full-scale world."[78] The Writer is a boy-like object that avoids the problems of the full-scale world of boys—particularly the kinds of boys I look at in the next section of the book—destitute, damaged, criminal, illiterate boys. He embodies being and not being a boy.

As a somewhat miniaturized boy, he encodes one of the ways progress gets measured: for example, by the late eighteenth century, "what had once needed an entire clock tower could now be made to fit snugly into the palm of one hand." So with *L'écrivain*, "every one of these crafted components has been refined and miniaturized to fit completely inside the body of the boy himself."[79] Elsewhere, the popularity of "the diminutive, infantilized male" that appeared in early picture books, Kerry Mallan argues, signals "the shape-changing capacity of masculinity in visual representations of the male body [which] can be assessed particularly in relation to size." This capacity can in turn be traced back to "the male nude of classical, Renaissance, and post-Renaissance periods . . . frequently depicted with diminutive genitals,—which were consequently overcompensated for by large swords and other phallic iconography." Mallan explains that "in Lacanian terms, the fetish creates a substitute for the penis."[80] As noted above in regard to breeching, one finds such substitutions in paintings and engravings throughout the period—small whips and toy guns in the little hands of (often frocked) boys. This substitution of a phallic symbol for an invisible (or in the case of the automaton, absent) phallus is identifiable in the goose feather quill expertly handled by the Writer—who dips the pen in ink, shakes off the excess, then gets down to (re)producing what he has been programmed to write. In spite of his apparent age, he is contributing to the world as it was fashioned for well-off, able-bodied, right-handed men.

Along with this phallic substitution, we might again recall the gaze that the Writer "casts . . . the copy" from which he appears to imitate his letters. Douglas identifies this "look cast" by the automaton as especially uncanny.[81] The combination, then, of quill pen and look cast might well reflect Freud's argument that "the feeling of something uncanny is directly attached to . . . the idea of being robbed of one's eye. . . . A study of dreams, phantasies and myths has taught us that anxiety about one's eyes, the fear of going blind, is often enough a substitute for the dread of being castrated."[82] The boy machine, who does not have all the anatomical parts of a boy, does wield a pen, unlike many live boys—particularly those at the age he is meant to represent. Like all fetishes, the thing in the boy's hand is not the boy, but it demonstrates what the boy can do. However, not all boys were expected to do the same things—for example, read and write—nor was it generally desirable that they should in a system where such manual labor as chimney sweeping (as will be seen) required no book-related education and offered little to no progress for the boy.

Moving Parts and Other Boys

The Writer links prosperous children (especially boys) and the written word in ways that the eighteenth-century marketplace both recognized and fostered. Although John Newbery produced texts aimed at young misses, that the principal target reader was male is evident in his overall oeuvre. In Newbery's 1761 book *The Newtonian System of Philosophy . . . Collected and Methodized for the Benefit of the Youth of These Kingdom*, one "Tom Telescope" delivers lectures "To the Lilliputian Society" while standing on a table. This "outstanding text," which Mary Hilton observes "ensured that by the end of the eighteenth century the story of natural philosophy had entered deep into the family circle," appeared in numerous editions and translations, well into the nineteenth century.[83] On most frontispieces, little Tom holds a whip in his hand—another miniature child wielding an indicator of masculinity.

Tom gives his audience a lesson on "motion": "As to Motion, I may save myself and you the trouble of explaining that; for every boy who can whip his top knows what motion is as well as his master."[84] It is a commonplace idea that boys and motion go together like a horse and carriage. Edward Gibbon observed, "The felicity of a school-boy consists in the perpetual motion of thoughtless and playful agility," while Mary Wollstonecraft noticed that "boys love sports of noise and activity; to beat the drum, to whip the top, and to drag about their little carts."[85] Robert Southey (1774–1843) is credited with the ingredients poem that explains "little boys" are "made of.... snips and snails and puppy dog tails."[86] Again, these ingredients imply movement above all else (versus the static and consumable "sugar and spice and everything nice" that makes up girls). The Writer, a steady-handed little boy, conveys (and even embodies) ideas not only about boys who will civilize the world (in large part through writing) but also about creatures who themselves required direction and control. This boy is made not of snips and snails but of springs, cogs and cams, and wood and porcelain, steel, papier-mâché, and even rubies, and he is a precious collection of materials, mechanical genius, and invested time.

In the same year that the Jaquet-Droz exhibit appeared on the London scene— 1775–1776—there also appeared another book, again brought out by John Newbery's firm, which resonates with one answer to the exclusivity of such exhibits as the Jaquet-Droz automata: it is a book "by" another little Tom—Tom Thumb— England's own miniature boy: *Tom Thumb's Exhibition, Being an Account of Many Valuable and Surprising Curiosities Which He Has Collected in the Course of His Travels; for the Instruction and Amusement of the British Youth.*[87] The premise of this sixty-two-page text—taking up Henry Fielding's richly imagined character from the two-act play *Tom Thumb* (1730) and the three-act *Tragedy of Tragedies* (1733)[88]—is that wee Tom has established an exhibition of artifacts that will entertain and educate children and for which this book is the catalogue: "The exhibition is to be found at Mrs. Lovegood's, in Wiseman Buildings, at the end of Education Road. But Mr. Lovegood will not let anyone in unless they bow to him respectfully, hold a copy of the catalogue, are attended by respectable adults who can swear to the child's good behavior, and can read any part of this book fluently and exactly."[89] Once in, however, all children "will be allowed to roam at will, and will be given sweetmeats and oranges."

Among the wonders in the fictitious display (and illustrated with woodcuts in the book) is "an advice bird," which "sings and shows its plumage to good children, but turns into a vulture to savage the bad." Those artifacts teaching "moral lessons" here include a "Perspective Glass," which "shows what things are really like, so that alcoholic drinks, for example, appear as snakes and reptiles in the glass."[90] The picture of a thief, shown through the Perspective Glass, is seen "in the process of being executed."[91] As the Hockliffe Project notes, "The 'exhibition' format of this work was doubtlessly designed to cash in on the increasing popularity of collecting and museums in the late eighteenth century."[92] At three pence, the "catalogue" is a much smaller investment than attendance at the exotic *spectacle mécanique* then at Covent Garden and can be opened over and over again. Among the instructive tableaux "to be seen" at Tom Thumb's exhibition is one of a schoolboy at his desk, a "young jackanapes . . . leaning with his left arm upon the desk, and cramming an apple into his mouth with the other; mumbling the whole time (for his mouth appears too full to speak plain) to a boy on the opposite side, who looks as idle and inattentive as himself." This depiction of slovenly, lazy pupils could not contrast more sharply with the boy automaton sitting ramrod straight at an exhibition then on King Street, exercising his flawless penmanship and keeping his seemingly attentive eyes on his work.

(Re)production

As I have noted, scholars debate how we should read the larger narrative of the eighteenth century's intellectual investment in automata and why. What did it celebrate? Whom did it make anxious? Evidently, the answers varied. Minsoo Kang makes the important point that, unlike "Renaissance engineers [who] built their automata to look like devils, pagan gods, and monsters . . . Enlightenment mechanics like Vaucanson and the Jaquet-Drozs made them in the shapes of ordinary animals and people. . . . While the objects retained their wondrous aura, they represented the marvels of the machine in the everyday world, devoid of magical and supernatural entities."[93] Further, about the Jaquet-Droz inventions and others like it, Bruce Mazlish argues, "These mechanical figures were bathed, at the time of the Enlightenment, in the pure light of reason, and discussion of them took place in unambiguous 'scientific' terms. . . . Underlying this discussion, however . . . ran the fears of the automata, for they posed an 'irrational' threat to humans, calling into question their identity, sexuality (the basis of creation?), and powers of domination."[94] Mazlish is among those who relate the automata and their makers to the hyperanxiety of "unnatural" reproduction later evidenced in Mary Shelley's *Frankenstein*, where "the scientist has . . . taken the place of woman. She has been displaced from the acts of conception and birth. It is the man, Frankenstein, who creates sexlessly."[95] Indeed, in *The Frankenstein of 1790 and Other Lost Chapters of Revolutionary France*, Julia V. Douthwaite argues "the Jaquet-Droz musician . . . could seem to demonstrate vitalist principles. . . . As she played music, her chest filled with air, and her eyes seemed to be fixed on her listeners in sympathetic feeling."[96] This "seemed" speaks to an important debate about the nature of life itself, along with what would one day be called homeostasis (upon which clockwork depends) and wherein vitalism—one word for the source of life—resides.

As mysterious and elusive as the source of life was, regularity and predictability were at the heart of vitalism, which Julien Offray de La Mettrie in 1748 called the "principle, which moves whole bodies, as well as the separate parts," such that "it produces no irregular motions, as some have imagined, but preserves the utmost regularity, both in animals which are entire, and maintain vital warmth, as well as amongst those which are cold, and imperfect."[97] Reasoning akin to this, about life-versus-thing, and natural-versus-unnatural production, is also evident in regard to the machine I discuss here in particular, both as a writer—producing text from ink—and as a boy. For all of us, Judith Butler says, "language emerges from the body, constituting an emission of sorts."[98] Jaquet-Droz created a boy that emitted ink. As with miniaturization of the body and of the quill in the case of the automaton, we might borrow from Sandra Gilbert and Susan Gubar the question "is a pen a metaphorical penis?"[99] not only because this machine is a he, and he is a writer, but also because in some sense the Writer is a son—itself yet another definition of "boy."

Jaquet-Droz lost his wife, Marianne, who died in childbirth in 1755, and their infant daughter shortly after. The history pages of the current Jaquet-Droz watch company website note, with mythmaking pathos, that its founder "never remarried, devoting himself entirely to clockmaking."[100] As we know, the deaths of mother and babe were common, yet there is something both uncommon and poignant about a horologist whose spouse and child have stepped out of time, having then chosen to "devote himself entirely" to keeping time. The girl "Musician" automaton was named by her innovators Marianne, after Jaquet-Droz's wife. Certainly, one advantage of clockwork is that it can outlast life.

Harold Bloom, among others, argues that the technology of timekeeping changed how we think about ourselves—our history and our future—in relation to time: "It was just after Huygen's clock (1659) that Milton began to compose *Paradise Lost*, in the early 1660s," Bloom reminds us. He posits that "it is in *Paradise Lost* that temporality fully becomes identified with anxiety."[101] Jaquet-Droz's boy-like wonder arguably speaks to order and endurance as a mechanical answer to temporal anxiety. He is a child without original sin in the postlapsarian (time-anxious) world. Being an advertisement for the other mechanical creations of his father(s)—clocks featuring mechanical singing birds, barking dogs, shepherds, and other rare and costly devices such as snuffbox clocks and jeweled perfume bottles—what the Writer is selling is both wonder at the times in which they are living and the capacity to produce such mechanical wonders, and selling time itself. He is as I write this nearing his two hundred fiftieth birthday—having survived two centuries beyond his maker (and takes pride of place in tourist information about Neuchâtel). He will probably outlast us all.

Yet the little boy machine still looks vulnerable and, like a human, subject to decay starting with age. He suggests both a defiance of time and a paradoxical—boy-like—vulnerability. This duality reinforces the possibility of reading the Writer within this context of offspring, brainchild born from a triumvirate of timekeepers: Jaquet-Droz and his only son Henri-Louis Jaquet-Droz, and apprentice-turned-partner Jean-Frédéric Leschot (whom Pierre had adopted as a child). By devising, assembling, and taking care of the Writer, Jaquet-Droz *père* is in a position analogous to a blameless Dr. Frankenstein.[102] While knowledge of anatomy is essential to the automatist, the horror associated with that other Enlightenment profession, anatomy (which eminent anatomist Felix Vicq d'Azyr [1748–1794] described as "torn and bloody members, infectious and unhealthy odors, the ghastly machinery of death")[103] is entirely absent in the clean, whole, and beautiful product that is *L'écrivain*. Mineral or sperm oil that kept parts running smoothly was not blood (although whales were killed for the latter).

In 2011, when the three automata finally toured China—a dream of Jaquet-Droz not realized in his lifetime—"in front of the watch connoisseurs in Beijing, the Writer penned the words '*Jaquet-Droz en Chine*,' or 'Jaquet-Droz in China.'"[104] To quote Butler again, here with respect to the performative aspect of human gender, "all signification takes place within the orbit of the compulsion to repeat."[105] Although referred to throughout the original advertisement as "it"—arguably to emphasize the mechanical ingenuity (and lack of trickery) of the Writer—it is also the representation of a boy child passing on the father's name both in the very proof of its existence and by writing the patronymic down. As Timothy Kaufman-Osborn posits of cultural artefacts, "Through labor, what was hitherto merely a proto-self externalizes itself, fashions an object whose objectivity testifies to the reality of the subject called into being via that act."[106] The written word is a cultural artifact. In the case of *L'écrivain*, one artifact—an automatic boy—engenders another—the written word—both of which carry on the legacy of the progenitor.

God in the Machine

It now comes to light that the question concerning the character of the being of things, to be singular and "this one," is completely and entirely hung up in the question concerning being. Does being still mean to us being created by God. If not, what then?   —Heidegger, What Is a Thing?

The machine in question, like other automata, not only demonstrates reproduction of a son without the female body. The inventor-father invests in the machine, but is God in the machine? This question tugs at the coat sleeves of self-conscious modernity and was certainly one of the reactions to automata at the time, as in the criticism with which this machinery met, cited above ("mere toys, and an unworthy waste of great genius"; "Swift making riddles"). Of course, if God works, it is in mysterious ways, so why not mechanical? In fact, "automata... helped Descartes perceive the universe and the natural world as a great clockwork machine set in motion by God... the premise of the mechanical philosophy."[107] This in turn set the stage for William Paley's 1802 watchmaker analogy for the Creator. Moreover, as Dominic Green reminds us, other "enlightenment metaphors were mechanical: God as the divine watchmaker; or, in Leibniz's image, the Cartesian mind and body as two clocks, synchronised but separate."[108] However, this does not mean that such metaphors were without complication; Paley's teleology was itself evidence of the anxiety produced by the sophistication of clockwork and of automata that trouble life and its origins.[109]

In 1783, not long after Jaquet-Droz caused a sensation with his *spectacle mécanique*, children's writer Dorothy Kilner (who was, incidentally, living in London in 1776 when the spectacle was there) wrote in *Letters from a Mother to Her Children* that "it is God who changes the milk and the bread which little babies eat, into *blood*, and *flesh*, and *bones*, and *hair*, and *nails*."[110] As standard as this reminder to be grateful to the Creator is, the very detailed itemization of the body here, together with the transformation of food into flesh, makes Kilner's explanation itself uncanny—a kind of reverse transubstantiation. Every life, according to Kilner's formula, is miraculous, and so can be traced to *the* miracle maker. Everything—everyone—begins with God the father. Surely, however, this certainty is troubled when something is someone. Simon Schaffer notes of the significance of Jaquet-Droz's Writer that, once programmed, "he works on his own." Of course, this phrasing gets to the heart of the appeal—and the dismissal—voiced in the long eighteenth century about automata: the machines are in some ways too good to be true.[111] The Writer certainly fits this category as a boy as well.

Those scholars who work on object theory frequently cite Richard Steele's *Spectator* no. 155, where the essayist laments, "The world is mercenary even to the buying and selling of our very Persons."[112] On some level the Writer speaks to such dangerous consumerism; perhaps he foreshadows that version of Western children's culture that Jack Zipes criticizes in his book *Sticks and Stones*: "Everything we do to, with, and for our children is influenced by capitalist market conditions and the hegemonic interests of ruling corporate elites. In simple terms, we calculate what is best for our children by regarding them as investments and turning them into commodities."[113] Yet in the 1770s the Writer, I suggest, was a model of commodity-turned-child. While Simon Schaffer points out that the Writer is "a device in the form of a small boy," other boys in this book represent boys in the form of devices.

Any precocious child from whom come words beyond his years always troubles the liminality between child and adult. And the child character who knows things others, including adults, do not know—that child sells books. Of course, such a character—like the Writer automaton—is not a real child at all. Given the price of admission, far fewer children would have seen the Jaquet-Droz exhibit than did adults, for all it would have enchanted and unnerved them. *L'écrivain* is a "representation of a child," as the advertisement states, mostly for adult consumption. As such, it is no mere doll: it is a tool, even as it wields another tool, the quill pen. In using and being a "tool," the Writer performs the act of writing while also performing boyhood.

Jaquet-Droz's representation of a boy therefore teases out further considerations regarding *boy* as *tool*. Michael Polanyi's reading of Heidegger as applied to the boy machine opens up more possibilities: "While we rely on a tool or a probe, these are not handled as external objects.... We pour ourselves out into them and assimilate them as part of our own existence. We accept them existentially by dwelling in them."[114] The phenomenal Writer could never be "a thing in itself."[115] There is too much invested in both the idea and the object of this boy.

In an analysis of a later likeness of a boy, Carlo Collodi's "The Adventures of Pinocchio" (1883), Anna Panszczyk notes, "To write about the animation of toys is to engage with the cultural expectations of what that animation looks like and the fact that such animation is often associated with the phrase and, therefore, the idea of toys 'coming to life.' And it is that 'coming,' that movement from one state of being (toy, object) to another state of being (human, living) which not only reinforces the idea that the animated plaything occupies a liminal state that is temporary and thus not permanent, but also reinforces the idea that such a liminal state looks human."[116] Jaquet-Droz's Writer, a century before Pinocchio, conveyed the liminality between object and human, along with—being a boy-shaped thing—the liminality of boyhood itself as something unfinished, something being worked on by every live boy. At the same time, *L'écrivain* will never be a man. In a curious way, this makes him the perfect boy in the inevitably imperfect sense that "to be a boy means to be a flawed, inchoate, or incomplete man."[117]

Our species has a long history of investment in not-alive items, a history with which Thing Theory concerns itself. Arguably, this rich area of inquiry is increasingly fascinating because things are becoming more like us, more *us*, than before—becoming our eyes, our voices, taking aim at our enemies. Even so, for much of human history we have wanted things like us. In 1668, Samuel Pepys confided in his diary about an affecting puppet performance he had just experienced, "It was pretty to see, and how that idle thing doth work upon people that see it, and even myself too."[118] Perhaps the pretty, idle thing took the diarist back to his own boyhood, embodying the return of the repressed. Nearly a century later, those who came to see the Jaquet-Droz exhibit in Covent Garden encountered a "representation of a boy," who produced and reproduced visible language. He seemed to concentrate. He wrote carefully, precisely, and apparently of his own volition, not like most little boys at all.

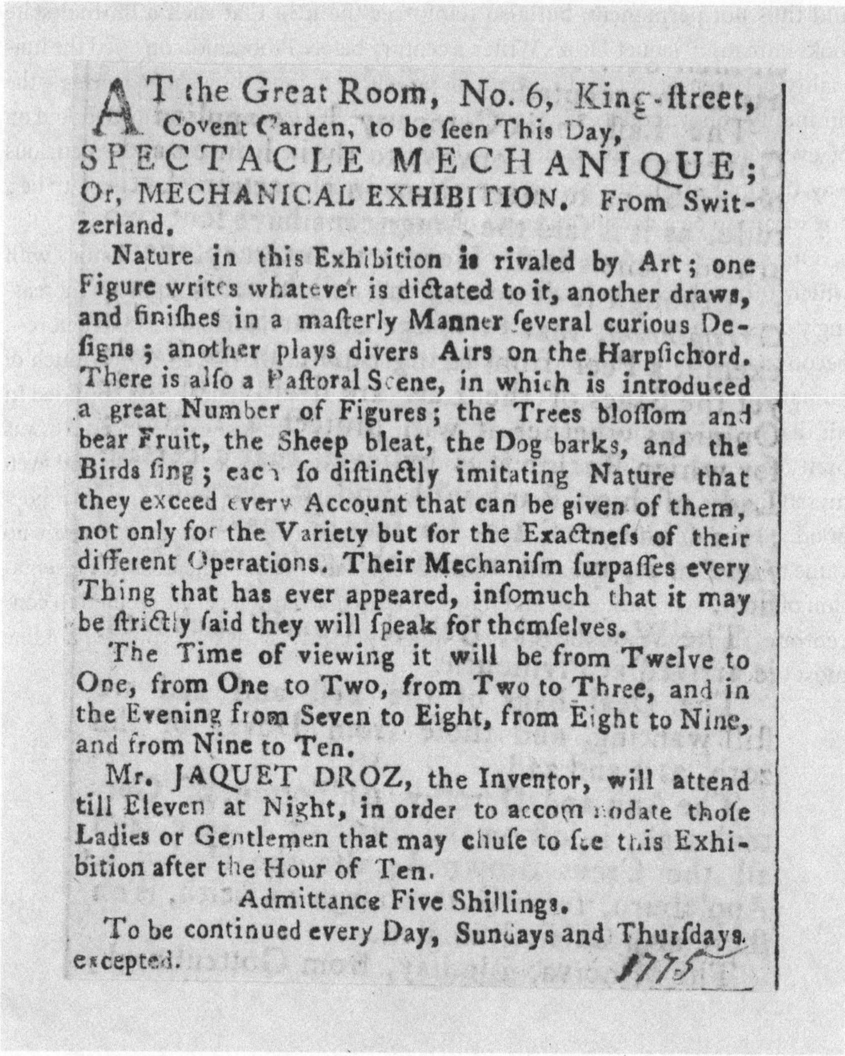

AT the Great Room, No. 6, King-street, Covent Garden, to be seen This Day, SPECTACLE MECHANIQUE; Or, MECHANICAL EXHIBITION. From Switzerland.

Nature in this Exhibition is rivaled by Art; one Figure writes whatever is dictated to it, another draws, and finishes in a masterly Manner several curious Designs; another plays divers Airs on the Harpsichord. There is also a Pastoral Scene, in which is introduced a great Number of Figures; the Trees blossom and bear Fruit, the Sheep bleat, the Dog barks, and the Birds sing; each so distinctly imitating Nature that they exceed every Account that can be given of them, not only for the Variety but for the Exactness of their different Operations. Their Mechanism surpasses every Thing that has ever appeared, insomuch that it may be strictly said they will speak for themselves.

The Time of viewing it will be from Twelve to One, from One to Two, from Two to Three, and in the Evening from Seven to Eight, from Eight to Nine, and from Nine to Ten.

Mr. JAQUET DROZ, the Inventor, will attend till Eleven at Night, in order to accommodate those Ladies or Gentlemen that may chuse to see this Exhibition after the Hour of Ten.

Admittance Five Shillings.

To be continued every Day, Sundays and Thursdays excepted.

1775

Figure 3.1. "At the Great Room, No. 6, King-street, Covent Garden, to be seen this day, Spectacle Machanique; or Mechanical Exhibition from Switzerland," Handbill by Henri-Louis Jaquet Droz from Bodleian Library Digital Archives. Public domain.

Figure 3.2. Photo of Jaquet-Droz's *L'Ecrivain*, December 27, 2005, at the *Musée d'Art et d'Histoire* of Neuchâtel, in Switzerland. https://commons.wikimedia.org/wiki/File:Automates-Jaquet-Droz-p1030495.jpg. CeCILL license.

CHAPTER 4

The Boy in the Chimney

SWEEPS' APPRENTICES, SUFFERING BODIES, AND JONATHAN SWIFT

tool 1 (a) . . . a mechanical implement for working upon something, as by cutting, striking, rubbing, or other process, in any manual art or industry.
—Oxford English Dictionary

tool. n.f. A hireling; a wretch who acts at the command of another.
—*Samuel Johnson,* A Dictionary of the English Language

Tristram Shandy's father worried about how breeches would constrict his boy, and how they might construct him—either as a gentleman or a "beast." Ellenor Fenn's *School Dialogues* explored a different confinement, whereby the boy in grammar school learned to use the tools of reading, writing, and discernment in order to get on in the world, and to avoid being a tool for someone else. Pierre Jaquet-Droz's clockwork boy performed gender, age, and social status, even as the child-shaped machine wielded another freighted tool, the pen. While each of these boys speaks to some aspect of male childhood in the long eighteenth century, it is some aspect of privileged boyhood. Yet as Dianne Payne reminds us, notwithstanding "some trickledown from the ideas of Locke and Rousseau about education and upbringing, the life experiences, the limited education and the drudgery within casual labor and apprenticeship that epitomized the early years of poor children were vastly difference from the experiences and life-styles of their richer contemporaries."[1] Mary Abbott puts it bluntly: "With an heir in prospect, landowners and their ladies set up cradles, acquired linen, and hired nurses. Poor couples dreaded another hungry mouth."[2]

The boy to whom I now turn, the chimney sweep's apprentice, was not educated, although he could have been the same age as Fenn's little pupil, Sprightly; nor was he valuable like the automaton from Switzerland. Like both of them, and like Tristram, this "climbing boy" would have worn breeches (or later in the century trousers)—except when at times in the course of his work he wore nothing. Rather than using a pen, this boy labored with tools such as the "switch" (brush) and "tuggy" (soot cloth). In doing so, he was made into a kind of tool himself in the cause of order, efficiency, and safety for others. Robert Holden states the situation explicitly: "Early in the eighteenth century a practice seemingly peculiar to England *transformed* small boys . . . into human brushes."[3] Climbing boys' bodies took on and took in the filth they were cleaning away, becoming signifiers revelatory of that filth.

The young sweep's apprentice was also rhetorically constructed—both as the most miserable (and untrustworthy) of children and eventually in activist writing aimed at alleviating the plight of the climbing boy, writing that decried the inhumanity with which the boy's soot-blackened body was treated. In addition to ambiguities of age and complications of gender, the word "boy" has also historically been a racialized (and racist) word; so too did the history of the chimney sweep's boy take on racial tropes in texts that dwelt on Blackness, servitude, and suffering. Here I address the history of the sweep's apprentice in responses to that much-troped boy, along with the intersectionality in writings about him and the transatlantic slave trade. Finally, the work of Jonathan Swift threads through this chapter: Swift's musings on brushes, brooms, and those whose very labor damaged and dehumanized them and turned them into tools, elucidate the ways in which others later looked at the climbing boy—and all the ways they refused to look at him.

Conditions of the Sweeps

In Samuel Pepys's diary account of the days following the Great Fire of London in September 1666, the "poor catt taken out of a hole in the chimney . . . with the hair all burned off the body and yet alive" reads as a symbol of London itself: damaged, denuded, yet surviving.[4] A significant portion of the city was rebuilt in the years following the conflagration, including with far more coal-burning chimneys, which "needed a stronger draught . . . and therefore narrower flue, than wood-burning ones, particularly in grander houses where the air passage was hindered as the flue turned through several angles to reach a central stack."[5] At the same time, "such chimneys rapidly filled with soot and needed frequent cleaning, yet were impassible to brushes."[6] Although elsewhere in Europe and in Scotland a lead ball and brush were lowered on a rope to clean smaller chimneys, in England the practice was to send a small child up the chimney.[7] Not surprisingly, the boys whose business it was to do this squeezing and cleaning—sweeps' apprentices—lived dangerous lives, often not lasting beyond boyhood itself.

Already by 1700 in London there were an estimated twenty thousand apprentices working across all trades, a large proportion of whom were adolescents. In the seventy-eight London city livery companies, the age at which most apprenticeships began fell as the century progressed—from just under seventeen years to just under fifteen by 1810. Parish-sponsored apprentices were younger, starting at an average age of twelve.[8] Sweeps' apprentices, mostly parish-sponsored as well, were still in a category to themselves: usually between five and ten years old, some were as young as four, reflected in the poet Charles Lamb referring to the singularity of such boys by calling them "premature apprenticements."[9] Even when indenture papers existed, however, such apprenticeships were often nominal: most masters effectively bought a boy for a lump sum from a poor family, widow, orphanage, or workhouse. This was because the work was so dangerous that the boy's advancement and his life were both less certain than in other trades.[10]

These children were permanently filthy, enduring deformed spines and twisted knees from wedging themselves into the chimneys and climbing awkwardly upward. Cancer of the scrotum, called "sooty warts," was endemic, as were blindness, suffocation, and injury or death from fire—either accidental from an ember still burning in the flue, or one lit under the boy by a master to make him finish the job.[11] Simon Dickie notes that "leisured classes took it for granted that manual laborers became deformed, often in specific and recognizable ways."[12] However, while much of London was filthy, violent, and clamorous with the voices of beggars, and many were recognizably deformed by labor, Tim Hitchcock notes that sweeps were beyond the possibility of being "member[s] of the respectable poor."[13] Rather, they were among the most derided and shunned members of society. Peter Ackroyd identifies the climbing boys in his biography of the city as "the most harshly treated of all London children."[14]

We tend to associate child chimney sweeps with the nineteenth century—with Charles Dickens's *Oliver Twist* (1838) and Charles Kingsley's *The Water Babies* (1862–1863).[15] However, Benita Cullingford's *British Chimney Sweeps: Five Centuries of Chimney Sweeping* (2000) names the very long period in which this practice was a part of life and a cause of death.[16] The nature of the work performed by children in general shifted over the eighteenth century in significant ways apart from narrower chimney designs. Scholarship on adolescence in the early modern period like that of Ilana Krausman Ben-Amos shows most children worked at agrarian or other labor alongside their family as soon as they were physically able to do so (fetch water, sweep floors) prior to entering service, sometimes doing so as young as ten.[17] Hugh Cunningham identifies the period after 1750 as one in which the state intervened in child-related matters to a far greater extent, largely for their protection.[18] Even so, childhood itself grew harder as "increased urbanization and industrialization led plebeian children . . . away from work supervised by their families or neighbors, and towards work in factories, often supervised by unfamiliar adults."[19] Joan Lane makes a point about the "rising visibility" of climbing boys as subjects of good works because the trade's "obvious abuse of the concept of apprentice was important because the children, unlike those in factories, were seen by the general public, plying their trade in city streets."[20]

Injuries, youth, and seemingly indelible filth contributed to this visibility, yet it produced few results for a very long time. Well-informed reports by indefatigable philanthropist Jonas Hanway in 1773 and 1779, for example, forwarded the Chimney Sweeper's Act of 1788, but met with no enforcement of higher age restriction—a lack of enforcement that continued well into the nineteenth century.[21] This was because the work the boys did was important, and they were not. Already the largest city in Europe by 1760, London reached a million inhabitants by the end of the century and just kept growing. Ash and soot produced by burning coal was profuse and dangerous and had to be removed; soot had a variety of uses, such as in fertilizer; and there were too many poor children. In this sense, the problem and the solution were both ubiquitous.

Those who get rid of waste seem ever in danger of being swept up and discarded with it. Sophie Gee's work on waste in the literature of the eighteenth century posits that "waste is animated by paradoxes. It is empty but full. Abject but life-intended. It putrefies, and it proliferates. Perhaps most importantly, we want to dispose of it, and we long to hold on to it."[22] Such descriptors are also applicable to childhood; even as most of us experience it, "we want to dispose of it, and we long to hold on to it." In a culture (like so many) that venerated manhood above other genders it identified, boyhood held a unique place in this opposition between preservation and disposal, and between taking notice and disregarding. The specific waste work of sweeps' boys seems especially relevant to the paradox Gee identifies with waste itself: society wanted to do away with the labor of these boys and wanted to hold onto it. The boys were thus visible and invisible at once.

Protest and Polemics

Despite the more accurate qualifier of "apprentice," which differentiates the boy from both a journeyman and a master sweep, the terms "chimney sweep" and "sweep" were often used as shorthand to refer to the boy rather than the grown man because there were so many climbing boys. The youth and, more specifically, smallness of the child that made him especially useful could make him pitiable. William Blake's famous poem "The Chimney Sweeper" in *Songs of Innocence* presents such a boy, "sold" into the trade "very young," and the piece by the same name in Blake's *Songs of Experience* shows another—exploited, ignored, and in misery. This "sweeper" is not a man, and "clothed ... in the clothes of death" he never will be.[23]

As campaigns against other injustices began to find voice within the discourse of sensibility, a number of writers took up the cause of this boy both prior to and following the abolition of the slave trade by Britain in 1807 (chattel slavery continued until the 1830s). Efforts to abolish the slave trade and the use of young boys as sweeps in the English-speaking world coincided for a number of reasons, including the increase in racialized justifications for slavery in the latter part of the century. Anne-Julia Zwierlein points out that the Black orphan child was formulated as "a sentimental icon" in countless texts at the end of the eighteenth century and beginning of the nineteenth.[24] Defenses of climbing boys like Blake's "little black thing amongst the snow" rendered such boys' situation analogous to that sentimental icon. Adriana Silvia Benzaquén notes that "to some degree, the experiences of slave children were no different from those of poor and working children in Europe and the colonies: hard work, little or no time for play or leisure, harsh discipline and physical punishment, malnutrition and diseases, and premature death."²⁵ Claire Lamont notes that "the portrayal of the chimney-sweep as a black man goes back at least to the sixteenth century."²⁶ However, this polemicizing in aligning the oppression of sweeps' boys and enslaved Black people was itself new.

While profuse, the alignment of the two was not always overt. The most well-known previously enslaved man of the late eighteenth century was Olaudah Equiano (ca. 1745–ca. 1797), an Ibo from northeastern Nigeria who was kidnapped and enslaved around the age of eleven.²⁷ In time Equiano learned to read and write, gained experience as a seaman, and was eventually sold to a British naval officer in Virginia. After more than a decade in slavery he was able to buy his freedom and settle in England, where he lectured and wrote for the British abolitionist movement. Equiano's memoir, *The Life of Olaudah Equiano or Gustavus Vassa, the African*, was published posthumously in London in 1789 and followed by numerous editions and translations, after which Equiano lingered in the British cultural imagination in a literary-historical space, particularly in the imaginations and writings of abolitionists.

The preface to the 1814 edition (probably written by the publisher, James Nichols) draws a striking analogy between the privileged life from which the African boy had been taken and a privileged English boyhood: had Equiano been an English memoirist, the preface suggests, such a writer "would not be backward in informing [readers] of his being the son of an Esquire. On this account he would naturally think himself entitled to greater commiseration, than would be claimed by a youth whose father had been a poor chimney-sweeper."²⁸ The latter is evidently the lowest position from which an English boy might begin his life, a position from which it seems there is nowhere to fall. In addition to drawing on a common understanding of the situation of the sweep, the writer of the 1814 preface was likely thinking at this time of the relationship between calls for abolition of the slave trade and movements still underway for an end to the practice of having young boys sweep chimneys. His analogy both draws on a shared understanding with his reader of lowliness of the chimney sweep's boy and mentions the English-born child most identifiable by his darkened skin.

Notably, in the late seventeenth and early eighteenth centuries, a regular practice of kidnapping British citizens "to feed the needs of the newly emergent transatlantic imperial trade" was replaced in the eighteenth with African slavery.²⁹ Tim Fulford argues that "lacking a public voice himself, [the climbing boy] gave doctors, reformers, philanthropists and poets voices to articulate the deepest fears of a nation that was exploiting people at home and abroad in its pursuit of wealth and comfort."³⁰ Chief among these public articulations was a collection by many hands titled *The Chimney-Sweeper's Friend and Climbing-Boys Album*, brought out in 1824 by Scottish poet and abolitionist James Montgomery (1771–1854).³¹ The miscellany appeared not long after a damning—although again ineffectual—"Report from the Committee of the House of Commons on the Employment of Boys in Sweeping of Chimneys" in 1817.³² Montgomery's own verse polemics identified the boys as beings cut off from compassion and fellow-feeling:

> Who loves the climbing boy?—Who cares
> If well or ill I be?
> Is there a living soul that shares
> A thought or wish with me?[33]

Montgomery is evidently appealing to readers to prove they have "living souls" and to remember that the climbing boy has a soul as well.

Having brought out poems celebrating the abolition of slavery in the decade before, Montgomery compared the abject young boys to "kidnapped and sold" "Africans" in this book.[34] Given the bitter living and working conditions of the sweeps, along with the soot on their skin, it is not surprising to find these sympathetic strains running between the two discourses. Britons had abolished slavery abroad, so "if, the argument ran, Britons could acknowledge their brotherhood with black Africans and ban the trade in their bodies, surely they could see their still greater kinship with the black boys at home."[35] Charles Lamb, again, employed the comparison to sentimental effect in his 1822 essay "The Praise of Chimney-Sweepers," where he wrote, "I reverence these young Africans of our own growth ... dim specks—poor blots—innocent blacknesses."[36] The combination of visibly darker skin and suffering—discussed further below—was used to argue for the freedom of both groups: for instance, Marcus Wood points out that "the first substantial printing of William Blake in North America," which tellingly included not only "The Little Black Boy" but also "The Chimney Sweeper," was in William Lloyd Garrison's 1842 *Anti-Slavery Standard*.[37] Slavery would not be abolished in America until 1865.

In England, Anja Müller finds in illustrated prints "a curious correspondence between the black servant boy and the chimney sweep, starting with their similarities in outward appearance, which sometimes accounts for misreadings ... or confusions" about which boy was which.[38] Yet Müller sees the very frequency with which "the black boy and the chimney sweep are, in a sense, exchangeable" indicative of a range of reactions to these children, and so as being open to different readings—from expressions of sympathy to jests devoid of sympathy.[39] As such, there *could* be an indictment of the position in prints depicting these boys, but not necessarily.

A case in point is Thomas Rowlandson's *The Trades of London* (1820), which I think evidences this kind of ambivalence. Most of his forty-three images depict adults working, looking contented, and indeed seeming sociable in doing so (shoe blacking, delivering the post, selling milk or hot cross buns), and they present children as mostly happy (buying the buns or dancing to the tune of a bagpipe). There are two prints that show miserable-looking children who are not being cared for by others. Alike in subjects, the prints differ in their depictions of boys who swept for a living.

In the first print, two sweeps' apprentices are following their master. What is arresting here is how inhuman—apparently simian—the boys appear to be. While the boys actually look more like chimpanzees—apes—than like monkeys, a chain that seems to be attached to the first apprentice reinforces the connection to monkeys, then owned by some as exotic pets and "generally kept on chains and attached to a ring in the floor."[40] Whereas monkeys had long been employed to satirize human vanity and misplaced pride (one thinks of Rochester), here the association with a lowly climbing boy makes another point. Rather than indicting our species, the resemblance to nonhuman animals instead argues for the resemblance of a specific group (sweeps' boys) to nonhuman animals. The nature of otherness with which the sweeps' boys are depicted entails racist stereotypes as well as echoing how "depictions of colonial populations, from Native Americans to Africans, had stressed their outlandish differences—in appearance, manners, cuisine, social organization, and language."[41] Janet Sorenson is here discussing portrayals of Scottish Highlanders, yet the list applies to the abject poor in England as well, including sweeps, who were seen as outlandish due to their appearance, as well as their "cant" mode of speech.

Anne Lafont has demonstrated that "artistic production and discourse in the eighteenth century produced tools of observation and analysis that allowed human beings to be differentiated as well as implicitly classified on a moral scale, an enterprise that would later veer into explicit racism." Beginning in this period, it was skin color, specifically, that became "the major site of division of the human species."[42] Lafont focuses on depictions in portraiture of African page boys and other servants. While Jaquet-Droz's automaton was a beautiful (and silent) boy, the deeply *unheimlich* nature of the sweeps in Rowlandson's print goes well beyond skin color as determined by ashes and dust; the very bodies of the boys as well as their faces are inhuman. If it were not too early to do so, the temptation would be to read them as organ grinders' monkeys, even down to the hats on the boys' heads. David Bindman notes, "Philosophical arguments deployed against slavery were invariably based on the universality of human nature, or brotherhood of man, which in turn rested on the implicit moral difference between man and animal."[43] Have the inhuman conditions of their work rendered the climbers in Rowlandson's print bestial, or does the print imply the boys are suited by nature to the work?

The impulse to read the print in figure 4.1 as merely mocking all sweeps is complicated, however, by the second print of a "poor sweeper" boy in Rowlandson's *Trades of London* series. Here the shabby child is both more human in facial features and seemingly as pale as the unsympathetic, well-fed woman who ignores him. This sweep is begging (as sweeps were widely known to do), yet the satiric target is clearly the woman bustling past him. These two prints combined indicate the ambivalence with which such boys were seen—either as beneath human consideration or as pitiable. That the "sweeper boy" in this second print is probably a street sweeper (his broom is not the brush used by chimney sweeps) emphasizes how far beneath every other profession was that of the boy in the chimney. Their contrast, too, points to how dark skin could represent a striking sign of suffering through brutal, unjust labor, or could be treated as invisible. It is this range of responses to the boy in the chimney that now takes us back to the beginning of the century and to more general observations on how getting rid of the waste created by humanity lays waste to humanity—a paradox that also comments obliquely on these throwaway sweeps' boys.

Prior to Protest: Reading Sweeps through Jonathan Swift

Jonathan Swift's parodic 1703 *Meditation upon a Broomstick* begins as a reflection on an object. Like the author whom he parodies, Robert Boyle, Swift soon turns his object into an emblem of human weakness.[44] Whereas Boyle's *Occasional Reflections upon Several Subjects* (1665) interpreted the material world as richly symbolic of the lessons taught in the gospel (for instance, about mutability, mortality, salvation), Swift's *Meditation* is decidedly secular. Yet it, too, is about humility and mutability and—despite the wry humor that drives the piece—about suffering:

> A Meditation upon a Broomstick
>
> THIS single Stick, which you now behold ingloriously lying in that neglected Corner, I once knew in a flourishing State in a Forest: It was full of Sap, full of Leaves, and full of Boughs: But now, in vain does the busy Art of Man pretend to vye with Nature, by tying that withered Bundle of Twigs to its sapless Trunk: It is now at best but the Reverse of what it was; a Tree turned upside down, the Branches on the Earth, and the Root in the Air: It is now handled by every dirty Wench, condemned to do her Drudgery; and by a capricious Kind of Fate destined to make other Things clean and be nasty it self. At length, worn to the Stumps in the Service of the Maids, it is either thrown out of Doors or condemned to the last Use of kindling a Fire. When I beheld this, I sighed, and said within my self Surely mortal Man is a Broomstick . . .[45]

The *Meditation* goes on to satirize age, its indignities, and the vain efforts by which man tries to stave them all off, time and intemperance nevertheless and inevitably leaving him "a withered Trunk."

Although *Meditation upon a Broomstick* is both parodic and burlesque, Swift's essay comments on all those human tools worn down in the service of others. The figure of the climbing boy has not hitherto entered the conversation about Swift's essay, yet this boy is a figure especially suited to the paradox Swift presents of the cleaning tool begrimed and, more to the point, a tool destroyed in being used.[46] The *Meditation*, along with other writing by Swift in which brooms, sweeping, and sweepers appear, can be read with reference to the lives of the chimney sweeps described above—boys whose lives, although brief, mirrored Swift's famous description of the broomstick.

Scholars have examined how the *Meditation* plays with pessimistic notions of what makes a "Mortal Man," what makes him vulnerable and, given that this is Swift, what awaits a satirist who dares to sweep into the corners of the muck-ridden world. Christopher Fox has pointed out that "Swift was a brilliant controversialist with a unique ability to become what he attacked and then to burrow from within."[47] Whereas Fox is taking note of Swift's political writings, we see such burrowing from within also in the fate of the broomstick, once "full of Sap, full of

Leaves, and full of Boughs," and the speaker's lament that it is "by a capricious Kind of Fate, destined to make other Things clean and be nasty it self." Again, inescapably "worn to the Stumps in the Service of the Maids, it is either thrown out of Doors, or condemned to its last Use of Kindling a Fire."[48] A broomstick (or broomstaff, or besom) is for Swift a sign of the human being depleted, of a body suffering damage and indignity in order to rectify external disorder, and of natural life rendered unnatural. Repeatedly he used this clean/unclean paradox to consider both the human condition and what satire uncomfortably achieves.[49] Michael Seidel sees the end of Swift's *Meditation* as being "not unlike the ending of *Gulliver's Travels*," because there too Swift "invests a series of surrogates, sacrificial satiric brooms, to do his dirty work for him."[50] Fredric V. Bogel, too, points out that Swift's meditative "broom-stick has its counterparts, in 'The Lady's Dressing Room,' in Celia's combs and basin, which are agents of grooming and cleanliness but are themselves 'Filled up with dirt.'"[51] "Agents of grooming and cleanliness" are unavoidably the martyrs of the material world—sacrificial objects attendant upon human lives. And, Swift argues here and elsewhere, such lives are both cleaned and contaminated by agents of grooming and cleanliness.

One effect of the *Meditation* is that the broomstick is animated into a kind of doll or puppet in the hands of its master (or mistress). The broom represents a topsy-turvy mortal man, with his feet (roots) now in the air, and his head (branches) on the earth. I alluded to puppets in my previous chapter on Ellenor Fenn's rhetorical schoolboys. In considering dolls and puppets, objects that represent humans, Julie Park demonstrates how "through building its global market economy, attended and facilitated by the exploration and colonization of exotic lands, eighteenth-century England directed a marvelous narrative about material objects and their relationship with human subjects."[52] A broomstick, used to dispose of dirt and itself fairly disposable, was by no means exotic or marvelous—although the besom does hold a place in witch lore. No longer alive as part of a tree, yet seemingly puppet-like, it is not dead either, but rather a semiliving tool, "handled by every dirty Wench." As such, Swift's broomstick represents both the relationship between human subjects and material objects and the relationship between human subjects and other human subjects. In the case of the chimney sweep, the distance between symbolic sign and its object was also minimal: sweeps both wielded and were objects that cleaned up filth and were begrimed and damaged by the act. Their doing was their undoing.

For Swift, brushes, brooms, and mops all serve a dually useful and ignominious function as creators of dirt as much as (or more than) removers of it. Brooms and brushes can be metonymic, then, because so many of those who wield tools are tools. We see more of this kind of person-thing confusion in Swift's mock-aubade "A Description of the Morning" (1709), where we meet a boy and a woman whose tasks are sweeping and scrubbing:

The Slip-shod 'Prentice from his Master's Door
Had par'd the Dirt, and sprinkled round the Floor.

> Now *Moll* had whirl'd her Mop with dext'rous Airs,
> Prepar'd to scrub the Entry and the Stairs.[53]

"Slip-shod 'Prentice" brings both assonance and consonance to the verb "sprinkled," while "mop" is a slant rhyme for "*Moll*," a reminder in prosody that what these people do, they do every morning. Worth recalling here is that "there was no provision for street cleaning, so each householder had to clear the area directly in front of his door, moving the dirt out into the traffic."[54] Dirt therefore shifted back and forth between spaces. This is cyclical, infinite filth.

After the slip-shod apprentice and Moll in the "Description" we encounter another boy—this one sweeping to find old nails—followed by a coal seller and a chimney sweep:

> The Youth with broomy Stumps began to trace
> The Kennel-Edge, where Wheels had worn the Place.
> The Small-coal Man was heard with Cadence deep;
> Till drown'd in shriller Notes of *Chimney-sweep*.[55]

The "broomy stumps" wielded by the youth refer to the worn-down straws of his broom, yet they seem also like worn-down legs. Like the ruts in the earth "where Wheels had worn the place," each person wielding mop or broom is confined within his or her sphere; each performs the same function in the same place each day. Indeed, even with the cacophony of the morning there is an element of the automatic herein—of men, women, and children as machines. "*Chimney-sweep*" names the person and what he does—the boy worker advertising his service. Since his notes are "shrill," the sweep in Swift's poem, like that in Blake's later verses, is a very young boy.[56]

What Bogel has identified as Swift's theme of "Purification and its Discontents" has been examined from various critical angles.[57] If we consider the plight of the chimney sweeps, the tragicomic fate of the broomstick in Swift's *Meditation* "kindling a Fire" is rendered merely tragic when applied to the real-life throwaway boys (sources too of purification, and its discontents). They, too, were like Swift's broomstick: tools "destined to make other Things clean, and be nasty" themselves. They were also often burnt.

Swift does not write tragedy, however. Nor does he simply write abjection. He writes ambivalence—an attitude we find in writings about boyhood itself as a subset of masculinity, a stage on the way to manhood from infancy, or a state of perpetual servitude. Recall Swift's use of human "tools" in *Remarks on a Letter to the Seven Lords*, quoted in my introduction, here: "A tool, and an instrument, in the metaphorical sense, differ thus: the former is an engine in the hands of knaves; the latter in those of wise and honest men."[58] Doubtless master sweeps, like any other tradesmen who took on apprentices, and parents, too, could be knaves, or wise and honest. A sooty chimney, however, was in need of tools to make it safe, including one conforming to Samuel Johnson's second definition of "tool" in the *Dictionary*: "a hireling; a wretch who acts at the command of another."[59] In this case, it is a poor boy.

We meet with another dirty mop (which may as well be a broom) in Swift's other urban mock-georgic, "A Description of a City Shower" (1710). Here, the weather in London wears out the poet even as it invades him (or "you") when "that Sprinkling which some careless Quean / Flirts on you from her Mop, but not so clean":

> Ah! Where must needy Poet seek for Aid,
> When Dust and Rain at once his Coat invade?
> Sole Coat, where Dust cemented by the Rain
> Erects the Nap, and leaves a cloudy Stain.[60]

All of these pieces, conflating brooms and mops and those who wield them, unavoidably implicate reader along with speaker. It is the commingled rain, street dirt, and detritus from this tool wielded by "some careless Quean[s]" that raises it all up again, a mixture that results in the stained coat. The speaker wears the city. As Swift wrote these words, especially when newly designed chimneys spelled safety, the practice of having children clean chimneys might have seemed no more avoidable than a city shower, although the city—unlike the shower in this urban anti-eclogue—is a human construction. Sweeps all wore the city, but its stain invaded their very skin.

The dean was to conflate different kinds of sweeping and grime in a more transparent conceit involving chimney sweeps proper among the surrogates listed in "A Letter of Advice to a Young Poet" (1720). It is a moment that also anticipates the ferocious brilliance of Lemuel Gulliver's eventual dismissal of all and sundry among his own species: "Neither do I make exceptions as to satirical poets and lampoon writers in consideration of their offices; for though, indeed, their business is to rake into kennels, gather up the filth of streets and families (in which respect they may be . . . as necessary to the town as scavengers and chimney-sweeps), yet I have observed, they too have themselves, at the same time, very foul clothes, and, like dirty persons, leave more filth and nastiness than they sweep away."[61] Having mentioned sweeps comically along with scavengers and his principal target, hack writers, Swift acknowledges that sweeps are "necessary to the town." However, one would not choose to spend time with either. Nor would one choose to observe them too closely.

Yet Swift was a curiously observant man. He was also, as Sean Shesgreen notes, both "keenly interested in the lower orders" and "largely unsympathetic" to them.[62] This is undeniable in reading Swift's oeuvre, as is, perhaps, Brian A. Connery's insightful comment that "among both the higher and the lower orders, Swift was often out of his class."[63] Sweeps' apprentices were boys so low as to be essentially beneath class, which is why it was easy to use and dehumanize them. This is also why Swift's repeated overlapping of people and tools is a way into interrogating the overlapping outrage of others writing about the conditions of those so low on the social scale as to be invisible: in urban spaces especially, the coal-dusted "sweeps" and, further away, African victims of slavery—those who suffered most desperately from empire building and were most objectified by it. Alongside outrage on behalf of both, ambivalence about one group sometimes echoes ambivalence about the other. This is why Swift's work is useful, too.

"Kindling Flames for Others to Warm Themselves By"

The ill-fated broomstick in the *Meditation* spends its last days "in slavery to the Maids" prior to being reduced to "kindling Flames for others to warm themselves by."[64] These "least deserving" women with the power to enslave men represent a joke about gender relations, yet the myriad references to slavery in Swift's collective works suggest there is more to it than that. In political writings about Ireland and England, and the multiple targets of *Gulliver's Travels*, for example, Carole Fabricant argues, Swift dwelt on "the complex interdependencies between tyrant and slave," because he "at all times displayed a healthy appreciation for the reality of stone walls."[65] Further, "confinement for Swift was an external act as well as a state of mind; it was a physical condition defined by architectural structures or geographical spaces, and political conditions produced by specific forms of oppression."[66] Although climbing boys' labor obviously took them from chimney to chimney, the confined nature of a chimney need not be pointed out. We also know that many suffocated to death there. What prison is narrower than a chimney, which James Montgomery described in *The Chimney-Sweeper's Friend* as prison cell and torture chamber combined: "Rougher than harrow-teeth within, / Sharp lime and jagged stone"?[67] As mentioned, climbing boys often worked naked to prevent clothing being shredded.[68] Harrow teeth, tools for breaking up and smoothing out soil, would shred skin as the boy scraped the soot from the jagged stone walls.

The breaking down of the human body is also, in the case of both Swift's *Meditation* and the sweep's apprentice, part of the oppression of the male body. The theme of male sterility in Swift's broomstick essay appears with the very beginnings of the broom qua broom: "that withered Bundle of Twigs [tied] to its sapless Trunk." Having been "full of Sap, full of Leaves, and full of Boughs" it is now effectively emasculated. Similarly, in *Gulliver's Travels*, the disturbing "solution" proposed to control the revolting Yahoos is castration, which Gulliver suggests to his Houyhnhnm masters: "That this invention might be practiced on the younger Yahoos here."[69] The cancerous scrotums of young boys who spent their daylight hours imprisoned in chimneys would achieve the same ends as castration on Yahoos, and as withering age did for mortal man previously "full of sap" in the *Meditation*: climbing boys who survived sweep's carcinoma would be unlikely to reproduce.[70]

Moreover, whatever else the Yahoos represent, they are also, in comparison to their "master" Houyhnhnms, not only more bestial but more childlike—not in the sense of innocent, but rather in that of exhibiting the fear, caprice, and violence of the young child. The feces-flinging, aggressive adult male Yahoos (whatever Gulliver's eventual conclusion is) are not men. They are something like monkeys, something like boys. A similar ambiguity, I think, is reflected in the relationship drawn between young chimney sweeps whose plight often precluded them from growing into men (and as such, from being as threatening as men) and enslaved African males who complicated what was understood as true manhood—who were not allowed to be men, either, even in abolitionist tracts.[71] Manhood was thus either prevented from coming about or denied as being. As regards childishness, the plaintive *peep*, *cheep*, and *sweep* sounds attributed to the climbing boys in poems and essays about them combine the nature of the work with images of the boys as hatchlings or chicks, which says much about the boys themselves saying little. Although onomatopoeic references to sounds the boys made were, as in the case of Blake's poems, intended to increase pathos, they have the potential to dehumanize too.

Swift's description of the incomprehensible Yahoos upon Gulliver's first sight of them—as bestial humanoids—is reminiscent of European descriptions of West Africans. Elaine L. Robinson pursues this resemblance, asking, "What other purpose could the Houyhnhnms' Yahoos serve, but as racism's black victims?"[72] For Robinson, who reads Swift's sermons and his use of the Queen Anne *Book of Common Prayer* in *Gulliver* to argue that Swift advocated true rather than false Christianity, "the Yahoos are black people, and . . . Swift is protesting the African trade."[73] While accepting in part Robinson's interpretation, I read the Yahoos as a more fluid problem: Swift himself later used the term *Yahoos* for individuals he loathed.[74] Michael Seidel states, "Jonathan Swift invented the word [Yahoo] as the degenerate moniker for the most irredeemable creatures on earth ever to sling excrement."[75] Surely, the Yahoos cannot then merely "be Black people."

Rather than accepting wholesale Robinson's argument, I agree with J. A. Richardson, who interprets Gulliver himself as one who "can be both right and wrong, sometimes simultaneously, because he and his situation do not suggest a coherent definition of human nature."[76] Importantly, as Richardson argues, Swift "frequently uses 'slave' and its cognates in ways that imply the slave's consent or complicity in enslavement."[77] For example, Richardson notes that the starving hordes in Ireland (who were not enslaved people) are partly responsible for their own suffering in *A Modest Proposal*: "Although its irony relies upon the recognition that trading in people is wrong, and although it forces readers to confront their position as members of society engaged in such trading, it also reinforces a key justification for slavery."[78] While it is therefore tempting to argue that Swift broadly indicts systemic suffering inflicted by one nation, class, or race on the people of another, I do not think that he allows the reader enough distance from the dirt, grime, and stench—of the Yahoos or of the poor or of the enslaved—to be satisfied with one way of thinking about them. These layers of ambivalence can well complicate our reading of the much smaller yet real issue of the abuse that was endemic in the sweeps' trade. That trade not only involved dangerous labor done for bed and board (and these most often inadequate) but also was built on powerless bodies that were troped by abolitionists as being "Black" bodies, both because of the boys' darkened skin but also because, unlike other apprentices, they were bought outright.

The socioeconomic system that Lemuel Gulliver tries to explain to his Houyhnhnm master describes his native land as one where "the rich Man enjoyed the Fruit of the poor Man's Labour, and the latter were a Thousand to one in Proportion to the former. That the Bulk of our People was forced to live miserably, by labouring every day for small Wages to make a few live plentifully."[79] Swift is not lamenting through Gulliver that the bulk of people must labor; he is, however, making clear that the "proportion" between rich and poor is unjust and that something *is* wrong with "the bulk of [any] people" being "forced to live miserably."

Troped Bodies, Black and Blackened

As Vincent Carretta notes, "For most of the eighteenth century, certainly the first half, slavery was perceived primarily as an economic concern, not a moral problem, and the initial basis of African slavery was predominantly financial rather than racial."[80] Efforts to end the slave trade and the use of young boys as sweeps in the English-speaking world coincided for a number of reasons, including the increase in racialized justifications for slavery. Contrasting the sort of enslavement he grew up with in Africa to the transatlantic trade, Olaudah Equiano's antislavery memoir testified to the tendency of the latter "to debauch men's minds, and harden them to every feeling of humanity!" As a result of such degradation of mind and compassion, severe "punishments of the slaves on every trifling occasion" were not only "frequent" but "well known."[81] This was more than callousness. With the extent of the slave trade, and the fact that it was a trade that encouraged cruelty, there can be no mistaking the widespread sadism Equiano identifies in those bereft of humanity who were given the power to torture and kill.

A similar relationship between nominal and legal ownership and cruelty is evidenced in K. H. Strange's documentation of personal accounts by men who had once been climbing boys, detailing brutality by adults who felt they "had a right to do as they pleased" with the children they had "purchased."[82] John Locke's argument in favor of contracts—"as soon as compact enters, slavery ceases" because of a check to the "despotical, arbitrary power" permitted without a contract[83]—is worth recalling here since climbing boys' compacts were most often based on a lump sum paid for the unlimited labor of the child. The misery and danger for which chimney sweeping was notorious are further pointed to by the fact that in America, following the abolition of enslavement in 1865, Black men and boys "slave or free . . . became involved [in sweeping], so the white men and boys gave up the trade which society despised so much."[84]

In *Bringing the Empire Home: Race, Class, and Gender in Britain and Colonial South Africa* (2004), Zine Magubane reads depictions of Black bodies as hinging upon suffering as spectacle—spectacle that "was marked by the elasticity the viewer was allowed in formulating a response. One could be alternately shocked, disgusted, aroused, amused, or any combination thereof. The only thing stable about the suffering black body, therefore, was the fact of its existence."[85] Specifically, Magubane reads "anti [Anglo-Boer] war discourses produced by working class activists" to show that "the manner in which the suffering of black and white bodies was juxtaposed in these texts served to redirect toward white bodies—specifically the bodies of white working-class men—the empathy and outrage that presumably should have been directed toward and expressed on behalf of the suffering black bodies."[86] Obviously such elasticity was rooted in traditions of racism working their way through previous centuries.

Magubane's take on "the fungible nature of blackness" in the discourse in colonial South Africa complicates the appearance of the suffering "Black bodies" in the campaign on behalf of child sweeps in England, reminding us that efforts to frame the climbing boys' position as one of domestic slavery, however well intentioned, could have had the effect of watering down full appreciation of the magnitude of the slave trade.[87] For instance, in Charles Lamb's essay about "young Africans of our own growth," he poetically implies that the chimney sweeps of Britain both were and were not Black. They are "dim specks—poor blots—innocent blacknesses." A "blot" can be rubbed away. "Innocent blacknesses" means "blackness" is imposed rather than innate, but also suggests punishment where none is warranted (again an indication of the apprenticeship as imprisonment). Yet it also problematizes "blackness" that is not a "speck" or a "blot."[88]

Although the suffering inflicted on individuals and peoples by the slave trade is a world apart from that of London's climbing boys, an elasticity in the range of responses to the latter is reflected in the tropes employed by writers like Blake, in an effort to elicit pity and outrage for "the little black thing among the snow."[89] Those who wrote about chimney sweeps in the period, either as mere guttersnipes in the urban landscape or sentimentalized as Lamb's "poor blots—innocent blacknesses,"[90] suggest why it took a long time to effect change for the sweeps—because the viewer was allowed elasticity in formulating a response to them as well. The connections drawn between the protracted horror that was the slave trade and the practice of sending children up chimneys go some way to explaining the variety of rhetorical approaches employed on behalf of the latter (very often, again, by writers who labored to end both).

As for the soot that identified the boys (accompanied often by ruined knees, curved spines, persistent coughs, and burns) social historians remind us of how thoroughly unwashed almost everyone was.[91] Yet sweeps—referred to as "the black Fraternity"—were remarked upon as beyond the very possibility of cleanliness. Even at night, the boys slept in cold cellars on the bags they had filled with soot. Their filth represented the threat of more filth, for brushing up against a sweep would be sullying, even though they were beneath notice. At the same time, boys as a demographic were conventionally and in general associated with having dirty faces; the soot-palled sweeps were familiar, yet rendered foreign and defamiliarized by their trade.

In responding to James Montgomery's appeals for poetry to call attention to the plight of the young sweep, bluestocking Joanna Baillie (who had subscribed to Equiano's memoirs) revealed a skepticism about the nature of protest and polemic: "You forget," she wrote to Montgomery, "that I firmly believe any verses whatever would do harm instead of good."[92] Her argument alerts Montgomery to the danger of sentiment impeding rather than inciting action—a position that might well reflect what Magubane sees in representations of the Black suffering body in colonialism as de facto. Indeed, Lamb's essay, again, stands as a case in point, urging his reader to give a penny or more to climbing boys. Yet, he enjoyed the whiteness of the sweep's toothy smile in his dark face, and "like[d] to meet a sweep... not a grown sweeper—old chimney sweepers are by no means attractive—but one of those tender novices, blooming through their first negritude, the maternal washings not quite effaced from the cheek—such as come forth with the dawn, or somewhat earlier, with their little professional notes sounding like the *peep peep* of a young sparrows; or liker to the matin lark should I pronounce them, in their aerial ascents not seldom anticipating the sun-rise?"[93] Youth and dark skin combine in that phrase "blooming in their first negritude" to emphasize both innocence and innocuousness; the phrase also naturalizes and—despite Lamb's overall aim—reifies the work the young boys did. "If it be starving weather," Lamb urged the gift of two pennies, as "the demand on thy humanity will surely rise to the tester."[94] This undoubtedly encouraged many readers to do so, but it does not address the system. Instead, Lamb's position aligns boy sweeps in England and enslaved Africans in yet another way—from a position of curious, well-meaning, but ultimately detached observer.[95]

Advocates for the wretched climbing boy had more than one problem with which to contend: not only was chimney sweeping an essential service, but the children who did the work were, more often than not, criminal because they were destitute. The presumption of dishonesty is another connection to other people exploited for labor and to tropes of external "blackness" as a sign of vice.[96] With respect to enslavement and vice, as Equiano testified, brutality engendered brutality. Ann Cline Kelly has explored how Swift perceived the Irish as being enslaved by the English: "The profound metamorphosis produced by prolonged servitude morbidly fascinated Swift. Sometimes he despaired that bondage to the English had uprooted every vestige of humanity and rationality in the Irish: continually brutalized, they become brutes—often quite unrecognizable as men."[97] Such unrecognizability—as in Thomas Rowlandson's print of monkey-faced, dark-skinned sweeps' apprentices—dehumanizes human bodies further. It also commodifies them.

Those who believed the ends justified the means in regard to sweeps carried on an argument about inevitable sacrifices for the greater good. As enslaved peoples were treated as tools of the empire, sweeps were tools of domestic England—a dehumanizing conflation evident in the protest poem penned in 1824 by John Holland on behalf of the climbing boy:

> Sold into slavery, doom'd to be a wretch,
> His flexile form, so exquisitely nerved,
> Goaded with curses, or at the rope's end,
> Must henceforth, as an animate machine,
> Be used, and treated vilely, day by day.[98]

Vile treatment being the norm "day by day" reinforces the trope of the climbing boy as slave at the same time as the endless repetition of the treatment renders the boy "animate machine." Indeed, theories of the mechanized body we encountered in the previous chapter lent themselves to unsentimentality about the working bodies of the poor. Roy Porter points out that "investigators were spurred to view living creatures mechanistically, as ingenious contraptions made up of skillfully articulated components (bones, joints, cartilage, muscles, vessels, functioning as levers, pulleys, cogs, pipes and wheels.... The body became a *machine carnis*, a machine of the flesh."[99] The description of the child in the chimney in the poem, as more tool than boy, decries a scenario both extreme and commonplace. Such commonplace "doom" again underlies Immanuel Kant's argument that society must move toward a "kingdom of ends"—a world in which humans are treated as ends in and of themselves, rather than as means to an end for others.[100] The London of the sweep's apprentice was far from such a kingdom. Rather, the boy who was nothing but a means to an end—a living tool—demonstrated why such a kingdom was needed, and how far the civilized, enlightened world was from creating it.

Dirty Work

Swift neither sentimentalized the chimney sweep nor proposed solutions for such a boy's plight. The world as he and his readers saw it was, after all, postlapsarian, and so bound to be a vale of tears. But he also refused to let the troublesome sight of the wretched portion of humanity equal invisibility in his aim to disconcert readers.[101] In his nonsatiric role as churchman, Swift delivered sermons on compassion and justice for the downtrodden: "Let not those, on whom the bounty of Providence hath bestowed wealth and honours, despise the men who are placed in a humble and inferior station; but rather, with their utmost power, by their countenance, by their protection, by just payment of their honest labour, encourage their daily endeavours for the support of themselves and their families."[102] There were few stations more "humble and inferior" than that of the climbing boy. Swift's collective, ambivalent meditations on the tools wielded by those who clean up filth, therefore, and how the relationship between groups of people connected by work dehumanizes one of those groups is useful for reading later works by Montgomery, Lamb, Shaftesbury, and others who made appeals on behalf of the climbing boys based on Christian charity and *caritas*.

Critical of those reformers who, at the end of the century and into the next, strove to alleviate the sufferings of chimney sweeps, Tim Fulford argues that most of these reformers imposed "mental, spiritual, and physical imprisonment" on the boys through a complicity between "technologized benevolence and evangelical Christianity" in workhouses and Sunday schools.[103] Fulford applauds Blake, for one, for "see[ing] through" and condemning the plans for social improvement that "perpetuate repression in the process of providing comfort."[104] Close to a century earlier, Swift did not condemn, but he did interrogate the proclivity to inflict suffering and to perpetuate repression, and he was certainly alert to hypocrisy: again from Swift's *Meditation*, broom-like man "sets up to be a universal Reformer and Corrector of Abuses ... and raiseth a mighty Dust where there was none before, sharing deeply all the while, in the very same Pollutions he pretends to sweep away."[105] The protracted length of time it took for significant reform to correct widespread abuses of the climbing boys proves how little the lives of destitute children changed over the eighteen and early nineteenth centuries compared to those of the middling and upper classes.

It would not have been in Swift's nature to preempt Montgomery with the sentimental, rhetorical "Who loves the climbing boy?" Yet variations of such questions run through Swift's satires about bodies sullied, worn down, and broken by labor. The reader is provoked to consider and implicated in the price of cleaning things up. Gee points out "the sheer difficulty of explaining how Swift's satires work dramatizes the way they trick us into experiencing the madness he represents— the confused insanity of not being able to tell the difference between waste and value."[106] The late eighteenth-century movement toward sensibility at once was a corrective to this "not being able to tell the difference" and, at times, brought a different kind of confusion to the notion of value—something we might read in Lamb's "reveren[t]" look at chimney sweeps "blooming through their first negritude."[107] All that being said, manifestations of "not being able to tell the difference between waste and value" drive us still. We clutter and declutter and clutter, inhabiting a kingdom of things.

Swift's musing on the "capricious kind of fate" both of the broomstick and of "mortal man" worn down "to the stumps" and thrown like kindling on the fire is a fitting way of thinking about the climbing boys who were enrobed in soot, twisted, and poisoned in the course of their work. The dilemma of the chimney sweep—in some cases truly burned to death—is that *some* human life was not too costly a price to pay for the fires to keep burning for well over a century after the *Meditation upon a Broomstick*. Indeed, apprenticing small boys to clean chimneys was not unlike the system proposed by Swift's projector in the 1729 *Modest Proposal*, for "preventing the Children of poor People . . . from being a Burden to their Parents or Country; and . . . making them beneficial to the Publick."[108]

Figure 4.1. *Rowlandson's characteristic Sketches of the Lower Orders, intended as a companion to the New Picture of London*. 1820.C.58.cc.1(2) page 12. Used by permission of the British Library.

Figure 4.2. *Rowlandson's characteristic Sketches of the Lower Orders, intended as a companion to the New Picture of London.* 1820.C.58.cc.1(2) page 19. Used by permission of the British Library.

CHAPTER 5

The Boy in the Gallows

CRIME, PUNISHMENT, BROADSHEETS, AFTERLIVES

Tool 1 (b) *in* Criminals' slang, *any weapon.*
—Oxford English Dictionary

Even the fiercest of creatures have their use.
—*Ellenor Fenn,* The Rational Dame

We have just looked at a boy endangered by a form of labor associated with London more than any other European city in the eighteenth and nineteenth centuries. The present chapter again considers an endangered boy, and again he was a sweep's apprentice, but this time it was not the chimney that endangered him—or not directly. He was also, himself, a threat to others, having degenerated from apprentice to thief, to prisoner in court, to a boy in the gallows. Recall John Arbuthnot's observation that "the external accidents to which males are subject (who must seek their food with danger) do make a great havock of them."[1] Whereas Arbuthnot did not mention crime being one of these dangers, it was a significant one. Then, as now, more male children than female children were prosecuted for crime, and males were punished more harshly.[2] As potential agents of violence, boys—whether naughty torturers of birds, wily, possibly aggressive pickpockets, or lawless rebels—signified a threat.[3] Boys as Arbuthnot sees them are thus unsafe in both senses of the word—because of what happen to them, and because of what they might do. Boys needed saving, including from themselves.

Whereas climbing boys might share the "capricious kind of fate" of Swift's broomstick, the boy in this chapter is especially associated with mischief—a word much used in stereotyping boys, yet also a punishable crime. I am interested here in the variety of mischief linked to boyhood, particularly in regard to how male children who committed crimes were depicted as a demographic—including among boy workers and, within the machinery of state law enforcement, as tools of the criminal element. Like Fenn's schoolboy Sprightly, the figure of the criminal boy could serve rhetorical and didactic ends in print; like the chimney sweep's climbing boy, he was visible and invisible, worthless, and yet functioned to further different agendas. Moreover, the criminally delinquent boy picks up on and complicates Tribunella's identification of boyhood as having "always constituted a kind of problem. To be a boy means to be a flawed, inchoate, or incomplete man, and boyhood involves the fundamental paradox between the privileges of maleness and the subaltern of youth, class or race."[4] As a criminal, such a boy might be set apart from men in his access to the property and persons on whom he might carry out an offense and the punishment he might receive; yet, at the same time, he was treated more like a man than a law-abiding boy would be.

The labor in which juvenile delinquents, real or unreal, were engaged before—and which often facilitated—the crimes that condemned them relates to the genre in which such tales are most often told, a "crossover" publication different from those hitherto discussed, although aimed at a wide readership. This is the informal broadsheet, also known as a broadside: a sheet of paper printed on one side only, forming one large page. Sold on street corners by hawkers who sometimes sang out their contents, broadsheet publications were cheaply printed and sold and most often devoted to the sensational.

I take here the case of "The Dreadful Life and Confession of a Boy Aged Twelve Years, Who Was Condemn'd to Die at Last Old Bailey Sessions," which purportedly occurred in November 1829 (see figure 5.1; the date is added by hand and therefore speculative). The story told on this sheet speaks to a tradition of ambivalence about boy criminals—and boy workers—throughout the long eighteenth century. This boy was named Thomas King.

The Dreadful Life and Confession

The history of such ephemera as "The Dreadful Life and Confession" represents a broad association between impoverished male children and crime, as well as speaking to the financial cost to merchants of boys and boy gangs. Not only theft of property from the former by the latter, however, is at issue. There is a clear relationship between the importance of labor in the story told by the broadsheet and others like it, and the role of paid labor for boys and a descent to crime and punishment—not merely crime and punishment that happened subsequent to or instead of labor but that were in part consequences of labor.

The prose account in the left-hand column reports that Thomas King's parents "encouraged their only son in lying, stealing &c." We learn that he was seven years old when "the parish humanely bound him an apprentice but his wickedness soon caused his master to discharge him—he was afterwards bound to a chimney-sweeper in the borough." However, the master sweep "soon repented having taken him, for he plundered every place that he was sent to work at, for which not only correction but imprisonment ensued. His master being an honest man brought him twice back with some property he had stolen which obtained him pardon, and prevented him from being transported." The broadside echoes other narratives of a child's descent into crime—the honest master who cannot override bad parenting and the damning influence of other boys. Nature and nurture combine in the boy taking on a life of crime and its consequences, for we are told, "His parents made him desert from his master, and bound him to a gang of thieves who sent him down the chimney of a jeweller in Swallow street, where he artfully unbolted the shop window, out of which his companions cut a pane of glass, and he handed a considerable quantity of articles to them; but the noise he made alarmed the family, and he was taken into custody, but the others escaped. He was tried at last Old Bailey Sessions, found Guilty, and sentenced to die in the 12th year of his age." The next and final paragraph of the report is confusing, as the reader learns that "*after his sentence the confession he made struck those around him with horror, stating the particulars of several murders and robberies*" (emphasis mine). The report concludes with the predictable "hope" that the example of Thomas King will serve as "a lasting warning to the world at large."

In keeping with conventions of criminal broadsides, where the prose account is matter-of-fact, the tone of the verse in the right-hand column offers pathos. Here we find tears among the onlookers, the boy called "poor" and "little" throughout, and appeals to maternal sensibility:

> Give ear ye tender mothers dear,
> And when this tale you read.
> Of a little boy of twelve years old,
> 'twill make your hearts to bleed.

Dramatically, even

> The Court was drown'd in tears,
> To see a child so soon cut off
> All in his infant years.

Now in verse, rather than confessing more heinous crimes—as he does in prose—Thomas "begg'd and pray'd for life / When his sentence was made known." As with the prose account, bad parenting is blamed in the poem, which then concludes by aiming the cautionary tale at others of Thomas's generation:

> Be warn'd my little children dear,
> By this poor boy's downfall,
> Keep from dishonest courses clear
> And GOD will bless you all.
> O think of this poor little boy,
> Lament his woeful state.
> Condemn'd to die on a gallows high,
> How dreadful is his fate.

As noted above, both the dual format and subject matter are common to the genre, as is the woodcut accompaniment.[5] In fact, the figures depicted in the print show that the woodcut here was decidedly from an earlier era—perhaps itself older by a century (see the clothing in figure 5.1).[6]

Numerous copies of this broadsheet are extant. The British Library note for its copy states, "The piece was used as a rhetorical device by supporters of moral reform to highlight the crimes of boys and girls generally. The text of the broadsheet was certainly recycled in similar publications."[7] Another printing of the same text, with minimal changes in spacing, font, and ornamentation, but using the same woodcut, would later be produced by James Catnach of Monmouth Street (1792–1841), the most prolific broadsheet printer of the period, who also made his name in farthing and halfpenny books for children.[8] In every printing the claim is that the trial has just taken place, "at the last Old Bailey sessions." Another alternately titled but otherwise identical version of the story, told in broadsheet format, names the culprit Thomas Mitchel. Prior to these, a truncated version of the song alone appears on a broadsheet dated for February 1820, there claiming that the (now unnamed) boy was only nine years old.[9]

Despite the conventions adhered to in the broadsheet, including a shift in tone from the prose to the poetry, the incongruence of publication date and woodcut provenance, and the dubious borrowing among printers, it is still striking how the condemned prisoner in the prose account and the one in the poem seem like different boys—the first hardened, the latter a repentant and "poor little boy." Where the two genres of "Confession" dovetail is in transforming Thomas into a conventional warning to those who may be tempted to make the same errors.[10] It is the cautionary tale that matters most in "The Dreadful Life and Confession" of Thomas, not whether it was factual. Instead, when other sources documenting crime are consulted, the oft-repeated tale begins to tip the scales away from authenticity. In the records of the Old Bailey sessions themselves, no twelve-year-old failed sweep's apprentice condemned to death exists (nor any nine-year-old)—called Thomas King or Thomas Mitchel or any other name—not for 1829, nor for any other year between 1674 and 1913.[11] He is a fictional delinquent apprentice, a fictional thief and murderer, and a fictional boy.

Boys to Men

As a boy once apprenticed to a chimney sweep, Thomas is obviously among the desperately poor, yet V.A.C. Gatrell has noticed how in the ballads and broadsides aimed largely at the poor themselves, "significantly, the only affliction not dwelt on in the songs was poverty. Poverty was the taken-for-granted backdrop to all plebeian devices and ingenuities."[12] Arguably, then, it is not the misery or poverty of the profession of sweeping chimneys (which we have seen was well understood) but apprenticeship writ large that Thomas represents (and which makes him interesting together with his youth); and it is lack of compliance as an apprentice about which other boys are being warned. Whereas the poor parenting and bad companions that come up in this tale are established elements of the narrative of a boy gone bad, so too is ingratitude for apprenticeship and failure in a trade.

The ostensible companion piece to the actual work getting done in apprenticeship was that the boy learn a trade to become a journeyman, then a master (which we have seen was harder for sweeps' apprentices than for others). Despite Daniel Defoe's idealistic assertion in 1726, "the State of apprentices is not a state of servitude now, and hardly of subjection,"[13] but rather "a Master is a Parent,"[14] Philip Rawlings points out that apprentices "had a tradition of radicalism and solidarity."[15] This is unsurprising given that apprenticeship entailed seven years of indentured service—for most officially beginning at the age of fourteen—but as we have seen this varied widely according to the trade and individual situations.

The seven years of apprenticeship represented if not always realized the time of growth from boy to man. As Deborah Simonton observes, this time "marked achievement of manhood" at the end of their service, which acquired a particular significance validating their masculinity."[16] That stage of life taken up by apprenticeship was, quite logically, both a productive one in terms of doing and learning and a problematic one in terms of growing out of boyhood. Marcia Pointon notes that "John Locke thought the passage from boyhood to manhood 'the most hazardous step in all the whole course of Life.'"[17] Whereas Locke was not talking about the poorer classes, it is of course this very liminal passage of time that was covered by any apprenticeship. Rebellion and rule- or lawbreaking, linked to what Locke labeled with opprobrium "warm blood," took numerous forms among apprentices, from absconding with the master's candlesticks to absconding with his wife or daughter, to violent crime against the family or others.[18] The bill of indentures signed by a parent or guardian (or the parish) forbade the boy "playing cards or dice, frequenting taverns or alehouses, or committing fornication."[19] As Vincent DiGirolamo notes, "Such behavior obviously was common enough to require proscription."[20] Once a master printer himself, Samuel Richardson would decry "the present depravity of servants" in the 1734 *Apprentice's Vade Mecum: or, Young Man's Pocket-Companion*, wherein Richardson set out the training, obligations, and appropriate behavior of apprentices in the press.[21] At the same time, we have seen that apprentices were vulnerable to abuse and not all were taught adequately to help them realize their potential and to gain eventual independence. Many ran away, breaking the contracts of their indentures.

As a result of the gap between the ideal and the reality of apprentice life, it is common to read of a boy turned thief by way of the access his job allowed him to homes—either the home he has been given by his own master or one in which he does a job. Whereas "for most of the criminals in popular literature, their apprenticeship is presented as a casual anchoring biographical fact . . . which ultimately has little bearing on his story. There are, however, a number of figures who are presented specifically as errant apprentices, whose revolt is inextricably bound with their position in society."[22] As testified to by the tale of Thomas, and as research by Joan Lane, Cheryl L. Nixon, and Tim Hitchcock as well as prison documents from the period itself demonstrate, apprenticeship—an ostensible path of upward mobility—could instead be a slippery slope downward. I have noted apprenticeship facilitated theft from a master or family and at the same time could lead to violence perpetrated by one of the parties against the other—itself a means to theft or the result of personal resentments or madness. (Dickens argued this most fully in *Oliver Twist* [1838].)[23] The proportion of adult males in early modern London who were apprentices is estimated at anywhere from 10 to 40 percent.[24] Peter Linebaugh records "two-fifths of those hanged at Tyburn in the eighteenth century had started an apprenticeship."[25] Craig Patterson tells us "the pages of criminal biography swarm with apprentices gone bad."[26] The subjects of such stories are usually grown men, however evident their childhood flaws might be made in the storytelling. One of the most popular plays of the century was George Lillo's 1731 *The London Merchant*—in which an apprentice, George Barnwell, first steals from his master, Thorowgood, then murders his own uncle. The movement from theft to murder in Lillo's play was a commentary on how lesser crimes (and sins) lead to greater ones, for boys as well as men.

Thomas King's boyhood—about to be ended by execution—is intended to increase the sadness of the broadside tale. His chimney sweeping beginnings are not only common but apt. As John Waller notes of the many apprentices who outgrew their ability to climb and had no other resource to fall back on, "about the only thing climbing flues did qualify sweeps for . . . was house burglary."[27] Recall John Holland's 1824 appeal on behalf of the chimney sweep's boy, quoted previously:

> Sold into slavery, doom'd to be a wretch,
> His flexile form, so exquisitely nerved,
> Goaded with curses, or at the rope's end,
> Must henceforth, as an animate machine,
> Be used, and treated vilely, day by day.[28]

Although the usage of the boy "as an animate machine" refers to the sweep's work, including the cleaning by which a boy might be lowered down a chimney on a rope, another possibility emerges with the image "at the rope's end." It is another way of describing death at the gallows.

In fact, the broadsheet "The Dreadful Life and Confession" shows young Thomas King as having been effectively "bound" as some sort of apprentice three times: first, "humanely" by the parish to a master whose trade we do not know, then "to a chimney-sweeper in the borough," and finally in effect, by his parents, "to a gang of thieves who sent him down the chimney of the jeweller." The descent down the chimney for nefarious purposes is a double breach of trust, since he is using skills learned at one trade (from his second master, "an honest man") to steal from a shopkeeper in another trade.

Nature of the Crimes

Ingratitude and corruption evidenced by the fallen apprentice in particular were seen as a bridge between threats to private property, threats to English bodies, and threats to England itself. Peter King shows that the early nineteenth century witnessed strenuous debates in Parliament and within committees formed to address rising juvenile crime. Here, "forms of juvenile behavior from gambling to

Sabbath-breaking worried contemporaries, but it was 'juvenile depredators,' juveniles who stole property, that formed the primary target of their concerns."[29] Anyone could be associated with property crime, but the fallen apprentice is a figure associated with the transition from work to crime as well as from property crime to violent crime. The rise of both over the period is reflected in the soaring number of crimes made capital offences in the second half of the eighteenth century.[30]

As a person whose liminality included boy-man and laborer-criminal, so too did the average apprentice straddle the worker-beggar divide. Numerous vagrancy laws give the impression that the culture was trying to enforce and reinforce a perception of work and crime being activities opposed to one another.[31] As idleness tempts and ultimately condemns, so industry saves; Isaac Watts made this plain to children and their parents in 1715 in "Against Idleness and Mischief":

> In Works of Labour or of Skill
> I would be busy too:
> For Satan finds some Mischief still
> For idle Hands to do.[32]

In the preamble to the bill of 1779 to modify the British penal system, reformers John Howard and William Blackstone worked on the same principle. They envisioned imprisonment at least in part as serving some of the aims of apprenticeship: in a good prison, they argued, the convicted is able "to correct himself and to acquire the habit of work."[33] "Vagrancy" is chiefly conceived of as wasting time, idleness (at an extreme, sloth—a deadly sin).

However, honest work and dishonest gain were not, for much of the population of London, two halves of a binary; they were, as in the case of young Thomas, the same side of the coin. Take, for instance, begging, which I have noted most climbing boys did. In *Down and Out in Eighteenth-Century London*, Tim Hitchcock highlights the relationship between begging and the need to appear to be working: "To make a living on the streets of London the poor needed an excuse to be there, a justification that kept the heavy hand of the constable and the watchman from fingering their ragged collars. A basket, tripod, and bottle of oil, a few laces, a mackerel, or some cabbage nets, were both a means of making money in themselves, sold to whomever would buy, and a badge that proclaimed a purpose to a beggar's wanderings."[34] More to the point in the present discussion, begging—like apprenticeship—had a gendered element that affected crime and punishment: "Most London apprentices were male, while most domestic servants were female," Hitchcock notes, adding, "Boys, who were expected to be self-reliant, had a difficult time claiming the sympathy of almsgivers, outside the structured spaces provided by ritual [i.e., Christmas boxes]. Their begging behaviour was both extremely visible and frequently unacceptable. As a result they needed props to legitimise it. The girls and women who laboured as servants in the houses of middling-sort London did not need to reinforce their claim to charity in this way. Their begging was largely invisible [because confined to the household they served], and certainly more frequently tolerated."[35]

Not surprisingly, therefore, "masters of this economy of makeshift were the shoeblacks and linkboys, the crossing sweepers and runners of casual errands"— employment most associated with youths. Naturally, the more mobile and transitory the employment, the more problematic it was.[36] There were attempts to suppress shoe blacking, Hitchcock notes, and to include it as one of many infractions of the vagrancy laws because of the occupation's links to begging and menacing (one would no more want shoe blacking rubbed onto one's clothing than soot), and because it could be—in part or entirely—an excuse, a fiction derived to mask a lack of activity, or a less legal activity, and to avoid detection.

Sweeps' boys were among the most notorious beggars, and for good reason. Being shoved up a chimney was not upward mobility. The horrors of the conditions in which such boys lived determined that as such an apprentice as broadsheet protagonist Thomas King would have been "at the bottom of the economic pile," receiving only bed and board for his work (if that).[37] "Apprentices who were 'out of their time' (aged 16), and who wished to remain in the chimney-sweeping trade, became journeymen. There were three categories: foreman, under-journeyman, journeyman-sweeper or boy."[38] However, as we have seen, for the majority of the climbing boys, merely to grow entailed quite literally growing out of their trade— beyond the confines of a chimney—into an uncertain future that contributed to begging as much as the uncertain present.[39]

Criminal Elements

If the line between work and begging was not always clear, neither was the line between work and more serious crime: underemployed or suspiciously employed boys and youths were deemed particularly dangerous. Messenger boys traversing the streets of the city turned pickpockets, and chimney sweeps turned extortionists— again at the very least "us[ing] the threat of their own dirtiness to encourage almsgiving on May Day."[40] Although the sweep's plight was to become a cause célèbre among some moral reformers, it is also clear these boys were not much sympathized with in general. Anja Müller observes that boy sweeps were usually unsentimentally "perceived and represented as part of an adolescent subculture that had been associated with apprentices and urban youths, and that was marked by potential subversiveness and riotousness."[41] Proof of this collective disrepute is not hard to find, including in the ballad written, sung, and sold following the death of the infamous highwayman Jack Hall, who died at Tyburn in 1707. Hall's execution ballad had tremendous longevity, as did the *Account and Memoirs* published after his death. V.A.C. Gatrell notes contemporary references to the tune of a popular ditty, *Chimney-sweep*, which was "Hall's alleged calling," although "the story that at the age of 7 his parents sold him to a chimney-sweeper" was "probably largely fictitious."[42]

Whether this was the case, Jack Hall's posthumous reputation enhances the relationship between chimney sweeps' apprentices-turned-criminals and both rising and falling—rising in wealth, in part because there was nowhere to fall to;

falling in the eyes of the law and contribution to society; rising in visibility, particularly to those who enjoyed or profited by criminal-hero tales; and falling to one's death at the end of the noose. There were many other unsafe and ill-paid jobs (that of cesspool-sewerman comes to mind);[43] yet, it is clear that "sweep's apprentice" was a shorthand term for unruly boys with so little to lose it made them dangerous. *The London Tradesman* in 1747, while acknowledging the unhappiness of the parish children who mostly occupied this "Black Fraternity" of the sweeping trade, called it "the greatest nursery for *Tyburn* of any Trade in *England*."[44] Early childhood and death, then, were commingled in and associated with the very trade.

In William Hogarth's street prints and other publications such boys are unruly and violent—at least pugnacious, at worst sadistic. All of these characteristics set them apart from any impulse to sentimentalize childhood. Rather, being part of the workforce, and "countering any notion of childhood innocence, these boys offer a condensed and concentrated image of a corrupt adult world."[45] Müller points out the words added to the depiction of animal abuse in Hogarth's "The First Stage of Cruelty":

> While various Scenes of sportive Woe
> The Infant Race employ:
> And tortur'd Victims bleeding shew
> The Tyrant in the Boy.

For Müller, "the perspective offered in *The Four Stages of Cruelty* is clearly gendered as male: only male children are the violent perpetrators and later, as adults, the cruel offenders."[46] This gendering of criminality and the tendency toward crime (particularly cruelty) matters. The seeds thereof were evident even among privileged boys in Ellenor Fenn's *School Dialogues*, where Sprightly admonished schoolmate Savage, "a goose can feel pain as well as a boy."[47] When Sprightly is later reminded by the head boy that "we are naturally prone to evil" he is also being reminded of the "nature" of boys in particular.[48]

The unruliness associated with unorganized or unsupervised youth was of grave concern to authorities. So was the *organization* of young apprentices, which could result in wider acts of subversiveness. For instance, the 1719 weavers' protests, enacted because of the import of raw silk from India and China, had been realized in part by "the custom of nailing people" by their clothing, described by Linebaugh as carried out by the youngest member of the trade: "Armed with hammers and a quantity of nails, apprentice boys hammered the silk skirts and coattails of the Quality into the wooden fronts of the pastry shops where they paused to examine the holiday cakes."[49] Here, then, we find boys both armed with tools and serving as tools for the agenda of their elders. The apprentices marred the property of would-be customers in order to demonstrate against the means of production of their trade being taken out of their masters' hands. In this case, labor solidarity harnessed boyish size and speed to carry out mischief.

Whereas Thomas King is not taking part in organized protest, his choices (such as they have been) do counter honest labor and involve collective action. Recall that one of Thomas King's chief problems was the "companions" in the "gang" with whom he undertook his final caper.[50] As Aparna Gollapudi, drawing on the work of Tim Hitchcock, observes, visibility and fear were for a long time associated with the "Black Guard"—"one of the most ubiquitous terms used for street children in early eighteenth-century London."[51] Given that sweeps were referred to as the "Black Fraternity," linguistic coloration itself unites the two communities. What threat is a twelve-year-old boy? If he stands for both a large number of like-minded, desperate boys and the men that they will all grow to be, he is a threat.

Punishment

The severity of the penalty levied upon Thomas King in the broadsheet, the vagueness of "several murders and robberies," to which he purportedly confesses, and the timing of Thomas's confession (after his sentence) both ring false and emphasize that the theft for which he was apprehended was the ostensible cause of death. Such a sentence for this crime was indeed the law. However, as fearsome as the specter of the fallen (and apprehended) apprentice is, had Thomas actually existed, it is unlikely such a boy would have been sentenced to death for theft alone.[52] Although the age of criminal responsibility for most crimes was seven, Gatrell has found that "of 103 Old Bailey death sentences passed on children under 14 for theft between 1801 and 1836, none was executed."[53] Instead, a young criminal received a whipping or was branded with a "T" on the thumb for thief (sometimes the brand was on the cheek). And, unless violent, a boy younger than fourteen almost always ended up paying for his crimes with labor, in a workhouse or in the colonies, where the indenture was normally for seven years (the amount of time one would also serve as an apprentice).

The broadsheet states that up to that moment Thomas had twice avoided transportation because of his honest master having "obtained him pardon," but transportation still would have been the likely result of his most recent transgression, the theft from the jewelers. The poor were far more likely to be transported than criminals of the middle class, and following the Transportation Act of 1718, children were transported along with adults to the colonies—the American colonies until 1766 and, after 1787, to the penal colonies of Australia.[54] Because the period between these dates saw overcrowded prisons and a failed attempt to transport prisoners to West Africa, male convicts also started to be sent to Prison Hulks in accordance with the Act of 1775, "punished by being kept to hard labour in the raising of sand, soil and gravel, and cleaning the river Thames, or any other service for the benefit of the navigation of the said river."[55] A boy like Thomas was more likely to have been consigned to one of these hulks on the Thames in 1829 than hanged for theft.

That having been said, however, Peter King has found "a pronounced shift away from dealing with youthful offenders by quiet summary measures and toward full adult-type indictments." This means that while the proportion of children who were executed was less, a number of new vagrancy acts were passed in the 1820s, and "assize records appear to indicate that the defense of *doli incapas* [incapable of crime] for certain categories of age had been largely eroded and that many more children were being found guilty in the 1820s than in the 1790s."[56] The resurrection of the broadside tale about Thomas, possibly from several years earlier, might well reflect this discrepancy between harsh sentence and commuted punishment, to remind readers that children could be executed according to the law.

Malatia Supplet Aetatem

Referring to the official accounts of the clerical ordinary at Newgate Prison, Craig Patterson notes that "from the perspective of criminal narrative, a silent criminal told no story; not only did he fail to justify God and vindicate man, but he also refused to participate in the narrative project, refused to become its subject."[57] From this standpoint, Thomas King is the subject of a successful narrative, justifying his own death sentence with "several murders and robberys" by confessing to them. The odd "particulars of several murders" tacked on to his account suggest a way of explaining away the excessive punishment for one so young, at the same time intimating that the cautionary tale told by the broadsheet is a tall tale. That being said, Gollapudi identifies the significant "gray area" of the child within the eight- to fourteen-year-old range in the long eighteenth century: "As William Blackstone puts it, 'the capacity of doing ill or contracting guilt, is not so much measured by years and days, as by the strength of the delinquent's understanding and judgement. For one lad of eleven years old may have as much cunning as another of fourteen; and in these cases the maxim is *malatia supplet aetatem*, that is, malice supplies the age.'"[58] Gollapudi points to the wording "that frequently occurs in the Old Bailey trials, where a child is 'an Old Offender, though young in years.'"[59] What "supplies the age" for the twelve-year-old Thomas King, making him deserving of punishment as a fourteen-year-old, is the malicious nature of crimes committed in his youth. Categorically, this position is supported by one of Rousseau's cautions in the 1762 *Émile*. Where elsewhere the philosopher emphasizes illness and other misfortunes that might endanger a child, here he argues that the child endangers: "The most dangerous period of human life is that from birth to the age of twelve. This is the time when error and vices germinate without one's yet having any instrument for destroying them; and by the time the instrument comes, the roots are so deep that it is too late to rip them out."[60]

Again, it is impossible to overlook gender in the midst of this, for punishment was different even if laws were—for theft and most violent crime—the same for male and female offenders.[61] Heather Shore's exhaustive work on nineteenth-century juvenile offenders confirms that they were mostly male.[62] Indeed, Emma Watkins finds that in the period between 1816 and 1850 (wherein our broadsheet falls), of the young offenders (between seven and fourteen) who were tried and condemned at the Old Bailey to transportation to Australia, there were 1,333 boys, and only 77 girls. This reflects a similar difference in the treatment of men and women awaiting trial at the prison.[63] Thomas King's boyhood obviously matters. In fact, as Judith Butler notes with reference to stories about boys, "Since the sixteenth century 'Tom' had functioned as a quasi-proper name for what is masculine, as in 'Tom-All-Thumbs,' or 'Tom-True-Tongue.'"[64] (Recall Tom Telescope and Tom Thumb in my discussion about the automaton as well as Newbery's intended boy audience of the *Little Pretty Pocket-Book* represented by Little Master Tommy.) The Thomas of the broadsheet has lived "the dreadful life" and told a dreadful "confession *of a boy*" (emphasis mine)—with the boyhood of the offender making both all the more "dreadful" than the execution of an adult and yet implicitly not as dreadful as if the offender had been a girl.

Nor should we ignore that although almost none were carried out, death sentences were given to children under fourteen for theft in the early nineteenth century.[65] The execution—or lack thereof—of the verdicts surely was meant to be elided in the message of their sentencing.[66] It is not so surprising that while it was common for children's sentences to be amended from death to some other punishment, condemnations to death as reported in the sensational broadsheets *remained* death in the public imagination. Unlike the original death sentence (and in the case of the broadsheet, the carrying out of it) the reduced sentence was not advertised, leaving the boys in such reports as characters who were effectively dead to the reader. Given the discrepancy in how boy criminals and girl criminals were treated—the former considered more likely to reoffend and punished more severely—we can read the figure of the boy convict as a tool of instructive oppression in a cautionary tale to other such boys (and parents) stressing death as a foregone conclusion. As noted by the authors of *Harnessing the Criminal Corpse* (2018), "cultural productions such as art and literature used the criminal corpse to evoke strong emotional reactions, which could be turned to comic effect or developed as horror. But the existence of cultural works around the criminal body also constituted part of what made it such a fearful, repulsive and powerful thing."[67] The Thomas King broadsheet is such a cultural work. Based on the criminalized child's body, it connects power, violence, gender, and class to youth.

Recollecting Spectacle

The story of terrorism is written by the state and it is therefore highly instructive. The spectators must certainly never know everything about terrorism, but they must always know enough to convince them that, compared with terrorism, everything else must be acceptable, or in any case more rational and democratic.
    —*Guy Debord,* Comments on the Society of the Spectacle

Debord is here discussing the spectacle culture of the 1960s, so the use of "democratic" is at best anachronistic for the period under discussion in this book, and broadsheet publication was no direct tool of the British government; however, the story of the boy thief hanged by the neck until he died entails a form of terrorism—in extended use "the instilling of fear or terror; intimidation, coercion, bullying."[68] Gatrell has found that although only "about 7000 of the 35000 [criminals] condemned to death were actually hanged between 1770 and 1830 . . . the scaffold loomed hugely in the popular imagination before 1830. We meet it at every turn: in ballads, Punch and Judy shows, broadsides, and woodcuts."[69] As long as London executions remained public, "crowds of 3000–7000 were standard," and it was to be expected that "compilations of criminal biographies were steady earners for publishers."[70] Gatrell makes a convincing case for entrenched ideas about the gallows in private minds and public culture: "In street ballads and street entertainment, remembering and imagining wove a collective idea of the scaffold in the space between print and orality."[71] Judith Flanders has shown "how crime in the 19th century—particularly gruesome murder and executions—served as entertainment in both fiction and real life," as evidenced again by broadsheets and cheap pamphlets.[72]

As "The Dreadful Life and Confession" testifies, however, "the tone of these communications was far from uniform."[73] Of course, Foucault argues that a large-scale shift from execution to imprisonment throughout Europe in the late eighteenth and early nineteenth centuries hinged upon new ideas about didactic punishment. In this "period when the entire economy of punishment was redistributed" including "disappearance of torture as a public spectacle," Foucault asserts that it became understood that "the publicity of punishment . . . must open up a book to be read."[74] Broadsheet publications like the one discussed here did not even have to be opened; moreover, they were available on street corners and were themselves sold by hawkers who were otherwise or simultaneously begging and avoiding vagrancy charges, who were poor, and who were often too old or disabled to do anything else.[75] Paul Slade notes "the sellers would pin their stock of ballads up on a board behind them and chant or sing a few choice verses to attract a crowd, sometimes accompanying themselves on a fiddle. Often, the singers were blind men, who would presumably have found it hard to earn a living in any other way."[76] Such sellers kept themselves fed by publicizing punishment in order to avoid it—for vagrancy or worse.

London hangings, formerly carried out at Tyburn, were moved to Newgate Prison in 1783, and their attraction as public entertainment waned (in 1868 they were moved inside the prison grounds). Arguably, in such cautionary tales as that of Thomas King, fictional execution made for a kind of play or replacement execution. Frances Dolan has traced a high degree of skepticism and discernment in responses to "true tales" back through the seventeenth century, identifying engaged reading practices and literary analysis.[77] Her findings undoubtedly apply to a portion of those who took in stories like that of Thomas; however, it is a story that I argue appeals to different kinds of "truth." Gatrell observes that the "huge sales" enjoyed by execution broadsheets, despite "the fact that the sheets were repetitive and their moralizing intrusive and formulaic," come down to their being "symbolic substitutes for the experiences signified or the experiences watched."[78] On one hand, starvation, disease, and dangerous work in the beginning of the nineteenth century meant that by "1839 almost half the funerals in London were of children under the age of ten," so the death of one more would mean little.[79] On the other hand, the story of Thomas King, a twelve-year-old symbolic substitute, appears to mean something and calls for scrutiny on the grounds of his sensationalized criminal boyhood. The replacement of torture of a prisoner with narrative incarceration was a didactic deterrent: "Around each of these moral 'representations,' schoolchildren will gather with their masters and adults will learn what lessons to teach their offspring. The great terrifying ritual of the public execution gives way, day after day, streets after street, to this serious theatre, with its multifarious and persuasive scenes."[80] Broadsheet death sentences shared some didactic ends with imprisonment as Foucault conceptualizes it; however, his point about "schoolchildren" and "offspring" becomes itself more pointed when the sentence is passed on a boy.

The range of effects such published accounts could have—including as incitement to crime through sensationalizing—is demonstrated by Sir John Fielding recommending that "authorities should clamp down on the street ballad-singers."[81] So, a tale like Thomas's could elicit compassion, or it could offset compassion a reader might feel for young chimney sweeps—the broadsheet seems to want it both ways (as many of them did). At the same time, the story of the failed apprentice contributes to a larger discourse that includes legal, moral, and educational arguments about children and how far they might be reformed, as well as how much work could be wrung from the child's body, whatever the state of his soul. I have argued that boys have historically represented a particular kind of currency, both valuable and expendable—valuable because of gender, expendable because of youth. The criminal boy's story might run the gamut from trivial to tragic. His death becomes a means to the end of warning other boys, and other parents, and it profits those in the ephemeral print trade. It makes the boy, finally, useful.

All the Potentially Guilty

At mid-eighteenth century, Voltaire was among those who voiced protest against state executions by pointing out "that a man after he is hanged is good for nothing, and that the punishments invented for the welfare of society should be useful to that society. It is clear that twenty vigorous thieves, condemned to hard labour at public works for the rest of their life, serve the state by their punishment; and their death would serve only the executioner."[82] However, as Foucault again argues, punishment was useful to the state in other ways, for "punishment is directed above all at others, at all the potentially guilty. So these obstacle-signs that are gradually engraved in the representation of the condemned man must therefore circulate rapidly and widely: they must be accepted and redistributed by all; they must shape the discourse that each individual has with the other and by which crime is forbidden to all by all.... Thus the convict pays twice; by the labour he provides and by the signs that he produces."[83] Foucault has been criticized for placing too much emphasis on power—particularly state, or sovereign, power. Nevertheless, Thomas King, the condemned twelve-year-old, is an "obstacle sign" who pays not with his labor but with his imaginary life, and Foucault's highlighting of rapid and wide circulation is fitting with respect to the broadsheet story we know to have been printed at least thrice. Thomas is a warning of the worst that might happen to any boy who strays from honest labor (being one kind of tool—"a person used by another for his own ends" or perhaps "an unskilful workman"), who instead dares use the skills of lawful labor—navigating a chimney—to commit crimes (being another kind of tool: "in *Criminal's slang*, any weapon").[84] The broadside story—a tool of communication—conveys a message about the weaponizing of boys by those who would use them as such. Thomas standing in for every poor criminal boy is a means to attract and entertain readers with a combination of what they expect from the genre and what they expect from such a boy.

Real Life

Criminal boys like Thomas King did, of course, exist, even if Thomas probably did not. In consulting trial proceedings at the Old Bailey, I have looked at the record of one 1777 trial that has not yet received attention, at which four chimney sweeps' apprentices (out of five accused) were indeed found guilty of shoplifting from a jeweler. The boys, named Ditcher, Foster, Miles (or Malloy), and Clark, gave their ages as between nine and eleven years old.[85] When their master, Joseph Vandecum, testified that he was a chimney sweeper, the court asked him, "How many of these boys have you?" The sweep replied tellingly, and perhaps truly, "Seven or eight, or more, I don't know how many."[86] In 1773, philanthropist Jonas Hanway would demand a change in his report on the chimney sweeping trade: "No Chimney-Sweeper should be permitted to keep as apprentices or servants . . . a greater number than four effective boys, under sixteen years of age, at one and the same time."[87] It was not unheard of for a master to have as many as twenty climbing boys under his care—one of the many reasons why Hanway complained that "justice . . . in respect to the boy, is asleep."[88]

Joseph Vandecum, the master of the four climbing boys found guilty in 1777, was chastised for playing an indirect role in their illegal activities—that of neglect. The proceedings include significant words from the judge: "It is a shameful thing that these boys at this age are left without the eye of any master to take care of them; and this is the consequence they are now brought here to answer for being thieves; it is a scandalous thing in the master, he is as criminal as the boys, they are generally kept starving, and left at their own will to do whatever they please." The master sweep responded with, "There is no such thing as starving in our business."[89] That of course was another fiction. Malnourishment made boys ideal for fitting into the narrow flues of chimneys, and sweeps' apprentices regularly begged for food.[90]

Ditcher, Foster, Miles, and Clark were found guilty of grand larceny and sentenced to "Whipping"—a common punishment for such a crime. In the *Annual Register*, a respected reference work of long standing, this theft is also recorded for the same year (1777); however here, in the heavy bound tome of the *Register*, the punishment has changed, and these (now unnamed) thieving sweeps' boys are recorded as having been condemned to "death."[91] Contrary to what actually occurred—in both sentencing and its realization—they had become tools of the press—as well as victims of rumor—to deter others, and because death sells. Punishment inflation, whether as a result of gossip, incomplete knowledge, or deliberate half-truths, was evidently not confined to sensationalistic broadsheets.

Cumulatively, officially, and unofficially lasting and ephemeral texts reflect the system that defines, prohibits, and punishes the criminal boy. Capital punishment ended time for the condemned. To end the life of a child is to punish by taking away more years of life than the criminal would have had left were he an adult. Such severity is intended to translate, paradoxically, into the clichéd "lasting warning" that the broadsheet claims to provide, however ephemeral the medium, "to the world at large." As such, Thomas King is a liminal character—in the sense of both being "both dead and alive" and being someone who "lives beyond the pale of society, of structure."[92] Because he could not reconcile to the demands of his apprenticeship, nor to the ethical/legal system, he was a doomed boy.

The exhortation made to readers of "The Dreadful Life and Confession"—to "think of this poor little boy" and "Lament his woeful state"—is conventional but not as important as that "lasting warning to the world at large," embodied by a body that never was, but was rather constructed as itself ephemeral and disposable, created to personify a warning to laboring-class boys most of all. Crime historian Peter King argues that in eighteenth-century views of childhood "despite various differences (between evangelical and romantic views, for example), the propertied classes had almost all embraced a more child-centered approach by 1820. . . . However these attitudes were not generally extended to the children of the labouring sort until after 1830."[93] The story about Thomas King, if not new in 1829, then certainly resurrected in that year, is less about a boy than about the threat posed to the propertied classes by children of the laboring sort.

Crossover Genres

A broadsheet tale such as this one also approximated the only literature for children (or for anyone) that a sweep might have encountered—and only then if he'd heard it sung or read out by hawkers. Other forms of biographies of fallen apprentices included pamphlets—usually, as mentioned, produced by Newgate ordinaries who profited from the manuscripts—swelling with repentance and clear warnings to others against sin. Broadsheets were pithier. In London by 1776 there was a newspaper "sold daily for every 24 persons aged 15 or over."[94] Added to which, a system of "hue and cry" put into place in the 1770s by Sir John Fielding, the Bow Street magistrate, whereby any bystander could implicate himself in the apprehension of a criminal, effectively turned the press, and newspapers in particular, into an instrument of the law, advertising details of crimes and criminals to large numbers of readers and would-be thief catchers not only in London but across the country.[95] As a corollary to such advertisements seeking information, crime broadsheets argued via narrative closure (death sentences) that the system based on collective curiosity and scrutiny worked.

Even more widely, broadsheets spoke to the almost insatiable hunger for the printed word. Mary Hilton argues for the breaking down of boundaries between genres with an expansion of print culture, along with the new money economy of the mid-eighteenth century: "Varying social and literary practices . . . now meant that genre offered a fluid intellectual resource that writers could begin to use creatively. In fact textual heterogeneity at mid-century was bewildering, as enterprising publishers such as John Newbery and Samuel Richardson encouraged new literary approaches."[96] Discussing early eighteenth-century children's literature, Matthew Grenby makes a convincing argument about "a socially diverse market" for numerous rags-to-riches stories, such as "Newbery's most celebrated productions . . . about a child's rise from poverty to wealth."[97] However, Grenby has shown that by the beginning of the nineteenth century "once the market for children's books had become more established, most publishers began to dispense with the [earlier] notion that they were catering for an audience that spanned the entire social spectrum. In particular, the moral tale, ever more dominant, began to take only affluent children for its protagonists, and to present the world as seen only from their point of view."[98] Broadsheets were arguably one of the genres that filled this vacuum in the space between the classes.

Because they catered even to the semiliterate among the curious, broadsheets speak to the fact that there was pervasive anxiety among the gentry about reading by the end of the eighteenth century: "Not only could the children of the vast new number of poorer citizens grow up to become an unbridled mob, but now a large unaccountable number of the poorer classes were openly and flagrantly literate. Historical evidence points to a widespread ability to read amongst all communities, however impoverished and backward in this period, most people having access to the written word if they so chose."[99] Such anxiety argues for efforts at policing through the written word. The impact of broadsides is borne out by the fact that Sunday school reformist Hannah More attempted to counter and compete with them in *Cheap Repository Tracts*—more than two hundred moral, religio-political tracts issued in series from 1795 to 1817, and reissued in collected editions until the 1830s. Whereas in their chapbook format More's tracts were clearly a response to the craze for chapbooks, both formats represented a widening of the readership among the less affluent at whom broadsheets were aimed. More saw the dialogue-format tracts, initially countering sympathy for the French Revolution and aimed specifically at the lower orders, as an alternative to just the kind of publication to which Thomas King's story belongs. Several tracts in More's collection are about and directed to apprentices, such as *The Cheapside Apprentice*, whose narrator, on the eve of being taken to the gallows, begs, "Attend, ye young men, who are about to enter into trade, for to you I write my story."[100]

One can also imagine a parent reading the story of Thomas King to a son in order to frighten him into better behavior—like one of the "puppets" in Ellenor Fenn's *School Dialogues for Boys* with the added usefulness of being (as far as they know) a real boy. The idea of pain, instantly associated with crime—something "forbidden to all by all"—depends upon widespread knowledge of the pain that has been inflicted. However, as we have seen, stories like that of Thomas King were not directed—as Grenby concludes later children's books and chapbooks of the period were—at the "the new generation of protagonists" who "command[ed] servants [and] were not the sort of children likely to receive charity, but to give it."[101] Rather, the broadsheet was broad sweeping, aimed at anyone who could read or be read to: adults and children, servants and laborers, as well as their masters. As a vehicle for the moral tale, the broadsheet did not undergo the gentrification that Grenby identifies but instead conflated and confused genre and target audience in order to reach the widest possible market.

In contrast, books were unequivocally aimed at the middling classes or above. One such book, *Juvenile Philosophy*, sees a mother explicating Hogarth's wildly popular series of prints "Industry and Idleness" to her two sons: "These plates, or engravings, which I have in my hand, contain the history of two boys; one idle, the other industrious. I mean no allusions (*seeing Thomas appear fretful*): they were both beyond your ages, and both apprentices, which, probably, you will never either of you become."[102] In the mother's lesson, the apprentices to a silk weaver are the puppets (as they were for Hogarth) at a remove from the privileged boys who are in a position to sit and have their mother read to them. What Hogarth analogized, the mother makes plain: "For it is a certain fact, that idleness and wickedness produce poverty, ignominy, and sometimes untimely death; and that industry and integrity procure competency, respectability, and tranquility of mind through the whole of life, and at that awful period when guilt is armed with all its terrors."[103] The wages of sin is both death and what awaits the sinner after death. Idleness and wickedness are again paired, leaving no space for the application of industry to wickedness. That "awful period" of facing death is seen in Hogarth's penultimate—and probably most popular—plate: "The Idle 'Prentice executed at Tyburn."[104] Everyone knew that this conclusion was far more likely than the twelfth and final plate, in which the industrious apprentice becomes Lord Mayor.

In *Juvenile Philosophy* little Thomas who listens to his mother explain Hogarth's pictures comes to improve his attitude to schoolwork and appreciate learning. Safe in the knowledge that his class protects him from the apprenticeship in the lesson, he has still learned that lesson.

At the same time, because the broadsheet was published as something that has happened "at last Old Bailey sessions"—whether readers took this as fact—it might have had a greater impact as a threat than other texts aimed at children (and these, literate and privileged children) such as Henry Sharpe Horsley's didactic poem "A Visit to Newgate" (1828), where a father brings his sons to the prison, first to observe a wretched "little boy" who is there "for thieving, you must know," before moving on to the spectacle of "some poor men ... doom'd to die":

This was matur'd full-grown crime,
    Its end, and its reward;
Reproaches in full stature stood,
    And death to fainting aw'd.[105]

The less freighted final quatrain of Isaac Watts's warning in verse "Against Idleness and Mischief" is all-encompassing regarding the child reader's time, concluding with a veiled reference to after the child's time on earth:

> In books, or work, or healthful play
> Let my first years be past,
> That I may give for every day
> Some good account at last.[106]

Thomas King's cautionary "Dreadful Life and Confession" is the very opposite of the "good account" Watts's child anticipates giving to the Creator, "at last" for the good of his soul. At the same time, the choice among pastimes available to the speaker in the poem, including "books" and "healthful play" alongside "work," is far more pleasant than the work a climbing boy had to do to keep body and soul together.

Social Contracts and Ponderous Machinery

In 1764, Italian economist Cesare Beccaria posed a question: "Is death as a penalty really *useful and necessary* for the security and good order of society?"[107] His position that it was neither useful nor necessary was based on public good, for "crimes are only to be measured by the injury done to society."[108] Beccaria's position—like Voltaire's calculation of the usefulness of a laboring body versus a body executed by the state—was part of a serious debate about capital punishment that has not yet entirely disappeared, for "useful" and "necessary" are debatable terms.

Those adjectives Cesare Beccaria employs to dispute capital punishment—"useful and necessary"—might well describe a tool. Punishment by authority has always been one tool for maintaining that authority. Even Ellenor Fenn's concluding dialogue in her *School Dialogues, for Boys* involves a discussion between a mother and a schoolmaster which shows the central, and sometimes only, purpose of punishment:

> LADY: Punishment rarely reclaims an offender.
> SAGE: If it *ever* did, yet it would have *this* use;—it might deter others from following a bad example.[109]

Elsewhere in Fenn's oeuvre, we find an explanation pertaining to the animal world that seems to apply to humans in criminal broadsheets: "Even the fiercest creatures have their use."[110]

Our fallen apprentice Thomas has no advocate, unlike Dickens's Oliver Twist, whose story began in serialization in 1837, not long after the "Dreadful Life and Confession" broadside appeared: "'But even if he has been wicked,' pursued Rose in defense of the boy, 'think how young he is; think that he may never have known a mother's love, or the comfort of a home; that ill-usage and blows or the want of bread, may have driven him to herd with men who have forced him to guilt. . . . For mercy's sake, think of this, before you let them drag this sick child to a prison, which in any case must be the grave of all his chances of amendment.'"[111] The "grave of all his chances of amendment" argues that prison turned petty criminals into hardened criminals. Criminal broadsheets make the same assumption, but in these the protagonist dies.

The apparently false report of Thomas King "Condemn'd to Die at Last Old Bailey Sessions" argues that even as the state condemned fewer criminals to death at the start of the nineteenth century, something "useful and necessary for the security and good order of society" *was* widely identified at least in sentencing to death (usually) fictional boys. In fact, Josephine McDonagh identifies "a discourse of child sacrifice, in which murder of a child, or children, in one way or another is valued as a positive or virtuous act ... in evidence until the end of the nineteenth century."[112] Whereas satire such as Jonathan Swift's child cannibalism in *A Modest Proposal* makes up part of McDonagh's argument, in her research surveying a broad variety of writings from the period, "rather than encountering a society that is progressively kinder in the attitudes it expresses towards children, less tolerant of infant death or violation, less willing to engage with the rhetoric of child sacrifice, we find instead a society that continued to maintain highly complex and ambiguous attitudes to [child] death and its symbolic potential."[113] The broadside about Thomas King, I suggest, pushes this complexity and ambiguity further, opening up questions about the symbolic potential of the dead boy as a warning to other boys, to those responsible for their upbringing, and to those who employed them.

As the eighteenth century moved into the nineteenth, juvenile crime—real or imagined—proliferated.[114] Uwe Böker maintains that across Europe, and influenced by the revolution in France, "from 1780 onwards a change took place, and it involved the construction of the concept of juvenile delinquency and an emphasis on the guardian's responsibility. Authority, control, and education were seen to a greater extent as efficient means of socializing the young."[115] Several years after the broadside about Thomas, Mary Carpenter's 1853 polemic *Juvenile Delinquents: Their Condition and Treatment* identified official agencies of law prevention aimed at the same demographic: "What a fruitless conflict has the law, with all its ponderous machinery, its active and vigilant agents, its denouncing bench of magistrates, here waged against a boy!"[116] The "ponderous machinery" and "active and vigilant agents" are clearly intended as foils to the frailty of a "boy." Similarly, that the law is "waged" implies warfare—unequal warfare, which she is pointing out is not war at all. Carpenter's indictment of the legal system demonstrates that forces for social improvement were at work, with and alongside those pushing for changes to chimney sweeps' conditions, to better these boys' chances and increase their worth by acknowledging they had any worth at all.

Taking note of the "remarkable upsurge in historical studies of crime" in recent decades, Paul Baines has noted that "crime history has for some been a way of attacking power and privilege."[117] I am conscious of doing so again, here. I am also conscious that eighteenth- and nineteenth-century genres of "crime history" were themselves more concerned with power and privilege than has been fully understood. And concerned with gender. Debates about delinquency speak to traditions of constructing boys as a particular threat to society, and part of the history of gender politics that we do well to recall. Statistics of criminality, conviction, and incarceration of young male offenders are much easier to keep track of now,[118] but stories from the past that blend fact and fiction, sensationalism and moralizing, warning and a sense of the inevitable criminality of the most vulnerable young males are not so easy to measure, nor are the effects of such cultural mythmaking as easily mapped out. Lucy Andrew traces the rise of "the criminal-centric penny dreadful" to a rise in literacy among the middle classes at the mid-nineteenth century, particularly working-class boys. Concerned adults saw such literature as sensationalizing criminality and corrupting those readers.[119] The broadsheet about Thomas King, however cheap and however maudlin, does not make the boy a hero.

Because Thomas King did not earn his keep, or keep chimneys safe, he failed to be the kind of tool that his trade required, so he was made into another. We have seen Zine Magubane discuss the "fungible" suffering Black body. It is an adjective brought into current parlance with the object theory of Bill Brown, who frequently employs the word "fungible," a term chiefly related to law and finance: "Of a good that has been contracted for: that can be replaced by another identical item without breaking the terms of the contract. More generally: interchangeable, replaceable."[120] Whereas the unique marvel that was Jaquet-Droz's automated Writer—although estimated as being worth hundreds of pounds in 1774—was in a real way priceless and irreplaceable, Thomas King was entirely "fungible"—interchangeable with and replaceable by thousands of poor boys who either reached or did not reach manhood in London in the long eighteenth century.

Ultimately, while the value of Jaquet-Droz's automated boy lay in his seeming to be alive, Thomas King is a boy whose value lay in his seeming to be dead. Finally, "The Dreadful Life and Confession" demonstrates that the role of the sweep's apprentice, increasingly decried as being dangerous to the boy by late eighteenth- and early nineteenth-century social reformers, was also, like other haphazard and inadequate employment, a threat to the property of employers and to a nation of shopkeepers that nevertheless needed such work done. What the condemned Thomas King represents is a threat larger than one "poor little boy." The broadsheet transforms him from a child trained to use tools in a chimney to a tool used by a gang of thieves for plunder, to a cautionary, rhetorical tool conveying that the wages of sin, and of crime, is death.

Figure 5.1. "The Dreadful Life and Confession of a Boy Aged Twelve Years." British Library Shelfmark 74/1888.c.3(119). Public domain.

CHAPTER 6

The Boy in the Printing Press

PRINTER'S DEVILS AND UPWARD MOBILITY

Boy, n. (a.1.) A male servant, slave, assistant, junior employee, etc.
—Oxford English Dictionary

Boys do not come apprentices to play, but to work; not to sit idle, and be doing nothing, but to mind their master's business, that they may learn how to do their own. —Daniel Defoe, *The Complete English Tradesman*

The boy in this final chapter is another urban male identified with skin blackened by his trade—not by soot this time but by printer's ink. While again lending itself to jests that dirtiness (and boyhood) invite, this troped "blackness" now connotes communication and profit alongside myths about the print trade itself. The young "printer's devil" was assigned the most menial of jobs, yet he had the capability to advance in skill and rise in stature in what was itself a rising trade. Such potential, like the very designation "printer's devil," nevertheless bespoke ambivalence, which was increasingly complicated by late modern shifts in—and the decline of—apprenticeship through the nineteenth century.

In considering the extent to which the printer's devil was a tool of the press, we encounter youths across a wide spectrum, from errand-running scamps to grown men. In fact, the malleability and capaciousness of the term "printer's devil" characterizes this apprentice as a type of elastic or mutable boy. Being young, male, and dirty, he is a figure available for belittling and is linked both with tools of the press trade and with "blunders"—like so many boys—and yet invested with possibility beyond that of other trades in contributing to the influential world of print and the other worlds print influenced. Although upward mobility was ostensibly the trajectory of all apprentices, who would in time advance to journeyman, then master, we have seen this trajectory was by no means universal.

Intersections

The prologue of Thomas Holcroft's 1791 comedy *The School for Arrogance* is spoken by a news hawker who plans to attend the play at the Theatre Royal, Covent Garden. First touting his wares, which include printed accounts of fires, earthquakes, murders, and rapes, advertisements for tinctures and cures, lists of bankruptcies, the Newgate calendar, and a prisoner's dying speech, the prologist enthusiastically turns to the subject of the upcoming play:

> Oh! I'll be there! With Jack, our printer's devil!
> We're judges, we! Know when to clap, or cavil!
> We've heard our pressmen talk of, of—of Rome and Greece!
> And have read Harry-Harry-Harry Stotle's master piece!
> When we have paid our shilling, we're the town!
> As wisely can find fault as those who pay their crown!
> Nay we, like them, if it be bad or good,
> Can talk, as fast as, as—as if we understood!¹

Here we see that the playhouse caters to a diverse paying audience (in contrast, for example, to the five shillings paid by every visitor to see Pierre Jaquet-Droz's automatons some fifteen years earlier). Yet, shilling-paying spectators like Holcroft's speaker, along with crown-paying audience members at the playhouse, are leveled insofar as claiming the right to have an opinion. Because of Holcroft's use of the news hawker and his friend the printer's devil, the printing house is similarly associated with leveling. While amusing, the speech (penned, after all, by the playwright) also conveys authorial anxiety about being judged by one's inferiors.² The news hawker and the printer's devil embody the combination of print-dependent employment and glaring ignorance for which those who did the menial jobs of the press were satirized. The stuttered rendering of Aristotle as "Harry-Harry-Harry Stotle" signals phonetics rather than literacy because they have (mis)heard the name, not "read" the "masterpiece," as the Englished, low name becomes a malapropism indicative of oxymoronic trades.

Such juxtapositions of presswork, vacuity, and error were already familiar to eighteenth-century readers and playgoers, who were educated by poems, novels, and plays that themselves decried the floods of ink and low standards epitomized by satires—in other words, expenditures of ink and paper lamenting the waste of ink and paper.³ As much as "Jack, our printer's devil" mentioned in the prologue is not a reliable judge, he belongs to the press, and he will judge something that is materially within his province even though it is intellectually beyond him. As such, the printer's devil signals an intersection between art and trade, humanity and machinery, the life of the mind and that of manual labor. He is also, being traditionally the youngest apprentice in a printing press, at the intersection of boyhood and manhood.

Devilish Nomenclature

The term "printer's devil" has a history embedded in that of the press itself. Samuel Johnson issued an ironic warning about the lasting stain of print in a *Rambler* essay that partly explains the hellish term: "What has once passed the press is irrevocable . . . and the printing-house may properly be compared to the infernal regions, for the facility of its entrance, and the difficulty with which authors return from it."[4] In linking the permanence of print and the precarious reputation of the author in 1750, Johnson was drawing upon an old discourse wherein print was perceived as a black art, mysterious and potentially dangerous. His conceit of entering "the infernal regions" also describes print as both sin and punishment combined. Superstition about the press had become largely parodic by the inky mid-eighteenth century when Johnson wrote, yet the craft that turned manuscript into print and reproduced the text ad infinitum was still regarded with a kind of trepidation in which mysticism and pragmatism each played a part.

Elizabeth Eisenstein argues that the printing press—in so many ways an "agent of change" for the Protestant Reformation and scientific revolution—also functioned as a catalyst for witch trials and murders in the seventeenth century through the publication of accusations of witchcraft, fomenting fear, and violence. As Eisenstein points out, still "in the eighteenth century . . . [the wooden hand press] was endowed with quasi-mystical powers and was the focal point of elaborate mythologizing. Graphic evidence that pagan gods were associated with Gutenberg's invention is not hard to find," as testified to by the gargoyles in devil form carved above the entrances of printing houses, many of which survive throughout Europe to this day.[5] Bargains with the devil made by Faust (and Marlowe's Dr. Faustus in 1570) hold a prominent place within this tradition, along with a story that William Caxton (d. 1491) had an assistant named Deville. The legacy of such mythology entails a tradition of mischief within and related to the press that was easy to draw upon through the years. Francis Bond Head's 1833 burlesque *The Printer's Devil; or, A Type of the Old One* sees the titular character, aptly named Nick, banter and boast among fellow apprentices in other trades, revealing in an aside, "Printer's Devils, in these times, do as much mischief as our great namesake."[6] It turns out that this Nick really is a demon in the service of "Old Scratch."

Not all references to the devil's influence on print were tongue-in-cheek, then. Sarah Wall-Randell has looked closely at the depiction of books themselves (particularly the encyclopedia in Marlowe's play), whose "bookish context" compared to the German legend it rewrites "suggests further deepening of the complexity of early modern attitudes toward print technology, attitudes so much less rational, practical, orderly than most recent book-history scholarship has imagined them."[7] Through the centuries among printers themselves there lingered the suspicion that the nasty demon Titivillus haunted print shops, inverting type and misspelling or deleting words. Because of this assortment of negative associations, a "printer's devil" refers not only to the worker but also to an error in print that seems to come out of nowhere and leap onto the page—perplexing, frustrating, unaccountable, and—to use Johnson's freighted word for allowing one's work to be put into print—"irrevocable." So the invisible printer's devil was blamed, and the errors themselves were called printer's devils (cleanliness being, after all, next to godliness). The apprentice "printer's devil," a tool of the press, thereby carried with him nomenclature colored both by those unaccountable typographical mistakes and by the mischievous spirit that meddled with the press.

The Youngest Apprentice

Being the errand boy in the printing office, usually the youngest apprentice, the printer's devil was accustomed to being labeled "little dirty devil," "imp," and "sprite," which Emma L. Greenwood notes all spring from his "infernal renown."[8] At the same time, the young devil's name referred to hard-earned grubbiness: Joseph Moxon tells us in his oft-printed *Mechanick Exercises* that this apprentice "took printed sheets off the tympan. He mixed tubs of ink and fetched type. He took worn and broken lead type that had been thrown into a 'hellbox,' to the furnace for melting and recasting." In the course of such work, Moxon elaborates, "These Boys do in a Printing-House, commonly black and Dawb themselves: whence the Workmen do Jocosely call them *Devils*; and sometimes *Spirits*, and sometimes *Flies*."[9] With his plethora of nicknames, such a boy did both expected tasks and whatever came up. A century and a half after Moxon, former printer's devil turned journalist and playwright Douglas William Jerrold explained that this "devil is a drudge . . . a young and sweating devil. There is no employment too dirty for him—no weight too heavy for his strength—no distance too far for him to walk, no, not walk, but to run, or fly."[10] Reflecting on Diderot's *Encyclopédie* (1751–1766), Robert Darnton emphasizes "real printing shops were dirty, loud and unruly—and so were real printers. The presses creaked and groaned. The ink balls filled with wool soaked in urine gave off a fierce stench."[11] It was the boy apprentices who tanned the soft leather for the beater balls (with which to apply the ink) in vats of human urine to keep the balls supple (surely providing urine as well), turning the balls over and "stomping on them with bare feet," while all of the pressmen "waded about in filthy paper, swilling wine." These older men also "torment[ed] apprentices with practical jokes."[12] Apprentices, particularly the youngest among them, were commonly the butt of such jokes in any trade (and still are).

"Printer's devil," therefore, is an elastic name—one that alludes to the quasi-mystical secrets of a mechanical craft as well as to the errors that seemed not quite human—and, at the same time, is a title that mocks the least powerful person in the profession, even as it associates him with the particular and sometimes peculiar power of print. As a repository for the ink that has not ended up on the page, the "devil" carried on his person the detritus of the trade, like any laborer is apt to do (he would also have had grease stains from the machines and possibly burns—as would others at work in the press).

The boys being called not only "devils" but also "flies" relates to both their speed (flying about) and again their telltale ink-blackened skin. One apocryphal story explaining the provenance of the term "printer's devil" combines boyhood and mistrust, along with mistreatment of such an apprentice in racialized terms: "Aldus Manutius (1449–1515) the celebrated Venetian printer, had a small [B]lack slave whom the superstitious believed to be an emissary of Satan. To satisfy the curious one day he said publicly in church, 'I, Aldus Manutius, printer to the Holy Church, have this day made public exposure of the printer's devil. All who think he is not flesh and blood come and pinch him.' Hence, in Venice arose the somewhat curious sobriquet of the printer's devil."[13] It is interesting that this tale is about proving the enslaved boy or man was *not* an "emissary of Satan," yet the "curious sobriquet" stuck. Unlike truly apprenticed printer's devils in England in the eighteenth century, Manutius's slave would have had no opportunity to become a master printer himself. In the tale he is both a human tool in the service of his master and the sign of his own servitude.

I have noted the importance of apprenticeship to running England. Recall the estimate of twenty thousand apprentices working in London alone by 1700, a large proportion of these working for the eighty-nine guilds of the city by midcentury.[14] W. J. Rorabaugh lists among the benefits of apprenticeship writ large the practice being "a system of education and job training by which important practical information was passed from one generation to the next; it was a mechanism by which youth could model themselves on socially approved adults; it was an institution devised to insure proper moral development through the master's fatherly responsibility for the behaviour of his apprentice; and it was a means of social control imposed upon potentially disruptive male adolescents."[15] We have seen failures in this system in the previous two chapters, particularly as regards chimney sweeping, for which apprenticeships were often no more than nominal (and which did not have a guild). Yet the trades and crafts wherein a boy might enter apprenticeship were numerous, including positions with coopers, weavers, cobblers, tinkers, bricklayers, tailors, drapers, merchants, furniture makers, pastry cooks, chemists, druggists, stationers, tanners, brassiers—each trade with its own secrets and codes, and status among the others.

Alongside the quasi-mystical associations of print in the eighteenth century, there yet endured some sense of newness about that trade (compared, for example, to the blacksmith trade that Dickens's Pip would later walk away from in *Great Expectations* [1861]). Most English printers joined the powerful Worshipful Company Stationer's Guild, the primary livery of the book trade, although there are exceptions—Edmund Curll being a notable one. In the first decade of the eighteenth century, "364 individuals became freemen (or, occasionally, freewomen) of the Stationer's Company . . . while 661 apprentices were bound to Company Members, of whom 293 completed their terms."[16] As we have heard so often about the eighteenth century, print was on the rise: James Raven explains that the number of working printers in Britain rose from "70 master printers working in London in 1700 . . . to over 250 active presses in London, Edinburgh, Glasgow and Dublin by 1760." By 1818, this number was very nearly matched by presses in London alone.[17] We can therefore conservatively estimate the number of printer's devils having been in the hundreds in any given year.

Promise and Advancement

For when you are a master made,
Then you are made a man.
    —Francis Bond Head,
      The Printer's Devil

Being on the rise, print could raise a boy to new heights, so that, alongside the toil and sweat in depictions of the apprentice, we find promise. A collection of *Curious Facts and Anecdotes* (1790) refers to the compositor (who set type) as "the lowest of all the humble retainers of literature . . . excepting the Printer's devil."[18] Humble as the latter is, however, the language used to speak of him is not merely dismissive, disgusted, or pitying, as we encountered in works about chimney sweeps' boys. The "humble retainer" still works for "literature." Similarly, in *Memoirs of a Printer's Devil* (1793), the anonymous author first goes so far as to call the work he endured as a boy "abject slavery," before explaining how, "in the first periods of my service I was necessarily occupied in what may be called the drudgery of learning, in which I obtained the appellation of a Printer's Devil, in the full extent and meaning of the phrase. . . . Yet I will never disown the title."[19] Such qualifiers to "abject slavery" belie the term. The drudgery here is not merely for the sake of his master's profit, but necessary for the boy, who is "occupied" with "learning." Furthermore, this memoirist refers to the papers his guardians signed as "an application to a tradesman in a LITERARY PROFESSION."[20]

Given the ideal presumed or eventual literariness of the profession, reading was indispensable for this boy who, it is important to note, might or might not advance to—and then through—the position of compositor. In her work on the press from 1750 to 1850, Greenwood notes that "in theory at least, printing required a high degree of literacy. Compositors had to take copy from authors' manuscripts, correcting spelling and grammar as they went, and their ability to read classical languages was considered desirable. . . . In practice, however, few would-be apprentices met these high standards."[21] Nevertheless, we can assume that most boys who went into the trade were competent in the more basic of these requirements. Further, a boy in the official position of printer's devil (rather than merely one taken on as an errand boy *without* indenture papers) was already in a situation of some envy: "Because the first years of apprenticeship were generally unpaid, with wages starting only part-way through the term and usually only at a very low rate, rising only towards the end of the term . . . apprenticeship was not a feasible option for the poorest households which relied on the income of children."[22] Such apprenticeship was reserved for those in middling families, but also—due to primogeniture—a necessity for many second, third, and later sons of more well-off families. Indeed, a boy might well qualify for such an apprenticeship at the completion of the sort of grammar school education we saw young Sprightly embarking upon in Fenn's *School Dialogues, for Boys*. Such a boy could hope to become a master printer himself; he might even turn out to be an author to boot, as John Nichols (editor of the *Gentleman's Magazine*) and Samuel Richardson had both done.[23] Richardson's own father was a joiner who improved his son's prospects by apprenticing him in the printing trade.

Despite association with dirty clothing and skin, therefore, printer's devils—far from being the outcasts that sweeps' boys were—had plum employment. Christopher Flint indicates, "In the period between the lapse of government licensing in 1695 [when the monopoly of the Stationer's Guild on book production was lessened] and the advent of industrialized book production in the early nineteenth century ... publishing [was] a specialist commercial undertaking."[24] Greenwood notes an advertisement for a press apprentice in 1770 "referring to printing as a 'genteel profession.'"[25] Overall, at the master level "printing was nearly as elite a trade as silver-smithing, and it required a relatively large amount of capital to buy a press and types in order to open a shop."[26] Not only intelligence, ambition, and competency but also great luck and, in most cases, investors would be required for achieving success after serving an apprenticeship.

Working for seven years and thereby earning one's independence from any apprentice arrangement illustrates how closely aligned were professional status and the end of a kind of prolonged boyhood.[27] As such, the arrangement both extended and blurred the limits of boyhood, varying according to the trade and individual circumstances (and one of the reasons for the reputation for rebellion that characterized depictions of apprentices, as noted in the previous chapter). A series of letters in 1711 from one younger son of his family, Thomas Huddlestone, serving an apprenticeship with a merchant in Italy, speaks in strong terms of his longing for the apprenticeship to end. "Perhaps one day [I will call] myself a man," he writes to his mother; and to his employer: "I am sensible that 'tis in your power to make me a man, you need only recommend me to your friends & Correspondents." Huddlestone, then a young man, went so far as to contrast being a "man" with being one who "must end [his] days in Servitude." His lament is another reminder of the conflation of "boy" and "servant." Attempting some means of policing when manhood might begin, in the 1734 *Apprentice's Vade Mecum* Richardson elaborates on the prohibition in place against marrying with the lexicon of boyhood, for "one may come to have a Family of Children while he himself is but a Boy, and while he is deprived of the honest Means of maintaining them, which may put him upon vile and base Practices to support it." The terms of such contracts regularly stipulated that the apprentice "shall not commit Fornication, nor contract Matrimony within the said Term."[28] Again, boyhood and manhood are therefore delineated not by a given age or by sexual maturity (or activity) but by subservience. A male with a family that he cannot support remains a boy. Employing encomium to urge both apprentices and the merchant class to stay the course, Richardson calls them "so necessary and serviceable a Set of People, who by their Industry and Labour are to be consider'd as the most useful Underwheels of the Commonwealth, that keep the great Machine of Trade and Manufacture going."²⁹ He was himself well-versed in printer's apprentices, whose employment could be fraught in particular ways, as print was a vehicle for a wide range of ideas: "honest" and "base," noble and ignoble, orderly and disruptive.

Reading, Peeping, and Class

Surely a defining feature of the ambivalent attitude demonstrated toward printer's devils hinges upon the combination of trade and education, mechanical labor and qualified literacy—the latter being a quandary for those who for one reason or another wished the laboring class to be able to read (the Bible, for example) but not to read indiscriminately. As we have seen with broadside publication history, a growing readership troubled many in the higher echelons with the potential of economic and political unrest. Johnson famously warned against the reading of novels, which he believed much misled "the young, the ignorant, and the idle," a trio of adjectives descriptive especially of the stereotypical apprentice and other servants (however hardworking they were in reality).³⁰ I have noted Hannah More aimed her *Cheap Repository Tracts* at the poor who were already influenced not only by other, sensationalistic broadsides but some too by Thomas Paine's democratizing polemics, which More opposed.³¹ Anything might come out of a printing press. As such, it is not surprising that printer's devils came to be associated with mischief ensuing from reading, and reading beyond one's ken.

Related to this, printer's devils were depicted as being by and large untrustworthy. Even the author of the 1793 *Memoirs* admits, tongue-in-cheek, "We Printer's Devils have a strong propensity to peep into other Men's Works. This will be acknowledged a laudable curiosity."³² Similarly, in Head's burlesque *The Printer's Devil*, the titular apprentice, Nick, boasts, "In my capacity now of Printer's Devil, like a tax-gather [sic], I can get in any where—I lurk upon a lady's couch, in the light form of a voluptuous novel—get in under the patriot's pillow, as a violent pamphlet against all order—entertain a politician at his breakfast, as a newspaper—the people, as an inflammatory placard; or puffing play bill. Of all the Devil's machines, the printing press is the most useful."³³ Thus, the devil inhabits liminal spaces and transgresses with a measure of permission. Playing on the old tropes about infernal machinery, Nick's statement also underscores the role played by the press in inciting individuals as well as the hydra-headed "people" with passion, and thereby opposing reason. The apprentice and printed text conflate here, with neither being containable. The press has its devil, and the Devil has his press.

"Nick's" powers of disruption via novel, pamphlet, newspaper, and placard also highlight the cooperative agency necessary in producing printed texts—a (here) negative cooperation that one finds reflected in lists of those who make up unthinking mobs, where printer's devils appear with some frequency. (Recall Thomas Holcroft's news-hawker speaking for himself and the printer's devil Jack: "When we have paid our shilling, we're the town!") Similarly, "An Elegiac Epistle" in the 1779 journal *Literary Fly* bemoans a contemptible mob made up of "Commissioned prentices and half-pay waiters, / Of printer's devils, devilish whores, coal heavers."[34] The same devils indicate incongruity and disorder in a poem by Mary Robinson, *Modern Manners*, where "dainty ladies strut in male attire, / And printer's devils emulate the lyre."[35] Here, the women in men's clothing and printer's devils playing at Orpheus are meant to be unseemly and ludicrous—moreover, aberrant— such that the latter are no more connoisseurs or creators of poetry than women in the trappings of masculinity are men. (The conflation of the two also might suggest that neither women nor printer's devils are *men*.)

In 1765, George Alexander Stevens employed a similar juxtaposition in a satirical series of lectures on physiognomy to indicate diminishment of quality going hand-in-glove with a population increase in the metropolis. Stevens laments those "who begged their way up to London on foot, where they were in hopes that the merit of their works would recommend them" along with the overall results: "(to prevent starving) Architecture turned bricklayer's labourer to a Chinese builder, Painting, was a grinder of colours to a paper stainer, Poetry turned Printer's Devil, Music sung ballads about the streets, and Astronomy cried Almanacks."[36] In Stevens's inventory, with "Poetry turned Printer's Devil," artistry is elided in trade, beauty is at the mercy of jobbing, and everyone is in it for the money. Printer's devils are the reductio ad absurdum of the printing press. Taking sheets off the tympan or mucking about with errands (or urine-soaked leather balls) for the printing house are activities as far from poetry as can be.

Bad Press: Secrets, Lies, and Vanity

All that being said about absurdity and illiteracy, the ink-marked skin of the printer's devil was also formulated as a sign publishing much attended by strife, rhetoric, ambition, politicking, and lies. With each of these the devil himself has been associated.[37] As printed material became more readily available and affordable to "the town," concern about reading that fomented unrest extended even to reading *about the trades*. Although the indentures sworn to by an apprentice included that he would keep his master's secrets, decline in secrecy and mystery resulted from an increase in the selling of diverse craft secrets began to occur at the end of the eighteenth century, as "technological advancement . . . made it more important for craftsmen to acquire new technologies than to maintain old secrets. A weaver might thus choose to sell his secrets in order to raise the capital to buy textile machinery."[38] Boys who worked in the printing press were doubly exposed to such temptations, as "the decline of secrecy was also encouraged by rising literacy among craftsmen, a wider dissemination of information in books, pamphlets, and newspapers, and the ability, for the first time, of a craftsman to make money by selling craft secrets to the public through the press."[39] This rendering of what ought to be private into material for public consumption is, of course, the chief danger of print for those who wish to hold onto both information and power. In Samuel Foote's play *The Devil on Two Sticks* (1768), the real devil facetiously assures a young printer's devil who promises to intercept political secrets for him, "Come, who knows but in a little time, if you are a good boy, you may get yourself committed to Newgate." In this world where ignominy is fame, when the boy expresses fear that his youth will prevent the aforementioned legal sentence, he is reassured, "Not at all: I have seen lads in limbo much younger than you. Come, don't be faint-hearted; there has many a printer been raised to the pillory from as slender beginnings."[40] As such, the youthful "good boy," who is obviously a bad boy—who in real life might be maimed or killed by spectators if "raised to the pillory"—is suddenly not that different from the sweep's apprentice-turned-thief who winds up in the gallows.

Apart from secrets, another danger associated with print is the publication of falsehood. Benjamin Franklin (a printer's devil at the age of twelve, and later famous for his honesty as a master printer) would often joke, "'Tis a Pity Lying is a Sin, it is so useful in Trade."[41] An essay in the 1752 series *Lady's Curiosity; or, Weekly Apollo* draws a specific connection between dishonesty in print and these young press apprentices in the press: "As to the inferior order among us, called *Flies*, employed in taking news-papers off the press, they are of latter extraction, being no older than news-papers themselves."[42] This time the explanation for the secondary nickname (flies) is no longer ink blackness nor flying rapidly from task to task. Instead, the members of this "inferior order" of apprentices were originally called "*Lies*, taken from the papers they so took off; and the alteration occasioned thus: To hasten these boys, the pressmen used to cry *Flie, Lie*, which naturally fell into one single word *Lie*."[43] As such, the very term "printer's devil" becomes shorthand for both the revelation of unseemly truths, and for fake news.

While the moniker "printer's devil" suggests transgressive literary acts, this devil was also associated with excessive and vanity printing (those floods of wasted ink). In a 1798 comedy by Charlotte Turner Smith, a lawyer named Period is admonished by his uncle for neglecting his duties at Old Bailey and dabbling in the press instead: "Why, when I was in London, your chambers was beset with printer's devils, bringing proof sheets, as you call'd em, of your Tour to Wandsworth; with Remarks during a Voyage to Battersea.' Ads-death! Is this the way to rise at the Bar?"[44] Every press, including those producing dry legal documents, would have had at least one printer's devils in its employ, yet the figure of the devil is most used to mock frivolous and unnecessary publication and time wasting. The mention of a devil signals what ought not to be—or at least what ought not to be put into print: the secrets of those who would keep them dark, slander, sedition, scandal, or self-aggrandizement.

The extent to which lesser or unworthy work appeared in print, combined with the young printer's devils also being called "flies," is also of interest because of the insect imagery we encounter in criticism of the period attacking the preservation in ink of claptrap or nonsense, most notable in the first half of the eighteenth century. One anonymous epigram "On Printing" in the *Gentleman's Magazine* concludes that print preserves "Dulness and maggots, calumny and lies."[45] Best known for this kind of thing is Alexander Pope, who used insect and arachnoid imagery to send up poetasters and other pretenders to authorship, as here in the "Epistle to Arbuthnot":

> Who shames a Scribbler? Break one cobweb thro',
> He spins the slight, self-pleasing thread anew;
> Destroy his Fib, or Sophistry; in vain,
> The Creature's at his dirty work again.[46]

The "dirty work" is the spinning—the scribbler's writing—yet it also fits as a description of ink work done in the printing press.

Pope's conflation of insubstantiality, falsehood, and dirt is evident again later in the poem where the imagery is more diverse, targeting the writings of "small critics" whose work, such as it is, is preserved in the "amber" of print:

> Pretty! In amber to observe the forms
> Of hairs, or straws, or dirt, or grubs, or worms;
> The things, we know, are neither rich nor rare,
> But wonder how the Devil they got there?[47]

Pope might even have had in mind the young printer's devils in thus wording the speaker's "wonder" at "how the Devil" such rubbish came to be printed. "Grubs" are larvae—not even insects, but insects in immature form (embryonic, or child insects). As has often been observed, the mention of "grub" cannot but evoke Grub Street—named elsewhere in the poem—a locale that Pat Rogers notes had an "unhappy alliance with jailbirds, rakehells and small-time anarchists."[48] Where print and crime are bedfellows—via either libel or, at least, print and the sort of misdemeanor against taste of which Pope complains—a printer's devil (like any boy or any apprentice) might be an apprentice both in trade and in crime.

As the products that came out of a press tended to vary beyond those produced in other trades (like barrels, shoes, cloth), the printer's devil reflects both the ambivalence and the polyvalence of the press itself. This youth functioned as yet another emblem of something Sophie Gee sees "treasured" in writings about London: "urban filth" conveyed as an especially literary trope.[49] One thinks again of Swift's flood of detritus in the "Description of a City Shower," where the "needy Poet" is bespattered in the deluge that culminates in the tercet,

> Sweepings from butchers' stalls, dung, guts, and blood,
> Drowned puppies, stinking sprats, all drenched in mud,
> Dead cats, and turnip tops, come tumbling down the flood.[50]

The "City Shower" is like Pope's *Dunciad*, which Gee also argues "calls attention to its own interest in unwanted surplus and to its preoccupation with the distinction between waste and profitable abundance."[51] Pope and Swift (who profited from printing their work) repeatedly link the *press* to the return of what should be *re*pressed (or, more so, with what is regurgitated). Of course, the problem identified by the Scriblerians and others was that much of what was written that made its way into print could be both: waste in terms of lacking in value, and profitable abundance.

P(l)aying the Devil

Pope's *Dunciad*, decrying and rejecting dullness in all its forms, sees dullness triumph in the final line, so "Universal darkness covers all." In the later edition, that darkness "buries all." While the latter conclusion is more stygian, the former is more inky.[52] Christopher Flint has noticed such associations in how Laurence Sterne "indulged his fascination with publishing" in *Tristram Shandy*: "Perhaps the most recondite allusion occurs when Yorick complains that spreading the lamp-black too thickly 'would make a very devil of it,' as it calls to mind both the notorious black page eulogizing Yorick himself in Sterne's own book, and the errand boys known as 'printer's devils' who handled the recently inked sheets and thus came to be covered in black."[53] Flint's observation—and what he reads in Yorick's complaint—signals mourning and absence; the blackened page is seen, yet there is nothing to see. Like the nickname "printer's devil," the lamp-black and ink show print aligned with the infernal regions, or perhaps more accurately, print aligns with the "darkness visible" of Milton's pre-pandemonium space where lie the fallen angels—created to be sources of light before rebellion brought them down.

As little as the boy apprentices in the press had to do with the gangs of criminal boys mentioned in the previous chapter, their demonic nomenclature still associates them with darkness and damage, albeit the darkness of the press. Manushag Powell points out that eighteenth-century periodical essays also intertwine the press and the demonic, "tak[ing] pleasure in identifying and exploring a darkly humorous connection between the stains of the printer's devil and the shadow of death and the underworld."[54] Like Elizabeth Eisenstein, Powell examines a piece in the *Grub-Street Journal* from October 1732, accompanied by a satirical three-part woodcut titled *The Art and Mystery of Printing Emblematically Displayed*, wherein various press workers are masked with animal heads. The specific press being targeted is that of Edmund Curll, notorious for his piracies. Curll is depicted here with the head of Janus, while other figures have the head of an ass, a boar, a greyhound, or the devil. An owl perches above the scene.[55] In the illustration, Powell points out, "Death and life, human and unhuman, serious and scandalous are all gathered together as the signs and symbols of the print trade."[56] These symbolic inversions sound like all of those diverse elements "gathered together" in the term "printer's devil" itself—a figure who is depicted in this woodcut wearing a humble garment and hanging up the wet sheets of print, a figure whose name is also a sign and symbol of the print trade. In the comic dialogue that accompanies the woodcut, printer's devils are referred to as "black gentry"—a tongue-in-cheek juxtaposition that speaks to tensions involving print and social class, labor to produce texts, and leisure to read them. The implications of the "black gentry," even as satirical, are an improvement on what was expected for the lives of the "black fraternity" used for chimney sweeps, and the "black guard" used for amorphous gangs of criminal boys.

Powell does not address the likely youth of the masked devil in her analysis of the woodcut and essay. Yet it is indeed interesting that the least powerful person in the trade goes by the moniker that best represents its complexities. The combination of a lack of power with the motivation to rise is one associated with youth. In the *Journal* dialogue one apprentice urges his brethren, "Let us not be ashamed of our name," for "we may justly attain, as many of our predecessors have done, to the dignity of Printers" and "have an opportunity of using others, as much like poor Devils, as we ourselves have been used by them."[57] From the articulation of this goal, Powell concludes, "in time, everyone becomes a devil to someone else in the letters trade."[58] The "everyone" encompasses laborers like the devils, older apprentices, compositors, journeymen, master printers, booksellers, and even authors; yet the case that "everyone becomes a devil to someone else" in such a homosocial space is also a reminder of the pranks played by the older men in the press on the apprentices, and more broadly of youth's subjection to age and the power of men over boys.

Boys in Waiting

When Douglas Jerrold sentimentalized the role of the eighteenth-century printer's devil in his memoir, he ennobled the boy by literary association: "Consider . . . the Devil, for instance, who carried the proofs of 'The Vicar of Wakefield' to Goldsmith . . . the Devil, the constant Devil, who took copy from Johnson; Defoe's Devil; Dryden's Devil . . . the legions of Devils who have visited the sons of genius and of wretchedness."[59] Here is a combined defense and romanticizing of the past through the medium of the boy who is ignorant of the longevity awaiting the words that were placed in his care: "Reader, do not . . . think the Printer's Devil only a nasty, dirty little boy. Though he be drudge to the press, he *is of* the press; here, should you even once in your life attempt the perils of type, treat our subject courteously, liberally—give the Devil more than his due."[60] While there is still a tongue-in-cheek mystique associated with the Devil in Jerrold's reminiscing, now it is the mystique of ancestral authors who relinquished the fruits of their labors to dirty little hands. There is a legacy of dignity in this drudgery.

In addition to the nature of the presswork that caused a printer's devil to be nasty and dirty, however, he was also frequently thought of as troublesome precisely because he was typically the one waiting on the author to finish a work expected by the printer. Jerrold, again, distinguished between "a youth running with a proof from the press of Guttenberg [sic], or Caxton," whom he called "a messenger of state; the bearer of a miracle of art; the part and parcel of a mysterious body" when "the Devil was somebody to be respected," and "the Printer's Devil of the nineteenth century" who was "in the social scale, estimated at very little above the errand boy."[61] The long period in between Gutenberg and the nineteenth century, however, evinced plenty of irritation rather than respect for the young apprentice.

Powell states that the boy's moniker, in addition to ink stains "and the shadow of death and the underworld," might be attributable to the fact that such a devil's "presence at their lodgings was an unwelcome reproach to overdue authors."[62] "An unwelcome reproach" is not what men expect from boys—quite the reverse.

The relationship between these two groups of males is intriguing (assuming most authors to be male, and certainly those I have found who complain about the devils waiting on them are male). Such protests are only half jesting, like those in Johnson's *Rambler* essays, and one we find in Robert Lloyd's 1763 "Dialogue between the Author and His Friend":

> While scarce at night I start to bed,
> Without a couplet in my head,
> And in the morning when I stir,
> Pop comes a Devil "Copy Sir."

Lloyd's use of the devil here is paradoxical because even as he complains, the speaker of the poem identifies himself as a genuine author; the hierarchy and the obligation are contained in the two words "Copy Sir."[63] Yet the servant in this moment becomes the taskmaster. Whereas people were accustomed to being waited on by boys—link boys to light the way through the streets, errand boys to fetch onions from the market or hail a cart or deliver a message, young shoe blacks, boys sweeping the streets and gutters, and full-time attendants such as footboys for the wealthier sorts—most customers were not waited on in quite this way. Mention of a printer's devil by an author becomes, therefore, an objective correlative encompassing both abjection of that which is dirty and fear of that which is unfinished, and being called out as an author who is caught up in both—that which is dirty and that which is unfinished. The boy in the printing press who might rise to the status of printer is himself unfinished, like any boy who might, or might not, become a man.

The pressure to produce "copy" speaks not only to the horror awaiting the author on the unfinished or blank page but also to the sense of an author's writing moving away and beyond her or his control, toward permanence (into Johnson's "infernal regions" again). At the same time, a complaint about an annoying "devil" suggests power held by those other nonauthorial agents, from bookseller down to devils themselves. Flint notes that "increasingly the book came to be a thing in and of itself, divorced from what had earlier been perceived as an intimate set of relations," such that "textual corruption emanates not only from the author or compositor, but also from myriad agents seemingly sprung into existence by the mechanical means of producing published matter. These printing-house figures become unsavory anonymous creatures whose work both creates and destroys: the *horses* (or pressmen), *asses* (or compositors), *flies* (or sheet removers) and *devils* (or errand boys).... The nicknames themselves suggest a dehumanizing process that infects the literary work with a kind of satanic self-destruction."[64] Evidently, those caricatured tropes betrayed amused anxiety, but also anxious amusement. Cumulatively, worry in the period about all the hands involved in getting a text to its reader anticipates critics like Jerome McGann's still-trenchant appeal "to take greater account of the other coding networks which operate at the documentary and bibliographical levels of literary work."[65] Even now, when we consider patrons, printers, and booksellers in such coding networks, there is not much mention of printer's devils (or flies). This is, again, because they were relatively ignorant of the business they were about, and because they were young.

Glorious Print?

Denis Diderot's collaborative *Encyclopédie* not only outlines printing as "the technique of impressing on paper the forms of letters from moveable type cast in a mould" but also lauds it as "that art which so favours the advancement of the Sciences, which increase in perfection as the amount of knowledge increases."[66] Such pleasure in a "mechanic art" shows enthusiasm for the great Enlightenment project, a sentiment shared by David Hume, who was certain that one "advantage of industry and of refinements in the mechanical arts is that they commonly produce some refinements in the liberal [arts]; nor can one be carried to perfection without being accompanied, in some degree, with the other."[67] Going further, the author of *Memoirs of a Printer's Devil* justifies his volume with the assertion "were any individual possessed of accurate knowledge in a new branch of the liberal or mechanic arts, such an one would feel a great degree of pleasure . . . communicating the results of his studies; from the degree of property he is thereby invested with; and from the natural propensity in man to be doing good."[68] The lowly printer's devil could learn an advanced mechanical art—and so, arguably, could advance the cause of progress. At the same time, that knowledge is power was testified to by trials, imprisonments, and even executions on the grounds of printing of texts deemed seditious and libelous.[69] We can thereby see the same type of *concordia discors* of boyhood itself meet in the young devil. Just as the written—and, more pointedly, the printed—word could be a source of anything from libel to enlightenment (not that these are mutually exclusive), a boy employed in the press could be a mere tool, a mediocrity, or a triumphant success.

Rags to Riches

Samuel Johnson, again, also lets us know the elasticity of the term "printer's devil" as regards the value of such a position and shows that it might include females: Boswell's *Life of Johnson* recounts that "once, when the conversation turned on [John] Campbell, Johnson mentioned that he had married 'a printer's devil.' This remark was made to the painter Joshua Reynolds, who expressed surprise: "'Why, I thought a printer's devil was a creature with a black face and in rags.' 'Yes, Sir,' Johnson responded, 'But I suppose he had her face washed, and put clean clothes on her. *(Then looking very serious, and very earnest.)* And she did not disgrace him.'"[70] Johnson's defense of Campbell's wife suggests that it was a profession from which an apprentice could rise and clean up nicely, and that such a past—such a beginning—was not inevitably a disgrace. A good printer's devil, however physically besmeared by the trade, did have the chance to become a successful, influential, and dignified printer.

A study of "printers' wealth on death" in England reveals a "mean of around one hundred and forty pounds in the period 1775–99 to well over nine hundred pounds in the period 1825–50."[71] It is therefore not surprising that published memoirs by printers through the late eighteenth and nineteenth centuries are numerous in comparison to those by masters in other professions, nor that the lowliness of the boy entering the craft is emphasized in these memoirs as a foil to his subsequent rise. More than anything else, the rise of newspapers fueled the recuperation and renovation of the term "printer's devil," thus it was reimagined as the lowly seed in tales of phenomenal growth.[72] On both sides of the Atlantic, nineteenth-century success stories use "printer's devil" as a kind of substitute for the word "rags" in the expression "rags to riches," for example in Benjamin Franklin's (unfinished) *Autobiography* (1790) and Bruce Michelson's *Printer's Devil: Mark Twain and the Publishing Revolution* (2006).[73] In England such tales, increasingly tied to nationalism, celebrated economy and dissemination of culture, whereas in America talking about the press would become synonymous with nationalism as defined more overtly by "freedom," democracy, and enterprise. Needless to say, the press has also been a vehicle for misogyny, proslavery diatribes, colonialism, and xenophobia in general (just as the internet is now). Most appealing, however, are stories like that of Isaiah Thomas of Boston, whose indentures as a printer's devil were signed in 1756 when he was six years old; by the age of thirty-four, master printer Thomas would own seven working presses.[74]

The Boy Problem: Delinquents and Machine Tenders

Isaiah Thomas was not the norm, of course, but the exception (as rags-to-riches stories are). Research shows by the start of the nineteenth century, as apprenticeship declined (apart from parish-run apprenticeships of pauper boys like sweeps), much of it became limited mostly to wealthier boys.[75] As wage labor became more common, it also grew more difficult to set up with a master, and to acquire a position with a press was no small expenditure for the boy's family. Greenwood compares "an image of hard work and self-improvement as presented in printers' autobiographies" with "perceptions that they came to the trade not as children but as teenagers, from 'respectable' families after a good education, and that printing was a 'genteel' trade with conditions of work that were suitably amenable."[76] However, in England, and especially London, "the concentration by the public press on negative representations of printers' apprentices, in spite of the existence of much good behaviours, coincides with an increasing fear of juvenile delinquency in the late eighteenth and early nineteenth centuries, stemming from the widespread assumption that criminal activity amongst youngsters was on the rise."[77] This reflects the increased, generalized fear about juvenile delinquency we saw in the last chapter from which no young apprentice seemed free.

While printer's devils were widely known to count among their number a majority of very young men or boys, what we come away from depictions of them with is the image of a kind of man-child—volatile and troublesome—Eric Tribunella's "inchoate or incomplete man."[78] Complicating this image of the printer's devil is that proliferation of these apprentices came to be resented by others in the printing trade. So, from the name for the youngest apprentice to the failure of apprenticeship itself, boys could be a problem for the men in the printing trade who had been boys before them. This shift in labor culture was felt across virtually all sectors of industry, as Doris Grumbach explains, whereby "the idea of advancement and learning through apprenticeship gave way to the slow and uncertain progress of the unskilled labourer. The unrealistic romance of a vision of skilled and contented artisans carrying on the arcane traditions of a craft was at an end."[79]

Unskilled labor (obviously often performed by men) was frequently called "boy labor," and its presence, twinned with increased mechanization, led to complaints sounded from England, America, New Zealand, and elsewhere, particularly by trade unions, about the boy labor surplus reducing wages and making it difficult to regulate the trade and for grown men to earn a living wage.[80] With industrialization, the transformation from craft to factory meant that craftsmen "were to be replaced by unskilled machine tenders—boys hired as 'apprentices,'" but not trained that way.[81] As a result, their older and/or skilled counterparts suffered, especially notable with the depression of 1837: "In trade after trade the pressures of a national market and the introduction of machinery pushed craftsmen into unemployment."[82] An essay by Edward Edwards, librarian and secretary of the London Society of Compositors, pulled no punches in 1850. Titled *On the Distressed State of the Printing Trade, Proving It to Be Mainly Attributable to Excessive Boy Labour*, the piece deplored how "the business has been inundated with boy labour. That is the tornado that has swept from before us the property which an all-wise God gave to each of us."[83] Edwards claimed this surplus had been a problem since the seventeenth century.[84] The all-wise God he mentioned as providing property "to each of us" might well evoke thoughts of printer's devils living down to their name—indeed, as not being part of God's will. Moreover, one can see how such pressure from some trades contributed to the push for mandatory schooling, to keep boys out of the labor force.

That said, the steadfast importance of print contributed to some traditional relationships enduring in altered forms. Rorabaugh notes that although "the total destruction of a craft [such as shoemaking] it turned out, provoked surprisingly few reactions," printing evolved to "occup[y] a peculiar middle ground," in terms of increased mechanization accompanied by apprenticeship.[85] Charles More discovered "in the second half of the [nineteenth] century . . . new-style apprenticeship was associated in particular with five growing industries: engineering, iron-ship-building, building, woodworking, and printing." As such, printing "remained far and away the biggest defender of the traditional seven-year term."[86] This means that printing remained a better trade to be in than most (which itself partly accounts for the "excessive boy labour"). To contextualize the labor market at the mid-nineteenth century, worth taking into consideration is the age at which a parliamentary *Children's Employment Commission Report* (1843) concluded most laboring children were then beginning full-time work: "in general, regular employment commences between seven and eight."[87] Doubtless, presses had errand-running little boys doing the work their predecessors had done a hundred or more years before who fell into this age range, but not in the same proportion as in other trades.

We certainly see in the discourse on the "boy problem" a reifying of what Tribunella points out: "Boys are supposed to possess male privilege, and yet their youth complicates their ability to claim the rewards of maleness or manhood."[88] Beyond conditions of indentures, which had not changed substantially over time, more subtle prescriptive language codified manpower in the nineteenth century in ways that reflected on the place of boys in the labor force. In 1802, for example, the Philadelphia Typographical Society, "attempted to set uniform practices and prices in order to legislate their objective to 'act as men toward men'"[89] Coming a year after William Wordsworth declared that a poet was "a man speaking to men," in the "Preface to *Lyrical Ballads*," one wonders whether, as Wordsworth's use of "man" and "men" was masculinizing poetry, the Typographical Society's use of "men" was reinscribing age boundaries for print.[90]

Botches

Transatlantic complaints about "boy labour" noted above were less strictly (or overtly) about age than about skill. As such, the term could apply to a wide range of males. The nuances involved in the "boy problem" therefore draw upon the third definition of "boy" in Johnson's *Dictionary*: "A word of contempt for young men, as noting their immaturity."[91] This attribute-based boyhood might never be outgrown.[92]

As late as 1887 U.S. Commissioner of Labour John Tobin, indicating again a general skepticism about boy workers, noted, "Every mechanic knows he has not much to fear from those skilled in his own trade. But he does fear the botches, the boys who worked at the trade but did not learn it."[93] Tobin's singling out of "boys who worked at the trade but did not learn it" speaks to a breakdown of the legitimate apprenticeship system; it also echoes Pope's warning in the *Essay on Criticism*: "A little learning is a dangerous thing."[94] Note that botches and boys are equated in Tobin's warning: "he does fear the botches, the boys who worked at the trade." Indeed, the word "botch" refers not only to "a flaw, imperfection or blemish" but also to "an unskilful or incompetent worker."[95] This aligns with the *OED* definition for the human *tool*: 3. b.: "(esp. qualified by *poor* or the like.) An unskilful workman; a shiftless person."[96] Arguably, such linguistic compression (for botch as well as for tool) speaks to the same type of semi-lighthearted mistrust evident in the term "printer's devil"—the perplexing cause of mistakes, the typographical mistakes themselves, and the boy who did not actually write the copy or even most of the time set the type, yet who—because he was at the bottom of the trade and because boys are so strongly associated with mischief—shared the name of those errors themselves.

The discourse about such boys also demonstrates a lack of clarity in terms of both just what the printer's devil role encompassed and what the age range for such a devil was or should be—reinforcing the negative connotations of the term "devil" over the innocuous. The printer's devil therefore reminds us of the very problem of boyhood's nebulous parameters. Johnson's definition of adolescence provides another touchstone, here: "The age succeeding childhood, and succeeded by puberty; more largely, that part of life in which the body has not yet reached its full perfection."[97] Johnson's definition of adolescence, which occurs before puberty, underscores a general confusion about boyhood—recall among the ways he defined "boy" was "one in the state of adolescence; older than an infant, yet not arrived at puberty or manhood," which offers the same time frame for "boy" as for adolescent, albeit with different wording. For neither of these people has "the body... reached its full perfection," perfection evidently (and again) being manhood. No wonder Johnson allowed that boyhood, at least, was "perhaps an arbitrary word."[98]

Technologies

The quip by Irish poet Thomas Moore from 1835, "Though an angel should write, still 'tis devils must print," seems a mere extension of Samuel Johnson's complaint about "the infernal regions" of the press, yet by the mid-nineteenth century the muddy waters of the print industry were obviously muddier with respect to who such devils were.[99] One fascinating development beginning at the mid-nineteenth century was a "hobby that sometime blurred the line between work and fun," that is, modified presses devised and marketed to small businesses and individuals. Indeed, "between 1852 and 1875, at least twenty-eight presses were patented for the use of boys, or at least amateurs." These modified technologies and how they were marketed seem to have been responding to and profiting from the excess of boy labor available to large-scale presses, with one advertisement urging "Boys. Don't be satisfied, and don't rest till you own a printing Press, and see for yourself the fun there is in it. One word for it, you will never want for amusement or pocket money after you get a Press."[100] Whereas the promise of "pocket money" is questionable, it also identifies such boys as not needing to earn their living. As such, they belong to a higher class than boys who do and are no threat to men in that position either. At the same time, hobby presses reflect more than the rise of print itself, but of print in the lives of children and particularly boys. In England in response to the 1850 and 1855 Public Libraries Acts, "the earliest known provision" for children was "a reading department for boys in Manchester Public Library in 1862."[101]

Eisenstein observes, "At present the idea of the printer's devil is as quaint as a classical allusion, a black-faced newsboy, or the use of hot type itself."[102] Even chimney sweeps' apprentices can seem quaint, if depicted as such. In noting that "ambivalence about communications technology seems just as strong today as it was in the past," Eisenstein's comment opens up our sense of the ambivalence directed toward the boys who did the dirtiest jobs in the early printing press. The persistence of ambivalence about technology is worth considering now, again, including with references to boys' relationships to technology, and to books (too much of one, too little of the other, a dichotomy created between them, rather than recollecting that books were technology too).[103]

Francis Bacon specified three Chinese inventions that "changed the whole face and state of things throughout the world" as being "printing, gunpowder, and the compass."[104] Like so many inventions, all three have been used to do good and to do harm. Those boys who grew to manhood in the early and late modern eras while learning the publishing business from the ground up got their hands dirty with the tools of a trade and learned the secrets of a craft, and many ultimately liberated themselves from indenture through a system that, by and large, worked. Some of these men, like those in any other profession, helped those who worked under them, guided and taught them to be truly useful to themselves and others. Others made the next generation of boys who came their way into mere means to an end. Like the printing press itself, printer's devils played a part in the cause of liberty, but not of everyone.

Conclusion

1. e. to go off the tool: *to leave the workman's hands.*
—Oxford English Dictionary

Jean-Jacques Rousseau's insistence that "the man must be considered in the man, and the child in the child" reflects his belief that too much was being asked of children, particularly boys, who were not valued for their youth so much as derided for and being hurried out of it.[1] Despite an evolution in how we think about childhood, boyhood remains the "arbitrary word" Samuel Johnson called it for reasons including its beginning, duration, and end; our developing understanding of cognitive, emotional, and physical development; and attitudes about gender that range from denying the existence of innate masculinity to impassioned defenses of it. The privilege or lack thereof and where a boy lives in the world, how much education he receives, when he begins working for a living, and what that work entails, still all vary extensively. What is a boy, and what is he good for? And what is good for him?

The stirring beginning to Immanuel Kant's 1784 essay "What Is Enlightenment?" equates the unenlightened man with a child by calling enlightenment "man's emergence from his self-imposed nonage."[2] The German term Kant employs, *Unmündigkeit*, means not having attained the age of majority, or legal adulthood.[3] For the philosopher, moving beyond *Unmündigkeit* is largely a matter of resolving to do so, whereas "nonage is the inability to use one's own understanding without another's guidance. This nonage is self-imposed if its cause lies not in lack of understanding but in indecision and lack of courage to use one's own mind without another's guidance. . . . Laziness and cowardice are the reasons why such a large part of mankind gladly remain minors all their lives, long after nature has freed them from external guidance. They are the reasons why it is so easy for others to set themselves up as guardians. It is so comfortable to be a minor."[4] Kant is here hoping to provide readers with intellectual tools to achieve their own enlightenment, even as he makes an argument for rising above "laziness and cowardice." The first of these flaws, incidentally, is also the most common complaint one finds against apprentices and servants in England through the eighteenth and nineteenth centuries. The same insults were directed toward schoolboys, the first coming chiefly from the adults in charge of them, the second by their peers. Of course, many were lazy. Most states of prolonged tutelage were not self-imposed, however, or certainly not exclusively so. For a great many children as well as adults, it was not "comfortable to be a minor" at all. Emerging from it was not a matter of choice.

Work by social historians in recent decades complicates further our sense of just what Kant was asking for, and what he was pushing against, by urging all of his readers to strive to overcome or outgrow nonage, as well as the imperative to "treat humanity . . . as an end and never simply as a means."[5] Boys are one segment of humanity that has historically complicated these ideals. As Deborah Simonton notes, training of apprentices "was about gendered division of labour," in the long eighteenth century, and as such as far-reaching effects on "masculinity and femininity throughout society."[6] We have seen how apprenticeship, as valuable and indeed necessary as it could be for a boy, also complicated the youth's ability to outgrow living his life under another's guidance, and we have seen that some schooling might train a boy not to use his own mind. Poverty and criminal "nurseries," including prison, could teach the boy to remain oppressed by another. Further, recall how Alexandra Shepherd puts manhood itself in perspective by contextualizing how few men were men in the early modern era: "Besides being a qualitative set of attributes, manhood was approached in advice literature as a distinct stage in the life cycle. . . . Parenting manuals, father-son advice, sermons, and tracts on ageing approached manhood as an ideal to which young men should aspire and from which old men would decay. Manhood was thereby portrayed as the golden mean of existence, although it was also deemed a fleeting phase. Theoretically limited to a mere ten or twenty years of the life cycle it was, as a consequence, restricted to a minority of men at any one time."[7] On top of the chronological golden mean of manhood itself, we find idealistic precepts like that of Peter Shaw, physician to King George II, who opined in 1755 that most important in men's lives were the qualities of "courage, magnanimity, labour, and difficulty."[8] Shaw's list, particularly the last two demands of manhood, raises questions about the difference between men and boys, for most of whom both "labour and difficulty" began long before they could be called men. Nor was magnanimity a quality available to all, even with great age. The restrictions and prescriptions of manhood itself remind us, again, of Thomas A. King's emphasis on agency in a period when "children, servants, apprentices, students, some adult men, slaves, and women were all property of some other men."[9] As Elizabeth Foyster argues, "The patriarchal ideal had costs for men's as well as women's lives."[10]

Counted along with these costs, boys have historically been a particular kind of currency, both valuable and expendable—valuable because of gender, expendable because of youth. Such a boy's story might run the gamut from trivial to tragic. I have sought to point out the costs for boys—and the cost measured in boys—of the patriarchal ideal, in looking at depictions of growth from nebulous boyhood to nebulous manhood in this period and to explore what these say about the usefulness of boys, from carriers of family names and inheritors of education and wealth to poor bodies used up by labor, to criminal scapegoats in the defense of property and law and, more hopefully, workers of technologies by which progress could be achieved. These stories are important because they contribute to the larger intertwined narratives of childhood, masculinity, patriarchy, feminism, labor, crime and punishment, and binary gender construction, among others. I have also called attention to the ways in which boy subjects in print, art, and automata were variously constructed as tools—human and object—the young male depicted as implement, apparatus, machine, or machine tender. Certainly, the boy's labor held value, as "the Enlightenment concept of work was a highly positive one."[11] Beyond the boys whose stories appear in this book were also the boy soldiers, sailors, farmers, and errand runners in every profession, making themselves useful.

At the same time, as Rainer Emig notes, "Bodily integrity, masculinity studies generally agree, is a major test of masculinity, and its only legitimate violation is bloodshed in situations of attack or defense."[12] What does this integrity as a test of masculinity mean in terms of the ways in which work violated bodily integrity? For, even when biological maleness came with privilege (as it still does), it also came with risks to that very biological self (as it still does); an extreme early modern example being the professional castrati, singers in the enormously popular Italian opera *seria*. It is estimated that "five thousand European boys lost the use or very existence of their testicles each year of the eighteenth century, most of them in Italy," the goal being "to create the possibility that neutered boys would later become rich and famous."[13] Like Pierre Jaquet-Droz's clockwork Writer, many of these boys traveled to England from the continent in order to perform (un)natural boyhood as spectacle. In service to others, they were and were not boys. The mutilation of male "tools" (bodily organs) to prevent development of the larynx and therefore the voice becomes a kind of synecdoche, representative of a host of sacrifices imposed on young males, like that of the child sweeps who cried *peep* and *cheep* to advertise their small bodies as being fit for narrow flues. The damage to the genitalia of choirboys—even in the hopes of enriching them, their families, and their handlers like choirmasters—treats the male body very much as the means to an end: the act at once fixed and finished boyhood, prevented manhood even as the dreamed-of monetary gain was intended to make the man.

Other boys whose manhood was sacrificed to work, chimney sweeps' boys were canaries in the mine of the industrial revolution. They were not just workers but human tools. Whereas when Jaquet-Droz automated boy Writer traveled with his brethren across Europe to be displayed in England in 1776 he was met with wonder by most who saw him, skepticism by the world weary, and uneasiness by others, by 1829 Thomas Carlyle complained, "Our true Deity is Mechanism. It has subdued Nature for us, and we think it will do all other things." Carlyle's complaint, Roy Porter argues, testifies that "man the machine had ceased to be a controversial claim and had been reduced to a fact of life in the emergent world of manufactures."[14]

Tools were employed to prop up the male body, too. Among the associations aimed to assist people belonging to certain demographics (foundlings, sweeps' boys, widows, all of "the poor," etc.), the National Truss Society was formed in 1786, the Rupture Society a decade after that, both "to relieve poor ruptured persons by furnishing (under surgical direction) trusses for every kind of rupture, and bandages and necessary instruments for all cases of prolapses."[15] Some of these surgical appliances were fashioned out of elastic, others of fabric, leather, or steel.[16] Indeed, throughout Europe as other technology advanced, so did expertise and equipment in the form of trusses, crutches, elastic stockings, artificial limbs and eyes—a market stimulated not only by the march of progress but by the recurrent warfare of the period.[17] Although the Truss and Rupture Societies were established for persons of both sexes, hernias and prolapses tended then as now to afflict one sex more than the other: ten years after the latter was established a report claimed that "this malady exists in one person in eight through the whole male population of the kingdom."[18]

Despite the establishment of these institutions, Joan Lane notes that "apprentices still complained that they were 'bursten' as a result of the heavy work." She concludes, "As late as 1842 it was estimated that ten percent of the labouring population were sufferers, and in earlier centuries the proportion must have been even higher."[19] Here we see the male body, whether grown to full manhood or not, belabored and burdened with the "ruptures" about which George Nicholson warned parents in urging them not to put their small boys into breeches: a "sad condition" wherein "a boy must be hardly three years old but he must be a man... to make water he must pull and strain at his little pipe." The very first warning Nicholson listed for not hurrying the child into the trappings of manhood, however, was that once in breeches, the boy was "1. Pent up and shackled, and by way of compensation his mind is stuffed with opinion and folly."[20] There is an irony here in that rushing prematurely into manhood almost ensures the "nonage" Kant laments, given that a mind "stuffed with opinion and folly" is a mind less likely to develop "courage to use one's own mind without another's guidance."

A final insight into boyhood as a series of constructs within a wide range of lived experiences comes from a glance back at *Tristram Shandy*, the boy who "went into breeches" late in adolescence due to his parents' fear he would "look like a beast in 'em." As a man, Tristram wonders about the possibility of innatism versus Lockean certainty about the tabula rasa of the child's understanding of his world. Tristram ponders, "—the ideas of time and space—or how we came by those ideas,—or of what stuff they were made,—or whether they were born with us,—or whether we pick'd them up afterwards as we went along,—or whether we did it in frocks,—or not till we had got into breeches,—with a thousand other inquires and disputes about INFINITY, PRESCIENCE, LIBERTY, NECESSITY and so forth, upon whose desperate and unconquerable theories, so many fine heads have been turned and crack'd."[21] Contrasting the child in frocks with the child in breeches as he contemplates the origin of ideas about infinity, prescience, liberty, and necessity, Sterne might have been suggesting that boys (and therefore, surely, girls as well) are ordered and classified, taught the constraints of necessity, and of what stuff they are made, too soon.

Notes

INTRODUCTION

1. John Arbuthnot, "An Argument for Divine Providence, Taken from the Constant Regularity Observ'd in the Births of Both Sexes," *Philosophical Transactions (1683–1775)* 27 (1710–1712): 186–190. Elliott Sober's chapter, "Sex Ratio Theory, Ancient and Modern: An Eighteenth-Century Debate about Intelligent Design and the Development of Models in Evolutionary Biology," in *Genesis Redux: Essays in the History and Philosophy of Artificial Life*, ed. Jessica Riskin (Chicago: University of Chicago Press, 2007), 131–162, addresses the probabilities of Arbuthnot's claims, along with the doctor's disputants.

2. For twenty-first-century statistics of female infanticide, which is largely culture-based, see the documentary *It's a Girl: The Three Deadliest Words in the World*, directed by Evan Grae Davis (London: Shadowline Films, 2012), https://www.itsagirlmovie.com/.

3. Hugh Cunningham, *Children and Childhood in Western Society since 1500* (New York: Routledge, 2021); Colin Heywood, *A History of Childhood: Children and Childhood in the West from Medieval to Modern Times* (Cambridge: Polity, 2001); Anja Müller, ed., *Fashioning Childhood in the Eighteenth Century: Age and Identity* (New York: Routledge, 2006); Anthony Fletcher, *Gender, Sex and Subordination in England, 1500–1800*, rev. ed. (New Haven, CT: Yale University Press, 1999); Anthony Fletcher, *Growing Up in England: The Experience of Childhood, 1600–1914* (New Haven, CT: Yale University Press, 2010); Jane Humphries, *Childhood and Child Labour in the British Industrial Revolution* (Cambridge: Cambridge University Press, 2010).

4. Elizabeth E. Foyster, *Manhood in Early Modern England: Honour, Sex and Marriage* (New York: Routledge, 2014); Alexandra Shepherd, *Meanings of Manhood in Early Modern England* (Oxford: Oxford University Press, 2003); Mark Rothery and Henry French, eds., *Making Men: The Formation of Elite Male Identities in England, c. 1660–1900* (Basingstoke: Palgrave, 2012); Kenneth B. Kidd, *Making American Boys: Boyology and the Feral Tale* (Minneapolis: University of Minnesota Press, 2004); Ruth Mazo Karras, *From Boys to Men: Formations of Masculinity in Late Medieval Europe* (Philadelphia: University of Pennsylvania Press, 2003).

5. See Keith Thomas's defense of the use of literature as a historical source in "History and Literature" (Ernest Hughes Memorial Lecture, University College of Swansea, March 7, 1988).

6. Hannah Newton, *The Sick Child in Early Modern England, 1580–1720* (Oxford: Oxford University Press, 2012), 8. See too Anna-Christina Giovanopoulos, "The Legal Status of Children in Eighteenth-Century England," in Müller, *Fashioning Childhood*, 43–52.

7. Diane Payne, "Children of the Poor in London: 1700–1780" (PhD Diss., University of Hertfordshire, 2008). On confusion about the age of a child Payne notes that "early in the [eighteenth] century, obscurity in the law resulted in there being two different ages of consent simultaneously, ten and twelve" (13n278). Obviously, this issue affected girls. See Julie Gammon, "A Denial of Innocence: Female Juvenile Victims of Rape and the English Legal System in the Eighteenth Century," in *Children in Question: Children, Parents and the State*, ed. Anthony Fletcher and Stephen Hussey (Manchester: Manchester University Press, 1999), 74–95.

8. A. E. Simpson, *Masculinity and Control: The Prosecution of Sex Offenses in Eighteenth-Century London* (New York: New York University Press, 1984), 146.

9. Article 1 of the Convention on the Rights of the Child, adopted and opened for signature, ratification, and accession by General Assembly resolution, November 20, 1989, states, "For the purposes of the present Convention, a child means every human being below the age of eighteen years unless under the law applicable to the child, a majority is attained earlier." United Nations Human Rights Office of the High Commissioner, "Article 1," Convention on the Rights of the Child, https://www.ohchr.org/en/professionalinterest/pages/crc.aspx.

10. "There are three stages of adolescence—early adolescence from 12–14 years, middle adolescence from 15–17 years and late adolescence from 18 years and over. Neuroscience has shown that a young person's cognitive development continues into this later stage and that their emotional maturity, self-image and judgement will be affected until the prefrontal cortex of the brain has fully developed." Lucy Wallis, "Is 25 the New Cut-Off Point for Adulthood?," *BBC News*, September 23, 2013, https://www.bbc.com/news/magazine-24173194.

11. Samuel Johnson, *A Dictionary of the English Language* (London, 1773), s.v. "boyhood" and "boy" (2).

12. For instance, in the *Oxford English Dictionary* (*OED*), a child is "a young person of either sex below the age of puberty; a boy or girl." *OED*, 3rd ed., s.v. "child, n." (I.2.a.). There has been steady decline in the age of puberty over the centuries. See Cheryl L. Sisk and Sheri A. Berenbaum, eds., "Puberty and Adolescence," special issue of *Hormones & Behavior* 64, no. 2 (2013).

13. Payne, "Children of the Poor," 13–14.

14. John Locke, *An Essay Concerning Human Understanding. In Four Books* (1689; London, 1690); Jean-Jacques Rousseau, *Émile; or, On Education* (1762), trans. Allan Bloom (New York: Basic Books, 1979).

15. Johnson, *Dictionary* (1773), s.v. "boy" (3).

16. Eric Tribunella, "Boyhood," in *Keywords for Children's Literature*, ed. Philip Nel and Lissa Paul (New York: New York University Press, 2011), 22. See the *OED*, 3rd ed., s.v. "boy n.1 and int.*" (A.*n.1* 1.a.): "A male servant, assistant, junior employee, etc." Among the definitions for "boy" we find also "Used (chiefly by white people) with reference to non-white slaves and (in English-speaking colonies) to non-white servants, laborers, etc. Also as a form of address (esp. as a summons). Now *hist.* and *rare* (usually considered *offensive*)" 1(b) and "A male person of low birth or status; (as a general term of contempt or abuse) a worthless fellow, a knave, a rogue, a wretch."

17. Shepherd, *Meanings of Manhood*, 9.

18. Johnson, *Dictionary* (1773), s.v. "boy" (1). The lexicographer did not define either "child" or "girl."

19. While Butler has her detractors, a quarter of a century after *Gender Trouble* Thekla Morgenroth and Michelle K. Ryan "argue that there is great value in (again) promoting the ideas Butler puts forward in *Gender Trouble* to social psychologists." See "Gender Trouble in Social Psychology: How Can Butler's Work Inform Experimental Social Psychologists' Conceptualization of Gender?," *Frontiers in Psychology* 27 (July 2018).

20. See Susan Bordo, *Unbearable Weight: Feminism, Western Culture, and the Body* (Berkeley: University of California Press, 1993), and Martha Nussbaum, "The Professor of Parody: The Hip Defeatism of Judith Butler," *New Republic*, February 2, 1999. This is not to say Nussbaum is not sympathetic to the trans community. See *The Monarchy of Fear: A Philosopher Looks at the Political Crisis* (New York: Simon & Schuster, 2018), 130, passim.

21. Müller, introduction to *Fashioning Childhood*, 1–10, 4.

22. Foyster, *Manhood in Early Modern England*, 31.

23. The first instance of boyhood in the *OED* concerns itself with this failing: "1577 J. Northbrooke *Spiritus est Vicarius Christi: Treat. Dicing* 22 'All the life (to be ydle) in thy childehoode, in thy boyehoode, in thy youth, in thy age.'"

24. Joy Damousi, "Writing Gender into History and History into Gender: *Creating a Nation* and Australian Historiography," in *Gender and History: Retrospect and Prospect*, ed. Leonore Davidoff, Keith McClelland, and Eleni Varikas (Oxford: Blackwell, 2000), 199.

25. Judith Kegan Gardiner, *Masculinity Studies and Feminist Theory* (New York: Columbia University Press, 2002), and Michael Kimmel, *The Gendered Society* (Oxford: Oxford University Press, 2000), 5.

26. Foyster, *Manhood in Early Modern England*, 39.

27. Much has changed since students in a children's fiction course taught by Perry Nodelman in the early 2000s were asked to think about constructions of boyhood. Nodelman's students were "distressed" at a "focus on questions of masculinity," because "girls, in their minds, were clearly the victims of stereotypes. Boys were just boys, allowed to be whomever they wanted to be, enjoying the freedom from stereotypes that girls can only envy." Nodelman, "Making Boys Appear: The Masculinity of Children's Fiction," in *Ways of Being Male: Representing Masculinities in Children's Literature and Film*, ed. John Stephens (New York: Routledge, 2002), 1.

28. James Kim, "'Good Cursed, Bouncing Losses': Masculinity, Sentimental Irony, and Exuberance in *Tristram Shandy*," *The Eighteenth Century: Theory and Interpretation* 48, no. 1 (2007): 3.

29. Stephen Orgel, *Impersonations: The Performance of Gender in Shakespeare's England* (Cambridge: Cambridge University Press, 1996), 61.

30. Natalie Zimon Davis, "Women's History in Transition: The European Case," *Feminist Studies* 3 (1976): 90.

31. Rothery and French, *Making Men*, xx.

32. No symbol combines danger and utility as a knife does—a fusion that this tool has in common with the young male body.

33. *OED*, s.v. "tool, *n.*" (2.a.), first published 1913.

34. Pope, "Epistle to Arbuthnot," in *The Poems of Alexander Pope: A Reduced Version of the Twickenham Text*, ed. John Butt (New Haven, CT: Yale University Press, 1963), 597–612, lines 334–337. Henceforth I follow the convention of citing this as *Shorter Twickenham*.

35. Swift, *A Pamphlet Entitl'd Some Remarks on a Letter to the Seven Lords of the Committee Appointed to Examine Gregg* (1711), in *The Works of the Rev. Jonathan Swift*, vol. 5, ed. Thomas Sheridan et al. (London, 1801), 393. Swift employs the pejorative use of knave, "a dishonest unprincipled man; a cunning unscrupulous rogue; a villain"; yet worth recalling is how class-based the word is, also referring to an attendant—boy or man.

36. Indeed, as the *Urban Dictionary* notes, the term is one of abuse, most often for men (and boys), even now becoming more common in the United Kingdom and elsewhere. Of particular interest are two of the definitions here: "Tool: (noun) 2.) Someone whose ego FAR exceeds his talent, intelligence, and likeability. But, of course, he is clueless regarding that fact. He erroneously thinks he is THE MAN! [and] 4.) Someone who acts like a dick, because ... well ... he's compensating." These definitions encompass both masculinity and a lack thereof, pointing to the vexed relationship between the idiomatic term and masculinity. https://www.urbandictionary.com/define.php?term=Tool.

37. Paula R. Backscheider, *Revising Women: Eighteenth-Century "Women's Fiction" and Social Engagement* (Baltimore: Johns Hopkins University Press, 2002), 7. Backscheider cites Xavière Gauthier, Monique Wittig, and Julia Kristeva among feminist theorists who discuss this positioning of woman as gap, as vessel.

38. In contemporary use of the word "tool" as an insult, it is certainly gendered. I thank Sarah Winters for pointing out that one rarely seems to hear a girl or woman criticized for being a "tool."

39. Immanuel Kant, *Observations on the Feeling of the Beautiful and the Sublime*, trans. John T. Goldthwaite (Berkeley: University of California Press, 2003), 77.

40. Mary Astell, *A Serious Proposal to the Ladies, for the Advancement of Their True and Greatest Interest. In Two Parts. By a Lover of Her Sex*, pt. 1 (London, 1697), 8.

41. Alexander Pope, "Epistle II. To a Lady," line 41, in *Shorter Twickenham*, 559–569; Jonathan Swift, "The Lady's Dressing Room," in *The Essential Writings of Jonathan Swift*, ed. Claude Rawson and Ian Higgins (New York: Norton, 2010), 603–606, line 144.

42. Pope, "The Rape of the Locke," in *Shorter Twickenham*, 217–242, l. I.99–100.

43. William Morris, "The Beauty of Life" (1880), in *William Morris on Art and Socialism*, ed. Norman Kelvin (Mineola, NY: Dover, 1999), 53.

44. Laura Mulvey, "Visual Pleasure and Narrative Cinema," *Screen* 16, no. 3 (Autumn 1975): 6–18, http://www.jahsonic.com/VPNC.html.

45. John Berger, *Ways of Seeing: Based on the BBC Television Series with John Berger* (London: BBC and Penguin, 1973), 47.

46. Aparna Gollapudi, "Personhood, Property Rights, and the Child in John Locke's *Two Treatises of Government* and Daniel Defoe's Fiction," *Eighteenth-Century Fiction* 28, no. 1 (Fall 2015): 25–58, 40, 42.

47. Tribunella notes that whereas "boy" has been used for far longer, the word "boyhood" became widely employed only in the nineteenth century in children's literature. Tribunella, "Boyhood," 21.

48. Denis Diderot, "Encyclopedia," trans. Philip Stewart, in Encyclopedia of Diderot & d'Alembert Collaborative Translation Project (Ann Arbor: Michigan Publishing, University of Michigan Library, 2002).

49. See Clorinda Donato and Robert M. Maniquis, eds., *The Encyclopédie and the Age of Revolution* (Boston: G. K. Hall, 1992), and Kurt P. A. Ballstadt, *Diderot: Natural Philosopher* (Oxford: Voltaire Foundation, 2008).

50. Seth Lerer, *Children's Literature: A Reader's History, from Aesop to Harry Potter* (Chicago: University of Chicago Press, 2008), 151.

51. Peter Walmsley, "The Enlightenment Worker: An Introduction," *Eighteenth-Century Fiction* 23, no. 2 (Winter 2010–2011): 264.

52. For children and farm labor, see K. D. M. Snell, *Annals of the Labouring Poor: Social Change and Agrarian England, 1660–1990* (Cambridge: Cambridge University Press, 2012).

53. Bill Brown, *A Sense of Things: The Object Matter of American Literature* (Chicago: University of Chicago Press, 2003), 38.

54. See Christopher Flint, "Speaking Objects: The Circulation of Stories in Eighteenth-Century Prose Fiction," *PMLA* 113, no. 2 (March 1998): 212–226, and Freya Johnston, "Little Lives: An Eighteenth-Century Sub-genre," *Cambridge Quarterly* 32, no. 2 (2003): 143–160.

55. Preface to Joseph Moxon and Theodore L. De Vinne, *Mechanick Exercises; or The Doctrine of Handy-works*, 3rd ed. (London, 1703).

56. Stephens, *Ways of Being Male*, x.

57. Bordo, *Unbearable Weight*, 38.

58. *OED*, s.v. "tool, *n.*" (2.b.), first published 1913.

59. Payne, "Children of the Poor," 13.

60. Sarah Fielding's linked stories/novel *The Governess, or Little Female Academy* (Dublin, 1749), aimed at girls, is probably the first school story per se.

61. Most of the boyhood explored in this book centers upon London, "the wonder city," as Roy Porter calls it, "a European marvel" that "dominated the nation like no other capital" in the eighteenth century. Roy Porter, *London: A Social History* (Cambridge, MA: Harvard University Press, 1995), 131. Regarding urban labor especially, as well as crime, apprenticeship, and the printing press, London was at the heart of the matter, with three-quarters of a million inhabitants by 1760, a number rising to 1.4 million by 1815.

62. Arbuthnot, "Argument for Divine Providence."

CHAPTER 1 — THE BOY IN BREECHES

1. Manuals "advised parents to make toilet training early and rigorous, a matter of exerting adult will on the willful child. By the eighteenth century and into the nineteenth, the effect of Enlightenment thinking was to get parents to see child training as a rational (rather than a necessarily moral) process. Structure and rigid scheduling dominated the child-training regime of the first half of the nineteenth century." Jay Mechling, "Toilet Training," in *Encyclopedia of Children and Childhood: In History and Society*, ed. Paula S. Fass (New York: Macmillan, 2004), http://www.faqs.org/childhood/Th-W/Toilet-Training.html.

2. Fletcher, *Gender, Sex, and Subordination*, 298.

3. Laurence Sterne, *The Life and Opinions of Tristram Shandy, Gentleman* (1759; Oxford: Oxford University Press, 2009). Text references are to page numbers in this edition and are made parenthetically throughout the rest of the chapter. Elements of this chapter first appeared in my article *"Tristram Shandy*, Boyhood, and Breeching," *Eighteenth-Century Fiction* 28, no. 1 (2015): 85–107, https://muse.jhu.edu/article/595358.

4. Norton's work on the Phutatorius episode addresses a different aspect of breeches: stoicism. He argues that "we should be wary of dismissing any of Sterne's 'sunshiny' digressions, especially one that concerns this particular piece of anatomy." Brian Michael Norton, *Fiction and the Philosophy of Happiness: Ethical Inquiries in the Age of Enlightenment* (Lewisburg, PA: Bucknell University Press, 2012), 26.

5. Philippe Ariès, *Centuries of Childhood: A Social History of Family Life* (New York: Vintage, 1960), qtd. in Heywood, *History of Childhood*, 39.

6. Cynthia Wall, *The Prose of Things: Transformations of Description in the Eighteenth Century* (Chicago: University of Chicago Press, 2006), 137ff.

7. Patricia Fara, *Pandora's Breeches: Women, Science and Power in the Enlightenment* (London: Pimlico, 2004). See too Dror Wahrman, *The Making of the Modern Self: Identity and Culture in Eighteenth-Century England* (New Haven, CT: Yale University Press, 2004).

8. See Anna Clark, *The Struggle for the Breeches: Gender and the Making of the British Working Class* (Berkeley: University of California Press, 1995). Lynn Hunt and Margaret Jacob note that slang used to describe sodomites included "breeches-clad bawds" and

"penchant for breeches" in "Somatic Affects: The Affective Revolution in 1790s Britain," *Eighteenth-Century Studies* 34, no. 4 (2001): 493.

9. In Johnson, "to wear the breeches" is "to usurp the authority of the husband." *Dictionary* (1755), s.v. "breeches," doi.https://johnsonsdictionaryonline.com/views/search.php?term=breeches.

10. Into the twentieth century small boys continued to wear frocks (also called short frocks, frock coats, or coats). One nineteenth-century storybook has a family rejoice over a bag of secondhand clothing, for "Sammy had never worn boy's clothes, as it had been more convenient and economical to have him take those his sisters had grown out of." Upon Sammy putting on breeches, the sisters dance about declaring, "He looks like a real boy!" Madeline Leslie, *Jack the Chimney Sweeper: And Other Stories for Children* (Boston, 1859), 84.

11. In the case of *Tristram Shandy*, scholars have paid a great deal of attention (as they are invited to do) to the preoccupation with what is inside breeches: Tristram's accidental circumcision at the age of five, Uncle Toby's injured groin, and Walter Shandy clapping "both his hands upon his cod-piece . . . when any thing hugely tickled him" (412).

12. Mark Breitenberg, *Anxious Masculinity in Early Modern England* (Cambridge: Cambridge University Press, 1996), 151–152.

13. Terry Castle, *Masquerade and Civilization: The Carnivalesque in Eighteenth-Century English Culture and Fiction* (Stanford, CA: Stanford University Press, 1986), 22. Castle describes "the she-male, or man dressed in women's clothes . . . in the traditional festivity known as the hobby-horse or hoodening game" who was frequently representative of "parodic motherhood." Castle quotes a description in *Gentleman's Magazine* (February 1771) of two men dressed as "two great girls, one in a white frock, with her doll." I would argue that, given how boys were dressed when small, not every foray into a frock was about pretending to be female; surely some had at heart the return to asexual babyhood.

14. About the severity of Tristram's wound, see Ross King, "*Tristram Shandy* and the Wound of Language," in *Laurence Sterne's* Tristram Shandy: *A Casebook*, ed. Thomas Keymer (Oxford: Oxford University Press, 2006), 123–146.

15. Which is why detractors of the 1560 Geneva Bible focused on that anachronistic translation of what Adam and Eve fashioned from fig leaves: "Then the eyes of them both were opened, and they knew that they were naked, and they sewed fig tree leaves together, and made themselves breeches" Genesis 3: 3–7, GNV.

16. The word "beast" also carried class connotations since boys from the laboring classes were generally breeched earliest; certainly, beasts have been employed as tools for humans.

17. Jonathan Lamb, *Sterne's Fiction and the Double Principle* (Cambridge: Cambridge University Press, 1989), 150.

18. For seventeenth-century spermism—the theory of embryo generation in which a mother is mere incubator, the father the "creator"—and its lingering influence, see David M. Friedman, *A Mind of Its Own: A Cultural History of the Penis* (New York: Free Press, 2001), 78–80.

19. George Nicholson, *On Clothing* (Manchester, 1797), 37. Matthew Grenby states that among John Locke's "aims was to remove the children of the middle and upper class from the influence of their social inferiors." Grenby, *The Child Reader, 1700–1840* (Cambridge: Cambridge University Press, 2011), 109. Locke's advice about raising children applied primarily to those in higher classes who would have servants. For example, "servants should be hinder'd from making court to [children] by giving them strong drink, wine, fruit, playthings, and other such matters, which may make them in love with their conversation." Locke, *Some Thoughts Concerning Education*, Harvard Classics vol. 37, *Locke/Berkley/Hume*, pt. 1: *Locke* (New York: Collier, 1909–1914), §69.

20. Nicholson, *On Clothing*, 38. The garment about which Nicholson complains would have been somewhat different from what Tristram wore. See Anne Buck, *Dress in Eighteenth-Century England* (New York: Holmes & Meir, 1979), 205.

21. Donelle R. Ruwe, "Benevolent Brothers and Supervising Mothers: Ideology in the Children's Verses of Mary and Charles Lamb and Charlotte Smith," *Children's Literature* 25 (1997): 94.

22. Anna Laetitia Barbauld, *Lessons for Children, from Two to Three Years Old* (London, 1778–1779), n.p.

23. Barbauld, *Lessons for Children*, 72.

24. Barbauld, *Lessons for Children*, 73–74.

25. Barbauld, *Lessons for Children*, 80–81.

26. Charles Lamb and Mary Lamb, "Going into Breeches," in *Poetry for Children* (London, 1809).

27. Lamb and Lamb, "Going into Breeches," lines 15–20.

28. Ruwe, "Benevolent Brothers and Supervising Mothers," 97.

29. Lamb, "Going into Breeches," lines 21–26.

30. Lamb, "Going into Breeches," lines 29–34.

31. Lamb, "Going into Breeches," lines 35–48.

32. Lamb, "Going into Breeches," lines 5–14.

33. *OED*, 3rd ed., s.v. "boy, *n.1* and *int.*" (A.1.d.), last modified December 2008, https://www.oed.com/view/Entry/22323.

34. Locke, *Some Thoughts Concerning Education*, §15.

35. Tribunella, "Boyhood," 22.

36. Johnson, *Dictionary* (1755), s.v. "boy."

37. "In the first half of the century girls wore for the brief period of infancy simple frocks of linen or muslin, fastening at the back and with a sash at the waist. At the age of three or four they put on a stiff, back-fastening bodice, boned and shaped like the stays of their mothers, with a separate skirt, the form of the stiff-bodied gown of earlier fashion, which gave them a fashionable adult shape until they changed to adults gowns when they were thirteen or fourteen. In everyday dress the frocks continued to be worn." Buck, *Dress in Eighteenth-Century England*, 205. Obviously, the constriction and even danger of wearing stays added further trials to womanhood and girlhood.

38. Locke, *Some Thoughts Concerning Education*, §35.

39. Coleridge to Robert Southey, November 1801, in Samuel Taylor Coleridge, *Collected Letters*, vol. 2: *1801–1806*, ed. Earl Leslie Griggs (Oxford: Clarendon, 1956), 774.

40. Daniel Defoe, *The History and Remarkable Life of the Truly Honourable Col. Jacque* (1722), ed. S. H. Monk (London: Oxford University Press, 1965), 28.

41. Mary Barber, *Poems on Several Occasions* (London, 1734 [1735]; reprint, [S. l.]: Gale ECCO, Print Editions, 2010), 13. See too Chantel Lavoie, "The Boy in the Text: Mary Barber, Her Son, and Children's Poetry in *Poems on Several Occasions*," *ABO: Interactive Journal for Women in the Arts, 1640–1830* 11, no. 1 (June 2021).

42. Barber, *Poems on Several Occasions*, 16.

43. *OED*, s.v. "breech, *v.*" (2), first published 1888.

44. Ruwe, "Benevolent Brothers and Supervising Mothers," 94.

45. Karras, *From Boys to Men*, 11. James Kim sees Sterne's novel as dwelling on "the loss of traditional forms of phallic authority and the encroachment of effeminacy on male identity." Kim, "'Good Cursed, Bouncing Losses,'" 6.

46. Anthony Fletcher, *Growing Up in England: The Experience of Childhood, 1600–1914* (New Haven, CT: Yale University Press, 2010), 15.

47. So much so that Pointon identifies in portraiture of the period "a gulf not only between masculinity and femininity but also between ungendered infancy and gendered youth." Marcia Pointon, *Hanging the Head: Portraiture and Social Formation in England* (New Haven, CT: Yale University Press, 1993), 172.

48. William Blakey, *Essay on the Manner of Preserving Children and Grown Persons from Ruptures* (London, 1792), 28.

49. Further, as Thomas Keymer points out, the serial publication of *Tristram Shandy* allowed Sterne to poke fun at "both *Critical* and *Monthly* reviewers with the author's fate 'to be settled by The Reviewers of My Breeches.'" Keymer, *Sterne, the Moderns and the Novel* (Oxford: Oxford University Press, 2002), 102.

50. Worth noting is that "machine" was a euphemism for condom.

51. Elizabeth W. Harries, "Words, Sex, and Gender in Sterne's Novels," in *The Cambridge Companion to Laurence Sterne*, ed. Thomas Keymer (Cambridge: Cambridge University Press, 2009), 116. James Kim argues, "Tristram may speak in the voice of the perpetual adolescent, but the fact remains that there are really no young people in Sterne, only old men grappling with their obsolescence." See Kim, "'Good Cursed, Bouncing Losses,'" 9.

52. Julie Park, *The Self and It: Novel Objects in Eighteenth-Century England* (Stanford, CA: Stanford University Press, 2010), xv.

53. To Juliet McMaster, one of the themes this metaphor reflects is that "the very disjunction of mind and body furnishes a vision of life, and a source of pain and laughter." McMaster, *Reading the Body in the Eighteenth-Century Novel* (Basingstoke: Palgrave Macmillan, 2004), 17.

54. Tristram's breeches and his "vile cough" are frequently referenced in close proximity. Among instances of breeches representing the narrator's overall state is the exclamatory "O Trim! would to heaven thou had'st a better historian!—would!—thy historian had a better pair of breeches! O—ye criticks! will nothing melt you?" (288), which reminds us how far Tristram has fallen from the discussion of all the options for fashioning his first breeches.

55. Brian Michael Norton, "The Moral in Phutatorius's Breeches: *Tristram Shandy* and the Limits of Stoic Ethics," *Eighteenth-Century Fiction* 184, no. 4 (2006): 419.

56. Robert A. Erickson, "'The Books of Generation': Some Observations on the Style of the English Midwife Books, 1671–1764," in *Sexuality in Eighteenth-Century Britain*, ed. Paul-Gabriel Boucé (Manchester: Manchester University Press, 1982), 77.

57. Erickson, "'Books of Generation,'" 77.

58. James Wolveridge, *Speculum matricis, or The Expert Midwives Handmaid* (1670), qtd. in Robert A. Erickson, *Mother Midnight: Birth, Sex, and Fate in Eighteenth-Century Fiction (Defoe, Richardson, and Sterne)* (New York: AMS Press, 1986), 205. Erickson cites William Sermon's midwifery book of 1671, *The Ladies Companion*, about the umbilical cord: "a common saying among the hearty good women . . . to the Midwife, if it be a boy, make him good measure, but if a girl tye it short." The practice and the joke also speak to how gender *is* written onto the body at birth. See also Louis Landa, "The Shandean Homunculus: The Background of Sterne's 'Little Gentleman,'" in *Restoration and Eighteenth-Century Literature: Essays in Honour of Alan Dugald McKillop*, ed. C. Carroll Camden (Chicago: University of Chicago Press, 1963), 52.

59. Paul-Gabriel Boucé explicates a "most extraordinary anatomical myth," originating with Aristotle, "which established a size-relationship between the nose and the penis" revisited in *Tristram Shandy* with "a seemingly inexhaustible source of puns, jokes, innuendos and spicy *doubles entendres*." Boucé, "Some Sexual Beliefs and Myths in Eighteenth-Century Britain," in *Sexuality in Eighteenth-Century Britain*, 31.

60. Erickson, *Mother Midnight*, 206.

61. Samuel Beckett, *Waiting for Godot* (New York: Grove Press, 2011), 103, lines 2724–2725.

62. Thomas Gray, "Ode on a Distant Prospect of Eton College" (1747), in *Broadview Anthology of British Literature: The Restoration and the Eighteenth Century*, ed. Joseph Laurence Black (Peterborough, ON: Broadview Press, 2006), 3:604–605.

63. Gray, "Ode on a Distant Prospect of Eton College," lines 29–30.

64. Gray, "Ode on a Distant Prospect of Eton College," lines 38–40.

65. Lucius Annaeus Seneca, *Epistles 66–92*, trans. R. M. Gummere (Cambridge, MA: Harvard University Press, 1917), epistle 90. See too Scott R. MacKenzie, "Breeches of Decorum: The Figure of a Barbarian in Montaigne and Addison," *South Central Review* 23, no. 2 (2006): 99–127, http://www.jstor.org/stable/40039933.

66. John Dunton, *A Voyage round the World* (1691; Cambridge: Chadwyck-Healey, 1997), 29–30. Paul Salzman argues that "it was quite probably Dunton who gave Sterne the idea of beginning a narrative prior to the birth of the hero." Salzman, *English Prose Fiction, 1558–1700: A Critical History* (Oxford: Clarendon, 1985), 302. The Widow Wadman kicking away the corking pin used to fasten the bottom of her night shift is another such moment of breaking a sac in order to create bipedal freedom (428). This unfolding response from the woman who loves Toby contrasts with the misogyny McMaster sees in Walter Shandy, who "tries to persuade his wife to undergo delivery by Caesarian—an operation always fatal in the eighteenth century: he's willing to have his wife cracked open like a nutshell for the safe delivery of his son." Juliet McMaster, "'Uncrystalized Flesh and Blood': The Body in *Tristram Shandy*," *Eighteenth-Century Fiction* 2, no. 3 (1990): 211. See, too, William Smellie's remarkable "Mother Machine," created to train male midwives, discussed in Brandy Lain Schillace, "Mother Machine: An 'Uncanny Valley' in the Eighteenth Century," *The Appendix* 1, no. 2 (2013).

67. See Scott MacKenzie's article on the ambiguity of Montaigne's final sentence in his essay *On Cannibals*: "All this is not too bad, but then they do not wear breeches." MacKenzie, "Breeches of Decorum," 102.

68. The entry in the *OED* includes "A garment covering the loins and thighs . . . distinguished from *trousers* by coming only just below the knee, but dialectally (and humorously) *breeches* includes *trousers*." OED, s.v. "breech, n." (1), first published 1888.

69. Norton, *Fiction and the Philosophy of Happiness*, 33.

70. Gail Kern Paster, *The Body Embarrassed: Drama and the Discipline of Shame in Early Modern England* (Ithaca, NY: Cornell University Press, 1993), 163.

71. I am grateful to an anonymous peer-reviewer for *Eighteenth-Century Fiction* for this wording.

72. Again, a common trope linking maleness and efficacy. Presumably, when Alexander Pope was insulting Prime Minister Robert Walpole's wit, he was also insulting his manhood with the claim that there were "no rules / Of honour" that bound Pope "not to maul His Tools, / Sure if they can not cut, it may be said, / His Saws are toothless, and his Hatchet lead." Alexander Pope, "Epistle to the Satires II," in *Shorter Twickenham*, 700, lines 147–1.149.

73. Erickson, *Mother Midnight*, 207. The relationship between adults and their children is mirrored in dress: "children's clothing was in part made from the parents' old clothing, in part bought second hand." Buck, *Dress in Eighteenth-Century England*, 180. Although Tristram's breeches are not made in this way, the cultural fact resonates with his early lament against a world as "a vile, dirty planet . . . made up of the shreds and clippings of the rest" (9).

CHAPTER 2 — THE BOY IN SCHOOL

1. Rare was the kind of exhortation that came from Rousseau to delay formal schooling. See Rousseau, *Émile*, 107.

2. Tribunella, "Boyhood," 22.

3. Mary Hilton, *Women and the Shaping of the Nation's Young: Education and Public Doctrine in Britain, 1750–1850* (Aldershot: Ashgate, 2007), 203. Peter Kirby argues that the proportion of children being "schooled" in the eighteenth century, and even through most of the nineteenth, has been overestimated. This contradicts the position that schooling "ended the nation's commitment to child labour." Rather, schooling "remained an uncompensated expense upon working-class families until 1891 when attendance was made free." Kirby, *Child Labour in Britain, 1750–1870* (New York: Palgrave Macmillan, 2003), 112.

4. Educational institutions and charitable projects proliferated as their difference blurred in the second half of the century. In 1756, the Marine Society, "for educating poor destitute boys to the sea," was established in Bishopsgate Street.

5. Apropos a book set in Christ's Hospital charity school—aimed at men readers—which complicates the figure of the schoolboy, see Chantel Lavoie, "Romancing the Purse and Sexualizing the Schoolboy in *The Fortunate Blue-coat Boy* (1770)," *English Studies in Canada* 44, no. 4 (2021): 115–132.

6. For an overview of the grammar school from its beginnings, see Donna Elaine Hobbs, "Telling Tales out of School: Schoolbooks, Audiences, and the Production of Vernacular Literature in Late Medieval England" (PhD diss., University of Texas at Austin, December 2012).

7. See David Stoker, "Establishing Lady Fenn's Canon," *Papers of the Bibliographical Society of America* 103, no. 1 (March 2009): 43–72.

8. See Mavis Reimer, "Traditions of the School Story," in *The Cambridge Companion to Children's Literature*, ed. M. O. Grenby and Andrea Immel (Cambridge: Cambridge University Press, 2009), and Beverly Lyon Clark, *Regendering the School Story* (New York: Routledge, 1996).

9. Lissa Paul, *The Children's Book Business: Lessons from the Long Eighteenth Century* (New York: Routledge, 2010), 96. See also Andrea Immel, "'Mistress of Infantine Language': Lady Ellenor Fenn, Her Set of Toys, and the 'Education of Each Moment,'" *Children's Literature* 25 (1997): 223.

10. Fenn, *School Dialogues, for Boys. Being an Attempt to Convey Instruction Insensibly to Their Tender Minds, and Instill the Love of Virtue*, 2 vols. (London, 1783), 1:xxiii and xxii. All parenthetical references throughout the rest of the chapter are to these two volumes.

11. Patricia Demers, ed., *From Instruction to Delight: An Anthology of Children's Literature to 1850* (Oxford: Oxford University Press, 2004).

12. Locke, *Some Thoughts Concerning Education*, §73.

13. Jackie Horne, *History and the Construction of the Child*, 112. Locke preferred "Breeding of a young Gentleman at home in his Father's sight, under a good Governor as much the best and safest way to this great and main End of Education [virtue]." Locke, *Some Thoughts Concerning Education*, §70. Sons from dissenting families were more often tutored or taught at home.

14. Joseph Bristow, *Empire Boys: Adventures in a Man's World* (Sydney: Unwin Hyman, 1991), 54.

15. Kristin Olsen, *Daily Life in the Eighteenth Century in England*, 2nd ed. (Westport, CT: Greenwood, 2002), 16. A majority of studies about the English boy at school begin with 1800. See John Chandos, *Boys Together: English Public Schools 1800–1860* (New Haven, CT:

Yale University Press, 1984), and T. W. Bamford, *The Rise of the Public Schools: A Study of Boys' Public Boarding Schools in England and Wales from 1837 to the Present Day* (London: Nelson, 1967).

16. Bristow, *Empire Boys*, 52.

17. Rothery and French, *Making Men*, 37.

18. Elizabeth Warriner to her son, George Warriner, 3 September 1796, qtd. in Rothery and French, *Making Men*, 38.

19. Locke called crying "a fault" and advised those who had the care of children "to compassionate them, whenever they suffer any hurt; but not to shew it in pitying them." *Some Thoughts Concerning Education*, §113.

20. Elizabeth Segel, "Domesticity and the Wide, Wide World," *Children's Literature* 8 (1980): 169.

21. Again, this shows both the influence of Anna Laetitia Barbauld's then recent (and ongoing) legacy of writing for small children and print conventions now aimed at them. Fenn's printer, John Marshall, was the preeminent publisher of children's literature in England from about 1780 to 1800. Harvey Darton, *Children's Books in England: Five Centuries of Social Life* (Cambridge: Cambridge University Press, 1982), 164.

22. This duality has been elucidated notably by Barbara Wall in *The Narrator's Voice: The Dilemma of Children's Fiction* (London: Palgrave, 1991) and Maria Nikolajeva in *Power, Voice and Subjectivity in Literature for Young Readers* (London: Routledge, 2010). A larger, related problem identified from a Marxist perspective is that voiced by Jack Zipes: "If we take the genitive case literally and seriously, and if we assume ownership and possession are involved . . . then there is no such thing as children's literature, or for that matter, children." Zipes, *Sticks and Stones: The Troublesome Success of Children's Literature from Slovenly Peter to Harry Potter* (New York: Routledge, 2002), 40.

23. Jacqueline Rose, *The Case of Peter Pan; or, The Impossibility of Children's Fiction* (1984; Philadelphia: University of Pennsylvania Press, 1992), 2.

24. Wall, *Narrator's Voice*, 79.

25. When his aunt was writing the book William Frere must have been just off to Felsted Grammar School in Essex, about fifty kilometers from his home in Roydon. Another book dedicated to Fenn's nephew William has not survived—*Master Meanwell's Rules*. David Stoker, "Ellenor Fenn as 'Mrs. Teachwell' and 'Mrs. Lovechild': A Pioneer Late Eighteenth-Century Children's Writer, Educator, and Philanthropist," *Princeton University Library Chronicle* 68, no. 3 (Spring 2007): 822.

26. See Plutarch, "The Life of Lycurgus," in *Plutarch's Lives*, vol. 1, trans. John Dryden (Boston: Little, Brown, 1906), 83–126: "It is confessed, on all hands, that the Spartans dealt with them very hardly; for it was a common thing to force them to drink to excess, and to lead them in that condition into their public halls, that the children might see what a sight a drunken man is; they made them to dance low dances, and sing ridiculous songs" (122). I am grateful to Jeremy Trevett for this reference.

27. First that of Jacques Amyot (1513–1593), then translated into English by Thomas North in 1578. Ruth Bottigheimer argues, "In terms of children's reading, the Battle of the Ancients and the Moderns can be understood as having two separate outcomes. . . . Boys' schoolbooks continued to purvey ancient classics: girls' schoolbooks incorporated modern fairytales." Bottigheimer, "Fairy Tales, Telemachus, and Young Misses Magazine: Moderns, Ancients, Gender, and Eighteenth-Century Book Publishing," *Children's Literature Association Quarterly* 28, no. 2 (Fall 2003): 173.

28. See Coppélia Kahn, *Roman Shakespeare: Warriors, Wounds, and Women* (New York: Routledge, 1997), 14. Kahn sees masculinity "as an ideology discursively maintained

through the appropriation of the Latin heritage for the early modern stage" (2). In part, she reads this appropriation as a rejection of native female Britain.

29. Edward Gibbon, *Miscellaneous Works: of Edward Gibbon, Esquire. With Memoirs of His Life and Writings, Composed by Himself: Illustrated from His Letters, with Occasional Notes and Narrative, by John Lord Sheffield. In Two Volumes*, vol. 1 (London, 1796), 147.

30. William Woolcombe to Henry Woolcombe, August 12, 1794, qtd. in Rothery and French, *Making Men*, 25. In 1683 John Dryden began his life of Plutarch and oversaw a translation of the *Lives* by several hands based on the original Greek. The most recent English translation when *School Dialogues* appeared was the six-volume *Plutarch's Lives from the Original Greek*, by John and William Langhorne from 1770. Single-volume editions for schoolboys existed as well.

31. Thomas Dyke Acland to Thomas Acland (Jr.), April 17, 1826, qtd. in Rothery and French, *Making Men*, 36. Worth recalling is that one of the three books that Frankenstein's creature finds and tries to learn from is Plutarch's *Lives*, the other two being Milton's *Paradise Lost* and Goethe's *The Sorrows of Young Werther*. For other classic texts in school, see Sonja Fieliz, "Tales of Miracle or Lessons of Morality? School Editions of Ovid's *Metamorphosis* as a Means of Shaping the Personalities of British Schoolboys," in Müller, *Fashioning Childhood*, 145–156.

32. Letter LXI from Samuel Richardson, *Pamela; or, Virtue Rewarded*, vol. 4 (1742; London, 1785), 626.

33. Andrew O'Malley, *Children's Literature, Popular Culture, and Robinson Crusoe* (London: Palgrave Macmillan, 2012), 31 and 30.

34. Qtd. in Pickering, *John Locke and Children's Books in Eighteenth-Century England* (Knoxville: University of Tennessee Press, 1981), 195.

35. J. H. Plumb, "The New World of Children in Eighteenth-Century Britain," *Past and Present* 67 (1975): 83. James Janeway's 1672 *A Token for Children: Being an Exact Account of the Conversion, Holy and Exemplary Lives, and Joyful Deaths of Several Young Children* was reprinted throughout the nineteenth century. For the comfort children might take from faith even in death, see Newton, *Sick Child*, 190–219, passim.

36. Robert Shoemaker, *Gender in English Society 1650–1850: The Emergence of Separate Spheres?* (London: Longman, 1998), 131.

37. KJV. Worth noting is the sympathy Fenn has for the reality of boys' lives in comparison to less secular work from earlier in the century like Abraham Chear's *A Looking Glass for Children* (London, 1708), which asks, "What are the Toyes, or Wanton Boyes / to an immortal Spirit?" 30.

38. Mavis Reimer argues, "After *Tom Brown's Schooldays* [1857], the main tradition of boys' school stories clearly functioned to create the gendered masculine subject, a subject closely connected to national and imperial imaginaries." Reimer, "Traditions of the School Story," 216. Fenn is still more concerned with the individual boy, his conduct, and his soul. The parental division of work along gendered lines, along with character-building effects (and those threats—or "temptations"—that remain unspoken) are all present in Tom Brown's father, the Squire's, internal monologue upon sending his son to school: "What is he sent to school for? Well, partly because he wanted so to go. If he'll only turn out a brave, helpful, truth-telling Englishman, and a gentleman, and a Christian, that's all I want." Thomas Hughes, *Tom Brown's School Days* (London: Harper and Brothers, 1911), chap. 4.

39. John Newbery, *A Little Pretty Pocket-Book . . . A New Attempt to Teach Children the Use of the English Alphabet, by Way of Diversion* (1744; London, 1770), 71.

40. Rothery and French, *Making Men*, 17.

41. The boys are tested on their knowledge of the gospels at Sprightly's school. William Van Reyk observes that "from the mid-1770s concerns began to emerge over whether the Classics were being taught to public school boys at the expense of religion, and it was suggested by many that to place a heavy emphasis on the Classics was to promote heathen morality." Van Reyk, "Educating Christian Men in the Eighteenth and Early Nineteenth Centuries: Public-School and Oxbridge Ideals," *Journal for Eighteenth-Century Studies* 32, no. 3 (2009): 431. See too Isabel Rivers, "Religion and Literature," in *The New Cambridge History of English Literature, 1660–1780*, ed. John Richetti (Cambridge: Cambridge University Press, 2005), 445–470.

42. Pope, *An Essay on Man*, in *Shorter Twickenham*, 501–547, ep. II, 217–220.

43. Grenby, *Child Reader*, 93.

44. Grenby, *Child Reader*, 93.

45. William Shakespeare, *As You Like It*, ed. Juliet Dusinberre, Arden Shakespeare (London: Thomson Learning, 2006), II.Iv.139–166.

46. Henry Fielding, *The History of Tom Jones, a Foundling*, vol. 1 (London, 1775), 289. Johnson includes in the *Dictionary* (1773), among other words with "boy" at their root, the adjective "'boyblind': Undiscerning, like a boy."

47. Mary Wollstonecraft, *A Vindication of the Rights of Woman*, ed. Eileen Hunt Botting (1792; New Haven, CT: Yale University Press, 2014), 190.

48. Two years after *School Dialogues* appeared Fenn founded a Sunday school in Dereham.

49. Tribunella, "Boyhood," 22.

50. William Godwin, "Private Education," essay 7 in *The Enquirer, Reflections on Education, Manners, and Literature* (London, 1797), 59.

51. John Tosh, *Manliness and Masculinities in Nineteenth-Century Britain: Essays on Gender, Family, and Empire* (London: Pearson Longman, 2005), 112.

52. Juliana Mary Buxton to John Jacob Buxton, April 23, 1801, qtd. in Rothery and French, *Making Men*, 45.

53. Mary Astell, *Some Reflections upon Marriage*, 2nd ed. (1700; London, 1703), 63–64. "Trains" means entrapments, snares.

54. Jonathan Swift, "An Essay on Modern Education," *The Intelligencer* 9 (1732), in *Miscellanies in Prose and Verse by Dr. Swift*, vol. 7 (London, 1742), 26. Italics indicate what Johnson quotes as his example in the *Dictionary* (1755).

55. Locke, *Some Thoughts Concerning Education*, §52.

56. Johnson told Boswell he was grateful to a schoolmaster who "beat a boy equally for not knowing a thing, as for neglecting to know it." In fact, "Johnson, upon all occasions, expressed his approbation of enforcing instruction by means of the rod." Boswell, *Life of Johnson*, 33. Louise Joy emphasizes, "Centuries' worth of moral and theological thought reinforced the attitude, enshrined in scripture, that 'He that spareth the rod, hateth his son; but he that loveth him, chasteneth him betimes' (Proverbs, XIII, 24), and both education theory and practice largely reified it." Joy, "Eighteenth-Century Children's Poetry and the Complexity of the Child's Mind," in *Literary Cultures and Eighteenth-Century Childhoods*, ed. Andrew O'Malley (New York: Palgrave Macmillan, 2018), 124.

57. Locke, *Some Thoughts Concerning Education*, §78.

58. A. S. Turberville, *English Men and Manners in the Eighteenth Century* (New York: Oxford University Press, 1957), qtd. in Henry L. Fulton, "Private Tutoring in Scotland: The Example of Mure of Dalwell," *Eighteenth-Century Life* 27, no. 3 (2003): 54. There had been six riots at Eton and five at Rugby prior to *School Dialogues*. Still ahead would be the 1793

"Great Rebellion at Winchester" and the 1797 rebellion at Rugby, at which the Riot Act was read. Rothery and French, *Making Men*, 15–16. In *Eminent Victorians* (New York: Random House, 1933), Lytton Strachey called the public school "a system of anarchy tempered by despotism . . . a life in which licensed barbarism was mingled with the daily and hourly study of the niceties of Ovidian verse" (204).

59. Teresa Michals, *Books for Children, Books for Adults: Age and the Novel from Defoe to James* (Cambridge: Cambridge University Press, 2014), 69.

60. Pope, "Epistle to Arbuthnot," in *Shorter Twickenham*, 599, line 40.

61. Reimer, "Traditions of the School Story," 211.

62. Richard Corbould and Samuel Springsguth, *Juvenile Philosophy; Containing Amusing and Instructive Discourses on Hogarth's Prints . . . Designed to Enlarge the Understandings of Youth, and to Impress Them at an Early Period with Just and Liberal Conceptions* (London, 1801), 64–65.

63. Sophia Woodley, "'Oh Miserable and Most Ruinous Measure': The Debate between Private and Public Education in Britain, 1760–1800," in *Educating the Child in Enlightenment Britain: Beliefs, Cultures, Practices*, ed. Mary Hilton and Jill Shefrin (Farnham: Ashgate, 2009), 21.

64. Rebecca Davies, *Written Maternal Authority and Eighteenth-Century Education in Britain: Educating by the Book* (Farnham: Ashgate, 2014), 7.

65. Foyster, *Manhood in Early Modern England*, 31.

66. Toni Bowers, "'A Point of Conscience': Breastfeeding and Maternal Authority in Pamela," in *Inventing Maternity: Politics, Science, and Literature, 1650–1865*, ed. Susan C. Greenfield and Carol Barash (Lexington: University Press of Kentucky, 1999), 14.

67. Carol Percy, "Disciplining Women? Grammar, Gender, and Leisure in the Works of Ellenor Fenn (1743–1813)," *Historiographia Linguistica* 33, no. 1–2 (2006): 109–137.

68. For a discussion of the same dual audience of a book at the end of World War I, see Lavoie, "*A Little Book for Mothers and Sons* (1919): A Church Army Book of Days for Boys and the Women Who Raised Them," *First World War Studies* 9, no. 1 (2018): 57–71.

69. One of William Hogarth's prints employs Solomon, Proverbs 10:1: "A wise son maketh a glad father: but a foolish son is the heaviness of his mother" (KJV).

70. Sarah Rangaratnam notes, "Each chapter [of *School Occurrences*] laments the results of one of the girls being either motherless, or having had an incompetent mother, and shows how the schoolmistress, Mrs. Teachwell, attempts to repair the damage done. . . . Ineffective parenting in early childhood has led to selfishness, impertinence, negativity, vanity." Rangaratnam, "Girls' Voices of the Eighteenth Century: The Development of a Genre for Young Female Readers, 1740–1800" (PhD diss., Wilfred Laurier University, 2018), 143.

71. See Anthony Fletcher's chapter on "Boyhood" in *Growing Up in England*, 12–22.

72. Sir Charles Grandison acknowledges, "My mother was an excellent woman: she had instilled into my earliest youth, almost inclined from infancy, notions of moral rectitude, and the first principles of Christianity; now rather ridiculed than inculcated in our youth of condition." Young Charles's mother's early death proves how important this instilling of principles "almost from infancy" was. Note the class bias implying that children "of condition" are more at risk of being overindulged. Samuel Richardson, *The History of Sir Charles Grandison*, vol. 2, in *The Novels of Samuel Richardson*, ed. William Lyon Phelps (New York: Croscup & Sterling, 1902), 62.

73. See too Elizabeth Segel, "'As the Twig Is Bent . . .': Gender and Childhood Reading," in *Gender and Reading: Essays on Readers, Texts and Contexts*, ed. Elizabeth Flynn and Patrocinio Schweickart (Baltimore: Johns Hopkins University Press, 1986), 171.

74. Michèle Cohen, *Fashioning Masculinity: National Identity and Language in the Eighteenth Century* (New York: Routledge, 1996), 105.

75. John Scott, *The School Boy's Sure Guide* (Edinburgh, 1774), a2.

76. Newbery, *Little Pretty Pocket-Book*, 7–8.

77. Grenby, *Child Reader*, 56.

78. O'Malley, *Children's Literature*, 25.

79. O'Malley, *Children's Literature*, 94. Authors for children such as Sarah Trimmer in *The Guardian of Education* (1802–1806) "expressed somewhat mixed feelings" about *Crusoe* as a didactic text. O'Malley, *Children's Literature*, 25. See too, however, O'Malley's interesting argument about how Robinsonades emphasized domesticity and the idea of home (and in various ways, femininity). O'Malley, *Children's Literature*, 44.

80. Anna Laetitia Barbauld would write to a friend, "You speak of beginning the education of your son. The moment he was able to form an idea his education was already begun.... This education goes on at every instant of time; it goes on *like* time; you can neither stop it nor turn its course." Barbauld, "What Is Education?," *Monthly Magazine*, March 1798, 167–171, from *Anna Laetitia Barbauld: Selected Poetry and Prose*, ed. William McCarthy and Elizabeth Kraft (Peterborough: Broadview, 2002), 321–332. Worth noting is Godwin's rueful observation: "go there; do that; read; write; rise; lie down; will perhaps forever be the language addressed to youth by age." Godwin, "Private Education," 53.

81. Rousseau, *Émile*, 79. See too Annie Smart, "'Bonnes mères qui savent penser': Motherhood and a Boy's Education in Rousseau's *Émile* and Epinay's *Letters à mon fils*," *New Perspectives on the Eighteenth Century* 3, no. 1 (Spring 2006): 21–31.

82. Isaac Watts, "Song 20," in *Divine Songs: Attempted in the Easy Language of Children* (London, 1715, lines 9–12.

83. Deborah Simonton, "Economy," in *A Cultural History of Childhood and Family in the Age of Enlightenment*, ed. Elizabeth Foyster and James Marten (London: Bloomsbury, 2014), 4:49–68 (49).

84. Joseph Addison and Richard Steele, "No. 56—Friday, May 4, 1711," *The Spectator*, from The Spectator Project: Hypermedia Research Archive of Eighteenth-Century Periodicals, Rutgers University Library, http://www2.scc.rutgers.edu/spectator/text/may1711/no56.html.

85. By 1783, few believed that cruelty to the least of God's creatures ended there. Although the practice of "stealing birds' nests was a common sport for eighteenth-century boys," it "was severely attacked within the wider context of a campaign against cruelty to animals." Anja Müller, *Framing Childhood in Eighteenth-Century English Periodicals and Prints, 1689–1789* (Surrey: Ashgate, 2009), 48.

86. Carol Percy, "Mid-century Grammars and Their Reception in the *Monthly Review* and the *Critical Review*," in *Grammars, Grammarians, and Grammar-Writing in Eighteenth-Century England*, ed. Ingrid Tieken-Boon van Ostade (Berlin: Mouton De Gruyter, 2008), 125. The model boy about whom Sprightly read in the parish registry, Jeremy Baldock, "had learned his Accidence, and great part of the Grammar Rules with such understanding, that he could almost pose any scholar" (*School Dialogues*, 1:80).

87. Two candidates were Robert Lowth, *A Short Introduction to English Grammar, with Critical Notes* (1762), and John Ash, *Grammatical Institutes; or, An Easy Introduction to Dr. Lowth's English Grammar* (1763). Lowth's popular grammar appears in Mrs. Teachwell's library in Fenn's 1784 *The Female Guardian*. Yet Karlijn Navest argues that "Fenn not only advised her young readers to read [John] Ash's grammar, but ... made considerable use of it while writing her own treatises on grammar." See Navest, "Ash's Grammatical Institutes and 'Mrs. Teachwell's Library for Young Ladies,'" in *Perspective on*

Prescriptivism, ed. John C. Beal et al. (Berlin: Peter Lang, 2008), 60. See too Carol Percy, "Paradigms Lost: Bishop Lowth and the 'Poetic Dialect' in His English Grammar," *Neophilologus* 81 (1997): 129–144.

88. Janet Sorenson, *The Grammar of Empire in Eighteenth-Century British Writing* (Cambridge: Cambridge University Press, 2000), 88.

89. Sorenson, *Grammar of Empire*, 65.

90. *The Child's Grammar* (1799) was "designed to enable ladies who may not have attended to the subject themselves to instruct their children." Fenn [pseud. Mrs. Lovechild], *The Child's Grammar* (Dublin, 1799), 26n.

91. Carol Percy, "'Nice' Grammarians: Making Distinctions of Class, Character and Gender In Women's Fiction, 1750–1830," *Women's Writing* 23, no. 1 (2006): 25.

92. David Stoker observes that Fenn was not well known as an author in her own lifetime, as her writings appeared either anonymously or pseudonymously. Stoker, "Ellenor Fenn as 'Mrs. Teachwell' and 'Mrs. Lovechild,'" 817.

93. Mitzi Myers, "Impeccable Governesses, Rational Dames, and Moral Mothers: Mary Wollstonecraft and the Female Tradition in Georgian Children's Books," *Children's Literature* 14, no. 1 (1986): 37. Mary Barber, whose poem about breeching on behalf of her son we saw in the first chapter, certainly used her title as mother of a boy to further her writing aims.

94. Fenn [pseud. Mrs. Lovechild], *The Rational Dame; or, Hints towards Supplying Prattle for Children* (London, [1790?]), vii, ix.

95. Both Percy and Immel have discussed Fenn's "Set of Toys," her "Grammar Boxes," wherein "each box contained cards bearing both text and pictures, and the whole was accompanied by a manual, *The Art of Teaching in Sport* [1784/85]." See Percy, "Disciplining Women?," 113 and 119, and Immel, "'Mistress of Infantine Language,'" 215–228. See too Jill Shefrin, "'Make It a Pleasure and Not a Task': Educational Games for Children in Georgian England," *Princeton University Library Chronicle* 60, no. 2 (Winter 1999): 64–65.

96. Davies, *Written Maternal Authority*, 45. In addition to their nephew William, the Fenns adopted and raise an orphaned heiress, Miss Andrews.

97. Fenn [pseud. Mrs. Lovechild], *Rational Sports . . . Designed as a Hint to Mothers How They May Inform the Minds of Their Little People Respecting the Objects with Which They Are Surrounded* (London, 1783), ix–x. The "real mother" here addressed is contrasted with "ladies who leave their offspring to imbibe the follies of the kitchen" (xvi–xvii); however, it is also evident that the "real mother" is contrasted at least in part with the author who has leisure to write and so provide the good—and busy—biological mother with a service.

98. Fenn [pseud. Mrs. Lovechild], *The Art of Teaching in Sport; Designed as a Prelude to a Set of Toys, for Enabling Ladies to Instill the Rudiments of Spelling, Reading, Grammar, and Arithmetic, under the Idea of Amusement* (London, [1796?]), 6.

99. Percy, "Disciplining Women?," 120ff. Taylor Walle notes "most of [Fenn's] books for children double as manuals for young children." See Walle, "'These Gentlemen's ill Treatment of our Mother Tongue': Female Grammarians and the Power of the Vernacular," *Tulsa Studies in Women's Literature* 35, no 1. (2017): 29.

100. Clark, *Regendering the School Story*, 69.

101. Percy, "Disciplining Women?," 120, passim.

102. Wayne C. Booth, *The Rhetoric of Fiction*, 2nd ed. (Chicago: University of Chicago Press, 1983), 397–398.

103. Wollstonecraft, *Vindication of the Rights of Women*, 116.

104. Susan Staves, *A Literary History of Women's Writing in Britain, 1660–1789* (Cambridge: Cambridge University Press, 2006), 249.

105. Myers, "Impeccable Governesses," 33. Davies argues that such maternal performativity could be demonstrably superior to maternity itself: of Sarah Fielding's novel *The Governess* (1749), Davies argues, "As a woman writing for children, Fielding takes the place of maternal governess in relation to child readers. She is, however, removed from the humiliating aspects of that servile role through her physical distance from her readership." Davies, *Written Maternal Authority*, 44. Fenn does not suggest any "humiliating aspects" of the mother's role in the *School Dialogues*, though the mother she addresses is without leisure time.

106. Walle, "'These Gentlemen's Ill Treatment,'" 29.

107. "Configuring themselves as the nation's teachers, they had reached out from the literary world to construct a variety of intellectual and pedagogical practices, propagating them through educational treatises, conduct books, popular guides, stories and handbooks." Hilton, *Women and the Shaping of the Nation's Young*, 2. See too Norma Clarke, "'That Cursed Barbauld Crew': Women Writers and Writing for Children in the Late Eighteenth Century," in *Opening the Nursery Door: Reading, Writing, and Childhood 1600–1900*, ed. Mary Hilton, Morag Styles, and Victor Watson (New York: Routledge, 2012), 91, passim.

108. Perry Nodelman, "Children's Literature as Women's Writing," *Children's Literature Association Quarterly* 13, no. 1 (1988): 32. For scholarship on collaborative works, especially between male authors and boys, in the nineteenth century, see Victoria Ford Smith's excellent *Between Generations: Collaborative Authorship in the Golden Age of Children's Literature* (Jackson: University Press of Mississippi, 2017).

109. Nodelman, "Children's Literature as Women's Writing," 32.

110. For example, Michel Foucault called "the sex of the schoolboy" "a public problem" in the eighteenth century. Foucault, *Discipline and Punish: The Birth of the Prison* (1977; New York: Vintage, 1995), 28.

111. Kristina Straub, "Men from Boys: Cibber, Pope, and the Schoolboy," *Eighteenth Century* 32, no. 3 (1991): 219–220.

112. Straub, "Men from Boys," 219, 232.

113. Backscheider, *Revising Women*, 7.

114. Terry Eagleton, *Literary Theory: An Introduction* (Minneapolis: University of Minnesota Press, 2008), 179.

115. *OED*, 3rd ed., s.v. "rhetorical *adj.*" (3), https://www.oed.com/view/Entry/165181.

116. Jackie Horne notes that "Greek and Roman mythology, and exemplary biography such as Plutarch's Lives of the Greeks and Romans, would have been familiar to many upper-class women, who could read such works in translation." Horne, *History and the Construction of the Child*, 221n. In the opening pages of *School Dialogues*, Fenn also quotes John Hoole's translation of Tasso's *Jerusalem Delivered* (1763) as well as Ramsay's *Life of Cyrus* (1728).

117. *OED*, 3rd ed., s.v. "rhetorical, *adj.*" (3).

118. This reading of Fenn is further complicated by what Heather Meek sees as a tension between "the emerging elevation of the 'natural mother'" whom "writers of conduct and medical manuals typically defined ... as nurturing, self-sacrificing, domestic, and committed utterly to her children," and the opposite—"the unnatural mother ... who assumed qualities of bodily excess and emotional changeability more consistent with the figure of the hysteric." See Meek, "Motherhood, Hysteria, and the Eighteenth-Century Woman Writer," in *Secrets of Generation: Reproduction in the Long Eighteenth Century*, ed. Raymond Stephanson and Darren Wagner (Toronto: University of Toronto Press, 2015), 238.

119. Fenn [pseud. Mrs. Teachwell], *School Occurrences: Supposed to Have Arisen among a Set of Young Ladies* (London, [1790?]), v–vi.

120. Percy, "Disciplining Women?," 135.
121. Park, *Self and It*, 164.
122. Park, *Self and It*, 173.
123. *OED*, 3rd, ed., s.v. "puppet, *n*.", https://www.oed.com/view/Entry/238792.
124. Richardson, *Pamela*, 607. Nevertheless, we have seen Pamela manage to write a collection of "nursery tales" and "stories" for her children. Richardson, *Pamela*, 633 and 626. See Julia Briggs's discussion of Pamela and Locke in "'Delightful Task!' Women, Children, and Reading in the Mid-Eighteenth Century," in *Culturing the Child, 1690–1914: Essays in Memory of Mitzi Myers*, ed. Donelle Ruwe (Toronto: Scarecrow Press, 2005), 73–75. Rebecca Davies, however, argues Pamela's "role as a mother merely involves passing knowledge [learned from her husband] into the receptive, rational vessel that is a *male* child's mind." Davies, *Written Maternal Authority*, 30.
125. Plutarch, *Lacaenarum Apophthegmata* [*Sayings of the Spartan Women*], *Moralia*, vol. 3, trans. Frank Cole Babbitt, Loeb Classical Library (Cambridge, MA: Harvard University Press, 1931), 3.5. See also Magdalena Myszkowska-Kaszuba, "The Only Women That Are Mothers of Men. Plutarch's Creation of the Spartan Mother," *Graeco-Latina Brunensia* 19, no. 1 (2014): 80. Spartan mothers were notorious for being "heartless."
126. Thomas A. King, *The Gendering of Men, 1600–1750*, vol. 1: *The English Phallus* (Madison: University of Wisconsin Press, 2004), 29.
127. James Janeway began his address to "Parents, School-Masters, and School-Mistresses" by drawing on the same myth: "I have often thought that Christ speaks to you as Pharaoh's daughter did to Moses' mother: Take this child and nurse it for me." Janeway, *A Token for Children: Being an Exact Account of the Conversion, Holy and Exemplary Lives, and Joyful Deaths of Several Young Children* (London, 1763), n.p.
128. Seventy-three years later, Hughes was no more direct in *Tom Brown's Schooldays*, when Tom's father wonders to himself: "Shall I go into the sort of temptations he'll meet with? No, I can't do that. Never do for an old fellow to go into such things with a boy. He won't understand me. Do him more harm than good, ten to one." As regards at least intergenerational sexuality involving schoolboys, Frances H. I. Henry has discussed how cases of what Lord Byron called "the crime not to be named among Christians" led to convictions: "An anonymous press campaign towards the end of November [1784]" was directed at William Beckford, for example, with "the tea-tables . . . full of the detection of B—kf—d in a scandalous affair with a [seventeen-year-old] boy at Mary[le]bone School. It is remarkable how many detections of this sort have happened of late" (anon agent to Lord Hardwicke). Elizabeth Carter and Elizabeth Montagu shared details of Beckford's "horrid behaviour." Henry, "Love, Sex, and the Noose: The Emotions of Sodomy in 18th Century England" (PhD diss., University of Western Ontario, 2019), 936–997. This case from the same year that *School Dialogues* appeared demonstrates the knowledge of the existence of sodomy involving schoolboys, including among the Bluestockings.
129. The late nineteenth century produced books for mothers not intended for childish eyes. One of these was Ellice Hopkins's critique of boarding schools, instructing women to advise their husbands to protect their sons from what they had suffered as schoolboys themselves. Hopkins delineated dramatically between the sexes, stating "women have to do with the fountain of sweet waters, clear as crystal, that flows from the throne of God; not with the sewers that flow from the foul imaginations and actions of men." Hopkins, *The Power of Womanhood; or, Mothers and Sons* (1899; New York: E. P. Dutton, 1901), 10.
130. Locke, *Some Thoughts Concerning Education*, §70.

CHAPTER 3 — THE BOY IN THE MACHINE

1. *OED*, 3rd ed., s.v. "manikin, *n.* and *adj.*" (1.a.), last modified September 2000, https://www.oed.com/view/Entry/113512.

2. Hilton, *Women and the Shaping of the Nation's Young*, 117.

3. Arriving in Paris in 1775 from his hometown of La Chaux-de-Fonds, the clockmaker in 1776 set up a workshop in London, where he entered into business with James Cox. The best account of Jaquet-Droz's career and the contents of his exhibit is in Marcia Pointon's *Brilliant Effects: A Cultural History of Gem Stones and Jewellery* (New Haven, CT: Yale University Press, 2009). See too Louis Sandoz, *Voyage de Pierre Jaquet-Droz à la cour du Roi d'Espagne, 1758–1759: d'après le Journal d'Abraham Louis Sandoz, son beau-père* (Geneva: Editions de la Baconnière, 1982).

4. This piece has been lost. Pointon reproduces a rare contemporary print of it in *Brilliant Effects*, 222.

5. The mechanism achieves what Simon Schaffer calls "materialized memory." Schaffer, *Mechanical Marvels: Clockwork Dreams*, directed by Nic Stacey (BBC Four, June 2013). A cam is "a projecting part of a wheel or other revolving piece of machinery, adapted to impart an alternating or variable motion of any kind to another piece pressing against it, by sliding or rolling contact. Much used in machines in which a uniform revolving motion is employed to actuate any kind of non-uniform, alternating, elliptical, or rectilineal movement." *OED*, s.v. "cam, *n.1*," first published 1888.

6. Pointon says that "the scribe took about four years to build." Four hours are required to program the automaton. Pointon, *Brilliant Effects*, 234.

7. See the beautifully photographed book *Jaquet-Droz* by Manuel Emch (New York: Assouline, 2007).

8. Alex Wetmore, *Men of Feeling in Eighteenth-Century Literature: Touching Fiction* (London: Palgrave Macmillan, 2013), 71.

9. Thomas Hobbes, *Leviathan* (1651; London, 1668), xxxvii.

10. Julien Offray de La Mettrie, *Man a Machine [L'Homme Machine]. Wherein the Several Systems of Philosophers, in Respect to the Soul of Man, Are Examin'd ... and a Full Detail Is Given of the Several Springs Which Move the Human Machine.*, 2nd ed. (1748; London, 1850), 11. For a useful synopsis of these debates in the seventeenth century, see chap. 3, "The Man-Machine in the World-Machine," in Minsoo Kang, *Sublime Dreams of Living Machines: The Automaton in the European Imagination* (Cambridge, MA: Harvard University Press, 2011), 103–145.

11. Kang, *Sublime Dreams*, 174. Adelheid Voskuhl explores contemporary descriptions of the Jaquet-Droz automata in calendars, almanacs, and journals. See Voskuhl, "Motions and Passions: Music-Playing Women Automata and the Culture of Affect in Late Eighteenth-Century Germany," in *Genesis Redux: Essays in the History and Philosophy of Artificial Life*, ed. Jessica Riskin (Chicago: University of Chicago Press, 2007), 303–305.

12. William Coxe, *Sketches of the Natural, Civil, and Political State of Swisserland* (London, 1779), 110. These automata became common as a way of insulting people: "Jaquet-Droz who has made a man of paste-board that plays tunes on a flute, would have made just such another actor," wrote one drama critic. See *Garrick in the Shades* (London, 1779), 18.

13. [William Coxe], *Observations on the Present State of Denmark, Russia, and Switzerland. In a Series of Letters* (London, 1784), 315–316.

14. Frances Burney, *Evelina; or, The History of a Young Lady's Entrance into the World* (Oxford: Oxford University Press, 2008), 77. See Julie Park's discussion of Evelina in *Self and It*, chap. 4, 123–160.

15. Barbara Benedict argues that in the long eighteenth century "the 'habit of curiosity,' collecting, is seen to demonstrate either the tasteful uses of wealth or the tasteless abuses of learning. It is wonder or it is skepticism." Benedict, "The 'Curious Attitude' in Eighteenth-Century Britain: Observing and Owning," *Eighteenth-Century Life* 14 (November 1990): 59–98: 59.
16. Pointon, *Brilliant Effects*, 22.
17. Schaffer, *Mechanical Marvels*. See https://www.youtube.com/watch?v=YAg66jrvpHA.
18. Schaffer, *Mechanical Marvels*, emphasis mine.
19. Bill Brown, "Thing Theory," *Critical Inquiry* 28, no. 1 (October 1, 2001): 3.
20. Chloe Wigston Smith examines *It* narratives and trade cards to argue that "the uncanny potential of embodied arguments" was deeply worrying to consumers, such that "object narratives, read in tandem with trade cards, suggest that the growth or distance between persons and things, as opposed to their collapse into each other, constitutes a central narrative in the period's commodity culture." Smith, "Clothes without Bodies: Objects, Humans, and the Marketplace in Eighteenth-Century It-Narratives and Trade Cards," *Eighteenth-Century Fiction: Trades* 23, no. 2 (Winter 2010–2011): 349.
21. Timothy V. Kaufman-Osborn, *Creatures of Prometheus: Gender and the Politics of Technology* (Lanham, MD: Rowman & Littlefield, 1997), 1.
22. Voskuhl, "Motions and Passions," 293–320. Terry Castle notes the association between the mysterious movement of mercury, the perception of women as mercurial, and automata. Castle, *The Female Thermometer: Eighteenth-Century Culture and the Invention of the Uncanny* (Oxford: Oxford University Press, 1995), 25. See too Brandy Lain Schillace, "'Reproducing' Custom: Mechanical Habits and Female Machines in Augustan Women's Education," *Feminist Formations* 25, no. 1 (2013): 111–137.
23. M. Norton Wise, "The Gender of Automata in Victorian Britain," in Riskin, *Genesis Redux*, 163.
24. Wise, "Gender of Automata," 163.
25. Park, *Self and It*, 125.
26. Wetmore, "Sympathy Machines: Men of Feeling and the Automaton," *Eighteenth-Century Studies* 43, no. 1 (2009): 37–54.
27. Wise, "Gender of Automata," 159.
28. So too is the Draughtsman described as a two-year-old; the taller girl musician is "ten or twelve years of age." Jaquet-Droz, *A Description of Several Pieces of Mechanism, Invented by the Sieur Jaquet-Droz, of . . . Switzerland. And Which Are Now to Be Seen at the Great Room, no. 6, in King-Street, Covent-Garden* (London, 1780[?]), 2. Kara Reilly calls the musician "the ideal aristocratic eighteenth-century teenager" in *Automata and Mimesis on the Stage of Theatre History* (New York: Palgrave Macmillan, 2011), 89. Such variation illustrates the discrepancy between size, demeanor, and capability or function.
29. Pointon, *Brilliant Effects*, 234.
30. Pointon, *Brilliant Effects*, 159.
31. Schaffer, *Mechanical Marvels*.
32. Lerer, *Children's Literature*, 84.
33. Although the Jaquet-Droz men created such objects as well. See Pointon, *Brilliant Effects*, 224, and A. Chapuis and E. Droz, *Les Automates: figures Artificielle d'Hommes et d'Animaux. Histoire et Technique* (Neuchâtel: Griffon, 1949).
34. Reilly, *Automata and Mimesis*, 88.
35. Benedict notes that "unlike hostility directed toward curiosity from the traditional, religious attack on indulgence," in the period "praise for [curiosity] tends to claim its usefulness." Such usefulness makes the word "curious" "a synonym for 'scientific' or 'learned' by means of empirical study.'" See Benedict, "'Curious Attitude,'" 61.

36. Regardless, I think, of his foreign origins, his male youth is by far more prominent.

37. Aileen Douglas, *Work in Hand: Script, Print, and Writing, 1690–1840* (Oxford: Oxford University Press, 2017), 80. Jaquet-Droz belonged to that community of French Calvinists who had settled in the Neuchâtel area.

38. George Bickham, *The Universal Penman. Engrav'd by George Bickham* (London, [1733[?]–1741), 29, lines 1–6.

39. Bickham, *Universal Penman*, line 8. Valentina K. Tikoff notes, "The ability to write joined reading and needlework in much female education" is manifested in the embroidered alphabet sampler. Tikoff, "Education," in Foyster and Marten, *Cultural History of Childhood and Family*, 93.

40. Testimony to this attitude appears in Wordsworth's derisive sonnet "Illustrated Books and Newspapers," wherein "Discourse was deemed Man's noblest attribute, / And written words the glory of his hand" (lines 1–2). However, "A backward movement surely have we here, / From manhood—back to childhood; for the age—/ Back towards caverned life's first rude career (lines 12–14). William Wordsworth, "Illustrated Books and Newspapers" (1846), in *Last Poems, 1821–1850*, ed. Jared Curtis, Cornell Wordsworth (Ithaca, NY: Cornell University Press, 1999), 405–406.

41. Voskuhl, "Motions and Passions," 304.

42. Rothery and French, *Making Men*, 12–13. There is something automatic in all these steps.

43. Jaquet-Droz, *Description of Several Pieces of Mechanism*, 2.

44. That being said, Locke's sense of young minds was nuanced as well, and he never sees them as mechanical learning machines: rather, "children should not have any thing like work, or serious, laid on them; neither their minds, nor bodies will bear it. It injures their healths; and their being forced and tied down to their books in an age at enmity with all such restraint, has, I doubt not, been the reason, why a great many have hated books and learning all their lives after." Locke, *Some Thoughts Concerning Education*, §149.

45. Zakiya Hanafi, *The Monster in the Machine: Magic, Medicine, and the Marvelous in the Time of the Scientific Revolution* (Durham, NC: Duke University Press, 2000), 93.

46. Schaffer, *Mechanical Marvels*.

47. Qtd. in Park, *Self and It*, 40.

48. Jaquet-Droz, *Description of Several Pieces of Mechanism*, 2.

49. For a thumbnail sketch of reading and writing—who did and did not do each, and when—see Merry E. Weisner, *Early Modern Europe, 1450–1789*, Cambridge History of Europe (Cambridge: Cambridge University Press, 2013), 1301–1335.

50. M. H. Abrams, *The Mirror and the Lamp: Romantic Theory and the Critical Tradition* (1953; Oxford: Oxford University Press, 1994), 10, emphasis mine.

51. Marjorie Swann, *Curiosities and Texts: The Culture of Collecting in Early Modern England* (Philadelphia: University of Pennsylvania Press, 2001), 149.

52. Schaffer, *Mechanical Marvels*.

53. Douglas, *Work in Hand*, 196.

54. Landlocked Switzerland was no colonizing power; however, the spread of Jaquet-Droz timepieces and the company name—particularly with the creation of objects both useful and beautiful—is another kind of intellectual-technological imperialism, and the boyishness of *L'écrivain* is a significant part of this.

55. Rousseau, *Émile*, 37.

56. Demers, *From Instruction to Delight*, 164.

57. Demers, *From Instruction to Delight*, 165.

58. Yet Rousseau's *scène lyrique*, *Pygmalion*, based on Ovid's tale, was written in Switzerland after *Émile* was banned in France in 1762. Frederick the Great had granted Rousseau

temporary refuge in Neuchâtel, where Jaquet-Droz created his automata. See Wendy C. Nielson, "Rousseau's *Pygmalion* and Automata in the Romantic Period," in *Romanticism, Rousseau, Switzerland: New Prospects*, ed. Angela Esterhammer et al. (New York: Palgrave Macmillan, 2015), 68–83. Nielson argues both that "Rousseau's version of Ovid's tale anticipates Romantic-era scepticism towards and fascination with automata as well as animated statues and corpses" and that "for Rousseau . . . automata represented the artificial nature of society" (68, 69).

59. Pope, "Epistle to Arbuthnot," in *Shorter Twickenham*, 597–612, line 128. Pope precedes this with the image of having been "dipp'd . . . in ink," line 126.

60. Rothery and French, *Making Men*, 19.

61. Rothery and French, *Making Men*, 19.

62. Marcia Pointon notes that the eighteenth-century Swiss "economy . . . depended on the sale of small-scale precious objects throughout Europe, the Levant, India, China and Japan." Pointon, *Brilliant Effects*, 221–222. I am grateful to Jenny McKenney for her observation on the grand tour.

63. Pointon, *Brilliant Effects*, 225.

64. Susan Stewart, *On Longing: Narratives of the Miniature, the Gigantic, The Souvenir, the Collection* (Baltimore: Johns Hopkins University Press, 1984), 155.

65. Lisha Pace, "Pierre Jaquet-Droz," History-Computer, December 6, 2022, http://history-computer.com/Dreamers/Jaquet-Droz.html.

66. Schaffer, *Mechanical Marvels*.

67. Five shillings was also the fee James Cox charged for admittance to his museum. He too disallowed servants, ostensibly as a security measure.

68. Plumb, "New World of Children," 85.

69. Stewart, *On Longing*, 57.

70. Pointon, *Brilliant Effects*, 223.

71. Gillen D'Arcy Wood, "Austen's Accomplishments: Music and the Modern Heroine," in *A Companion to Jane Austen*, ed. Claudia Johnson and Clara Tuite (Hoboken, NJ: John Wiley, 2011), 366.

72. When the prince-archbishop of Salzburg commissioned an extravagant mechanical town as part of the luxury offered at Hellburn Palace, it was the oppressed salt miners who designed and constructed the exhibition wherein automata "execute their tasks perfectly, mechanically, automatically," while the "aristocratic audience watches with the most minimal of movement." Schaffer, *Mechanical Marvels*.

73. Reilly, *Automata and Mimesis*, 181. Further, the steadiness and predictability of clockwork have long been related to males: consider Alfred Crosby's reminder of the sixteenth-century contribution to warfare, for example, which "reduced foot soldiers to quanta. They, even more than the men of the Greek phalance and Roman legion, learned to perform like automata. They began to do something we have considered characteristic of soldiers ever since: to march in step." Crosby, *The Measure of Reality: Quantification in Western Europe, 1250–1600* (Cambridge: Cambridge University Press, 1997), 7.

74. Schaffer, *Mechanical Marvels*. Whereas Michel Foucault argues that with labor and incarceration "a body is docile that may be subjected, used, transformed and improved," something else again was demonstrated with the mechanical bodies of these marvelous machines: "The celebrated automata . . . were not only a way of illustrating an organism, they were also political puppets, small-scale models of power: Frederick II, the meticulous king of small machines, well-trained regiments and long exercises, was obsessed with them." Foucault, *Discipline and Punish*, 136.

75. Locke, *Some Thoughts Concerning Education*, §149.

76. The importance of these habits was entrenched already by 423 BCE when Aristophanes described "the Discipline rare which flourished in Athens of yore": "First of all the old rule was preserved in our school that 'boys should be seen and not heard.'" Aristophanes, *The Clouds*, in *Aristophanes*, vol. 1, trans. Benjamin Bickley Rogers, Loeb Classical Library (New York: Putnam & Sons, 1924), 266–403, lines 960–961.

77. Melinda Alliker Rabb, *Miniature and the English Imagination: Literature, Cognition, and Small-Scale Culture, 1650–1765* (Cambridge: Cambridge University Press, 2019), 4–5.

78. Rabb, *Miniature and the English Imagination*, 123.

79. Schaffer, *Mechanical Marvels*.

80. Kerry Mallan, "Picturing the Male," in Stephens, *Ways of Being Male*, 25.

81. Douglas, *Work in Hand*, 196.

82. Sigmund Freud, *The Uncanny*, trans. David McClintock (1919; New York: Penguin, 2003), 91. Freud of course refers to the 1816/1817 story by E. T. A. Hoffman wherein "The Sandman" steals children's eyes. See Castle's application of Freud's reading to the eighteenth century in *The Female Thermometer*, 7, 37–38, and 128, passim.

83. Hilton, *Women and the Shaping of the Nation's Young*, 116.

84. Newbery, *The Newtonian System of Philosophy . . . Collected and Methodized for the Benefit of the Youth of These Kingdoms* (London, 1761), 5.

85. Gibbon, *Miscellaneous Works*, 31; Wollstonecraft, *Vindication of the Rights of Women*, 108.

86. Gloria T. Delamar, ed., *Mother Goose: From Nursery to Literature* (New York: Universe, 2000), 175–177. A snip is a small eel, and wiggly. In 1928, an advertisement for a new line of toys for "young housewives" touted small electrical appliances with the note, "Boys always have been liberally supplied with outfits and playthings which moved and worked, and which they could use constructively." *American Home* 1 (December 1928): 227, qtd. in Carroll Pursell, *From Playgrounds to PlayStation: The Interaction of Technology and Play* (Baltimore: Johns Hopkins University Press, 2015), 82.

87. This was republished in 1805 by John Harris (Ellenor Fenn's publisher).

88. Deborah Needleman Armintor reads Fielding's miniature Tom alongside "the remarkable eighteenth-century genre of anthropomorphic dildo poetry" in *The Little Everyman: Stature and Masculinity in Eighteenth-Century English Literature* (Seattle: University of Washington Press, 2011), 80–104.

89. Newbery, *Tom Thumb's Exhibition, Being an Account of Many Valuable and Surprising Curiosities Which He Has Collected in the Course of His Travels; for the Instruction and Amusement of the British Youth* (London, 1815).

90. Nigel Wood and Matthew Grenby, "Introductory Essay," in Newbery, *Tom Thumb's Exhibition*.

91. Newbery, *Tom Thumb's Exhibition*.

92. Wood and Grenby, "Introductory Essay," and "Book Data and Essay," in *Tom Thumb's Exhibition*.

93. Kang, *Sublime Dreams*, 121. As Victoria Nelson observes, "Puppets, the less clever ancestors of automata, were themselves frequently connection to religious belief." Nelson, *The Secret Life of Puppets* (Cambridge, MA: Harvard University Press, 2003), 246. Julie Park points out that puppets were often "visual critique[s] of religious enthusiasm" in *Self and It*, 171.

94. Bruce Mazlish, "The Man-Machine and Artificial Intelligence," *Stanford Humanities Review* 4, no. 2 (1995): 21–45.

95. Mazlish, "Man-Machine."

96. Julia V. Douthwaite, *The Frankenstein of 1790 and Other Lost Chapters of Revolutionary France* (Chicago: University of Chicago Press, 2012), 68.

97. Mettrie, *Man a Machine*, 58–59.

98. "The body is that upon which language falters, and the body carries its own signs, its own signifiers, in ways that remain largely unconscious." Judith Butler, *Undoing Gender* (New York: Routledge, 2004), 198.

99. Sandra Gilbert and Susan Gubar, *The Madwoman in the Attic: The Woman Writer and the Nineteenth-Century Imagination*, 2nd ed. (1979; New Haven, CT: Yale University Press, 2000), 3.

100. Jaquet-Droz, "History" (n.d.), http://www.jaquet-droz.com/en/history.

101. Harold Bloom, *Agon: Towards a Theory of Revisionism* (Oxford: Oxford University Press, 1982), 112.

102. While acknowledging Chris Baldick's argument that Mary Shelley's creature represents the disenfranchised poor of a segmented nation more than a critique of science, Kang argues in *Sublime Dreams* that the novel "also points to the dark side of Romantic science by imagining an uncanny event that occurs as a result of crossing the boundary between the animate and the inanimate" (219). See Baldick, *In Frankenstein's Shadow: Myth, Monstrosity, and Nineteenth-Century Writing* (Oxford: Clarendon, 1987), 33–35.

103. Félix Vicq d'Azyr, *Discours sur l'Anatomie et de la physiologie avec des planche coloriées représentant au naturel les divers organs de l'hommes et des animaux* (Paris: l'Imprimerie de France, F.A. Didot l'ainé, 1786), 1.

104. Other phrases he has been programmed to write include "Je pense donc Je suis" and "Bienvenue a Neuchâtel." Pointon, *Brilliant Effects*, 234.

105. Judith Butler, *Gender Trouble* (New York: Routledge, 1990), 145.

106. Kaufman-Osborn, *Creatures of Prometheus*, 49.

107. Reilly, *Automata and Mimesis*, 181; William Paley, *Natural Theology of Evidences of the Existence and Attributes of the Deity* (Philadelphia, 1802).

108. Dominic Green, "Towards the Best of All Possible Worlds," *Spectator*, no. 10 (September 2016).

109. Victoria Nelson has a much different reading of automata in the era: "Understanding the disguises of the supernatural in Western culture after the year 1700 means looking most of all at the larger idea of the machine and the mechanical—of which category human automation is only a single example, but a very crucial one." For Nelson, then, automata represent "historical transfer under way in which ideas about the transcendental soul attached to the human simulacrum were shifting from the context of the sacred into secular culture." Nelson, *Secret Life of Puppets*, 58 and 60. At the same time, Terry Castle argues, "It is difficult to avoid the conclusion that it was during the eighteenth century, with its confident rejection of transcendental exploration, compulsive quest for systemic knowledge, and self-conscious valorization of 'reason' over 'superstition,' that human beings first experience that encompassing sense of strangeness and unease Freud finds so characteristic of modern life." Castle posits that "the eighteenth-century invention of the automaton was also (in the most obvious sense) an 'invention' of the uncanny." Castle, *Female Thermometer*, 10–11.

110. Dorothy Kilner, *Letters from a Mother to Her Children, on Various Important Subjects*, vol. 1 (London, [1780?]), 28. Related to Kilner's explanation is another uncanny boy who was also more (and other) than a boy—Christ.

111. There were hoaxes perpetrated with so-called automata as well, most infamous of which is perhaps the Mechanical Turk, or Automatic Chess-player, unveiled in 1770 by Hungarian Wolfgang von Kempelen. It was debunked.

112. Richard Steele, "No. 155—Tuesday, August 28, 1711," *The Spectator*, The Spectator Project: A Hypermedia Research Archive of Eighteenth-Century Periodicals, Rutgers University Library, http://www2.scc.rutgers.edu/spectator/text/august1711/no155.html.

113. Zipes, *Sticks and Stones*, xi.

114. Michael Polanyi, *Personal Knowledge: Towards a Post-critical Philosophy* (1968; Sussex: Psychology Press, 1998), 61.

115. Immanuel Kant, *Prolegomena to Any Future Metaphysics*, trans. Paul Carus, 3rd ed. (1783; Chicago: Open Court, 1906), §32, https://www.gutenberg.org/files/52821/52821-h/52821-h.htm.

116. Anna Panszczyk, "The 'Becoming' of Pinocchio: The Liminal Nature of Collodi's Boy-Toy," *Children's Literature* 44, no. 1 (2016): 192.

117. Eric Tribunella notes that whereas "boy" has been used for far longer, the word "boyhood" became widely employed only in nineteenth-century children's literature. Tribunella, "Boyhood," 21.

118. Samuel Pepys, "Monday, Sept 28, 1668," in *The Diary of Samuel Pepys*, vol. 9, ed. Robert Latham and William Matthews (Berkeley: University of California Press, 2000), 313.

CHAPTER 4 — THE BOY IN THE CHIMNEY

1. Payne, "Children of the Poor," 13.

2. Mary Abbott, "Life Cycle," in Foyster and Marten, *Cultural History of Childhood and Family*, 113.

3. Robert Holden, *Orphans of History: The Forgotten Children of the First Fleet* (Melbourne: Text, 2000), 178.

4. Samuel Pepys, *The Shorter Pepys*, ed. Robert Latham (London: Penguin, 1985), 666.

5. Benita Cullingford, *British Chimney Sweeps: Five Centuries of Chimney Sweeping* (Lewes, DE: Guild, 2000), 18.

6. Tim Fulford, "A Romantic Technologist and Britain's Little Black Boys," *Wordsworth Circle* 33, no. 1 (2002): 36–42.

7. Other methods proposed for cleaning chimneys along with prizes offered for the invention of a new system met with resistance, as when House of Commons member Mr. Ommaney in 1817 "pointed out that if machinery supplanted boys, the boys would fall back on their parish for relief, and the poor-rates would soar and render the tax-payers indignant." George L. Phillips, "The Abolition of Climbing Boys," *American Journal of Economics and Sociology* 9, no. 4 (1950): 454. Girls only rarely did this work.

8. Emma L. Greenwood, "Work, Identity and Letterpress Printers in Britain, 1750–1850" (PhD diss., University of Manchester, 2015), 108. Ilana Krausman Ben-Amos notes that "age of entry into apprenticeship in provincial towns was probably lower than in London's largest companies"; however, Ben-Amos does not address the specific situation of chimney sweeps in *Adolescence and Youth in Early Modern England* (New Haven, CT: Yale University Press, 1994), 226. Over time, "Apprenticeship was less likely to involve the development of highly qualified, skilled labour power than to be the means of organizing the exploitation of young labour power." Peter Linebaugh, *The London Hanged: Crime and Civil Society in the Eighteenth Century* (London: Verso, 2006), 62. In the German States, sweeps did belong to guilds. Cullingford, *British Chimney Sweeps*, 40.

9. Charles Lamb, *The Works of Charles Lamb: To Which Are Prefixed, His Letters, and a Sketch of His Life*, vol. 2, ed. Thomas Noon Talfourd (New York: Harper & Brothers, 1838), 126.

10. Joan Lane, *Apprenticeship in England, 1600–1914* (London: UCL Press, 1996), 113.

11. Percival Pott first reported scrotal carcinoma in sweeps in 1775. See Nadia Benmoussa, John-David Rebibo, Patrick Conan, and Philippe Charlier, "Chimney-Sweeps' Cancer—Early Proof of Environmentally Driven Tumourigenicity," *Lancet: Perspectives, History of Medicine* 20, no. 3 (2019). K. H. Strange lists a number of reports at the beginning

of the nineteenth century, with details that speak to cruelty and sadism directed regularly at apprentices by adults who felt they "had a right to do as they pleased" with the children they had purchased. See Strange, *The Climbing Boys: A Study of Sweeps' Apprentices, 1773–1875* (London: Allison and Busby, 1982), 21–23, passim.

12. Simon Dickie, *Cruelty and Laughter: Forgotten Comic Literature and the Unsentimental Eighteenth Century* (Chicago: Chicago University Press, 2011), 96.

13. Tim Hitchcock, *Down and Out in Eighteenth-Century London* (London: Hambledon Continuum, 2004), 196 and 114. See too Kevin Siena's recent *Rotten Bodies: Class and Contagion in Eighteenth-Century Britain* (New Haven, CT: Yale University Press, 2019). Siena addresses the legacy of seventeenth-century plague(s) in Britain, particularly the pervasive fear of the poor as contagious, which makes the visibility of the climbing boy—scarred, burnt, and besmeared—of special interest.

14. Peter Ackroyd, *London: The Biography* (London: Vintage, 2001), 215.

15. Claire Lamont provides a useful synopsis of the drawn-out movement to outlaw use of children to sweep chimneys, and activism undertaken to hurry this movement along. Lamont, "Blake, Lamb and the Chimney-Sweepers," *Charles Lamb Bulletin* 76 (1991): 109–119. See too Niels van Manen's "The Regulation of Chimney Sweep Apprentices, 1770–1840," in *Childhood and Child Labour in Industrial England: Diversity and Agency, 1750–1914*, ed. Nigel Goose and Katrina Honeyman (Farnham: Ashgate, 2013), 97–114.

16. Coal was mined as early as the fifteenth century. By 1700 five-sixths of the world's coal was mined in Britain, much of it by women and children. See Jane Humphries, *Childhood and Child Labour in the British Industrial Revolution* (Cambridge: Cambridge University Press, 2010), 146–155.

17. Ben-Amos, *Adolescence and Youth*, 40–44. As Deborah Simonton reminds us, "children worked long hours in difficult conditions both before and after industrialization," in Simonton, "Economy," 50.

18. See chap. 5, "Children, Philanthropy, and the State in Europe, 1500–1860," in Hugh Cunningham, *Children and Childhood in Western Society since 1500* (New York: Routledge, 2021), 80–113, passim.

19. Horne, *History and the Construction of the Child*, 8.

20. Lane, *Apprenticeship in England*, 113. Jane Humphries points out that chimney sweeping was "widely publicized but numerically less important" than other trades, particularly factory work. Humphries, *Childhood and Child Labour*, 212. See too Katrina Honeyman, *Child Workers in England, 1780–1820* (Farnham: Ashgate, 2007).

21. Jonas Hanway, *The State of Chimney-Sweepers' Young Apprentices* (London, 1773), and Hanway, *The State of Master Chimney-Sweepers, and Their Journeymen; Particularly of the Distressed Boys, Apprentices, Who Are Daily Seen in the Streets of These Cities Staggering under a Load of Misery* (London, 1779). The Chimney Sweeper's Act, passed in 1788, decreed that no child under eight be sent out to work, along with other assurances, although the act was not heeded; in 1834 an act set fourteen as the minimum age for sweeps, with the same results. The seventh Earl of Shaftesbury (1801–1885) campaigned tirelessly for both the abolition of slavery and the passing of the Chimney Sweepers and Chimney Regulations Act in 1840 (in 1864 amended to the Chimney Sweepers Regulation Act). The act prohibited any person under twenty-one from being compelled or knowingly allowed to ascend or descend a chimney or flue for sweeping, cleaning, or scoring. This did not eliminate the trade, but it gave teeth to the fight to do so.

22. Sophie Gee, *Making Waste: Leftovers and the Eighteenth-Century Imagination* (Princeton, NJ: Princeton University Press, 2010), 108.

23. Blake, "The Chimney Sweeper," from *Songs of Innocence* (1789), lines 1–2, and "The Chimney Sweeper," from *Songs of Experience* (1794), line 7, in William Blake, *Songs of Innocence and of Experience* (1789 and 1794; Oxford: Oxford University Press, 1970).

24. Anne-Julia Zwierlein, "'Poor Negro-Girl,' 'Little Black Boy': Constructing Childhood in Eighteenth-Century Slave Narratives, Abolitionist Propaganda and Postcolonial Novels," *Zeitschrift fur Anglistik und Amerikanistik: A Quarterly of Language, Literature and Culture* 52, no. 2 (2004): 107–120.

25. Adriana Silvia Benzaquén, "World Contexts," in Foyster and Marten, *Cultural History of Childhood and Family*, 201.

26. See Lamont, "Blake, Lamb and the Chimney-Sweeper," 116.

27. Carretta has called into question the first part of Equiano's narrative, arguing he was born in South Carolina. See Carretta, *Equiano the African: Biography of a Self-Made Man* (Athens: University of Georgia Press, 2005).

28. From the preface to Olaudah Equiano, *The Life of Olaudah Equiano or Gustavus Vassa, the African* (1789; 1814; Mineola, NY: Dover, 1999), 7.

29. Gollapudi, "Personhood, Property Rights, and the Child," 40–41.

30. Fulford, "Romantic Technologist," 2.

31. James Montgomery, *The Chimney-Sweeper's Friend* (London, 1824), facsimile edition by Donald H. Reiman (New York: Garland, 1978).

32. When asked to contribute to the album, Charles Lamb replied that the Society for Ameliorating the Condition of Infant Chimney-Sweepers "have been labouring at it for these 20 Years & made few Converts. I think it was injudicious to mix stories avowedly colour'd by fiction with the sad true statements from the parliamentary records." Charles Lamb to James Montgomery, May 15, 1824, from Charles Lamb, *The Letters of Charles and Mary Lamb 1821–1842*, 2 vols., ed. E. V. Lucas (London: Methuen), 2:690–691.

33. Montgomery, *Chimney-Sweeper's Friend*, 398, lines 1–4.

34. Montgomery, *Chimney-Sweeper's Friend*, 12.

35. Fulford, "Romantic Technologist," 7.

36. Lamb, *Works of Charles Lamb*, 126; also included in Montgomery's miscellany.

37. Marcus Wood, *Slavery, Empathy, and Pornography* (Oxford: Oxford University Press, 2002), 193.

38. Anja Müller, *Framing Childhood in Eighteenth-Century English Periodicals and Prints, 1689–1789* (Surrey: Ashgate, 2009), 197.

39. Müller, *Framing Childhood*, 199.

40. Ingrid H. Tague, *Animal Companions: Pets and Social Change in Eighteenth-Century Britain* (University Park: Pennsylvania State University Press, 2015), 42. Incidentally, Samuel Johnson defines the verb "to boy" as "to act apishly, or, like a boy" in *Dictionary* (1755). David Bindman notes that "human-animal comparison . . . was a gift for caricaturists," naming Rowlandson in particular. Bindman, *Ape to Apollo: Aesthetics and the Idea of Race in the Eighteenth Century* (Ithaca, NY: Cornell University Press, 2002), 96.

41. Sorenson, *Grammar of Empire*, 37.

42. Anne Lafont, "How Skin Color Became a Racial Marker: Art Historical Perspectives on Race," *Eighteenth-Century Studies* 51, no. 1 (2017): 89–113.

43. Bindman, *Ape to Apollo*, 151.

44. Swift wrote his *Meditation* while working as secretary at the household of William Temple in Surrey. Edmund Curll pirated the essay in 1703; Swift had it printed in 1710. Robert Boyle's *Occasional Reflections upon Several Subjects* (1665) is a work that invited parody from the start by the not infrequent oddity of its "occasions." Kirsten Juhas,

"Introduction," in *A Meditation upon a Broomstick*, ed. Kirsten Juhas et al. (Münster: Ehrenpreis Centre for Swift Studies, November 2011).

45. Jonathan Swift, *A Meditation upon a Broomstick: According to the Style and Manner of the Honourable Robert Boyle's Meditations* (1703, 1710) in Rawson and Higgins, *Essential Writings of Jonathan Swift*, 159. All references are to this edition. See Valerie Rumbold's "Textual Account" of the *Meditation* in *The Cambridge Companion Edition of the Works of Jonathan Swift: Parodies, Hoaxes, Mock Treatises*, ed. Valerie Rumbold (Cambridge: Cambridge University Press, 2013), 635–639.

46. Unlike the broom Swift describes in his *Meditation*, a sweep would have used "either a flat circular brush or a brush known as a 'Turk's head,' which was short and sturdy." Cullingford, *British Chimney Sweeps*. Yet "brush" and "broom" were often interchangeable terms. One definition of "broom" is "an implement for sweeping, a besom: originally one made of twigs of broom, heather, etc., fixed to a 'stick' or handle; now the generic name for a besom of any material." *OED*, s.v. "broom, *n*." (3.a.), first published 1888. Under "brush," we find that "the *chimney-sweep's brush* and *dust brush* pass into a *besom*." *OED*, s.v. "brush, *n2*" (I.1.a.), first published 1888.

47. Christopher Fox, "Introduction," *The Cambridge Companion to Jonathan Swift*, ed. Christopher Fox (Cambridge: Cambridge University Press, 2003), 1.

48. Valerie Rumbold notes the "commonplace comparison" of the "sapless Trunk" and the worn-out man. Rumbold, "Textual Account," 13.

49. Bogel argues that Swift is always exploring "a connection between satirist and satiric object, a contamination that compromises their distinctness." Fredric V. Bogel, *The Difference Satire Makes: Rhetoric and Reading from Jonson to Byron* (Ithaca, NY: Cornell University Press, 2001), 65.

50. Michael Seidel, "Satire, Lampoon, Libel, Slander," in *The Cambridge Companion to Eighteenth-Century Literature, 1650–1750*, ed. Stephen Zwicker (Cambridge: Cambridge University Press, 1998), 55. Swift's references to "sluts," brooms, and besoms are explored in D. A. Kent's "Ubiquitous but Invisible: Female Domestic Servants in Mid-Eighteenth-Century London," *History Workshop* 28 (1989): 111–128.

51. Bogel, *Difference Satire Makes*, 115.

52. Park, *Self and It*, 3.

53. Swift, "A Description of the Morning," in Rawson and Higgins, *Essential Writings of Jonathan Swift*, 514, lines 5–8. Generally, the sprinkling of the floor involved sawdust. Swift may also have had in mind *Pilgrim's Progress* (1678): "Now, when he began to sweep, the dust began so abundantly to fly about, that Christian had almost therewith been choked. Then said the Interpreter to a damsel that stood by, Bring hither water, and sprinkle the room; the which, when she had done, it was swept and cleansed with pleasure. CHRISTIAN. Then said Christian, What means this? INTERPRETER. The Interpreter answered, This parlour is the heart of a man that was never sanctified by the sweet grace of the Gospel. The dust is his original sin, and inward corruptions, that have defiled the whole man. He that began to sweep at first is the law; but she that brought water, and did sprinkle it, is the Gospel." John Bunyan, *The Pilgrim's Progress* (1678; Oxford: Oxford University Press, 2009), 30. Swift wrote he had "been better entertained and more informed by a Chapter of *Pilgrim's Progress*, than by a long *Discourse* upon the *Will* and the *Intellect*, and *simple* or *complex Ideas*." From *A Letter to a Young Gentleman* (1720) in Rawson and Higgins, *Essential Writings of Jonathan Swift*, 251–63 (260). See also the print by Antoine Wierix (1555–1604), *The Christ Child Sweeping Monsters Out of the Believer's Heart*" (allegorical print, Wellcome Collection, London [1600?]), https://wellcomecollection.org/works/dswp5x26.

54. Leopold Damrosch, *Jonathan Swift: His Life and His World* (New Haven, CT: Yale University Press, 2013), 121.

55. Swift, "A Description of the Morning," in Rawson and Higgins, *Essential Writings of Jonathan Swift*, 515, lines 9–12.

56. See Damrosch, *Jonathan Swift*, 121. Even so, "Description of the Morning," as C. N. Manlove points out, "gives us little scope to reflect on . . . the miserable lives of servants or of the poor." Manlove, "Swift's Structures: 'A Description of the Morning' and Some Others," *Studies in English Literature, 1500–1900* 29, no. 3 (1989): 466.

57. Bogel, *Difference Satire Makes*, 106.

58. Swift, *Pamphlet Entitl'd Some Remarks on a Letter*, 393. Swift employs the pejorative use of *knave*: "a dishonest unprincipled man; a cunning unscrupulous rogue; a villain"; yet worth recalling is how class-based is the word, referring to an attendant, boy, or man. *OED*, 3rd ed., s.v. "knave, *n*." (3.a.), last updated June 2014, https://www.oed.com/view/Entry/103934.

59. Johnson, *Dictionary* (1755), s.v. "tool (2)."

60. Swift, "Description of a City Shower," in Rawson and Higgins, *Essential Writings of Jonathan Swift*, 515–516, lines 27–30.

61. Jonathan Swift, "A Letter of Advice to a Young Poet," in *The Works of Jonathan Swift . . . Containing Additional Letters, Tracts, and Poems*, vol. 9 (Edinburgh, 1824), 203.

62. Sean Shesgreen, "Swift, Reynolds, and the Lower Orders," in *Representations of Swift*, ed. Brian A. Connery (Newark: University of Delaware Press, 2002), 195. More to the point, in the dean's writing "the lower orders are treated in a spectrum of captious tones ranging from light irony to humorless savagery" (196).

63. Brian A. Connery, "Hints toward Authoritative Conversation: Swift's Dialogical Strategies in the Letters and the Life," in Connery, *Representations of Swift*, 161. We see such conflation in Swift's "On Poetry, a Rhapsody," where the poet is less qualified to "rise" than even "Beggar's Brat," "Bastard of a Pedlar Scot," or the "Boy brought up to cleaning Shoes, / The Spawn of Bridewell, or of Stews." In Rawson and Higgins, *Essential Writings of Jonathan Swift*, 647, lines 33–36.

64. Jonathan Swift, *A Meditation upon a Broomstick: According to the Style and Manner of the Honourable Robert Boyle's Meditations* (1703, 1710), in Rawson and Higgins, *Essential Writings of Jonathan Swift*, 159.

65. Carole Fabricant, *Swift's Landscape* (Baltimore: Johns Hopkins University Press, 1982), 43.

66. Fabricant, *Swift's Landscape*, 43.

67. "The Complaint," in Montgomery, *Chimney-Sweeper's Friend*, 7.

68. The boys being forced to climb naked is widely documented. See Henry Mayhew, *London Labour and the London Poor: A Cyclopaedia of the Conditions and Earnings of Those That Will Work, Those That Cannot Work, and Those That Will Not Work* (1861; Stansted: Wordsworth Press, 2008), 2:396.

69. Swift, *Gulliver's Travels*, in Rawson and Higgins, *Essential Writings of Jonathan Swift*, 311–502 (486).

70. Montgomery was to suggest as much by arguing not only the likelihood of an early death but that (even) "The gypsy may be loved, and love; / But I—but I must not." *Chimney Sweeper's Friend*, 400. With respect to the association between urban labor, ill health, and lack of sexual potency, Karen Harvey points out the extent to which eighteenth-century erotica was given a pastoral setting, to align love and sex against the strains and stains of urban life. See Harvey, *Reading Sex in the Eighteenth Century: Bodies and Gender in English Erotic Culture* (Cambridge: Cambridge University Press, 2004), 150ff.

71. See, for example, Melissa N. Stein, "Unsexing the Race: Lynching, Castration and Racial Science," in *Measuring Manhood: Race and the Science of Masculinity, 1830–1934* (Minneapolis: University of Minnesota Press, 2015), 217–250; and Paul Obiyo Mbanaso Njemanze, "Masculinity in the African Diaspora," *Journal of International Social Research* 6, no. 28 (2013): 222–227.

72. Elaine L. Robinson, *Gulliver as Slave Trader: Racism Reviled by Jonathan Swift* (Jefferson, NC: MacFarland, 2006), 58.

73. Robinson, *Gulliver as Slave Trader*, 6.

74. Jonathan Swift, "The Yahoo's Overthrow," in Rawson and Higgins, *Essential Writings of Jonathan Swift*, 659, lines 68–69.

75. Michael Seidel, "Systems Satire: Swift.com," in *The Cambridge History of English Literature, 1660–1780*, vol. 2: *Literary Genres: Adaptation and Reformation*, ed. John Richetti (Cambridge: Cambridge University Press, 2005), 235–258.

76. J. A. Richardson, *Slavery and Augustan Literature: Swift, Pope, Gay* (New York: Routledge, 2004), 137.

77. Richardson, *Slavery and Augustan Literature*, 123.

78. Richardson, *Slavery and Augustan Literature*, 136.

79. Swift, *Gulliver's Travels*, 472.

80. Vincent Carretta, *Unchained Voices: An Anthology of Black Authors in the English-Speaking World of the Eighteenth Century* (Lexington: University Press of Kentucky, 2003) 2.

81. Equiano, *Life of Olaudah Equiano*, 80 and 82.

82. See Strange, *Climbing Boys*, 21–23, passim. For the 1778 trial of a boy beaten to death by his master in Dublin, see James Kelly, "Chimney Sweeps, Climbing Boys and Child Employment in Ireland, 1775–1875," *Irish Economic and Social History Journal* 47, no. 1 (2020): 36–58.

83. John Locke, *Two Treatises of Government* (1689; London, 1821), II. §172.

84. Strange, *Climbing Boys*, 90–91.

85. Zine Magubane, *Bringing the Empire Home: Race, Class, and Gender in Britain and Colonial South Africa* (Chicago: University of Chicago Press, 2004), 103.

86. Magubane, *Bringing the Empire Home*, 104.

87. Regarding fiction produced later in the period, see Zwierlein, "'Poor Negro-Girl.'"

88. Lamb, *Works of Charles Lamb*, 126.

89. Blake, "The Chimney Sweeper," from *Songs of Innocence and of Experience*, line 1.

90. Charles Lamb, *Works of Charles Lamb*, 126.

91. Emily Cockayne, *Hubbub: Filth, Noise, and Stench in England, 1600–1770* (New Haven, CT: Yale University Press, 2007), 61.

92. Qtd. in J. B. Slagle, "Literary Activism: James Montgomery, Joanna Baillie, and the Plight of Britain's Chimney Sweeps," *Studies in Romanticism* 51, no. 1 (2012): 67. Baillie recommended "The old Scotch way of Cleaning Chimneys," with "two men, ropes, brooms, a blanket, and a long ladder." Qtd. in Slagle, "Literary Activism," 70.

93. Lamb, *Works of Charles Lamb*, 396.

94. Lamb, *Works of Charles Lamb*, 396.

95. Whether satire "was written for or against slavery," Marcus Wood sees "a position of amused detachment" in the words of Caucasian authors trying to write from *any* position about the Black body. Wood, "Black Bodies and Satiric Limits in the Long Eighteenth Century," in *The Satiric Eye: Forms of Satire in the Romantic Period*, ed. Steven Edward Jones (Basingstoke: Palgrave Macmillan, 2003), 56. See too Nicholas Hudson, "'Britons Never Will Be Slaves': National Myth, Conservatism, and the Beginnings of British Antislavery," *Eighteenth-Century Studies* 34, no. 4 (2001): 559–576.

96. See the 1798 *Encyclopedia Britannica* entry for "Negro": "Vices of the most notorious seem to be the portion of this unhappy race."

97. Ann Cline Kelly, "Swift's Explorations of Slavery in Houyhnhnmland and Ireland," *PMLA* 91, no. 5 (1976): 848.

98. John Holland, "An Appeal to the Fair Sex," from *The Chimney-Sweeper's Friend, and Climbing-Boy's Album*, arranged by James Montgomery (London, 1824), 282.

99. Roy Porter, *Flesh in the Age of Reason* (London: Allen Lane / Penguin, 2003), 51.

100. Immanuel Kant, *Grounding for the Metaphysics of Morals / On a Supposed Right to Lie Because of Philanthropic Concerns*, trans. James W. Ellington (1785; Indianapolis: Hackett, 1993), 4:439.

101. The same kind of argument regarding Swift's treatment of women (compared to their treatment by Pope) comes from Margaret Anne Doody: "The effect of Swift's humour is not to silence the woman but to force her into utterance." Doody, "Swift among the Women," *Yearbook of English Studies* 18 (1988): 72.

102. Jonathan Swift, "On the Poor Man's Contentment," in *The Prose Works of Jonathan Swift*, ed. Temple Scott (London: George Bell and Sons, 1903), 112.

103. Fulford, "Romantic Technologist," 8. See also Tim Fulford, Debbie Lee, and Peter J. Kitson, "Britain's Little Black Boys and the Technologies of Benevolence," in *Literature, Science, and Exploration in the Romantic Era: Bodies of Knowledge* (Cambridge: Cambridge University Press, 2004), 228–270, 267, passim.

104. Fulford, "Romantic Technologist," 8.

105. Swift, *Meditation upon a Broomstick*, 159.

106. Gee, *Making Waste*, 99.

107. Lamb, *Works of Charles Lamb*, 396.

108. Swift, *A Modest Proposal*, in Rawson and Higgins, *Essential Writings of Jonathan Swift*, 295–301 (295).

CHAPTER 5 — THE BOY IN THE GALLOWS

1. Arbuthnot, "Argument for Divine Providence," 188.

2. Clive Emsley, Tim Hitchcock, and Robert Shoemaker, "Historical Background—Gender in the Proceedings," in *The Proceedings of the Old Bailey: London's Central Criminal Court, 1674 to 1913*, version 7.0, https://www.oldbaileyonline.org/static/Gender.jsp.

3. See Charles and Mary Lamb's typical poem "The Butterfly," in which a brother's propensity to tear the wings off a butterfly is halted by his sister. The former chafes at the lecture but promises to "take care, / And try to be human." Qtd. in Demers, *From Instruction to Delight*, 317.

4. Tribunella, "Boyhood," 21.

5. See Simon Eliot, "The Business of Victorian Book Publishing," in *The Cambridge Companion to the Victorian Novel*, ed. Deidre David (Cambridge: Cambridge University Press, 2000), 41.

6. "Any printer hoping to use illustrations to spice up a broadside was well advised to keep a stock of images on hand, or even to acquire the stock of a late colleague." Alexandria Franklin, "Making Sense of Broadside Ballad Illustrations in the Seventeenth and Eighteenth Centuries," *Studies in Ephemera: Text and Image in Eighteenth-Century Print*, ed. Kevin D. Murphy and Sally O'Driscoll (Lewisburg, PA: Bucknell University Press, 2013), 170.

7. "Broadside on 'The Dreadful Life and Confession of a Boy Aged Twelve Years,'" Discovering Literature: Romantics and Victorians Collection Items, British Library Online, https://www.bl.uk/collection-items/broadside-the-dreadful-life-and-confession-of-a-boy-aged-twelve-years.

8. Catnach grew rich on murder reports published at his press, London's Seven Dials.

9. The Thomas Mitchel version is undated, without the woodcut, and printed by "Horsen" (although the British Library estimates 1829 for this as well). A subtitle here adds the boy "was tried on five different Indictments." See "Broadside on 'The Dreadful Life and Confession.'"

10. Gatrell points out the genre "almost always paid lip-service to conventional morality; their values were sentimental, not transgressive. The felon's repentance was central to their comment, and readers were warned against error." V.A.C. Gatrell, *The Hanging Tree: Execution and the English People 1770–1818* (Oxford: Oxford University Press, 1996), 156.

11. Tim Hitchcock, Robert Shoemaker, Sharon Howard, Jamie McLaughlin, et al., *London Lives, 1690–1800*, version 1.1, April 24, 2012, www.londonlives.org.

12. Gatrell, *Hanging Tree*, 133. At the same time, the particular *markedness* of sweeps made such boys stand out because they were known to extort money by threatening to dirty others with the soot on their bodies and clothes.

13. Daniel Defoe, *The Complete English Tradesman . . . Calculated for the Instruction of our Inland Tradesmen; and Especially of Young Beginners* (London, 1726), 20.

14. Defoe, *The Complete Family Instructor . . . with a Great Variety of Cases, Relating to the Setting Ill Examples to Children and Servants* (Liverpool, 1800), 177. Defoe argued that "men go apprentices while they are but boys; to talk to them in their first three or four years signifies nothing; they are rather to be taught submission to families, and subjection to their masters, and dutiful attendance in their shops or warehouses." *Complete English Tradesman*, 8–9. Otto Fenichel thought Defoe had "Apprentice Complex . . . a ready mode of enjoying dependence under a guise of future independence, temporary submission to the father's authority offering a means to becoming oneself a male in time." Fenichel, *The Psychoanalytic Theory of Neurosis* (1946; London: Routledge, 2017), 564 and 423.

15. Philip Rawlings, *Drunks, Whores, and Idle Apprentices* (New York: Routledge, 1992), 15.

16. Deborah Simonton, *A History of European Women's Work: 1700 to the Present* (New York: Routledge, 2002), 53.

17. Marcia Pointon, *Portrayal and the Search for Identity* (Chicago: University of Chicago Press, 2013), 77. Locke, however, directed his concern to that privileged boy subject to "great looseness, extravagancy, and debauchery which young men have run into as soon as they have been left loose from a severe and strict education into the wider world." Locke, *Some Thoughts Concerning Education*, §94.

18. Locke, *Some Thoughts Concerning Education*, §199.

19. Vincent DiGirolamo, "In Franklin's Footsteps: News Carriers and Postboys in the Revolution and Early Republic," in *Children and Youth in a New Nation*, ed. James Martin (New York: New York University Press, 2009), 50. The 1662 Act of Settlement had made poor children the responsibility of the parish where they were born.

20. DiGirolamo, "In Franklin's Footsteps," 50.

21. Samuel Richardson, *Apprentice's Vade Mecum: or, Young Man's Pocket-Companion . . . The Whole Calculated for the Mutual Ease and Benefit Both of Master and Servant; and Recommended to the Serious Consideration of All Parents, &c. Who Have Children That They Design to Put Out Apprentice* (Dublin, 1734). See too Alexander Pettit, "The Headwaters of Ooziness (Richardson the Polemicist)," in *New Contexts for Eighteenth-Century British Fiction*, ed. Christopher D. Johnson (Newark: University of Delaware Press, 2011), 74.

22. Craig Patterson, "Horrible Roberys, High-Way Men, and Murders: Defoe, Gay, Lillo, and the Popular Literature of Crime" (PhD diss., University of Toronto, 1994), 179. See too Alysa Levene, "'Honesty, Sobriety and Diligence': Master-Apprentice Relations in Eighteenth- and Nineteenth-Century England," *Social History* 33, no. 2 (2008): 183–200.

23. Emma Donoghue's wonderful novel *Slammerkin* (London: Virago, 2000) recounts a murder that took place in the Welsh Borders in 1763, where a onetime prostitute in domestic service ends up killing her mistress.

24. Patrick Wallis, Cliff Webb, and Chris Minns, "Leaving Home and Entering Service: The Age of Apprenticeship in Early Modern London," *Continuity and Change* 23, no. 3 (2010).

25. Linebaugh, *London Hanged*, 62.

26. Patterson, "Horrible Roberys," 178.

27. John Waller, *The Real Oliver Twist: Robert Blincoe—A Life That Illuminates an Age* (London: Icon Books, 2005), 63.

28. Holland, "Appeal to the Fair Sex," 282.

29. At the same time, violent crime "was notably absent from these contemporary discussions." Peter King, *Crime and Law in England, 1750–1840: Remaking Justice from the Margins* (Cambridge: Cambridge University Press, 2006), 75. See also Robert Shoemaker, "Male Honour and the Decline of Public Violence in Eighteenth-Century London," *Social History* 26, no. 2 (2001): 190–208. Shoemaker attributes a decline in homicides to a reimagining of masculinity itself as being not necessarily predicated on violence.

30. "England surpassed neighboring British, European, and American countries in the number of crimes classified as capital offenses (more than 200) and in the number of people hanged for them (7000 in London between 1770 and 1830)." Regina Hewitt, *Symbolic Interactions: Social Problems and Literary Interventions in the Works of Baillie, Scott, and Landor* (Lewisburg, PA: Bucknell University Press, 2006), 50.

31. The 1713 and 1744 acts divided vagrants into three broad classifications: "Idle and Disorderly Persons," "Rogues and Vagabonds," and "Incorrigible Rogues": "When presented at sessions, rogues and vagabonds could be re-classified as **Incorrigible Rogues** (primarily persistent and well-known offenders), and sentenced to between six months and two years further imprisonment and hard labour, and a further round of whippings. And if, having been condemned as an incorrigible rogue, the prisoner escaped, they could be transported for seven years. In practice the imposition of these punishments was markedly random." Hitchcock et al., *London Lives*, https://www.londonlives.org/static/Vagrancy.jsp.

32. Watts, "Song 20," in *Divine Songs*.

33. Foucault, *Discipline and Punish*, 123.

34. Hitchcock, *Down and Out*, 49.

35. Hitchcock, *Down and Out*, 183.

36. Hitchcock, *Down and Out*, 53. Linkboys carried flaming torches for pedestrians at night for a fee. The image on the cover of *Writing through Boyhood* is of a linkboy.

37. Hitchcock, *Down and Out*, 195.

38. See Cullingford, *British Chimney Sweeps*, 44.

39. William Tooke, Secretary for the Society for Superseding the Necessity of Climbing Boys, was interviewed by parliamentary committee in 1817:

Is there not in general a prejudice against children who have been brought up in that trade, when they have grown too big to be employed in it?
—Unquestionably; they are totally incapable, from previous habits of education or strength of body, to make themselves useful in any other vocation.
So that a boy who has outgrown his fitness for that business must be thrown upon the parish?
—Certainly.

Qtd. in Cullingford, *British Chimney Sweeps*, 174.

40. Hitchcock, *Down and Out*, 76.

41. Müller, *Framing Childhood*, 201.

42. Gatrell, *Hanging Tree*, 140. In the next century, the ballad was renamed "Sam Hall."

43. See Henry Mayhew's extensive list in *London Labour*.

44. R. Campbell, *The London Tradesman* (1747; New Abbot, UK: David & Charles, 1969), 328.

45. Müller, *Framing Childhood*, 185.

46. Müller, *Framing Childhood*, 186. Most of the boys around him are committing inhumane acts against animals. Müller does not address the child of the next verse, and at the center of Hogarth's engraving is the boy "of gentler Heart" who offers both his "Tears and Tart" to stop the cruelty being inflicted on the dog. This tearful boy is well dressed and well-off; the boy who refuses the tart in favor of exercising gleeful cruelty is ragged and poor (by his coat, a charity schoolboy of the parish of St. Giles). See Sean Shesgreen, *Engravings by Hogarth: 101 Prints* (New York: Dover, 1974).

47. Fenn, *School Dialogues*, 1:45.

48. Fenn, *School Dialogues*, 1:75. Erin Mackie traces a different aspect of the relationship between masculinity, privilege, and Restoration crime: "In extravagant fashion... the rake's masculinity asserts criminality as a status privilege." Ultimately, a "survival into late modernity of such a seemingly nostalgic and out-moded fantasy of fully licensed masculinity" shows "gender, not status, provides validation of delinquency." Mackie, "Boys Will Be Boys: Masculinity, Criminality, and the Restoration Rake," *Eighteenth Century* 26, no. 2 (2005): 132 and 145.

49. Linebaugh, *London Hanged*, 20.

50. A greater threat, then as now, was the dangerous adults—pimps and others who preyed on youth by running what Edward Gibbon Wakefield called "nurseries of crime." Wakefield, *Facts Relating to the Punishment of Death in the Metropolis* (London, 1831), 16–17.

51. Aparna Gollapudi, "Criminal Children in the Eighteenth Century and Daniel Defoe's *Colonel Jack*," *Philological Quarterly* 96, no. 1 (2017): 27–35 (30). Gollapudi's reading of Defoe's novel provides excellent background about criminal boyhood as well as nuanced analysis of Defoe's ambivalence about these boys' education, culpability, and morality.

52. In 1777, a fifteen-year-old named James Harris was hanged alongside the Reverend Dr. William Dodd. "Harris had stolen two half-guineas and some shillings from a stage coach: Dodd's forgery involved £4300." Clive Emsley, "Introduction," in *The Newgate Calendar* (Stansted, UK: Wordsworth Editions, 1997), xiv.

53. This is in keeping with trends in executions per convictions for adults. At the Old Bailey in the period 1826–1830 there were recorded 857 convictions, of which 90 percent were pardoned. Gatrell, *Hanging Tree*, appendix 2, 616.

54. Dickens's Jack Dawkins, the Artful Dodger in *Oliver Twist*, is transported for life.

55. The act "helped to give birth to a new idea in English penal methods—the idea of hard labour at home." William Branch, *The English Prison Hulks* (Chicago: Johnson, 1957), 3.

56. King, *Crime and Law in England*, 35.

57. Patterson, "Horrible Roberys," 197–198. The *Newgate Calendar* was first issued in 1773.

58. William Blackstone, *Commentaries on the Laws of England*, 4 vols. (London 1769), 4:22–23, qtd. in Gollapudi, "Criminal Children."

59. Gollapudi, "Criminal Children," 36.

60. Rousseau, *Émile*, 93. Charles Kingsley's *The Water Babies* would introduce another sweep's apprentice Tom who combined deprivation and depravity, one who "could not read nor write, and did not care to do either; and he had never washed himself, for there was no

water up the court where he lived. He had never been taught to say his prayers. He had never heard of God, or of Christ, except in words which you have never heard.... He cried when he had to climb the dark flues, rubbing his poor knees and elbows raw; and when the soot got into his eyes, which it did every day of the week; and when his master beat him, which he did every day in the week." Kingsley, *The Water Babies* (London, 1889), 1.

61. Garthine Walker's pivotal study reflects on how discourses of male and female violence were rooted in very different concepts of male and female honor. She also makes the argument that female property offenders suffered more severe sentences from the courts than scholars have assumed. Walker, *Crime, Gender and Social Order in Early Modern England*, Cambridge Studies in Early Modern British History (Cambridge: Cambridge University Press, 2003).

62. Heather Shore, *Artful Dodgers: Youth and Crime in Early Nineteenth-Century London* (Woodbridge: Royal Historical Society / Boydell Press, 1999).

63. Emma Watkins, "The Case of George Fenby," *Crime History*, June 5, 2015, https://WatkinsemmadWatkins.wordpress.com/2015/06/05/the-case-of-george-fenby/. See too Emma Watkins and Barry Godfrey, *Criminal Children: Researching Juvenile Offenders 1820–1920* (South Yorkshire: Pen and Sword, 2018). Peter King makes the case for a highly gendered discourse about delinquency: "The boys become thieves and the girls prostitutes," noted an 1817 parliamentary committee. King, *Crime and Law in England*, 89. Of course, girls were thieves and boys, prostitutes, too; yet the more usual stance identifies girls becoming property, while boys steal property.

64. Judith Butler, *Bodies That Matter: On the Discursive Limits of Sex* (Sussex: Psychology Press, 1993), 154. For further discussion of the ubiquitous name "Tom," see Daniel Hahn and Michael Morpurgo, *Oxford Companion to Children's Literature* (Oxford: Oxford University Press, 2015), 585–588. The main culprit in William Hogarth's *The First Stage of Cruelty* is called Tom Nero. For a similar point about the name Jack, see Andrew O'Malley, "Crusoe's Children: *Robinson Crusoe* and the Culture of Childhood in the Eighteenth Century," in *The Child in British Literature: Literary Constructions of Childhood, Medieval to Contemporary*, ed. Adrienne E. Gavin (New York: Palgrave Macmillan, 2012), 88.

65. A fourteen-year-old, John Bell, was hanged in 1831 for killing another boy, after which "nobody that age was hanged again. Yet both newspaper and broadside reports on Bell's case hardly mention his youth—only the fact that he had murdered another boy cruelly and for gain." Gatrell, *Hanging Tree*, 4.

66. Of transportation verdicts, too, Emma Watkins makes the point that "the key word here is *sentence*, as not all were sent" to the colonies. See Watkins, *Life Courses of Young Convicts Transported to Van Diemen's Land*, History of Crime, Deviance, and Punishment (London: Bloomsbury, 2020), 60ff.

67. S. Tarlow and Lowman E. Battell, "Folk Beliefs and Popular Tales," in *Harnessing the Power of the Criminal Corpse* [Internet]. Cham (CH): Palgrave Macmillan; 2018. https://www.ncbi.nlm.nih.gov/books/NBK513556/ doi: 10.1007/978-3-319-77908-9_8.

68. *OED*, 3rd ed., s.v. "terrorism" (2.b.), https://www.oed.com/oed2/00249602.

69. Gatrell, *Hanging Tree*, 7 and 122.

70. Gatrell, *Hanging Tree*, 7 and 114.

71. Gatrell, *Hanging Tree*, 119.

72. Judith Flanders, "Murder as Entertainment," in *Discovering Literature: Romantics & Victorians*, British Library Online, https://www.bl.uk/romantics-and-victorians/articles/murder-as-entertainment.

73. Gatrell, *Hanging Tree*, 119.

74. Foucault, *Discipline and Punish*, 7 and 111.

75. Hitchcock, *Down and Out*, 76. Further, as Hal Gladfelder notes, "the great mass of new reports, execution broadsides, trials, and canting books were written by badly paid and anonymous professional authors." Gladfelder, *Criminality and Narrative in Eighteenth-Century England: Beyond the Law* (Baltimore: Johns Hopkins University Press, 2001), 88. The impact of true or seemingly true stories should not be discounted. When Priscilla Wakefield wrote *Juvenile Anecdotes, Founded on Facts*, in 1795, she had "frequently heard Children raise against the influence of moral tales on their own conduct, that they were not true, but merely fictions to entertain." Wakefield was convinced "real anecdotes of characters their own ages, and dispositions . . . would probably reach their hearts with peculiar force." Qtd. in Pickering, *John Locke and Children's Books*, 58.

76. Paul Slade, "The Death hunters: British Broadsides." http://www.planetslade.com/broadside-ballads-1.html. See too Matt Brown, "The Gallows Ballads of Nineteenth-Century London," *Londonist*, April 2010, https://londonist.com/2010/04/the_gallows_ballads_of_19th_century. Also Lance Bertelsen's reading of Hogarth's *The Idle 'Prentice Executed at Tyburn* (1747): "In the hawker and her surroundings we find the abundant paradoxes linking official or commercial productions and popular responses to them: a legal demonstration of terror and control results in a chaotic festival fuelled by irreverence and gin; a printed 'Last Dying Speech' makes a marketable celebrity of a condemned man who has yet to speak; a ragged, dirty female carrying a child at the periphery of the crowd becomes a central symbol for popular print culture as she cries a minatory publication she probably cannot read to a socially mixed audience who will buy it more for entertainment than instruction." Bertelsen, "Popular Entertainment and Instruction, Literary and Dramatic: Chapbooks, Advice Books, Almanacs, Ballads, Farces, Pantomimes, Prints and Shows," in *The Cambridge History of English Literature, 1660–1780*, ed. John Richetti (Cambridge: Cambridge University Press, 2005), 61–86.

77. Frances E. Dolan, *True Relations: Reading, Literature and Evidence in Seventeenth-Century England* (Philadelphia: University of Pennsylvania Press, 2013).

78. Gatrell, *Hanging Tree*, 175.

79. Ackroyd, *London*, 653.

80. Foucault, *Discipline and Punish*, 113.

81. Simpson, *Masculinity and Control*, 68.

82. Voltaire, *Philosophical Dictionary* (1764), in *The Portable Enlightenment Reader*, ed. Isaac Kramnick (New York: Penguin, 1994), 534.

83. Foucault, *Discipline and Punish*, 108–109.

84. Yet another definition of "tool" being "a pickpocket; the member of a pair or team of pickpockets who actually picks pockets." *OED*, s.v. "tool, *n.*" (1.b.[b]) and (3.c.).

85. The trials were held at Old Bailey. See "15th October 1777," Old Bailey Proceedings: Accounts of Criminal Trials, from Hitchcock et al., *London Lives*, LL reference number t17771015-22.

86. "15th October 1777," Old Bailey Proceedings.

87. Hanway, *State of Master Chimney-Sweepers*, 29.

88. Hanway, *State of Master Chimney-Sweepers*, 9. Hanway and master sweep David Porter secured passage of an Act for the Better Regulation of Chimney Sweepers and Their Apprentices (1788). The act stated that no boy could be bound as apprentice before the age of eight. A clause that every master sweep must be registered was voted down in Parliament.

89. "15th October 1777," Old Bailey Proceedings.

90. Boswell recorded a conversation with Johnson, October 10, 1784: "We talked of the state of the poor in London—JOHNSON. Saunders Welch, the Justice, who was once High-

Constable of Holborn, and had the best opportunities of knowing the state of the poor, told me, that I under-rated the number, when I computed that twenty a week, that is, above a thousand a year, died of hunger; not absolutely of immediate hunger, but of the wasting and other diseases which are the consequences of hunger. This happens only in so large a place as London, where people are not known." Significantly, Johnson went on to assert, "What we are told about the great sums got by begging is not true: the trade is overstocked." Boswell, *Life of Johnson*, 1031.

91. The *Register* reports "18 condemned to death for various acts of theft" in the last Old Bailey Sessions, including "four chimney-sweepers boys, for shop-lifting." *Annual Register; or, A View of the History, Politics and Literature for the Year 1777* (London, 1785), 205.

92. John Clute and John Grant, eds., *The Encyclopedia of Fantasy* (London: Orbit, 1997), 581.

93. King, *Crime and Law in England*, 107.

94. Thomas Munck, *The Enlightenment: A Comparative Social History, 1721–1794* (London: Hodder Arnold, 2000), 112.

95. Gwenda Morgan and Peter Rushton, "Visible Bodies: Power, Subordination and Identity in the Eighteenth-Century Atlantic World," *Journal of Social History* 39, no. 1 (2005): 39. Whereas in England these criminals on the run were mostly runaway servants (although absentee husbands and other shirkers of responsibility appeared), in America they included convict (indentured) servants as well as enslaved people. A profitable "culture of advertising" ensured that "newspapers provided a cheap and locally-available means of publicising those who had been seized by suspicious authorities or had proved mutinous by leaving their posts without permission." Rushton, "Visible Bodies," 39.

96. Hilton, *Women and the Shaping of the Nation's Young*, 40.

97. Grenby, *Child Reader*, 73.

98. Grenby, *Child Reader*, 73. At the same time, "popular literature was not eclipsed in children's lives by the increased ubiquity of more respectable children's books" (111).

99. Hilton, *Women and the Shaping of the Nation's Young*, 134; see too David Vincent, *Literature and Popular Culture, 1760–1914* (Cambridge: Cambridge University Press, 1989), 23.

100. Hannah More, *The Cheapside Apprentice; or, The History of Mr. Francis H ... Shewing Also, How a Gay Life, May Prove a Short One; and That a Merry Evening May Produce a Sorrowful Morning* (Philadelphia, 1800; Ann Arbor: Text Creation Partnership, 2011), 3. More also printed "The Apprentice's Monitor; or, Indentures in Verse, Shewing What They Are Bound to Do." The subtitle (and advertisement) qualifies it as "Proper to be hung up in all Shops." This too is an "obstacle sign," reminding "EACH young Apprentice, when he's bound to Trade, / This solemn vow to GOD and Man has made." More, "The Apprentice's Monitor; or, Indentures in Verse, Shewing What They Are Bound to Do" (Bath, 1785; Ann Arbor: Text Creation Partnership with ECCO, 2011), lines 1–2.

101. Grenby, *Child Reader*, 74.

102. Corbould and Springsguth, *Juvenile Philosophy*, 6–7.

103. Corbould and Springsguth, *Juvenile Philosophy*, 73 and 8. As regards the profound difference in the rhetoric about idleness for different classes, see Sarah Jordan, "Idleness, Class and Gender in the Long Eighteenth Century," in *Idleness, Indolence and Leisure in English Literature*, ed. M. Fludernik and M. Nandi (London: Palgrave Macmillan, 2014), 107–128.

104. For the extent to which Hogarth's work was incorporated into children's literature, see Andrea Immel, "The Didacticism That Laughs: John Newbery's Entertaining Little Books and William Hogarth's Pictured Morals," *Lion and the Unicorn* 33 (2009): 146–166.

105. From Henry Sharpe Horsley, *The Affectionate Parent's Gift; and the Good Child's Reward* (1828), in Demers, *From Instruction to Delight*, 219–220.

106. Watts, "Against Idleness and Mischief," in *Divine Songs*, lines 13–16. All children were raised with a keen understanding that death could come at any time from illness or accident. Industrialization increased the chances: in 1832, in Manchester, the factory and mining city, a working-class boy lived an average of just seventeen years. Waller, *Real Oliver Twist*, 4.

107. Cesare Beccaria, "An Essay on Crimes and Punishment," in Kramnick, *Portable Enlightenment Reader*, 526.

108. Beccaria, "Essay on Crimes and Punishment," 528.

109. Fenn, *School Dialogues*, 2:138.

110. Fenn, *Rational Dame*, 23.

111. Charles Dickens, *Oliver Twist; or, The Parish Boy's Progress* (1838), chap. 30.

112. Josephine McDonagh, *Child Murder and British Culture, 1720–1900* (Cambridge: Cambridge University Press, 2003), 9.

113. McDonagh, *Child Murder and British Culture*, 9.

114. London experienced "a veritable deluge of recorded juvenile crime" in the 1820s—a decade in which "the proportion of 0–14 year olds in the national population reached its peak." King, *Crime and Law in England*, 110 and 91. A juvenile reformatory was recommended in 1817 by the Society for the Improvement of Prison Discipline and for the Reformation of Juvenile Offenders up to the age of seventeen. The first juvenile prison was the 1838 Parkhurst Prison on the Isle of Wight.

115. Uwe Böker, "Childhood and Juvenile Delinquency in Eighteenth-Century Newgate Calendars," in Müller, *Fashioning Childhood*, 141.

116. Qtd. in Hilton, *Women and the Shaping of the Nation's Young*, 199. Hilton also mentions a meeting of the Royal Society in 1855 at which a Mr. Elliot vociferated "juvenile offenders should be treated as all other offenders ... they must be hurt so that the idea of pain might be instantly associated with crime in the minds of *all* evildoers" (199, emphasis mine).

117. Paul Baines, "Crime Histories," *Eighteenth-Century Studies* 42, no. 1 (2008): 166.

118. One study of the more recent relationship between males and crime is Tim Newburn and Elizabeth A. Stanko, eds., *Just Boys Doing Business? Men, Masculinities and Crime* (East Sussex: Psychology Press, 1994).

119. Lucy Andrew positions the publication of *The Boy Detective* in 1865–1866 as a response to the glamorization of crime and criminality in penny dreadfuls. Andrew, *The Boy Detective in Early British Children's Literature: Patrolling the Borders between Boyhood and Manhood*, Critical Approaches in Children's Literature (London: Palgrave, 2017), 19–23.

120. *OED*, 3rd ed. s.v. "fungible, *adj.* and *n.*" (A), last updated September 2007, https://www.oed.com/view/Entry/75537; Brown, *Sense of Things*, 38.

CHAPTER 6 — THE BOY IN THE PRINTING PRESS

1. Thomas Holcroft, *The School for Arrogance* (London, 1791; ECCO, 2011). Other prologues were also delivered by printer's devils, such as Richard Cumberland's *The Fashionable Lover; A Comedy: As It Is Acted at the Theatre-Royal in Drury-Lane* (London, 1772).

2. That said, W. M. Verhoeven argues Holcroft "aimed at removing all social, political and economic inequalities and restrictions from society." See Verhoeven, "Politics for the People: Thomas Holcroft's Proto-Marxism," in *Re-viewing Thomas Holcroft, 1745–1809: Essays on His Works and Life*, ed. A. A. Markley and Miriam L. Wallace (London: Routledge, 2012), 200.

3. The rhetoric is ubiquitous. Consider the opening couplet of Mary Jones's "An Epistle to Lady Bowyer": "How much of paper's spoil'd! What floods of ink! / and yet how few,

how very few can think!" In *Poems by Eminent Ladies* (London, 1755), 1:112. For a broad discussion of Grub Street, its environs, and its legacy, see Pat Rogers's *Grub Street: Studies in a Subculture* (New York: Harper & Row, 1972).

4. Samuel Johnson, "XVI: Saturday, May 12, 1750," in *The Rambler: In Four Volumes*, vol. 1 (Philadelphia, 1827), 112–116 (112).

5. Elizabeth Eisenstein, "Gods, Devils, and Gutenberg: The Eighteenth Century Confronts the Printing Press," *Studies in Eighteenth-Century Culture* 27 (1988): 1. For an extended discussion of Protestantism and print, see Eisenstein's *The Printing Press as an Agent of Change*, 2 vols. (Cambridge: Cambridge University Press, 1980).

6. Francis Bond Head, *The Printer's Devil; or, A Type of the Old One* (London, 1833). One of Johnson's definitions of "devil" as a noun more generally is "a ludicrous term for mischief." *Dictionary* (1755), s.v. "devil" (3).

7. Sarah Wall-Randell, "Doctor Faustus and the Printer's Devil," *Studies in English Literature 1500–1900* 48, no. 2 (Spring 2008): 21.

8. Greenwood, "Work, Identity and Letterpress Printers," 37. As with other apprenticeship contracts, what the boy officially earned with his labor included training in a craft, lodging, board, washing, and clothing.

9. Joseph Moxon, *Mechanick Exercises; or, The Doctrine of Handyworks. Applied to the Art of Printing*, vol. 2 (London, 1683), 373. To add to the tropes of the printing house, it was called a "chapel," and errors in print referred to as "monks" and "friars."

10. Douglas Jerrold, "Sketches of the English," in *The Writings of Douglas Jerrold*, vol. 5 (London, 1853), 301. Jerrold began work as a printer's apprentice in 1816 at the age of thirteen, then in 1819 became a compositor for the *Sunday Monitor*.

11. Robert Darnton, *The Business of Enlightenment: A Publishing History of the Encyclopedie 1775–1880* (Cambridge, MA: Belknap, 1979), 242. Note Eisenstein's critique of Darnton's focus on the unpleasantness of the press: "Eighteenth-century Europeans were accustomed, as our more fastidious contemporaries are not, to the even fiercer stench made by human waste and to wading about in filthy streets dodging horse manure." In "Gods, Devils, and Gutenberg," 11. "Printer's devil" did not become a term for a compositor until early in the twentieth century.

12. "If a printer's devil took a turn at the press, one could coat the bar with glue or ink." Darnton, *Business of Enlightenment*, 243.

13. Samuel Grant Oliphaunt, *Queer Questions and Ready Replies*, 2nd ed. (Boston, 1887), 44.

14. Rawlings, *Drunks, Whores, and Idle Apprentices*, 15.

15. W. J. Rorabaugh, *The Craft Apprentice* (Oxford: Oxford University Press, 1988), xvii. As regards appeals to an apprentice readership, see Edel Lamb, "Youth Culture," in *The Ashgate Companion to Popular Culture in Early Modern England*, ed. Andrew Hadfield et al. (New York: Routledge, 2016), 31–38.

16. Ian Gadd, "Leaving the Printer to his Liberty: Swift and the London Book Trade 1701–1714," in *Jonathan Swift and the Eighteenth-Century Book*, ed. Paddy Bullard and James McLaverty (Cambridge: Cambridge University Press, 2013), 54.

17. James Raven, *The Business of Books: Booksellers and the Book Trade* (New Haven, CT: Yale University Press, 2007), 36.

18. Benjamin Goosequill and Peter Paragraph, *Curious Facts and Anecdotes, Not Contained in the Memoirs of Philip Thickness, Esq.* (London, 1790).

19. *Memoirs of a Printer's Devil; Interspersed with Pleasing Recollections, Local Descriptions and Anecdotes* (London, 1793), 92. Jim English proposes one Thomas Seldom in Gainsborough, Lincolnshire, as the author of the *Memoirs*. See English, "A Tentative Enquiry into the Identity of 'A Printer's Devil,'" *Quadrat* 11 (2000): 3–8.

20. *Memoirs of a Printer's Devil*, 14, 92 and 91. Caps in original.

21. Greenwood, "Work, Identity and Letterpress Printers," 48.

22. Greenwood, "Work, Identity and Letterpress Printers," 45. See too Henry French and Mark Rothery, "Male Anxiety among Younger Sons of the English Landed Gentry, 1700–1900," *Historical Journal* 62, no. 4 (2019): 967–995. They note, "Under the system of primogeniture, younger sons inherited only a small portion of the ancestral estate and, from the late seventeenth century, very rarely any land. They were positioned near the apex of social and gender privilege, but often reached adulthood fairly certain of a landless existence, uncertain of inheriting the resources to maintain this status, anxious about their capacity to earn their own livings and dependent on the honour of their families" (967).

23. John Nichols (1745–1826) was a printer, author, antiquarian, and editor of the *Gentleman's Magazine* for nearly forty years.

24. Christopher Flint, *The Appearance of Print in Eighteenth-Century Fiction* (Cambridge: Cambridge University Press, 2011), 2.

25. Classified ads, *Gazetteer and New Daily Advertiser*, July 2, 1770, qtd. in Greenwood, "Work, Identity and Letterpress Printers," 44.

26. Rorabaugh, *Craft Apprentice*, 7. Over the centuries, printers were able to hold onto "their high-status image as the elite of the working class." Seymour Martin Lipset, Martin Trow, and James S. Coleman, *Union Democracy: The Internal Politics of the International Typographical Union* (New York: Free Press, 1956), 30.

27. Until 1767, a parish apprenticeship normally lasted until the age of twenty-four for boys and twenty-one or marriage for girls, at which time the number of years was lowered by An Act for the Better Regulation of the Parish Poor Children, of the Several Parishes Therein Mentioned Within the Bills of Mortality. Hitchcock et al., *London Lives*, https://www.londonlives.org/static/IA.jsp.

28. Richardson, *Apprentice's Vade Mecum*, 13.

29. Thomas Keymer, *Richardson's "Clarissa" and the Eighteenth-Century Reader* (Cambridge: Cambridge University Press, 1992), 146–147. Richardson is discouraging both establishment of and attendance at playhouses. In the manual aimed at apprentices, Keymer suggests "the apprentice of whom Richardson writes is no ordinary cog in the machine. In the radically capitalist Commonwealth of the *Vade Mecum* [such an apprentice] not only guarantee[s] the present vitality of the trade, but also prepar[es] for his future responsibilities as a Citizen" (146–147). But there *were* plenty of ordinary cogs in the machine among the tens of thousands of apprentices in London.

30. Samuel Johnson, "IV: Saturday, March 31, 1750," *The Rambler* 1 (1750): 56–60 (57).

31. See Mona Scheuermann, *In Praise of Poverty: Hannah More Counters Thomas Paine and the Radical Threat* (Lexington: University Press of Kentucky, 2002). Again, in the play *The Printer's Devil*, demon Nick identifies "the principal use of our printing presses to teach this wholesome doctrine of universal property, and to forget the laws of *Meum* and *Tuum*." Head, *Printer's Devil*, 5. For a useful study of reading practices across the classes, see Eve Tavor Bannet, *Eighteenth-Century Manners of Reading: Print Culture and Popular Instruction in the Anglophone Atlantic World* (Cambridge: Cambridge University Press, 2017), 45, passim.

32. *Memoirs of a Printer's Devil*, 22.

33. Head, *Printer's Devil*, 10. The anonymous 1763 play *The Cabal* introduces a printer's devil named "Smut."

34. Mrs. Catherine Carrot (Greengrocer), "An Elegiac Epistle." *Literary Fly*, no. 4 (February 20, 1779). https://books.google.ca/books?id=KbdbAAAAQAAJ.

35. Mary Robinson [pseud. Horace Juvenal], *Modern Manners: A Poem in Two Cantos* (London, 1793), 19.

36. George Alexander Stevens, *The Celebrated Lecture on Heads: Which Has Been Exhibited Upwards of One Hundred Successive Nights, to Crouded Audiences, and Met with the Most Universal Applause* (London, 1765), 8. The noisiness of this list speaks to Pat Rogers's observation about what Pope does in *The Dunciad*, where too "literary incompetence is imaged by cacophony." Rogers, *Grub Street*, 62.

37. See John 8:44, AV. "Devil" is also slang for a lawyer and for the act we would now call the hazing of new military cadets. From Albert Barrère and Charles Godfrey Leland, *A Dictionary of Slang, Jargon & Cant, Embracing English, American, and Anglo-Indian Slang, Pidgin English, Tinker's Jargon and Other Irregular Phraseology*, s.v. "devil," (London 1889–1890), 305. *The Oxford Dictionary of Phrase and Fable* glosses "printer's devil" with the more general note that "a *devil* is a person employed in a subordinate position to work under the direction of or for a particular person," ed. Elizabeth Knowles (Oxford: Oxford University Press, 2016).

38. Rorabaugh, *Craft Apprentice*, 33.

39. Rorabaugh, *Craft Apprentice*, 33.

40. Samuel Foote, *The Devil upon Two Sticks: A Comedy, in Three Acts. As It Is Performed at the Theatre-Royal in the Haymarket* (London, 1778; ECCO, 2011), 34.

41. From Benjamin Franklin, "Lying Shopkeepers" (1730), qtd. in J. A. Leo Lemay, *The Life of Benjamin Franklin*, vol. 2: *Printer and Publisher, 1730–1747* (Philadelphia: University of Pennsylvania Press, 2006), 135.

42. Nestor Druid, Gent., *The Lady's Curiosity; or, Weekly Apollo* (London 1752), 197.

43. Druid, *Lady's Curiosity*, 197.

44. Charlotte Turner Smith, *What Is She? A Comedy in Five Acts* (London, 1799), 49.

45. Qtd. in Flint, *Appearance of Print*, 27.

46. Pope, "Epistle to Arbuthnot," in *Shorter Twickenham*, 597–612, lines 89–92.

47. Pope, "Epistle to Arbuthnot," lines 169–172.

48. Rogers, *Grub Street*, 124. The "grub" of the name refers to a ditch, not the insect.

49. Gee, *Making Waste*, 37.

50. Swift, "Description of a City Shower," in Rawson and Higgins, *Essential Writings of Jonathan Swift*, 515–516, line 27 and lines 61–63.

51. Gee, *Making Waste*, 77.

52. Pope, *The Dunciad*, in *Shorter Twickenham*, 317–342, line 356. See Harold Weber's argument that "the poem represents an anguished protest against the breakdown in traditional structures of memory, and a sustained critique of the new (or newly redesigned) institutions—library, museum, and academy—that print culture helped to erect in their place. At the same time, Pope's successive revisions of the poem transform it into the very type of textual archive that he despises." Weber, "The 'Garbage Heap' of Memory: At Play in Pope's Archives of Dulness," *Eighteenth-Century Studies* 33, no. 1 (1999): 3. See too Joanna Maciulewicz, *Representations of Book Culture in Eighteenth-Century English Imaginative Writing*, New Directions in Books History (London: Palgrave Macmillan, 2018), 79–119.

53. Flint, *Appearance of Print*, 37. Incidentally, mention of the oil and lamp black "with which the paper is so strongly impregnated" in *Tristram Shandy* occurs adjacent to the anecdote wherein Phutatorius experiences the hot coal down his breeches. See chapter 1.

54. Manushag N. Powell, *Performing Authorship in Eighteenth-Century Periodicals* (Lewisburg, PA: Bucknell University Press, 2012), 203.

55. *The Art and Mystery of Printing Emblematically Displayed* (etching on paper, 1732, British Museum, London), https://www.britishmuseum.org/collection/object/P_1868-0808-10094.

56. Powell, *Performing Authorship in Eighteenth-Century Periodicals*, 204. Elizabeth Eisenstein analyzes the essay and satirical print in chap. 4 of *Divine Art, Infernal Machine: The Reception of Printing in the West from First Impressions to the Sense of an Ending* (Philadelphia: University of Pennsylvania Press, 2011). Flint examines a number of essays from the period that emphasize print is a "mystery" in *Appearance of Print*, 9ff.

57. "The Art and Mystery of Printing Emblematically Displayed."

58. Powell, *Performing Authorship in Eighteenth-Century Periodicals*, 204. Greenwood argues that "the use of devil imagery was, however, fairly harmless by comparison with other aspects of young printers' representations which focussed more on their behaviour and attitudes than their appearance." "Work, Identity and Letterpress Printers," 37.

59. Jerrold, "Sketches," 304.

60. Jerrold, "Sketches," 306.

61. Jerrold, "Sketches," 301.

62. Powell, *Performing Authorship in Eighteenth-Century Periodicals*, 200.

63. A bit like Pope in the "Epistle to Arbuthnot," recalling how he "lisp'd in numbers and the numbers came," which innate gift has since led to the poet being besieged by poetasters and (other) idiots.

64. Flint, *Appearance of Print*, 34. Christopher Fanning is among those who point out with reference to the larger Scriblerian project (chiefly of Pope, Swift, Arbuthnot, and sometimes Gay), "attention to the material uses of writing [print] is accompanied by the alienation of the author from his work and his reader." See Fanning, "Small Particles of Eloquence: Sterne and the Scriblerian Text," *Modern Philology* 100, no. 3 (2003): 372. In Flint's discussion of nicknames, he distinguishes between "flies" and "devils." These were sometimes separate workers, although as we have seen in Moxon's *Mechanick Exercises*, not usually.

65. Jerome McGann, *The Textual Condition* (Princeton, NJ: Princeton University Press, 1991), 36 and 78.

66. Louis de Jaucourt, "Printing, History Of," trans. I. M. L. Donaldson, in *The Encyclopedia of Diderot & d'Alembert Collaborative Translation Project*, https://quod.lib.umich.edu/d/did/did2222.0000.090. Originally published as "Imprimerie," *Encyclopédie ou Dictionnaire raisonné des sciences, des arts et des métiers*, 8: 607–609 (Paris, 1765).

67. David Hume, "On Luxury" (1742), in Kramnick, *Portable Enlightenment Reader*, 491.

68. *Memoirs of a Printer's Devil*, xii–xiii.

69. Edmund Curll, Pope's publisher, was notorious for legal difficulties over his printing practices, including having stood in the pillory for seditious libel in 1728. See Paul Baines and Pat Rogers, *Edmund Curll, Bookseller* (Oxford: Oxford University Press, 2007). See also Tamara L. Hunt, "Servants, Masters and Seditious Libel in Eighteenth-Century England," *Book History* 20 (2017): 83–110.

70. Boswell, *Life of Samuel Johnson*, 1141.

71. Greenwood, "Work, Identity and Letterpress Printers," 102.

72. See Julie Hedgepeth Williams, *Three Not-So-Ordinary Joes: A Plantation Newspaperman, a Printer's Devil, an English Wit, and the Founding of Southern Literature* (Montgomery, AL: NewSouth Books. 2018). Later came Thomas Jefferson and Mark Twain—the latter of whom worked on a country paper that, Bruce Michelson notes, in the 1840s employed "apparatus and rituals essentially unchanged from what they had been two centuries before." Michelson, *Printer's Devil: Mark Twain and the American Publishing Revolution* (Berkeley: University of California Press, 2006), 2.

73. The evolving use of the apprentice's moniker is interesting in light of Greenwood's observation: "By the mid-nineteenth century, developments in printing technology had

largely done away with the particularly dirty work of earlier times (thereby nullifying the chief aspect of the printer's devil's identity); the term was said to have gone out of use amongst printers by 1857." "Work, Identity and Letterpress Printers," 26. See too Elizabeth Harris, *The Boy and His Press* (Washington, DC: Smithsonian Institution, 1992).

74. Ronald Schultz, "Printers' Devils: Decline of Apprenticeship in America," review of *The Craft Apprentice: From Franklin to the Machine Age in America* by W. J. Rorabaugh, *Reviews in American History* 15, no. 2 (1987): 26.

75. And these tended to be indentured to the more respectable professions like surgery. Charles Brooks, "Apprenticeship, Social Mobility and the Middling Sort, 1550–1800," in *The Middling Sort of People*, ed. Jonathan Barry and Charles Brooks (London: Palgrave, 1994), 67–68. Other workers, like carters, draymen, and street sweepers, had never had a system of apprenticeship, and, as noted, huge numbers of the young worked in agricultural jobs not categorized as apprenticeships, although they were similar to apprenticeships in reality.

76. Greenwood, "Work, Identity and Letterpress Printers," 31. Humphries suggests attitudes toward apprentices (and other young workers) were largely determined by their age: the younger, the more sympathy for the potential exploitation of the child; the older, the less sympathy was forthcoming for the unmanageable adolescent. At the same time, "While child labour has generally been condemned, the attitude to its combination with on-the-job training, as in an apprenticeship, is more ambivalent." Jane Humphries, *Childhood and Child Labour in the British Industrial Revolution* (Cambridge: Cambridge University Press, 2010), 256.

77. Greenwood, "Work, Identity and Letterpress Printers," 43.

78. Tribunella, "Boyhood," 22.

79. Doris Grumbach, "Printers' Devils and Other Apprentices," *Washington Post*, February 23, 1986.

80. See Peter Franks, *Print and Politics: A History of Trade Unions in the New Zealand Printing Industry, 1865–1995* (Victoria: Victoria University Press, 2001), 19, 38, and 62.

81. Rorabaugh, *Craft Apprentice*, 133–134. See too Robert Allen, "Technology," in *The Cambridge Economic History of Modern Britain*, vol. 1, ed. Roderick Floud, Jane Humphries, and Paul Johnson (Cambridge: Cambridge University Press, 2014), 292–320.

82. Rorabaugh, *Craft Apprentice*, 131.

83. Edward Edwards, *The Disease and the Remedy: An Essay on the Distressed State of the Printing Trade, Proving It to Be Mainly Attributable to Excessive Boy Labour: With Some Practical Observations Showing the Extent of the Distress, and Suggesting a Remedy for Its Gradual Amelioration: Accompanied by an Appeal to Master Printers and Newspaper Proprietors, to Aid in the Work of Reformation* (London, 1850).

84. See too Patrick Duffy, *The Skilled Compositor, 1850–1914: An Aristocrat among Working Men* (New York: Routledge, 2017), 56.

85. Rorabaugh, *Craft Apprentice*, 76.

86. Charles More, *Skill and the English Working Class, 1870–1914* (London: Croom Helm, 1980), 43. "Even in the twentieth century, the method of training remained disproportionately used by printers; in one town nearly half the total number of apprenticeships between 1935 and 1939 was to printing." Greenwood, "Work, Identity and Letterpress Printers," 32.

87. Qtd. in Greenwood, "Work, Identity and Letterpress Printers," 107.

88. Tribunella, "Boyhood," 25.

89. As early as 1776 in America, trade societies were forming, "some of which amounted to early unions" that, Michael Everton notes, "sought to regulate not only labor conditions but behavior." Everton, "The Would-Be-Author and the Real Bookseller," *Early American*

Literature 40, no. 1 (2005): 84. Typographical Society qtd. from Ethelbert Stewart, *A Documentary History of the Early Organization of Printers* (1902; Charleston, SC: BiblioBazaar, 2008), 11. For the extent to which the society tried—and failed—to regulate the apprentice-journeyman-printer trajectory, see Rosalind Reimers, *Printers and Men of Capital: Philadelphia Book Publishers in the New Republic* (Philadelphia: University of Pennsylvania Press, 1996), 43, passim.

90. William Wordsworth, "Preface to *Lyrical Ballads*" (1801), in *English Romantic Writers*, 2nd ed., ed. David Perkins (Orlando, FL: Harcourt Brace, 1995), 428.

91. Johnson, *Dictionary* (1755), s.v. "boy" (3).

92. See the *OED*'s use of "boy" as a verb: "*transitive*: To address (a person) as 'boy.' Esp. with a man as object, with belittling implication." The *OED* gives examples from as far back as the sixteenth century. *OED*, 3rd ed., s.v. "boy, v." (1.a.), last updated December 2008, https://www.oed.com/view/Entry/22325. Again, the word also has a racialized history. See the introduction, note 15.

93. John J. Tobin, *Third Biennial Report of the Bureau of Labor Statistics of California* (Sacramento, 1888), 212.

94. Pope, "Essay on Criticism" (1711), in *Shorter Twickenham*, 144–168, line 215.

95. *OED*, 3rd ed., s.v. "botch, n.2" (1) and (5.a.), last updated June 2016, https://www.oed.com/view/Entry/21840.

96. The word "devil" names mechanical tools as well: "11. a. Any of various instruments or machines which are fitted with a sharp edge, sharp teeth, or spikes, and typically used for tearing or other destructive work, *esp. (a)* a machine used for tearing open and cleaning wool, cotton, flax, and other fibres, in preparation for spinning; a willy (willy n.1 3); †*(b)* a machine used to tear up old cloth, rags, etc., for use as shoddy or for paper manufacturing (*obsolete*); †*(c)* a device used to cut or destroy the nets of fishermen at sea (*obsolete*)." Johnson, *Dictionary* (1755), s.v. "tool." Cf. devil's dust nt. 2.

97. Johnson, *Dictionary* (1755), s.v. "adolescence."

98. Johnson, *Dictionary* (1773) s.v. "boyhood."

99. Thomas Moore, *The Fudges in England* (London: Longman, 1835).

100. Pursell, *From Playgrounds to PlayStation*, 82.

101. Thomas Van Der Walt, "Librarianship," in *International Companion Encyclopedia of Children's Literature*, vol. 4, ed. Peter Hunt (London: Routledge, 2004), 812.

102. Eisenstein, *Divine Art, Infernal Machine*, 244.

103. See James Raven, *What Is the History of the Book?*, What Is History? (Cambridge: Polity, 2018).

104. Qtd. from Hugh Trevor-Roper, *The Crisis of the Seventeenth Century: Religion, The Reformation, and Social Change* (Indianapolis: Liberty Fund, 1968), 36n.

CONCLUSION

1. Rousseau, *Émile*, 80.

2. John Locke used this English word with respect to childhood development: "To inform the Mind, and govern the Actions of their yet ignorant Nonage, till Reason shall take its Place and ease them of that Trouble, is what the Children want, and the Parents are bound to." Locke, *Two Treatises of Government*, II §58. In 1747, Robert Campbell employed the term to describe apprenticeship in the *London Tradesman*: "He cannot bestow seven Years of his Nonage better than among those kind of Goods he resolves to deal in when settled" (282).

3. Immanuel Kant, "What Is Enlightenment?" (1784), trans. Mary C. Smith (Columbia University Library Online), hppt://www.columbia.ed/acis/eets/CCREAD/etscc/kant.html.

4. Kant, "What Is Enlightenment?"

5. Kant thought "the entire beautiful sex" was convinced that freedom is dangerous. See Robin May Schott, ed., *Feminist Interpretations of Immanuel Kant* (University Park: Pennsylvania State University Press, 1997).

6. Simonton, *History of European Women's Work*, 81.

7. Shepherd, *Meanings of Manhood*, 9.

8. Qtd. in Wahrman, *Making of the Modern Self*, 82.

9. King, *Gendering of Men*, 29.

10. Foyster, *Manhood in Early Modern England*, 3.

11. Christiana Payne, "Picturing Work," in *A Cultural History of Work in the Enlightenment*, ed. Ann Montenach and Deborah Simonton (London: Bloomsbury, 2020), 39–60, 39.

12. Rainer Emig, "Sentimental Masculinity: Henry Mackenzie's *The Man of Feeling* (1771)," in *Configuring Masculinity in Theory and Literary Practice*, ed. Stefan Horlacher (Leiden: Brill, 2015), 127–139, 134.

13. Friedman, *Mind of Its Own*, 82.

14. "Signs of the Times," *Edinburgh Review*, 1829, qtd. in Porter, *Flesh in the Age of Reason*, 374 and 375.

15. Herbert Frye, *The Royal Guide to the London Charities* (London, 1884), 302–303. See too Rob Hardy, "The Ruptured Poor," *Rough Draft*, July 7, 2008, http://rbhardy3rd.blogspot.com/2008/06/ruptured-poor.html.

16. Liliane Hilaire-Pérez and Christelle Rabier, "Self-Machinery? Steel Trusses and the Management of Ruptures in Eighteenth-Century Europe," *Technology and Culture* 54, no. 3 (2013): 460–502.

17. David M. Turner and Alun Withey, "Technologies of the Body: Polite Consumption and the Correction of Deformity in Eighteenth-Century England," *History* 99, no. 338 (2014): 775-796.

18. *Literary Panorama, and National Register*, vol. 2 (London, 1807), 990.

19. Lane, *Apprenticeship in England*, 43.

20. Nicholson, *On Clothing*, 37.

21. Sterne, *Life and Opinions of Tristram Shandy, Gentleman*, 150.

Bibliography

Abbott, Mary. "Life Cycle." In Foyster and Marten, *Cultural History of Childhood and Family*, 113.

Abrams, M. H. *The Mirror and The Lamp: Romantic Theory and the Critical Tradition*. 1953. Oxford: Oxford University Press, 1994.

Ackroyd, Peter. *London: The Biography*. London: Vintage, 2001.

Addison, Joseph. "No. 56—Friday, May 4, 1711." *The Spectator*. The Spectator Project: A Hypermedia Research Archive of Eighteenth-Century Periodicals, Rutgers University Library. http://spectator.libraries.rutgers.edu/text/may1711/no56.html.

Allen, Robert. "Technology." In *The Cambridge Economic History of Modern Britain*, vol. 1, edited by Roderick Floud, Jane Humphries, and Paul Johnson, 292–320. Cambridge: Cambridge University Press, 2014. https://doi.org/10.1017/CHO9781139815017.

Amnesty International. "Industry Giants Fail to Tackle Child Labour Allegations in Cobalt Battery Supply Chains." November 15, 2017. https://www.amnesty.org/en/latest/news/2017/11/industry-giants-fail-to-tackle-child-labour-allegations-in-cobalt-battery-supply-chains/.

Andrew, Lucy. *The Boy Detective in Early British Children's Literature: Patrolling the Borders between Boyhood and Manhood*. Critical Approaches in Children's Literature. London: Palgrave, 2017.

The Annual Register; or, A View of the History, Politics and Literature for the Year 1777. London, 1785. HathiTrust. https://babel.hathitrust.org/cgi/pt?id=njp.32101076875515.

Arbuthnot, John. "An Argument for Divine Providence, Taken from the Constant Regularity Observ'd in the Births of Both Sexes. By Dr. John Arbuthnott, Physitian in Ordinary to Her Majesty, and Fellow of the College of Physitians and the Royal Society." *Philosophical Transactions (1683–1775)* 27 (1710–1712): 186–190. http://www.jstor.org/stable/103111.

Ariès, Philippe. *Centuries of Childhood: A Social History of Family Life*. New York: Vintage, 1960.

Aristophanes. *The Clouds*. In *Aristophanes*, vol. 1, translated by Benjamin Bickley Rogers, 266–403. Loeb Classical Library. New York: Putnam & Sons, 1924.

Armintor, Deborah Needleman. *The Little Everyman: Stature and Masculinity in Eighteenth-Century English Literature*. Seattle: University of Washington Press, 2011.

The Art and Mystery of Printing Emblematically Displayed. Etching on paper, 1732. London: British Museum, https://www.britishmuseum.org/collection/object/P_1868-0808-10094.

Ash, John. *Grammatical Institutes; or, An Easy Introduction to Dr. Lowth's English Grammar.* London, 1763.

Astell, Mary. *A Serious Proposal to the Ladies, for the Advancement of Their True and Greatest Interest. In Two Parts. By a Lover of Her Sex.* Pt. 1. London, 1697. ECCO, Gale doc. no. CW0114597167.

———. *Some Reflections upon Marriage.* 2nd ed. 1700. London, 1703. From ECCO, Gale doc. no. CW0118997840.

Backscheider, Paula R. *Revising Women: Eighteenth-Century "Women's Fiction" and Social Engagement.* Baltimore: Johns Hopkins University Press, 2002.

Baines, Paul. "Crime Histories." *Eighteenth-Century Studies* 42, no. 1 (2008): 166–170.

Baines, Paul, and Pat Rogers. *Edmund Curll, Bookseller.* Oxford: Oxford University Press, 2007.

Baird, Ileana, and Christina Ionescu, eds. *Eighteenth-Century Thing Theory in a Global Context: From Consumerism to Celebrity Culture.* New York: Routledge, 2016.

Baldick, Chris. *In Frankenstein's Shadow: Myth, Monstrosity, and Nineteenth-Century Writing.* Oxford: Clarendon, 1987.

Ballstadt, Kurt P. A. *Diderot: Natural Philosopher.* Oxford: Voltaire Foundation, 2008.

Bamford, T. W. *The Rise of the Public Schools: A Study of Boys' Public Boarding Schools in England and Wales from 1837 to the Present Day.* London: Nelson, 1967.

Banister, Julia. *Masculinity, Militarism and Eighteenth-Century Culture, 1689–1815.* Cambridge University Press, 2018. https://doi.org/10.1017/9781108163927.

Bannet, Eve Tavor. *Eighteenth-Century Manners of Reading: Print Culture and Popular Instruction in the Anglophone Atlantic World.* Cambridge: Cambridge University Press, 2017.

Barbauld, Anna Laetitia. *Lessons for Children, from Two to Three Years Old.* London, 1778–1779. ECCO, Gale doc. no. CW0120057293.

———. "What Is Education?" *Monthly Magazine*, March 1798, 167–171. In *Anna Laetitia Barbauld: Selected Poetry and Prose*, edited by William McCarthy and Elizabeth Kraft, 321–332. Peterborough: Broadview, 2002.

Barber, Mary. *Poems on Several Occasions.* London: Rivington, 1734 (1735). Reprint, Gale ECCO, Print Editions, 2010.

Barrère, Albert, and Charles Godfrey Leland. *A Dictionary of Slang, Jargon & Cant, Embracing English, American, and Anglo-Indian Slang, Pidgin English, Tinker's Jargon and Other Irregular Phraseology.* London, 1889–1890.

Beccaria, Cesare. "An Essay on Crimes and Punishment." In Kramnick, *Portable Enlightenment Reader*, 525–532.

Beckett, Samuel. *Waiting for Godot.* New York: Grove Press, 2011.

Ben-Amos, Ilana Krausman. *Adolescence and Youth in Early Modern England.* New Haven, CT: Yale University Press, 1994.

Benedict, Barbara. "The 'Curious Attitude' in Eighteenth-Century Britain: Observing and Owning." *Eighteenth-Century Life* 14 (November 1990): 59–98.

Benmoussa, Nadia, John-David Rebibo, Patrick Conan, and Philippe Charlier. "Chimney-Sweeps' Cancer—Early Proof of Environmentally Driven Tumourigenicity." *Lancet: Perspectives, History of Medicine* 20, no. 3 (2019). https://doi.org/10.1016/S1470-2045(19)30106-8.

Benzaquén, Adriana Silvia. "World Contexts." In Foyster and Marten, *Cultural History of Childhood and Family*, 185–204.

Berger, John. *Ways of Seeing: Based on the BBC Television Series with John Berger.* London: BBC and Penguin, 1973.

Bertelsen, Lance. "Popular Entertainment and Instruction, Literary and Dramatic: Chapbooks, Advice Books, Almanacs, Ballads, Farces, Pantomimes, Prints and Shows." In *The Cambridge History of English Literature, 1660–1780*, edited by John Richetti, 61–86. Cambridge: Cambridge University Press, 2005.

Bickham, George. *The Universal Penman. Engrav'd by George Bickham*. London, [1733?]–1741. ECCO, Gale doc. no. CW0106410810.

Bindman, David. *Ape to Apollo: Aesthetics and the Idea of Race in the Eighteenth Century*. Ithaca, NY: Cornell University Press, 2002.

Blackstone, William. *Commentaries on the Laws of England*. 4 vols. London, 1769.

Blake, William. *Songs of Innocence and of Experience*. 1789 and 1794. Oxford: Oxford University Press, 1970.

Blakey, William. *Essay on the Manner of Preserving Children and Grown Persons from Ruptures*. London, 1792. ECCO, Gale doc. no. CW0107241577.

Bloom, Harold. *Agon: Towards a Theory of Revisionism*. Oxford: Oxford University Press, 1982.

Bogel, Fredric V. *The Difference Satire Makes: Rhetoric and Reading from Jonson to Byron*. Ithaca, NY: Cornell University Press, 2001.

Böker, Uwe. "Childhood and Juvenile Delinquency in Eighteenth-Century Newgate Calendars." In Müller, *Fashioning Childhood in the Eighteenth Century*, 135–144.

Booth, Wayne C. *The Rhetoric of Fiction*. 2nd ed. Chicago: University of Chicago Press, 1983.

Bordo, Susan. *Unbearable Weight: Feminism, Western Culture, and the Body*. Berkeley: University of California Press, 1993.

Boswell, James. *Life of Johnson*. London: Oxford University Press, 1953.

Bottigheimer, Ruth. "Fairy Tales, Telemachus, and Young Misses Magazine: Moderns, Ancients, Gender, and Eighteenth-Century Book Publishing." *Children's Literature Association Quarterly* 28, no. 2 (Fall 2003): 171–175.

Boucé, Paul-Gabriel, ed. *Sexuality in Eighteenth-Century Britain*. Manchester: Manchester University Press, 1982.

———. "Some Sexual Beliefs and Myths in Eighteenth-Century Britain." In Boucé, *Sexuality in Eighteenth-Century Britain*, 28–46.

Bowers, Toni. "'A Point of Conscience': Breastfeeding and Maternal Authority in Pamela." In *Inventing Maternity: Politics, Science, and Literature, 1650–1865*, edited by Susan C. Greenfield and Carol Barash, 138–158. Lexington: University Press of Kentucky, 1999.

Branch, William. *The English Prison Hulks*. Chicago: Johnson, 1957.

Breitenberg, Mark. *Anxious Masculinity in Early Modern England*. Cambridge: Cambridge University Press, 1996.

Briggs, Julia. "'Delightful Task!' Women, Children, and Reading in the Mid-Eighteenth Century." In *Culturing the Child, 1690–1914: Essays in Memory of Mitzi Myers*, edited by Donelle Ruwe, 67–82. Toronto: Scarecrow Press, 2005.

Bristow, Joseph. *Empire Boys: Adventures in a Man's World*. Sydney: Unwin Hyman, 1991.

"Broadside on 'The Dreadful Life and Confession of a Boy Aged Twelve Years.'" Discovering Literature: Romantics and Victorians Collection Items. British Library Online. https://www.bl.uk/collection-items/broadside-the-dreadful-life-and-confession-of-a-boy-aged-twelve-years.

Brooks, Charles. "Apprenticeship, Social Mobility and the Middling Sort, 1550–1800." In *The Middling Sort of People*, edited by Jonathan Barry and Charles Brooks, 52–83. London: Palgrave, 1994.

Brown, Bill. *A Sense of Things: The Object Matter of American Literature*. Chicago: University of Chicago Press, 2003.

——. "Thing Theory." *Critical Inquiry* 28, no. 1 (October 1, 2001): 1–22.
Brown, Matt. "The Gallows Ballads of Nineteenth-Century London." *Londonist*, April 2010. https://londonist.com/2010/04/the_gallows_ballads_of_19th_century.
Buck, Anne. *Dress in Eighteenth-Century England*. New York: Holmes & Meir, 1979.
Bunyan, John. *The Pilgrim's Progress*. 1678. Oxford: Oxford University Press, 2009.
Burney, Frances. *Evelina; or, The History of a Young Lady's Entrance into the World*. Oxford: Oxford University Press, 2008.
Burton, Robert. *Anatomy of Melancholy*. London, 1621.
Butler, Judith. *Bodies That Matter: On the Discursive Limits of Sex*. Sussex: Psychology Press, 1993.
——. *Gender Trouble*. New York: Routledge, 1990.
——. *Undoing Gender*. New York: Routledge, 2004.
The Cabal; as Acted at the Theatre in George-Street. London, 1763. ECCO, Gale doc. no. CW0110148218.
Campbell, R. *The London Tradesman*. 1747. New Abbot, UK: David & Charles, 1969.
Carretta, Vincent. *Equiano the African: Biography of a Self-Made Man*. Athens: University of Georgia Press, 2005.
——. *Unchained Voices: An Anthology of Black Authors in the English-Speaking World of the Eighteenth Century*. Lexington: University Press of Kentucky, 2003.
Carrot, Mrs. Catherine (Greengrocer). "An Elegiac Epistle." *Literary Fly*, no. 4 (February 20, 1779). https://books.google.ca/books?id=KbdbAAAAQAAJ.
Castle, Terry. *The Female Thermometer: Eighteenth-Century Culture and the Invention of the Uncanny*. Oxford: Oxford University Press, 1995.
——. *Masquerade and Civilization: The Carnivalesque in Eighteenth-Century English Culture and Fiction*. Stanford, CA: Stanford University Press, 1986.
Chandos, John. *Boys Together: English Public Schools 1800–1860*. New Haven, CT: Yale University Press, 1984.
Chapuis, A., and E. Droz. *Les Automates: figures Artificielle d'Hommes et d'Animaux. Histoire et Technique*. Neuchâtel: Griffon, 1949.
Chear, Abraham. *A Looking Glass for Children*. London, 1708. ECCO, Gale doc. no. CW0117990442.
The Chimney Sweepers and Chimneys Regulation Acts. 1840 and 1864.
Clark, Anna. *The Struggle for the Breeches: Gender and the Making of the British Working Class*. Berkeley: University of California Press, 1995.
Clark, Beverly Lyon. *Regendering the School Story*. New York: Routledge, 1996.
Clarke, Norma. "'That Cursed Barbauld Crew': Women Writers and Writing for Children in the Late Eighteenth Century." In *Opening the Nursery Door: Reading, Writing, and Childhood 1600–1900*, edited by Mary Hilton, Morag Styles, and Victor Watson, 91–103. New York: Routledge, 2012.
Clute, John, and John Grant, eds. *The Encyclopedia of Fantasy*. London: Orbit, 1997.
Cockayne, Emily. *Hubbub: Filth, Noise, and Stench in England, 1600–1770*. New Haven, CT: Yale University Press, 2007.
Cohen, Michèle. *Fashioning Masculinity: National Identity and Language in the Eighteenth Century*. New York: Routledge, 1996.
Coleridge, Samuel Taylor. *Collected Letters*, vol. 2: *1801–1806*. Edited by Earl Leslie Griggs. Oxford: Clarendon, 1956.
Connery, Brian A. "Hints toward Authoritative Conversation: Swift's Dialogical Strategies in the Letters and the Life." In Connery, *Representations of Swift*, 159–177.
——, ed. *Representations of Swift*. Newark: University of Delaware Press, 2002.

Corbould, Richard, and Samuel Springsguth. *Juvenile Philosophy; Containing Amusing and Instructive Discourses on Hogarth's Prints ... Designed to Enlarge the Understandings of Youth, and to Impress Them at an Early Period with Just and Liberal Conceptions.* London, 1801.

[Coxe, William]. *Observations on the Present State of Denmark, Russia, and Switzerland. In a Series of Letters.* London, 1784. ECCO, Gale doc. no. CW0104720844.

———. *Sketches of the Natural, Civil, and Political State of Swisserland.* London, 1779. ECCO, Gale doc. no. CW0105422414.

Crosby, Alfred W. *The Measure of Reality: Quantification in Western Europe, 1250–1600.* Cambridge: Cambridge University Press, 1997.

Cullingford, Benita. *British Chimney Sweeps: Five Centuries of Chimney Sweeping.* Lewes, DE: Guild, 2000.

Cumberland, Richard. *The Fashionable Lover; A Comedy: As It Is Acted at the Theatre-Royal in Drury-Lane.* London, 1772.

Cunningham, Hugh. *Children and Childhood in Western Society since 1500.* 3rd ed. New York: Routledge, 2021.

Damousi, Joy. "Writing Gender into History and History into Gender: *Creating a Nation* and Australian Historiography." In *Gender and History: Retrospect and Prospect*, edited by Leonore Davidoff, Keith McClelland, and Eleni Varikas, 194–206. Oxford: Blackwell, 2000.

Damrosch, Leopold. *Jonathan Swift: His Life and His World.* New Haven, CT: Yale University Press, 2013.

Darnton, Robert. *The Business of Enlightenment: A Publishing History of the Encyclopedie 1775–1880.* Cambridge, MA: Belknap, 1979.

Darton, Harvey. *Children's Books in England: Five Centuries of Social Life.* Cambridge: Cambridge University Press, 1982.

Davies, Rebecca. *Written Maternal Authority and Eighteenth-Century Education in Britain: Educating by the Book.* Farnham: Ashgate, 2014.

Davis, Evan Grae, dir. *It's a Girl: The Three Deadliest Words in the World.* London: Shadowline Films, 2012. https://www.itsagirlmovie.com/.

Davis, Natalie Zemon. "Women's History in Transition: The European Case." *Feminist Studies* 3 (1976): 83–103.

d'Azyr, Félix Vicq. *Discours sur l'Anatomie et de la physiologie avec des planche coloriées représentant au naturel les divers organs de l'hommes et des animaux.* Paris: l'Imprimerie de France, F.A. Didot l'ainé, 1786.

Debord, Guy. *Comments on the Society of the Spectacle.* Translated by Malcolm Imrie. 1988. London: Verso, 1998.

Defoe, Daniel. *The Complete English Tradesman ... Calculated for the Instruction of Our Inland Tradesmen; and Especially of Young Beginners.* London, 1726. ECCO, Gale doc. no. CW0107374956.

———. *The Complete Family Instructor ... with a Great Variety of Cases, Relating to the Setting Ill Examples to Children and Servants.* Liverpool, 1800. ECCO, Gale doc. no. CW0117169513.

———. *The History and Remarkable Life of the Truly Honourable Col. Jacque.* Edited by S. H. Monk. 1722. London: Oxford University Press, 1965.

Delamar, Gloria T., ed. *Mother Goose: From Nursery to Literature.* New York: Universe, 2000.

Demers, Patricia, ed. *From Instruction to Delight: An Anthology of Children's Literature to 1850.* Oxford: Oxford University Press, 2004.

Dickens, Charles. *Great Expectations.* 1861. Oxford: Oxford University Press, 2008.

———. *Oliver Twist; or, The Parish Boy's Progress*. 1838. https://www.gutenberg.org/files/730/730-h/730-h.htm.

Dickie, Simon. *Cruelty and Laughter: Forgotten Comic Literature and the Unsentimental Eighteenth Century*. Chicago: University of Chicago Press, 2011.

Diderot, Denis. "Encyclopedia" (1755). Translated by Philip Stewart. Encyclopedia of Diderot & d'Alembert Collaborative Translation Project. http://hdl.handle.net/2027/spo.did2222.0000.004.

DiGirolamo, Vincent. "In Franklin's Footsteps: News Carriers and Postboys in the Revolution and Early Republic." In *Children and Youth in a New Nation*, edited by James Martin, 48–66. New York: New York University Press, 2009.

Dolan, Frances E. *True Relations: Reading, Literature and Evidence in Seventeenth-Century England*. Philadelphia: University of Pennsylvania Press, 2013.

Donato, Clorinda, and Robert M. Maniquis, eds. *The Encyclopédie and the Age of Revolution*. Boston: G. K. Hall, 1992.

Donoghue, Emma. *Slammerkin*. London: Virago, 2000.

Doody, Margaret Anne. "Swift among the Women." *Yearbook of English Studies* 18 (1988): 68–92.

Douglas, Aileen. *Work in Hand: Script, Print, and Writing, 1690–1841*. Oxford: Oxford University Press, 2017.

Douthwaite, Julia V. *The Frankenstein of 1790 and Other Lost Chapters of Revolutionary France*. Chicago: University of Chicago Press, 2012.

Druid, Nestor. *The Lady's Curiosity; or, Weekly Apollo*. London, 1752.

Duffy, Patrick. *The Skilled Compositor, 1850–1914: An Aristocrat among Working Men*. New York: Routledge, 2017.

Dunton, John. *A Voyage round the World*. 1691. Cambridge: Chadwyck-Healey, 1997.

Eagleton, Terry. *Literary Theory: An Introduction*. Minneapolis: University of Minnesota Press, 2008.

Edwards, Edward. *The Disease and the Remedy: An Essay on the Distressed State of the Printing Trade, Proving It to Be Mainly Attributable to Excessive Boy Labour: With Some Practical Observations Showing the Extent of the Distress, and Suggesting a Remedy for Its Gradual Amelioration: Accompanied by an Appeal to Master Printers and Newspaper Proprietors, to Aid in the Work of Reformation*. London, 1850.

Eisenstein, Elizabeth L. *Divine Art, Infernal Machine: The Reception of Printing in the West from First Impressions to the Sense of an Ending*. Philadelphia: University of Pennsylvania Press, 2011.

———. "Gods, Devils, and Gutenberg: The Eighteenth Century Confronts the Printing Press." *Studies in Eighteenth-Century Culture* 27 (1988): 1–12.

———. *The Printing Press as an Agent of Change*. 2 vols. Cambridge: Cambridge University Press, 1980.

Eliot, Simon. "The Business of Victorian Book Publishing." In *The Cambridge Companion to the Victorian Novel*, edited by Deidre David, 36–61. Cambridge: Cambridge University Press, 2000.

Emch, Manuel. *Jaquet-Droz*. New York: Assouline, 2007.

Emig, Rainer. "Sentimental Masculinity: Henry Mackenzie's *The Man of Feeling* (1771)." In *Configuring Masculinity in Theory and Literary Practice*, edited by Stefan Horlacher, 127–129. Leiden: Brill, 2015. https://doi.org/10.1163/9789004299009_008.

Emsley, Clive. "Introduction." In *The Newgate Calendar*, by George Theodore Wilkinson, ix–xvi. Stansted, UK: Wordsworth Editions, 1997.

Emsley, Clive, Tim Hitchcock, and Robert Shoemaker. "Historical Background—Gender in the Proceedings." In *The Proceedings of the Old Bailey: London's Central Criminal Court, 1674 to 1913*, version 7.0. https://www.oldbaileyonline.org/static/Gender.jsp.

The Encyclopedia of Diderot & d'Alembert Collaborative Translation Project. Ann Arbor: Michigan Publishing, University of Michigan Library, 2002.

English, Jim. "A Tentative Enquiry into the Identity of 'A Printer's Devil.'" *Quadrat* 11 (2000): 3-8.

Equiano, Olaudah. *The Life of Olaudah Equiano or Gustavus Vassa, the African*. 1789; 1814. Mineola, NY: Dover, 1999.

Erickson, Robert A. "'The Books of Generation': Some Observations on the Style of the English Midwife Books, 1671-1764." In Boucé, *Sexuality in Eighteenth-Century Britain*, 74-94.

———. *Mother Midnight: Birth, Sex, and Fate in Eighteenth-Century Fiction (Defoe, Richardson, and Sterne)*. New York: AMS Press, 1986.

Everton, Michael. "The Would-Be-Author and the Real Bookseller." *Early American Literature* 40, no. 1 (2005): 79-110.

Fabricant, Carole. *Swift's Landscape*. Baltimore: Johns Hopkins University Press, 1982.

Fanning, Christopher. "Small Particles of Eloquence: Sterne and the Scriblerian Text." *Modern Philology* 100, no. 3 (2003): 360-392.

Fara, Patricia. *Pandora's Breeches: Women, Science and Power in the Enlightenment*. London: Pimlico, 2004.

Fenichel, Otto. *The Psychoanalytic Theory of Neurosis*. 1946. London: Routledge, 2017.

[Fenn, Ellenor, pseud. Mrs. Lovechild]. *The Art of Teaching in Sport; Designed as a Prelude to a Set of Toys, for Enabling Ladies to Instill the Rudiments of Spelling, Reading, Grammar, and Arithmetic, under the Idea of Amusement*. London, [1784/5]. 1785 ed. ECCO, Gale doc. no., CW0116744240.

———[pseud. Mrs. Lovechild]. *The Child's Grammar. Designed to Enable Ladies Who May Not Have Attended to the Subject Themselves to Instruct Their Children ... with Directions for Full Examination*. Dublin, 1799. ECCO, Gale doc. no. CB127841200.

———. *Cobwebs to Catch Flies; or, Dialogues in Short Sentences Adapted to Children from the Age of Three to Eight Years*. 2 vols. London, 1783. ECCO, Gale doc. no. CW0117078924 and CW0117079016.

———. *The Female Guardian. Designed to Correct Some of the Foibles Incident to Girls, and Supply Them with Innocent Amusement for Their Hours of Leisure*. London, 1784. ECCO, Gale doc. no. CW0114335183.

———[pseud. Mrs. Lovechild]. *The Rational Dame; or, Hints towards Supplying Prattle for Children*. London, [1790?]. ECCO, Gale doc. no. CW0112777753.

———[pseud. Mrs. Lovechild]. *Rational Sports ... Designed as a Hint to Mothers How They May Inform the Minds of Their Little People Respecting the Objects with Which They Are Surrounded*. London, 1783. ECCO, Gale doc. no. CB129502681.

———. *School Dialogues, for Boys. Being an Attempt to Convey Instruction Insensibly to Their Tender Minds, and Instill the Love of Virtue*. 2 vols. London, 1783. ECCO, Gale doc. nos. CW0112531545 and CW0111207898.

———[pseud. Mrs. Teachwell]. *School Occurrences: Supposed to Have Arisen among a Set of Young Ladies*. London, [1782-1783]. 1790 ed. ECCO, Gale doc. no. CW0116947275

Fielding, Henry. *The History of Tom Jones, a Foundling*. Vol. 1. London, 1775. ECCO, Gale doc. no. CW0116772389.

Fielding, Sarah. *The Governess, or Little Female Academy*. Dublin, 1749.

Fieliz, Sonja. "Tales of Miracle or Lessons of Morality? School Editions of Ovid's *Metamorphosis* as a Means of Shaping the Personalities of British Schoolboys." In Müller, *Fashioning Childhood in the Eighteenth Century*, 145–156.

Flanders, Judith. "Murder as Entertainment." In *Discovering Literature: Romantics & Victorians*. British Library Online. https://www.bl.uk/romantics-and-victorians/articles/murder-as-entertainment.

Fletcher, Anthony. *Gender, Sex, and Subordination in England, 1500–1800*. [1995] Rev. ed. New Haven, CT: Yale University Press, 1999.

———. *Growing Up in England: The Experience of Childhood, 1600–1914*. [2008] New Haven, CT: Yale University Press, 2010.

Flint, Christopher. *The Appearance of Print in Eighteenth-Century Fiction*. Cambridge: Cambridge University Press, 2011.

———. "Speaking Objects: The Circulation of Stories in Eighteenth-Century Prose Fiction." *PMLA* 113, no. 2 (March 1998): 212–226.

Foote, Samuel. *The Devil upon Two Sticks: A Comedy, in Three Acts. As It Is Performed at the Theatre-Royal in the Haymarket*. London, 1778. ECCO, 2011. https://quod.lib.umich.edu/e/ecco/004794420.0001.000/1:6?rgn=div1;view=toc.

Ford Smith, Victoria. *Between Generations: Collaborative Authorship in the Golden Age of Children's Literature*. Jackson: University Press of Mississippi, 2017.

Foucault, Michel. *Discipline and Punish: The Birth of the Prison*. 1977. New York: Vintage, 1995.

Fox, Christopher. "Introduction." In *The Cambridge Companion to Jonathan Swift*, edited by Christopher Fox. Cambridge: Cambridge University Press, 2003.

Foyster, Elizabeth A. *Manhood in Early Modern England: Honour, Sex and Marriage*. [1999] New York: Routledge, 2014.

Foyster, Elizabeth, and James Marten, eds. *A Cultural History of Childhood and Family in the Age of Enlightenment*. London: Bloomsbury, 2014.

Franklin, Alexandra. "Making Sense of Broadside Ballad Illustrations in the Seventeenth and Eighteenth Centuries." In *Studies in Ephemera: Text and Image in Eighteenth-Century Print*, edited by Kevin D. Murphy and Sally O'Driscoll, 169–194. Lewisburg, PA: Bucknell University Press, 2013.

Franks, Peter. *Print and Politics: A History of Trade Unions in the New Zealand Printing Industry, 1865–1995*. Victoria: Victoria University Press, 2001.

French, Henry, and Mark Rothery. "Male Anxiety among Younger Sons of the English Landed Gentry, 1700–1900." *Historical Journal* 62, no. 4 (2019): 967–995.

Freud, Sigmund. *The Uncanny*. 1919. Translated by David McClintock. New York: Penguin, 2003.

Friedman, David M. *A Mind of Its Own: A Cultural History of the Penis*. New York: Free Press, 2001.

Frye, Herbert. *The Royal Guide to the London Charities*. London, 1884. HathiTrust Digital Library. https://catalog.hathitrust.org/Record/102657406.

Fulford, Tim. "A Romantic Technologist and Britain's Little Black Boys." *Wordsworth Circle* 33, no. 1 (2002): 36–42. https://link.gale.com/apps/doc/A88610755/AONE.

Fulford, Tim, Debbie Lee, and Peter J. Kitson. "Britain's Little Black Boys and the Technologies of Benevolence." In *Literature, Science, and Exploration in the Romantic Era: Bodies of Knowledge*, 228–270. Cambridge: Cambridge University Press, 2004.

Fulton, Henry L. "Private Tutoring in Scotland: The Example of Mure of Dalwell." *Eighteenth-Century Life* 27, no. 3 (2003): 53–69.

Gadd, Ian. "Leaving the Printer to his Liberty: Swift and the London Book Trade 1701–1714." In *Jonathan Swift and the Eighteenth-Century Book*, edited by Paddy Bullard and James McLaverty, 51–64. Cambridge: Cambridge University Press, 2013.

Gammon, Julie. "A Denial of Innocence: Female Juvenile Victims of Rape and the English Legal System in the Eighteenth Century." In *Children in Question: Children, Parents and the State*, edited by Anthony Fletcher and Stephen Hussey, 74–95. Manchester: Manchester University Press, 1999.

Garrick in the Shades. London, 1779. ECCO, Gale doc. no. CW0112939638.

Gatrell, V.A.C. *The Hanging Tree: Execution and the English People 1770–1868*. Oxford: Oxford University Press, 1996.

Gee, Sophie. *Making Waste: Leftovers and the Eighteenth-Century Imagination*. Princeton, NJ: Princeton University Press, 2010.

Gibbon, Edward. *Miscellaneous Works: of Edward Gibbon, Esquire. With Memoirs of His Life and Writings, Composed by Himself: Illustrated from His Letters, with Occasional Notes and Narrative, by John Lord Sheffield. In Two Volumes*. Vol. 1. London, 1796. ECCO, 2011. https://quod.lib.umich.edu/e/ecco/004849601.0001.001/.

Gilbert, Sandra, and Susan Gubar. *The Madwoman in the Attic: The Woman Writer and the Nineteenth-Century Imagination*. 2nd ed. 1979. New Haven, CT: Yale University Press, 2000.

Giovanopoulos, Anna-Christina. "The Legal Status of Children in Eighteenth-Century England." In Müller, *Fashioning Childhood in the Eighteenth Century*, 43–52.

Gladfelder, Hal. *Criminality and Narrative in Eighteenth-Century England: Beyond the Law*. Baltimore: Johns Hopkins University Press, 2001.

Godwin, William. "Private Education." Essay 7 in *The Enquirer. From Reflections on Education, Manners, and Literature*. London, 1797.

Gollapudi, Aparna. "Criminal Children in the Eighteenth Century and Daniel Defoe's *Colonel Jack*." *Philological Quarterly* 96, no. 1 (2017): 27–53.

———. "Personhood, Property Rights, and the Child in John Locke's *Two Treatises of Government* and Daniel Defoe's Fiction." *Eighteenth-Century Fiction* 28, no. 1 (Fall 2015): 25–58.

Goode, Mike. *Sentimental Masculinity and the Rise of History, 1790–1890*. Cambridge: Cambridge University Press, 2009.

Goosequill, Benjamin, and Thomas Paragraph. *Curious Facts and Anecdotes, Not Contained in the Memoirs of Philip Thickness, Esq*. London, 1790. https://books.google.ca/books?id=QB4IAAAAQAAJ&d.

Goring, Paul. *The Rhetoric of Sensibility in Eighteenth-Century Culture*. Cambridge: Cambridge University Press, 2004.

Gray, Thomas. "Ode on a Distant Prospect of Eton College" (1747). In *Broadview Anthology of British Literature: The Restoration and the Eighteenth Century*, edited by Joseph Laurence Black, 604–605. Peterborough, Ontario: Broadview Press, 2006.

Green, Dominic. "Towards the Best of All Possible Worlds." Review of *The Dream of Enlightenment: The Rise of Modern Philosophy* by Anthony Gottlieb. *Spectator*, no. 10 (September 2016). https://www.spectator.co.uk/article/towards-the-best-of-all-possible-worlds.

Greenwood, Emma L. "Work, Identity and Letterpress Printers in Britain, 1750–1850." PhD diss., University of Manchester, 2015.

Grenby, Matthew. *The Child Reader, 1700–1840*. Cambridge: Cambridge University Press, 2011.

Grenby, Matthew, and Nigel Wood. Introductory essay to *Tom Thumb's Exhibition, Being an Account of Many Valuable and Surprising Curiosities Which He Has Collected in the Course of His Travels; for the Instruction and Amusement of the British Youth*. London, [1761] 1815. http://hockliffe.dmu.ac.uk/items/0239.html.

Grumbach, Doris. "Printers' Devils and Other Apprentices." *Washington Post*, February 23, 1986. https://www.washingtonpost.com/archive/entertainment/books/1986/02/23/printers-devils-and-other-apprentices/93d714b6-16ca-4d9d-bbac-0a748bfc4261/.

Hahn, Daniel, and Michael Morpurgo. *Oxford Companion to Children's Literature*. Oxford: Oxford University Press, 2015.

Hanafi, Zakiya. *The Monster in the Machine: Magic, Medicine, and the Marvelous in the Time of the Scientific Revolution*. Durham, NC: Duke University Press, 2000.

Hanway, Jonas. *The State of Chimney-Sweepers' Young Apprentices*. London, 1773.

———. *The State of Master Chimney-Sweepers, and Their Journeymen; Particularly of Distressed Boys, Apprentices, Who Are Daily Seen in the Streets of These Cities Staggering under a Load of Misery*. London, 1779. ECCO, Gale doc. no. CW0105766108.

Hardy, Rob. "The Ruptured Poor." *Rough Draft*, July 7, 2008. http://rbhardy3rd.blogspot.com/2008/06/ruptured-poor.html.

Harries, Elizabeth W. "Words, Sex, and Gender in Sterne's Novels." In *The Cambridge Companion to Laurence Sterne*, edited by Thomas Keymer, 111–124. Cambridge: Cambridge University Press, 2009.

Harris, Elizabeth. *The Boy and His Press*. Washington, DC: Smithsonian Institution, 1992.

Harvey, Karen. *Reading Sex in the Eighteenth Century: Bodies and Gender in English Erotic Culture*. Cambridge: Cambridge University Press, 2004.

Head, Francis Bond. *The Printer's Devil; or, A Type of the Old One*. London, 1833.

Heidegger, Martin. *What Is a Thing?* Translated by W. B. Barton. Chicago: Henry Regner, 1967.

Henry, Frances H. I. "Love, Sex, and the Noose: The Emotions of Sodomy in 18th Century England." PhD diss., University of Western Ontario, 2019. https://ir.lib.uwo.ca/cgi/viewcontent.cgi?article=9111&context=etd.

Hewitt, Regina. *Symbolic Interactions: Social Problems and Literary Interventions in the Works of Baillie, Scott, and Landor*. Lewisburg, PA: Bucknell University Press, 2006.

Heywood, Colin. *History of Childhood: Children and Childhood in the West from Medieval to Modern Times*. Cambridge: Polity, 2001.

Hilaire-Pérez, Liliane, and Christelle Rabier. "Self-Machinery? Steel Trusses and the Management of Ruptures in Eighteenth-Century Europe." *Technology and Culture* 54, no. 3 (2013): 460–502. https://doi.org/10.1353/tech.2013.0096.

Hilton, Mary. *Women and the Shaping of the Nation's Young: Education and Public Doctrine in Britain, 1750–1850*. Aldershot: Ashgate, 2007.

Hitchcock, Tim. *Down and Out in Eighteenth-Century London*. London: Hambledon Continuum, 2004.

Hitchcock, Tim, Robert Shoemaker, Sharon Howard, Jamie McLaughlin, et al. *London Lives, 1690–1800*. Online version 1.1, April 24, 2012. www.londonlives.org.

Hobbes, Thomas. *Leviathan*. 1651. London, 1668.

Hobbs, Donna Elaine. "Telling Tales out of School: Schoolbooks, Audiences, and the Production of Vernacular Literature in Late Medieval England." PhD diss., University of Texas at Austin, 2012. https://repositoriesss.lib.utexas.edu/bitstream/handle/2152/19594/hobbs_dissertation_20129.pdf?sequence=1.

Holcroft, Thomas. *The School for Arrogance*. London, 1791. ECCO, 2011. https://quod.lib.umich.edu/e/ecco/004889453.0001.000

/1:6?firstpubl1 = 1700;firstpubl2 = 1800;rgn=div1;sort=occur;subview=detail;type=simple; view=fulltext;q1=printer+s+devil.

Holden, Robert. *Orphans of History: The Forgotten Children of the First Fleet*. Melbourne: Text, 2000.

Holland, John. "An Appeal to the Fair Sex." In *The Chimney-Sweeper's Friend, and Climbing-Boy's Album*, arranged by James Montgomery, 277–287. London, 1824. https://books.google.ca/books?id=GwdgAAAAcAAJ.

Honeyman, Katrina. *Child Workers in England, 1780–1820*. Farnham: Ashgate, 2007.

Hopkins, Ellice. *The Power of Womanhood; or, Mothers and Sons*. 1899. New York: E. P. Dutton, 1901. https://books.google.ca/books?id=7hcEAAAAYAAJ.

Horne, George. *Sunday Schools Recommended, a Sermon, with an Appendix on the Method of forming and Conducting Them*. Oxford, 1786.

Horne, Jackie. *History and the Construction of the Child in Early British Children's Literature*. Farnham: Ashgate, 2011.

Horsley, Henry Sharpe. *The Affectionate Parent's Gift; and the Good Child's Reward* (1828). In Demers, *From Instruction to Delight*, 219–220.

Hudson, Nicholas. "'Britons Never Will Be Slaves': National Myth, Conservatism, and the Beginnings of British Antislavery." *Eighteenth-Century Studies* 34, no. 4 (2001): 559–576. https://doi.org/10.1353/ecs.2001.0044.

Hughes, Thomas. *Tom Brown's School Days*. London: Harper and Brothers, 1911. https://www.gutenberg.org/files/1480/1480-h/1480-h.htm.

Hume, David. "On Luxury" (1742). In Kramnick, *Portable Enlightenment Reader*, 491.

Humphries, Jane. *Childhood and Child Labour in the British Industrial Revolution*. Cambridge: Cambridge University Press, 2010.

Hunt, Lynn, and Margaret Jacob. "Somatic Affects: The Affective Revolution in 1790s Britain." *Eighteenth-Century Studies* 34, no. 4 (2001): 491–521.

Hunt, Tamara L. "Servants, Masters and Seditious Libel in Eighteenth-Century England." *Book History* 20 (2017): 83–110. https://doi.org/10.1353/bh.2017.0002.

Immel, Andrea. "The Didacticism That Laughs: John Newbery's Entertaining Little Books and William Hogarth's Pictured Morals." *Lion and the Unicorn* 33 (2009): 146–166.

———. "'Mistress of Infantine Language': Lady Ellenor Fenn, Her Set of Toys, and the 'Education of Each Moment.'" *Children's Literature* 25 (1997): 215–228.

Janeway, James. *A Token for Children: Being an Exact Account of the Conversion, Holy and Exemplary Lives, and Joyful Deaths of Several Young Children*. London, 1763. ECCO, Gale doc. no. CW0122573846.

Jaquet-Droz. "History." n.d. http://www.jaquet-droz.com/en/history.

Jaquet-Droz, Henri-Louis. *A Description of Several PIECES OF MECHANISM: Invented by the Sieur Jaquet-Droz of the Chaux de Fonds, in the County of Neuchâtel, Switzerland and Which Are Now to Be Seen at the Great Room, No.6, in King-Street, Covent Garden*. Bodleian Library, Oxford, John Johnson Collection.

———. *A Description of Several Pieces of Mechanism, Invented by the Sieur Jaquet-Droz, of . . . Switzerland. And Which Are Now to Be Seen at the Great Room, no. 6, in King-Street, Covent-Garden*. London, 1780[?]. ECCO, Gale doc. no. CW0108702426.

Jaucourt, Louis, chevalier de. "Printing, History Of." Translated by I. M. L. Donaldson. *Encyclopedia of Diderot & d'Alembert Collaborative Translation Project*. https://quod.lib.umich.edu/d/did/did2222.0000.090.

———. "Tool." *The Encyclopedia of Diderot & d'Alembert Collaborative Translation Project*. Translated by Ann-Marie Thornton. http://hdl.handle.net/2027/spo.did2222.0002.229.

Jerrold, Douglas. "Sketches of the English." In *The Writings of Douglas Jerrold*, vol. 5. London, 1853.

Johnson, Samuel. *A Dictionary of the English Language*. Vols. 1–2. London, 1773. ECCO, Gale doc. no. CW0110905602.

———. *A Dictionary of the English Language: A Digital Edition of the 1755 Classic by Samuel Johnson*. Edited by Brandi Besalke. Last modified June 14, 2017. http://johnsonsdictionaryonline.com.

———. *The Rambler: In Four Volumes*. Vol. 1. Edited by Alex Chalmers. Philadelphia, 1827. Hathi Trust Digital Library. https://catalog.hathitrust.org/Record/006056181.

Johnston, Freya. "Little Lives: An Eighteenth-Century Sub-genre." *Cambridge Quarterly* 32, no. 2 (2003): 143–160.

Jones, Mary. "An Epistle to Lady Bowyer." In *Poems by Eminent Ladies*, 112. London, 1755.

Jordan, Sarah. "Idleness, Class and Gender in the Long Eighteenth Century." In *Idleness, Indolence and Leisure in English Literature*, edited by M. Fludernik and M. Nandi, 107–128. London: Palgrave Macmillan, 2014. https://doi.org/10.1057/9781137404008_6.

Joy, Louise. "Eighteenth-Century Children's Poetry and the Complexity of the Child's Mind." In *Literary Cultures and Eighteenth-Century Childhoods*, edited by Andrew O'Malley, 117–138. New York: Palgrave Macmillan, 2018.

Juhas, Kirsten. "Introduction." In *A Meditation upon a Broomstick*, edited by Kirsten Juhas, Dirk F. Passmann, Hermann J. Real, and Sandra Simon. Münster: Ehrenpreis Centre for Swift Studies, November 2011. https://www.uni-muenster.de/imperia/md/content/englischesseminar/swift/a_meditation_upon_a_broomstick_introduction.pdf.

Kahn, Coppélia. *Roman Shakespeare: Warriors, Wounds, and Women*. New York: Routledge, 1997.

Kang, Minsoo. *Sublime Dreams of Living Machines: The Automaton in the European Imagination*. Cambridge, MA: Harvard University Press, 2011.

Kant, Immanuel. *Grounding for the Metaphysics of Morals / On a Supposed Right to Lie Because of Philanthropic Concerns*. Translated by James W. Ellington. 1785. Indianapolis: Hackett, 1993.

———. *Observations on the Feeling of the Beautiful and the Sublime*. Translated by John T. Goldthwaite. Berkeley: University of California Press, 2003.

———. *Prolegomena to Any Future Metaphysics*. 1783. Translated by Paul Carus. 3rd ed. Chicago: Open Court, 1906. https://www.gutenberg.org/files/52821/52821-h/52821-h.htm.

———. "What Is Enlightenment?" 1784. Translated by Mary C. Smith. Columbia University Library Online. hppt://www.columbia.edu/acis/eets/CCREAD/etscc/kant.html.

Karras, Ruth Mazo. *From Boys to Men: Formations of Masculinity in Late Medieval Europe*. Philadelphia: University of Pennsylvania Press, 2003.

Kaufman-Osborn, Timothy V. *Creatures of Prometheus: Gender and the Politics of Technology*. Lanham, MD: Rowman & Littlefield, 1997.

Kegan Gardiner, Judith. *Masculinity Studies and Feminist Theory*. New York: Columbia University Press, 2002.

Kelly, Ann Cline. "Swift's Explorations of Slavery in Houyhnhnmland and Ireland." *PMLA* 91, no. 5 (1976): 846–855. https://doi.org/10.2307/461560.

Kelly, James. "Chimney Sweeps, Climbing Boys and Child Employment in Ireland, 1775–1875." *Irish Economic and Social History Journal* 47, no. 1 (2020): 36–58.

Kent, D. A. "Ubiquitous but Invisible: Female Domestic Servants in Mid-Eighteenth-Century London." *History Workshop* 28 (1989): 111–128.

Keymer, Thomas, ed. *Laurence Sterne's* Tristram Shandy: *A Casebook*. Oxford: Oxford University Press, 2006.

———. *Richardson's "Clarissa" and the Eighteenth-Century Reader*. Cambridge: Cambridge University Press, 1992.

———. *Sterne, the Moderns and the Novel*. Oxford: Oxford University Press, 2002.

Kidd, Kenneth B. *Making American Boys: Boyology and the Feral Tale*. Minneapolis: University of Minnesota Press, 2004.

Kilner, Dorothy. *Letters from a Mother to Her Children, on Various Important Subjects*. Vol. 1. London, [1780?]. ECCO, Gale doc. no. CW0114554876.

Kim, James. "'Good Cursed, Bouncing Losses': Masculinity, Sentimental Irony, and Exuberance in *Tristram Shandy*." *Eighteenth Century: Theory and Interpretation* 48, no. 1 (2007): 3–24.

Kimmel, Michael. *The Gendered Society*. Oxford: Oxford University Press, 2000.

King, Peter. *Crime and Law in England, 1750–1840: Remaking Justice from the Margins*. Cambridge: Cambridge University Press, 2006.

King, Ross. "*Tristram Shandy* and the Wound of Language." In Keymer, *Laurence Sterne's* Tristram Shandy, 123–146.

King, Thomas A. *The Gendering of Men, 1600–1750*. Vol. 1: *The English Phallus*. Madison: University of Wisconsin Press, 2004.

Kingsley, Charles. *The Water Babies*. London, [1862–1863] 889.http://www.gutenberg.org/files/1018/1018-h/1018-h.htm.

Kirby, Peter. *Child Labour in Britain, 1750–1870*. New York: Palgrave Macmillan, 2003.

Knowles, Elizabeth, ed. *The Oxford Dictionary of Phrase and Fable*. Oxford: Oxford University Press, 2016.

Kramnick, Isaac, ed. *The Portable Enlightenment Reader*. New York: Penguin, 1994.

Kristeva, Julia. *Powers of Horror: An Essay on Abjection*. Translated by Leon S. Roudiez. New York: Columbia University Press, 1982.

Lafont, Anne. "How Skin Color Became a Racial Marker: Art Historical Perspectives on Race." *Eighteenth-Century Studies* 51, no. 1 (2017): 89–113. https://doi.org/10.1353/ecs.2017.0046.

Lamb, Charles. *The Letters of Charles and Mary Lamb 1821–1842*. 2 vols. Edited by E. V. Lucas. London: Methuen, 2019.

———. *The Works of Charles Lamb: To Which Are Prefixed, His Letters, and a Sketch of His Life*. Vol. 2. Edited by Thomas Noon Talfourd. New York: Harper & Brothers, 1838.

Lamb, Charles, and Mary Lamb. *Poetry for Children*. London, 1809.

Lamb, Edel. "Youth Culture." In *The Ashgate Companion to Popular Culture in Early Modern England*, edited by Andrew Hadfield et al., 31–38. New York: Routledge, 2016.

Lamb, Jonathan. *Sterne's Fiction and the Double Principle*. Cambridge: Cambridge University Press, 1989.

Lamont, Claire. "Blake, Lamb and the Chimney-Sweepers." *Charles Lamb Bulletin* 76 (1991): 109–123.

Landa, Louis. "The Shandean Homunculus: The Background of Sterne's 'Little Gentleman.'" In *Restoration and Eighteenth-Century Literature: Essays in Honour of Alan Dugald McKillop*, edited by C. Carroll Camden, 140–159. Chicago: University of Chicago Press, 1963.

Lane, Joan. *Apprenticeship in England, 1600–1914*. London: UCL Press, 1996.

Lavoie, Chantel. "The Boy in the Text: Mary Barber, Her Son, and Children's Poetry in *Poems on Several Occasions*" *ABO: Interactive Journal for Women in the Arts, 1640–1830* 11, no. 1 (June 2021). https://doi.org/10.5038/2157-7129.11.1.1260.

———. "*A Little Book for Mothers and Sons* (1919): A Church Army Book of Days for Boys and the Women Who Raised Them." *First World War Studies* 9, no. 1 (2018): 57–71.

———. "Romancing the Purse and Sexualizing the Schoolboy in *The Fortunate Blue-Coat Boy* (1770)." *English Studies in Canada* 44, no. 4 (2021): 115–132.

———. "*Tristram Shandy*, Boyhood, and Breeching," *Eighteenth-Century Fiction* 28, no. 1 (2015): 85–107. https://muse.jhu.edu/article/595358.

Lemay, J. A. Leo. *The Life of Benjamin Franklin*. Vol. 2: *Printer and Publisher, 1730–1747*. Philadelphia: University of Pennsylvania Press, 2006.

Lerer, Seth. *Children's Literature: A Reader's History, from Aesop to Harry Potter*. Chicago: University of Chicago Press, 2008.

Leslie, Madeline. *Jack the Chimney Sweeper: And Other Stories for Children*. Boston, 1859.

Levene, Alysa. "'Honesty, Sobriety and Diligence': Master-Apprentice Relations in Eighteenth- and Nineteenth-Century England." *Social History* 33, no. 2 (2008): 183–200.

Lillo, George. *The London Merchant; or, The History of George Barnwell. As It Is Acted at the Theatre Royal in Drury Lane*. 1731. London, 1776. ECCO, Gale doc. no. CW0107652785.

Linebaugh, Peter. *The London Hanged: Crime and Civil Society in the Eighteenth Century*. London: Verso, 2006.

Lipset, Seymour Martin, Martin Trow, and James S. Coleman. *Union Democracy: The Internal Politics of the International Typographical Union*. New York: Free Press, 1956.

The Literary Panorama, and National Register. Vol. 2. London, 1807. Hathi Trust Digital Library. https://babel.hathitrust.org/cgi/pt?id=chi.34333090.

Locke, John. *An Essay Concerning Human Understanding. In Four Books*. 1689. London, 1690.

———. *Some Thoughts Concerning Education*. Harvard Classics vol. 37. *Locke/Berkley/Hume*, pt. 1: *Locke*. New York: Collier, 1909–1914. https://www.bartleby.com/37/1/.

———. *Two Treatises of Government* (1689). Vols. 1–2. London: R. Butler, 1821. www.bartleby.com/169/.

Lowth, Robert. *A Short Introduction to English Grammar, with Critical Notes*. London, 1762.

Maciulewicz, Joanna. *Representations of Book Culture in Eighteenth-Century English Imaginative Writing*. New Directions in Book History. London: Palgrave Macmillan, 2018.

MacKenzie, Scott R. "Breeches of Decorum: The Figure of a Barbarian in Montaigne and Addison." *South Central Review* 23, no. 2 (2006): 99–127. http://www.jstor.org/stable/40039933.

Mackie, Erin. "Boys Will Be Boys: Masculinity, Criminality, and the Restoration Rake." *Eighteenth Century* 26, no. 2 (2005): 129–149.

Magubane, Zine. *Bringing the Empire Home: Race, Class, and Gender in Britain and Colonial South Africa*. Chicago: University of Chicago Press, 2004.

Mallan, Kerry. "Picturing the Male." In *Ways of Being Male: Representing Masculinities in Children's Literature and Film*, edited by John Stephens, 15–37. New York: Routledge, 2002.

Manen, Niels van. "The Regulation of Chimney Sweep Apprentices, 1770–1840." In *Childhood and Child Labour in Industrial England: Diversity and Agency, 1750–1914*, edited by Nigel Goose and Katrina Honeyman, 97–114. Farnham: Ashgate, 2013.

Manlove, C. N. "Swift's Structures: 'A Description of the Morning' and Some Others." *Studies in English Literature, 1500–1900* 29, no. 3 (1989): 463–472. https://doi.org/10.2307/450650.

Mayhew, Henry. *London Labour and the London Poor: A Cyclopaedia of the Conditions and Earnings of Those That Will Work, Those That Cannot Work, and Those That Will Not Work*. 1861. Stansted: Wordsworth Press, 2008.

Mazlish, Bruce. "The Man-Machine and Artificial Intelligence." *Stanford Humanities Review* 4, no. 2 (1995): 21–45. http://www2.psych.utoronto.ca/users/reingold/courses/ai/cache/mazlish.html.

McDonagh, Josephine. *Child Murder and British Culture, 1720–1900*. Cambridge: Cambridge University Press, 2003.

McGann, Jerome. *The Textual Condition*. Princeton, NJ: Princeton University Press, 1991.

McMaster, Juliet. *Reading the Body in the Eighteenth-Century Novel*. Basingstoke: Palgrave Macmillan, 2004.

———. "'Uncrystalized Flesh and Blood': The Body in *Tristram Shandy*." *Eighteenth-Century Fiction* 2, no. 3 (1990): 197–214. https://doi.org/10.1353/ecf.1990.0031.

Mechling, Jay. "Toilet Training." In *Encyclopedia of Children and Childhood: In History and Society*, edited by Paula S. Fass. New York: Macmillan, 2004. http://www.faqs.org/childhood/Th-W/Toilet-Training.html.

Meek, Heather. "Motherhood, Hysteria, and the Eighteenth-Century Woman Writer." In *Secrets of Generation: Reproduction in the Long Eighteenth Century*, edited by Raymond Stephanson and Darren Wagner, 238–257. Toronto: University of Toronto Press, 2015.

Memoirs of a Printer's Devil; Interspersed with Pleasing Recollections, Local Descriptions and Anecdotes. London, 1793. https://books.google.ca/books/about/Memoirs_of_a_Printer_s_Devil.html?id=UxBcxwEACAAJ.

Mettrie, Julien Offray de La. *Man a Machine [L'Homme Machine]. Wherein the Several Systems of Philosophers, in Respect to the Soul of Man, Are Examin'd . . . and a Full Detail Is Given of the Several Springs Which Move the Human Machine*. 1748. 2nd ed. London, 1850. ECCO, Gale doc. no. CW0120526618.

Michals, Teresa. *Books for Children, Books for Adults: Age and the Novel from Defoe to James*. Cambridge: Cambridge University Press, 2014.

Michelson, Bruce. *Printer's Devil: Mark Twain and the American Publishing Revolution*. Berkeley: University of California Press, 2006.

Miller, Naomi J., and Naomi Yavneh, eds. *Gender and Early Modern Constructions of Childhood*. Farnham: Ashgate, 2011.

Montgomery, James. *The Chimney-Sweeper's Friend*. London, 1824. Facsimile ed. by Donald H. Reiman. New York: Garland, 1978.

Moore, Thomas. *The Fudges in England*. London: Longman, Rees, Orme, Brown, Green & Longman, 1835. https://www.google.ca/books/edition/The_Fudges_in_England/4UM1AAAAMAAJ?hl=en&gbpv=0.

More, Charles. *Skill and the English Working Class, 1870–1914*. London: Croom Helm, 1980.

More, Hannah. "The Apprentice's Monitor; or, Indentures in Verse, Shewing What They Are Bound to Do." Bath, 1785. ECCO, 2011. In *Cheap Repositor Tracts* (1795–1817). https://quod.lib.umich.edu/e/ecco/004796394.0001.000/.

———. *The Cheapside Apprentice; or, The History of Mr. Francis H . . . Shewing Also, How a Gay Life, May Prove a Short One; and That a Merry Evening May Produce a Sorrowful Morning*. Philadelphia, 1800. Ann Arbor: Text Creation Partnership, 2011. https://quod.lib.umich.edu/e/evans/N27875.0001.001/.

Morgan, Gwenda, and Peter Rushton. "Visible Bodies: Power, Subordination and Identity in the Eighteenth-Century Atlantic World." *Journal of Social History* 39, no. 1 (2005): 39–64.

Morgenroth, Thekla, and Michelle K. Ryan, "Gender Trouble in Social Psychology: How Can Butler's Work Inform Experimental Social Psychologists' Conceptualization of Gender?" *Frontiers in Psychology* 27 (July 2018). https://doi.org/10.3389/fpsyg.2018.01320.

Morris, William. "The Beauty of Life" (1880). In *William Morris on Art and Socialism*, edited by Norman Kelvin, 35–55. Minneola, NY: Dover, 1999.

Moxon, Joseph. *Mechanick Exercises; or, The Doctrine of Handyworks. Applied to the Art of Printing*. Vol. 2. London, 1683. https://library.si.edu/digital-library/book/moxonsmechanicke21683moxo.

Moxon, Joseph, and Theodore L. De Vinne. *Mechanick Exercises; or The Doctrine of Handyworks*. 3rd ed. London, 1703.

Müller, Anja, ed. *Fashioning Childhood in the Eighteenth Century: Age and Identity*. New York: Routledge, 2006.

——. *Framing Childhood in Eighteenth-Century English Periodicals and Prints, 1689–1789*. Surrey: Ashgate, 2009.

Mulvey, Laura. "Visual Pleasure and Narrative Cinema." *Screen* 16, no. 3 (Autumn 1975): 6–18. http://www.jahsonic.com/VPNC.html.

Munck, Thomas. *The Enlightenment: A Comparative Social History, 1721–1794*. London: Hodder Arnold, 2000.

Myers, Mitzi. "Impeccable Governesses, Rational Dames, and Moral Mothers: Mary Wollstonecraft and the Female Tradition in Georgian Children's Books." *Children's Literature* 14, no. 1 (1986): 31–59.

Myszkowska-Kaszuba, Magdalena. "The Only Women That Are Mothers of Men. Plutarch's Creation of the Spartan Mother." *Graeco-Latina Brunensia* 19, no. 1 (2014): 77–92.

Navest, Karlijn. "Ash's Grammatical Institutes and 'Mrs. Teachwell's Library for Young Ladies.'" In *Perspective on Prescriptivism*, edited by John C. Beal et al., 59–82. Berlin: Peter Lang, 2008.

Nel, Philip, and Lissa Paul, eds. *Keywords for Children's Literature*. New York: New York University Press, 2011.

Nelson, Victoria. *The Secret Life of Puppets*. Cambridge, MA: Harvard University Press, 2003.

Newbery, John. *A Little Pretty Pocket-Book . . . A New Attempt to Teach Children the Use of the English Alphabet, by Way of Diversion*. 1744. London, 1770. ECCO, Gale doc. no. CW0116143876.

—— [pseud. Tom Telescope]. *The Newtonian System of Philosophy . . . Collected and Methodized for the Benefit of the Youth of These Kingdoms*. London, 1761. From ECCO, Gale doc. no. CW0122409707.

——. *Tom Thumb's Exhibition, Being an Account of Many Valuable and Surprising Curiosities Which He Has Collected in the Course of His Travels; for the Instruction and Amusement of the British Youth*. London, 1815. Hockliffe Project. http://hockliffe.dmu.ac.uk/items/0239.html.

Newburn, Tim, and Elizabeth A. Stanko, eds. *Just Boys Doing Business? Men, Masculinities and Crime*. East Sussex: Psychology Press, 1994.

Newton, Hannah. *The Sick Child in Early Modern England, 1580–1720*. Oxford: Oxford University Press, 2012.

Nicholson, George. *On Clothing*. Manchester, 1797. ECCO, Gale doc. no. CB126089224.

Nielson, Wendy C. "Rousseau's *Pygmalion* and Automata in the Romantic Period." In *Romanticism, Rousseau, Switzerland: New Prospects*, edited by Angela Esterhammer, Dianne Piccitto, and Patrick Vencent, 68–83. London: Palgrave Macmillan, 2015.

Nikolajeva, Maria. "The Identification Fallacy: Perspective and Subjectivity in Children's Literature." In *Telling Children's Stories: Narrative Theory and Children's Literature*, edited by Mike Cadden, 187–208. Lincoln: University of Nebraska Press, 2011.

——. *Power, Voice and Subjectivity in Literature for Young Readers*. London: Routledge, 2010.

Nixon, Cheryl L. *The Orphan in Eighteenth-Century Law and Literature: Estate, Blood, and Body*. Studies in Childhood, 1700 to the Present. London: Routledge, 2016.

Njemanze, Paul Obiyo Mbanaso. "Masculinity in the African Diaspora." *Journal of International Social Research* 6, no. 28 (2013): 222–227.

Nodelman, Perry. "Children's Literature as Women's Writing." *Children's Literature Association Quarterly* 13, no. 1 (1988): 31–34.

———. "Making Boys Appear: The Masculinity of Children's Fiction." In *Ways of Being Male: Representing Masculinities in Children's Literature and Film*, edited by John Stephens, 1–14. New York: Routledge, 2002.

Norton, Brian Michael. *Fiction and the Philosophy of Happiness: Ethical Inquiries in the Age of Enlightenment*. Lewisburg, PA: Bucknell University Press, 2012.

———. "The Moral in Phutatorius's Breeches: *Tristram Shandy* and the Limits of Stoic Ethics." *Eighteenth-Century Fiction* 184, no. 4 (2006): 405–423. http://dx.doi.org/10.1353/ecf.2006.0064.

Nussbaum, Martha. *The Monarchy of Fear: A Philosopher Looks at the Political Crisis*. New York: Simon & Schuster, 2018.

———. "The Professor of Parody: The Hip Defeatism of Judith Butler." *New Republic*, February 2, 1999. https://newrepublic.com/article/150687/professor-parody.

Oliphaunt, Samuel Grant. *Queer Questions and Ready Replies*. 2nd ed. Boston, 1887.

Olsen, Kristin. *Daily Life in the Eighteenth Century in England*. 2nd ed. Westport, CT: Greenwood, 2002.

O'Malley, Andrew. *Children's Literature, Popular Culture, and Robinson Crusoe*. London: Palgrave Macmillan, 2012.

———. "Crusoe's Children: *Robinson Crusoe* and the Culture of Childhood in the Eighteenth Century." In *The Child in British Literature: Literary Constructions of Childhood, Medieval to Contemporary*, edited by Adrienne E. Gavin, 87–100. New York: Palgrave Macmillan, 2012.

———, ed. *Literary Cultures and Eighteenth-Century Childhoods*. New York: Palgrave Macmillan, 2018.

Orgel, Stephen. *Impersonations: The Performance of Gender in Shakespeare's England*. Cambridge: Cambridge University Press, 1996.

Pace, Lisha. "Pierre Jaquet-Droz." History-Computer, December 6, 2022. http://history-computer.com/Dreamers/Jaquet-Droz.html.

Paley, William. *Natural Theology of Evidences of the Existence and Attributes of the Deity*. Philadelphia, 1802.

Panszczyk, Anna. "The 'Becoming' of Pinocchio: The Liminal Nature of Collodi's Boy-Toy." *Children's Literature* 44, no. 1 (2016): 192–218. http://muse.jhu.edu/article/619582.

Park, Julie. *The Self and It: Novel Objects in Eighteenth-Century England*. Stanford, CA: Stanford University Press, 2010.

Paster, Gail Kern. *The Body Embarrassed: Drama and the Discipline of Shame in Early Modern England*. Ithaca, NY: Cornell University Press, 1993.

Patterson, Craig. "Horrible Roberys, High-Way Men, and Murders: Defoe, Gay, Lillo, and the Popular Literature of Crime." PhD diss., University of Toronto, 1994.

Paul, Lissa. *The Children's Book Business: Lessons from the Long Eighteenth Century*. New York: Routledge, 2011.

Payne, Christiana. "Picturing Work." In *A Cultural History of Work in the Enlightenment*, edited by Ann Montenach and Deborah Simonton, 39–60. New York: Bloomsbury, 2020.

Payne, Dianne. "Children of the Poor in London: 1700–1780." PhD diss., University of Hertfordshire, 2008. https://pdfs.semanticscholar.org/56fb/8488a7fa38c356a87253ccc6f8719ae405eb.pdf.

Pepys, Samuel. "Monday, Sept 28, 1668." In *The Diary of Samuel Pepys*, vol. 9, edited by Robert Latham and William Matthews., 313–314. Berkeley: University of California Press, 2000.

———. *The Shorter Pepys*. Edited by Robert Latham. London: Penguin, 1985.

Percy, Carol. "Disciplining Women? Grammar, Gender, and Leisure in the Works of Ellenor Fenn (1743–1813)." *Historiographia Linguistica* 33, no. 1–2 (2006): 109–137. https://doi.org/https://doi.org/10.1075/hl.33.1.08per.

———. "Mid-century Grammars and Their Reception in the *Monthly Review* and the *Critical Review*." In *Grammars, Grammarians, and Grammar-Writing in Eighteenth-Century England*, edited by Ingrid Tieken-Boon van Ostade, 125–142. Berlin: Mouton De Gruyter, 2008.

———. "'Nice' Grammarians: Making Distinctions of Class, Character and Gender in Women's Fiction, 1750–1830." *Women's Writing* 23, no. 1 (2006): 9–32. https://doi.org/10.1080/09699082.2015.1103997.

———. "Paradigms Lost: Bishop Lowth and the 'Poetic Dialect' in His English Grammar." *Neophilologus* 81 (1997): 129–144.

Pettit, Alexander. "The Headwaters of Ooziness (Richardson the Polemicist)." In *New Contexts for Eighteenth-Century British Fiction*, edited by Christopher D. Johnson, 67–86. Newark: University of Delaware Press, 2011.

Phillips, George L. "The Abolition of Climbing Boys." *American Journal of Economics and Sociology* 9, no. 4 (1950): 445–462. www.jstor.org/stable/3483549.

Pickering, Samuel F., Jr. *John Locke and Children's Books in Eighteenth-Century England*. Knoxville: University of Tennessee Press, 1981.

Plumb, J. H. "The New World of Children in Eighteenth-Century Britain." *Past and Present* 67 (1975): 64–95.

Plutarch. *Lacaenarum Apophthegmata* [*Sayings of the Spartan Women*]. *Moralia*. Vol. 3. Translated by Frank Cole Babbitt. Loeb Classical Library. Cambridge, MA: Harvard University Press, 1931.

———. "The Life of Lycurgus." In *Plutarch's Lives*, vol. 1, translated by John Dryden, 83–126. Boston: Little, Brown, 1906. Online Library of Liberty. https://oll.libertyfund.org/titles/plutarch-plutarchs-lives-dryden-trans-vol-1.

Pointon, Marcia. *Brilliant Effects: A Cultural History of Gem Stones and Jewellery*. New Haven, CT: Yale University Press, 2009.

———. *Hanging the Head: Portraiture and Social Formation in England*. New Haven, CT: Yale University Press, 1993.

———. *Portrayal and the Search for Identity*. Chicago: University of Chicago Press, 2013.

Polanyi, Michael. *Personal Knowledge: Towards a Post-critical Philosophy*. 1968. Sussex: Psychology Press, 1998.

Pope, Alexander. *The Poems of Alexander Pope: A Reduced Version of the Twickenham Text*. Edited by John Butt. New Haven, CT: Yale University Press, 1963.

Porter, Roy. *Flesh in the Age of Reason*. London: Allen Lane / Penguin, 2003.

———. *London: A Social History*. Cambridge, MA: Harvard University Press, 1995.

Powell, Manushag N. *Performing Authorship in Eighteenth-Century Periodicals*. Lewisburg, PA: Bucknell University Press, 2012.

Pursell, Carroll. *From Playgrounds to PlayStation: The Interaction of Technology and Play*. Baltimore: Johns Hopkins University Press, 2015.

Rabb, Melinda Alliker. *Miniature and the English Imagination: Literature, Cognition, and Small Scale Culture, 1650–1765*. Cambridge: Cambridge University Press, 2019.

Rangaratnam, Sarah. "Girls' Voices of the Eighteenth Century: The Development of a Genre for Young Female Readers, 1740–1800." PhD diss., Wilfred Laurier University, 2018. https://scholars.wlu.ca/etd/2104.

Rauser, Amelia. *Caricature Unmasked: Irony, Authenticity, and Individualism in Eighteenth-Century English Prints*. Newark: University of Delaware Press, 2011.

Raven, James. *The Business of Books: Booksellers and the Book Trade*. New Haven, CT: Yale University Press, 2007.

———. *What Is the History of the Book? What Is History?* Cambridge: Polity, 2018.

Rawlings, Philip. *Drunks, Whores, and Idle Apprentices*. New York: Routledge, 1992.

Rawson, Claude, and Ian Higgins, eds. *The Essential Writings of Jonathan Swift*. London: Norton, 2010.

Reilly, Kara. *Automata and Mimesis on the Stage of Theatre History*. New York: Palgrave Macmillan, 2011.

Reimer, Mavis. "Traditions of the School Story." In *The Cambridge Companion to Children's Literature*, edited by M. O. Grenby and Andrea Immel, 209–225. Cambridge: Cambridge University Press, 2009.

Reimers, Rosalind. *Printers and Men of Capital: Philadelphia Book Publishers in the New Republic*. Philadelphia: University of Pennsylvania Press, 1996.

Reyk, William Van. "Educating Christian Men in the Eighteenth and Early Nineteenth Centuries: Public-School and Oxbridge Ideals." *Journal for Eighteenth-Century Studies* 32, no. 3 (2009): 425–437.

Richardson, J. A. *Slavery and Augustan Literature: Swift, Pope, Gay*. New York: Routledge, 2004.

Richardson, Samuel. *The Apprentice's Vade Mecum: or, Young Man's Pocket-Companion . . . The Whole Calculated for the Mutual Ease and Benefit Both of Master and Servant; and Recommended to the Serious Consideration of All Parents, &c. Who Have Children That They Design to Put Out Apprentice*. Dublin, 1734. ECCO, Gale doc. no. CB131332575.

———. *The History of Sir Charles Grandison*. Vol. 2 of 7. In *The Novels of Samuel Richardson*, edited by William Lyon Phelps. New York: Croscup & Sterling, 1902. Hathi Trust Digital Library. https://babel.hathitrust.org/cgi/pt?id=mdp.39015002714775.

———. *Pamela; or, Virtue Rewarded*. 1742. Vol. 4. London, 1785. ECCO, Gale doc. no. CW0115893630.

Riskin, Jessica, ed. *Genesis Redux: Essays in the History and Philosophy of Artificial Life*. Chicago: University of Chicago Press, 2007.

Rivers, Isabel. "Religion and Literature." In *The New Cambridge History of English Literature, 1660–1780*, edited by John Richetti, 445–470. Cambridge: Cambridge University Press, 2005.

Robinson, Elaine L. *Gulliver as Slave Trader: Racism Reviled by Jonathan Swift*. Jefferson, NC: MacFarland, 2006.

[Robinson, Mary] pseud. Horace Juvenal. *Modern Manners, a Poem in Two Cantos*. London, 1793. ECCO, Gale doc. no. CB132853188.

Rogers, Pat. *Grub Street: Studies in a Subculture*. New York: Harper & Row, 1972.

Rorabaugh, W. J. *The Craft Apprentice*. Oxford: Oxford University Press, 1988.

Rose, Jacqueline. *The Case of Peter Pan; or, The Impossibility of Children's Fiction*. 1984. Philadelphia: University of Pennsylvania Press, 1992.

Rothery, Mark, and Henry French, eds. *Making Men: The Formation of Elite Male Identities in England, 1660–1900*. Basingstoke: Palgrave, 2012.

———. *Man's Estate: Landed Gentry Masculinities, c.1660–1900*. Oxford: Oxford University Press, 2012.

Rousseau, Jean-Jacques. *Émile; or, On Education*. 1762. Translated by Allan Bloom. New York: Basic Books, 1979.

Rumbold, Valerie. "Textual Account." In *Meditation upon a Broomstick. The Cambridge Companion Edition of the Works of Jonathan Swift: Parodies, Hoaxes, Mock Treatises*, edited by Valerie Rumbold, 4–16. Cambridge: Cambridge University Press, 2013.

Ruwe, Donelle R. "Benevolent Brothers and Supervising Mothers: Ideology in the Children's Verses of Mary and Charles Lamb and Charlotte Smith." *Children's Literature* 25 (1997): 87–114.

Salzman, Paul. *English Prose Fiction, 1558–1700: A Critical History*. Oxford: Clarendon, 1985.

Sandoz, Louis. *Voyage de Pierre Jaquet-Droz à la cour du Roi d'Espagne, 1758–1759: d'après le Journal d'Abraham Louis Sandoz, son beau-père*. Geneva: Editions de la Baconnière, 1982.

Schaffer, Simon. *Mechanical Marvels: Clockwork Dreams*. Directed by Nic Stacey. First broadcast June 2013. BBC Four. https://www.youtube.com/watch?v=YAg66jrvpHA.

Scheuermann, Mona. *In Praise of Poverty: Hannah More Counters Thomas Paine and the Radical Threat*. Lexington: University Press of Kentucky, 2002.

Schillace, Brandy Lain. "Mother Machine: An 'Uncanny Valley' in the Eighteenth Century." *The Appendix* 1, no. 2 (2013). http://theappendix.net/issues/2013/4/mother-machine-an-uncanny-valley-in-the-eighteenth-century.

———. "'Reproducing' Custom: Mechanical Habits and Female Machines in Augustan Women's Education." *Feminist Formations* 25, no. 1 (2013): 111–137. https://doi.org/10.1353/ff.2013.0000.

Schott, Robin May, ed. *Feminist Interpretations of Immanuel Kant*. University Park: Pennsylvania State University Press, 1997.

Schultz, Ronald. "Printers' Devils: Decline of Apprenticeship in America." Review of *The Craft Apprentice: From Franklin to the Machine Age in America* by W. J. Rorabaugh. *Reviews in American History* 15, no. 2 (1987): 226–231.

Scott, John. *The School Boy's Sure Guide*. Edinburgh, 1774.

Segel, Elizabeth. "'As the Twig Is Bent...': Gender and Childhood Reading." In *Gender and Reading: Essays on Readers, Texts and Contexts*, edited by Elizabeth Flynn and Patrocinio Schweickart, 165–186. Baltimore: Johns Hopkins University Press, 1986.

———. "Domesticity and the Wide, Wide World." *Children's Literature* 8 (1980): 168–175. https://doi.org/10.1353/chl.0.0487.

Seidel, Michael. "Satire, Lampoon, Libel, Slander." In *The Cambridge Companion to Eighteenth-Century Literature, 1650–1750*, edited by Stephen Zwicker. Cambridge: Cambridge University Press, 1998.

———. "Systems Satire: Swift.com." In *The Cambridge History of English Literature, 1660–1780*, vol. 2: *Literary Genres: Adaptation and Reformation*, edited by John Richetti, 235–258. New Cambridge History of English Literature. Cambridge: Cambridge University Press, 2005. https://doi.org/10.1017/CHOL9780521781442.011.com.

Seidler, Victor J. *Transforming Masculinities: Men, Cultures, Bodies, Power, Sex and Love*. London: Routledge, 2006.

Seneca, Lucius Annaeus. *Epistles 66–92*. Translated by R. M. Gummere. Cambridge, MA: Harvard University Press, 1917. http://www.stoics.com/seneca_epistles_book_2.html.

Shakespeare, William. *As You Like It*. Edited by Juliet Dusinberre. Arden Shakespeare. London: Thomson Learning, 2006.

Shefrin, Jill, "'Make It a Pleasure and Not a Task': Educational Games for Children in Georgian England." *Princeton University Library Chronicle* 60, no. 2 (Winter 1999): 264–265.

Shelley, Mary. *Frankenstein; or, The Modern Prometheus*. 1818. Edited by D. L. Macdonald and Kathleen Scherf. Toronto: Broadview, 2012.

Shepherd, Alexandra. *Meanings of Manhood in Early Modern England*. Oxford: Oxford University Press, 2003.

Shesgreen, Sean. *Engravings by Hogarth: 101 Prints*. New York: Dover, 1974.

———. "Swift, Reynolds, and the Lower Orders." In Connery, *Representations of Swift*, 195–211.

Shoemaker, Robert. *Gender in English Society 1650–1850: The Emergence of Separate Spheres?* London: Longman, 1998.

———. "Male Honour and the Decline of Public Violence in Eighteenth-Century London." *Social History* 26, no. 2 (2001): 190–208.

Shore, Heather. *Artful Dodgers: Youth and Crime in Early Nineteenth-Century London.* Woodbridge: Royal Historical Society / Boydell Press, 1999.

Siena, Kevin. *Rotten Bodies: Class and Contagion in Eighteenth-Century Britain.* New Haven, CT: Yale University Press, 2019.

Simonton, Deborah. "Economy." In Foyster and Marten, *Cultural History of Childhood and Family*, 49–68.

———. *A History of European Women's Work: 1700 to the Present.* London: Routledge, 2002.

Simpson, A. E. *Masculinity and Control: The Prosecution of Sex Offenses in Eighteenth-Century London.* New York: New York University Press, 1984.

Sisk, Cheryl L., and Sheri A. Berenbaum, eds. "Puberty and Adolescence." Special issue of *Hormones & Behavior* 64, no. 2 (2013).

Slade, Paul. "The Death Hunters: British Broadsides" http://www.planetslade.com/broadside-ballads-1.html

Slagle, J. B. "Literary Activism: James Montgomery, Joanna Baillie, and the Plight of Britain's Chimney Sweeps." *Studies in Romanticism* 51, no. 1 (2012): 59–76.

Smart, Annie. "'Bonnes mères qui savent penser': Motherhood and a Boy's Education in Rousseau's *Émile* and Epinay's *Letters à mon fils.*" *New Perspectives on the Eighteenth Century* 3, no. 1 (Spring 2006): 21–31.

Smith, Chloe Wigston. "Clothes without Bodies: Objects, Humans, and the Marketplace in Eighteenth-Century It-Narratives and Trade Cards." Eighteenth-Century Fiction: Trades 23, no. 2 (Winter 2010–2011): 347–380.

Snell, K. D. M. *Annals of the Labouring Poor: Social Change and Agrarian England, 1660–1990.* Cambridge: Cambridge University Press, 2012.

Sober, Elliot. "Sex Ratio Theory, Ancient and Modern: An Eighteenth-Century Debate about Intelligent Design and the Development of Models in Evolutionary Biology." In Riskin, *Genesis Redux*, 131–162.

Sorenson, Janet. *The Grammar of Empire in Eighteenth-Century British Writing.* Cambridge: Cambridge University Press, 2000.

Staves, Susan. *A Literary History of Women's Writing in Britain, 1660–1789.* Cambridge: Cambridge University Press, 2006.

Steele, Richard. "No. 155—Tuesday, August 28, 1711." *The Spectator.* The Spectator Project: A Hypermedia Research Archive of Eighteenth-Century Periodicals, Rutgers University Library. http://www2.scc.rutgers.edu/spectator/text/august1711/no155.html.

Stein, Melissa N. "Unsexing the Race: Lynching, Castration and Racial Science." In *Measuring Manhood: Race and the Science of Masculinity, 1830–1934*, 217–250. Minneapolis: University of Minnesota Press, 2015.

Stephens, John, ed. *Ways of Being Male: Representing Masculinities in Children's Literature.* New York: Routledge, 2002.

Sterne, Laurence. *The Life and Opinions of Tristram Shandy, Gentleman.* 1759. Oxford: Oxford University Press, 2009.

Stevens, George Alexander. *The Celebrated Lecture on Heads: Which Has Been Exhibited Upwards of One Hundred Successive Nights, to Crouded Audiences, and Met with the Most Universal Applause.* London, 1765. ECCO, Gale doc. no. CW0107716211.

Stewart, Ethelbert. *A Documentary History of the Early Organization of Printers*. 1902. Charleston, SC: BiblioBazaar, 2008.
Stewart, Susan. *On Longing: Narratives of the Miniature, the Gigantic, the Souvenir, the Collection*. Baltimore: Johns Hopkins University Press, 1984.
Stoker, David. "Ellenor Fenn as 'Mrs. Teachwell' and 'Mrs. Lovechild': A Pioneer Late Eighteenth-Century Children's Writer, Educator, and Philanthropist." *Princeton University Library Chronicle* 68, no. 3 (Spring 2007): 817–850. https://doi.org/10.25290/prinunivlibrchro.68.3.0817.
———. "Establishing Lady Fenn's Canon." *Papers of the Bibliographical Society of America* 103, no. 1 (March 2009): 43–72.
Strachey, Lytton. *Eminent Victorians*. New York: Random House, 1933.
Strange, K. H. *The Climbing Boys: A Study of Sweeps' Apprentices, 1773–1875*. London: Allison and Busby, 1982.
Straub, Kristina. "Men from Boys: Cibber, Pope, and the Schoolboy." *Eighteenth Century* 32, no. 3 (1991): 219–239.
Swann, Marjorie. *Curiosities and Texts: The Culture of Collecting in Early Modern England*. Philadelphia: University of Pennsylvania Press, 2001.
Swift, Jonathan. "An Essay on Modern Education." *The Intelligencer* 9 (1732). In *Miscellanies in Prose and Verse by Dr. Swift*, vol. 7. London, 1742. ECCO, Gale doc. no. CW0116425524.
———. *Gulliver's Travels*. Oxford: Oxford University Press, 1998.
———. "A Letter of Advice to a Young Poet." In *The Works of Jonathan Swift . . . Containing Additional Letters, Tracts, and Poems*, vol. 9, 183–207. Edinburgh, 1824. http://books.google.ca/books?id=t9ViAAAAcAAJ.
———. "On the Poor Man's Contentment." In *The Prose Works of Jonathan Swift*, edited by Temple Scott, 202–210. London: George Bell and Sons, 1903.
———. *A Pamphlet Entitl'd Some Remarks on a Letter to the Seven Lords of the Committee Appointed to Examine Gregg* (1711). In *The Works of the Rev. Jonathan Swift*, vol. 5, edited by Thomas Sheridan et al., 373–400. London, 1801.
Tague, Ingrid H. *Animal Companions: Pets and Social Change in Eighteenth-Century Britain*. University Park: Pennsylvania State University Press, 2015.
Tarlow S., and Lowman E. Battell, eds. "Folk Beliefs and Popular Tales." In *Harnessing the Power of the Criminal Corpse* [Internet]. Cham (CH): Palgrave Macmillan; 2018. https://www.ncbi.nlm.nih.gov/books/NBK513556/. doi: 10.1007/978-3-319-77908-9_8.
Thomas, Keith. "History and Literature." Ernest Hughes Memorial Lecture, University College of Swansea, March 7, 1988.
Tikoff, Valentina K. "Education." In Foyster and Marten, *Cultural History of Childhood and Family*, 90–109.
Tobin, John J. *Third Biennial Report of the Bureau of Labor Statistics of California*. Sacramento, 1888. https://books.google.ca/books?id=_R8rAAAAYAAJ.
Tosh, John. *Manliness and Masculinities in Nineteenth-Century Britain: Essays on Gender, Family, and Empire*. London: Pearson Longman, 2005.
Trevor-Roper, Hugh. *The Crisis of the Seventeenth Century: Religion, the Reformation, and Social Change*. Indianapolis: Liberty Fund, 1968.
Tribunella, Eric. "Boyhood." In Nel and Paul, *Keywords for Children's Literature*, 22–25.
Turberville, A. S. *English Men and Manners in the Eighteenth Century*. New York: Oxford University Press, 1957.
Turner, David M., and Alun Withey. "Technologies of the Body: Polite Consumption and the Correction of Deformity in Eighteenth-Century England." *History* 99, no. 338 (2014): 775–796. https://doi.org/10.1111/1468-229X.12087.

Turner Smith, Charlotte. *What Is She? A Comedy in Five Acts*. London, 1799. ECCO, Gale doc. no. CW0114387051.

United Nations Human Rights Office of the High Commissioner. "Article 1." Convention on the Rights of the Child. https://www.ohchr.org/en/professionalinterest/pages/crc.aspx.

Van Der Walt, Thomas. "Librarianship." In *International Companion Encyclopedia of Children's Literature*, vol. 4, edited by Peter Hunt, 812–825. London: Routledge, 2004.

Verhoeven, W. M. "Politics for the People: Thomas Holcroft's Proto-Marxism." In *Reviewing Thomas Holcroft, 1745–1809: Essays on His Works and Life*, edited by A. A. Markley and Miriam L. Wallace, 197–217. London: Routledge, 2012.

Vincent, David. *Literature and Popular Culture, 1760–1914*. Cambridge: Cambridge University Press, 1989.

Voltaire, François-Marie Arouet de. *Philosophical Dictionary* (1764). In Kramnick, *Portable Enlightenment Reader*, 532–535.

Voskuhl, Adelheid. *Androids in the Enlightenment: Mechanics, Artisans, and Cultures of the Self*. Chicago: University of Chicago Press, 2013.

———. "Motions and Passions: Music-Playing Women Automata and the Culture of Affect in Late Eighteenth-Century Germany." In Riskin, *Genesis Redux*, 293–320.

Wahrman, Dror. *The Making of the Modern Self: Identity and Culture in Eighteenth-Century England*. New Haven, CT: Yale University Press, 2004.

Wakefield, Edward Gibbon. *Facts Relating to the Punishment of Death in the Metropolis*. London, 1831. https://books.google.ca/books?id=iGlBtAEACAAJ.

Wakefield, Patricia. *Juvenile Anecdotes, Founded on Facts*. London, 1795.

Walker, Garthine. *Crime, Gender and Social Order in Early Modern England*. Cambridge Studies in Early Modern British History. Cambridge: Cambridge University Press, 2003. https://doi.org/10.1017/CBO9780511496110.

Wall, Barbara. *The Narrator's Voice: The Dilemma of Children's Fiction*. London: Palgrave, 1991.

Wall, Cynthia. *The Prose of Things: Transformations of Description in the Eighteenth Century*. Chicago: University of Chicago Press, 2006.

Walle, Taylor. "'These Gentlemen's Ill Treatment of Our Mother Tongue': Female Grammarians and the Power of the Vernacular." *Tulsa Studies in Women's Literature* 35, no. 1 (2017): 17–43.

Waller, John. *The Real Oliver Twist: Robert Blincoe—A Life That Illuminates an Age*. London: Icon Books, 2005.

Wallis, Lucy. "Is 25 the New Cut-Off Point for Adulthood?" *BBC News*, September 23, 2013. https://www.bbc.com/news/magazine-24173194.

Wallis, Patrick, Cliff Webb, and Chris Minns. "Leaving Home and Entering Service: The Age of Apprenticeship in Early Modern London." *Continuity and Change* 23, no. 3 (2010). https://doi.org/10.1017/S0268416010000299.

Wall-Randell, Sarah. "Doctor Faustus and the Printer's Devil." *Studies in English Literature 1500–1900* 48, no. 2 (Spring 2008): 1–26.

Walmsley, Peter. "The Enlightenment Worker: An Introduction." *Eighteenth-Century Fiction* 23, no. 2 (Winter 2010–2011): 259–268.

Watkins, Emma. "The Case of George Fenby." *Crime History*, June 5, 2015. https://emmadwatkins.wordpress.com/2015/06/05/the-case-of-george-fenby/.

———. *Life Courses of Young Convicts Transported to Van Diemen's Land*. History of Crime, Deviance, and Punishment. London: Bloomsbury, 2020.

Watkins, Emma, and Barry Godfrey. *Criminal Children: Researching Juvenile Offenders 1820–1920*. South Yorkshire: Pen and Sword, 2018.

Watts, Isaac. *Divine Songs: Attempted in the Easy Language of Children.* London, 1715. http://www.gutenberg.org/cache/epub/13439/pg13439-images.html.

Weber, Harold. "The 'Garbage Heap' of Memory: At Play in Pope's Archives of Dulness." *Eighteenth-Century Studies* 33, no. 1 (1999): 1–19. https://doi.org/10.1353/ecs.1999.0060.

Weirex, Antoine. "The Christ Child Sweeping Monsters Out of the Believer's Heart." London: Wellcome Collection. https://wellcomecollection.org/works/dswp5x26.

Weisner, Merry E. *Early Modern Europe, 1450–1789.* Cambridge History of Europe. Cambridge: Cambridge University Press, 2013.

Wetmore, Alex. *Men of Feeling in Eighteenth-Century Literature: Touching Fiction.* New York: Palgrave Macmillan, 2013.

———. "Sympathy Machines: Men of Feeling and the Automaton." *Eighteenth-Century Studies* 43, no. 1 (Fall 2009): 37–54.

Williams, Julie Hedgepeth. *Three Not-So-Ordinary Joes: A Plantation Newspaperman, a Printer's Devil, an English Wit, and the Founding of Southern Literature.* Montgomery, AL: NewSouth Books, 2018.

Wise, M. Norton. "The Gender of Automata in Victorian Britain." In Riskin, *Genesis Redux*, 163–195.

Wollstonecraft, Mary. *A Vindication of the Rights of Woman.* 1792. Edited by Eileen Hunt Botting. New Haven, CT: Yale University Press, 2014.

Wood, Gillen D'Arcy. "Austen's Accomplishments: Music and the Modern Heroine." In *A Companion to Jane Austen*, edited by Claudia Johnson and Clara Tuite, 366–376. Hoboken, NJ: John Wiley, 2011.

Wood, Marcus. "Black Bodies and Satiric Limits in the Long Eighteenth Century." In *The Satiric Eye: Forms of Satire in the Romantic Period*, edited by Steven Edward Jones, 55–70. Basingstoke: Palgrave Macmillan, 2003.

———. *Slavery, Empathy, and Pornography.* Oxford: Oxford University Press, 2002.

Woodley, Sophia. "'Oh Miserable and Most Ruinous Measure': The Debate between Private and Public Education in Britain, 1760–1800." In *Educating the Child in Enlightenment Britain: Beliefs, Cultures, Practices*, edited by Mary Hilton and Jill Shefrin, 21–39. Farnham: Ashgate, 2009.

Wordsworth, William. "Illustrated Books and Newspapers" (1846). In *Last Poems, 1821–1850*, edited by Jared Curtis, 405–406. Cornell Wordsworth. Ithaca, NY: Cornell University Press, 1999.

———. "Preface to *Lyrical Ballads*" (1801). In *English Romantic Writers*, 2nd ed., edited by David Perkins, 423–434. Orlando, FL: Harcourt Brace, 1995.

Zipes, Jack. *Sticks and Stones: The Troublesome Success of Children's Literature from Slovenly Peter to Harry Potter.* New York: Routledge, 2002.

Zwierlein, Anne-Julia. "'Poor Negro-Girl,' 'Little Black Boy': Constructing Childhood in Eighteenth-Century Slave Narratives, Abolitionist Propaganda and Postcolonial Novels." *Zeitschrift fur Anglistik und Amerikanistik: A Quarterly of Language, Literature and Culture* 52, no. 2 (2004): 107–120.

Index

(Italicized page numbers indicate photographs and figures)

abolition, 14, 57, 87–89, 96–97, 176n21. *See also* slavery
Addison, Joseph. See *Spectator, The*
Andrew, Lucy, 124, 188n119
apprenticeship, 32, 107–112, 126, 142–143, 155n61, 175n8, 182n14, 190n29, 193n86; benefits of, 130; blurred limits of boyhood, 132; duration of indenture, 190n27; failed, 107, 117, 120, 130; failure of apprenticeship itself, 142; prohibition against marrying, 132; subversive and riotous apprentices, 111–112; work without apprenticeship, 193n75. *See also* boyhood and labor; child labor
Arbuthnot, John, 1, 12, 14, 15, 104, 151n1, 192n64. *See also* Pope, Alexander: "Epistle to Arbuthnot"
Aristotle's Masterpiece, 127
Ash, 165n87
Astell, Mary, 8–9, 44
automata, 2, 63, 65, 72, 73, 77–78, 115; as androids, 64, 67, 68, 71, 74; anxiety over, 70, 77, 79; automation of toys, 80–81; embodied meanings, 67, 68; exclusivity and luxury, 26, 73; and gender, 9, 11, 66–67, 77; hoaxes, 174n111; Manuel of Turin's automata, 72; mechanical ingenuity, 67; mechanical spectacle, 63, 65–68, 79; mechanization of labor, 73; and mimesis, 65, 71; miniaturization, 74, 78; as performing dolls, 64, 72, 73, 80, 92; as puppets, 66, 173n93, 174n109; as tools, 69, 148; and the uncanny, 66, 67, 74; unnatural reproduction, 77, 79.

See also Jaquet-Droz, Pierre, and his automata

Backscheider, Paula, 8, 58, 154n37
Baillie, Joanna, 98
Barbauld, Anna Laetitia, 20, 21, 33, 161n21; and abolitionism, 57; *Lessons for Children*, 20, 50; "What is Education," 165n80
Barber, Mary, 24, 166n93
Beccaria, Cesare, 122
Ben-Amos, Ilana Krausman, 86, 176n17
Benedict, Barbara, 170n15, 170n35
Bible, the, 32, 133, 156n15, 163n56, 164n69, 168n127; and the sacrifice of boys, 11; schoolboys tested on gospel knowledge, 163n41
Bindman, David, 90, 177n40
Blackstone, William, 110, 114
Blake, William, 14, 100; "The Chimney Sweeper," 87, 89, 93, 96, 98; "The Little Black Boy," 87, 89; pathos, pity, and outrage, 96, 98
Bogel, Fredric V., 92, 93, 178n49
Bordo, Susan, 5, 11–12
Boswell, James, 32, 140, 163n56, 186n90
boy, biological, 5, 13, 16; the male generative "tool," 27; and puberty, 3
boy, definitions of, 3, 152n16; according to Johnson, 23, 43; boy as manikin, 22, 63, 72; "boy" as military subordinate, 23; "boy" as pejorative term, 4, 10, 23; "boyhood" an arbitrary word, 3–4, 146, 154n47; flawed, inchoate, or incomplete man, 10, 23, 142; a male child, 4–5, 23; a man

boy (cont.)
  under construction, 1, 8, 10, 16, 24, 194n92; not a girl, 5, 23; not yet arrived at puberty, 3, 4
boy as beast: class connotations, 74, 152n16; cruelty and savagery, 51–52; lacking civilization, 19, 26, 49–50; in *Tristram Shandy*, 19, 26, 82, 147
boy as tool, 7–13, 62, 63; animate machine, 109
boy becoming a schoolboy, 31, 46; "schoolboy" as pejorative term, 41; school systems and world systems, 46
boyhood, construction of, 12, 153n27; abjection, 11, 57; boys' and mens' history elided, 1–2, 7; "boy" stands for whatever is needed, 8; class and economic value, 2, 3, 10, 11, 27, 33, 74; from domain of women to that of men, 26, 46, 49; excluded from personhood, 10, 11; from frock to breeches, 4, 13, 16–18, 19, 20, 23–24, 28, 75, 147, 157n37; laboring, 53, 86, 94, 119, 124, 133; limited male privilege, 8, 10, 26, 58; as male "other," 9; male privilege vs. subaltern class, 8, 105, 143; middle- and upper-class childhood, 13, 63, 68, 101, 109, 121, 124; over-indulgence, 164n72; privilege and education, 32; temporary and changing, 22; trope for writing woman, 57; when adulthood is achieved, 3, 13, 46, 147
boyhood, literary representations of, 2, 13, 14; Blake, 14; Defoe, 10; Dickens, 108–109; exemplary and cautionary uses, 2–3, 13, 14; Lillo, 109; Plutarch, 36. *See also* Fenn, Ellenor; Holland, John; Sterne, Laurence: *Tristram Shandy*
boyhood and criminality, 24, 104, 112, 113, 117, 124, 141, 188n114; begging, 110, 119, 120; broadsheets, 105, 107, 109, 121; cautionary tales, 114, 116, 117, 119, 120, 123, 124, 186n75; construction of juvenile delinquency, 123; conventional morality, 182n10; death sentences and retributive justice, 113, 119; discourse of child sacrifice, 123, 124; execution narratives, 115–116, 123, 186n75; failed apprenticeship, 107, 117, 120; glamorization of crime, 188n119; literacy and gentry anxiety, 120, 124; severity of punishments, 14, 104, 109, 113, 188n116; thief-catchers, 11; the uses of pathos, 106–107; the uses of sensationalism, 115
boyhood and education, 31; accounting for time, 50–51, 109, 121, 188n106; bad or idle companions, 41–43, 46; conduit to masculine authority, 58; developing good conduct, 31, 42; developing reason, 45; good habits not trifles, 47; habits of constancy, 70; improper indulgence, 44, 46; need to recognize vice, 43; parent educators, 33, 47–48; penmanship, 68–69; reading, 50; role of maternal educator, 33–34, 54–57, 59, 167n105
boyhood and education, in schools: Blue Coat schools, 32; charity schools, 160nn4–5; corporal punishment, 44; dame schools, 32; emphasis on classics, 32; Eton, 28, 32, 34, 45, 163n58; Felsted Grammar School, 161n25; grammar (private) schools, 32–34, 39, 44, 82, 130, 160n6; Harrow, 35, 38, 43, 45; harsh and indifferent teaching, 34; homosociality, 50, 58; obstinacy and rebellion, 44–45; preparation for school, 48; public schools, 32, 34, 39, 42, 61, 62, 163n41, 163n58; riots at schools, 44, 45, 50, 163n58; Rugby, 34, 163n58; separation from home and family, 34–35, 47; teaching grammar, 32, 52–53, 58, 70, 165n87; teaching spelling, 32; universities, 32, 56, 72; Westminster, 32, 34; Winchester, 34, 163–164n58
boyhood and labor: conflation of child and tools of trade, 14; industry vs. idleness, 110, 121, 187n103; juvenile crime as labor, 105; surplus of boy labor, 14, 142; uncivilized laboring boy as beast, 156n16; work with family, 32. *See also* apprenticeship; chimney sweeps and apprentices (climbing boys); printers' devil
Boyle, Robert, 91, 177n44
breeches, 29, 30, 31, 63, 65, 156n10, 159n67; the anatomical "tool" underneath, 25, 156n10; becoming a boy, 13, 84; breeching, 12, 16, 17, 19–20, 24, 68, 166n93; and concealment, 16; and corporal punishment, 24; creates and marks identity, 19; from frock to breeches, 4, 8, 13, 16, 24, 28, 32, 149; jests and puns, 27; as a normative act, 30; problems caused by, 19–20, 24–25, 27, 149; as rite of passage, 13, 17–18, 20, 23, 33, 49, 156n10; signifying maleness, 11, 17, 22, 26, 28; and transformative power, 16, 21–22, 27; unbreeched boys, 25, 27; vs. unfettered freedom, 27; women wearing, 7, 26, 30, 156n9
Breitenberg, Mark, 17–18
Brown, Bill, 11, 66, 124
Bunyan, John, *The Pilgrim's Progress*, 32, 39, 178n53
Butler, Judith, 5, 78–79, 114, 153nn19–20, 174n98

INDEX

Campbell, Robert, *The London Tradesman*, 113, 194n2
capital punishment, 109, 111–115, 118–119, 121, 123, 124, 184nn52–53, 185n65, 187n91; Beccaria and, 122; fictitious, 3, 14, 107, 113–115, 117; number of capital offenses, 110, 183n30; Voltaire and, 117, 121
Carretta, Vincent, 97, 177n27
Castle, Terry, 18, 67, 156n13, 170n22, 173n82, 174n109
Catnach, James, 107, 182n8
Caxton, William, 128, 138
child labor, 3, 12, 14, 90, 122, 129, 142–144, 148, 155n61, 176n17, 193n76; coal mining, 176n16; dangers of, 8, 85, 87; farm labor, 154n52, 193n75; and industrialization, 86, 143, 176n20. *See also* chimney sweeps and apprentices (climbing boys)
children, 155n1; books for, 20–23, 36–37, 50, 79, 120–121, 153n27, 187n98, 187n104; Bunyan's *Pilgrim's Progress*, 32; children naturally good or wicked, 47; constraint and confinement, 43; domestic education, 47; health, sickness, mortality, 34, 51, 162n35, 188n106, and military readiness, 22; primers, 32; separation of classes, 156n19; the spoiled child, 45, 47, 49, 60, 164n72; studies of, 2
chimney sweeps and apprentices (climbing boys): Act for the Better Regulation of Chimney Sweepers and Their Apprentices, 86, 176n21; apprenticeship, 85, 87; begging, 111; Blake's two versions of "The Chimney Sweeper," 87, 89, 96; *The Chimney-Sweeper's Friend*, 88, 95, 177n32; depicted as subhuman, 89–90; and highwayman Jack Hall, 111; Kingsley's *The Water Babies*, 84, 184n60; markedness of sweeps, 182n12; the most miserable of children, 85; paradoxes of waste, 87, 91; parallel between Black boys and sweeps, 89, 96–99; presumption of dishonesty, 99, 112; reform campaigns, 100, 175n7, 176n15, 177n32; Society for Superseding the Necessity of Climbing Boys, 183n39; "sold" into the trade, 87, 99; subversive and riotous, 111; and tropes of Blackness, servitude, suffering, 85, 87–89, 90, 97
chimney sweeps' tools: brushes (switches), 84, 85, 90, 178n46; child as tool (human brush, animate machine, 85, 99, 100; the "old Scotch way," 180n92; soot cloth (tuggy), 85
chimney sweeps' working conditions: beatings, 180n82; blindness, 86; burns and lacerations, 86, 176n13; cancer, 86, 95, 175n11; deformed spine and knees, 86; mortality, 85, 91, 95; naked work, 84–85, 179n68; suffocation, 86, 95
Clark, Beverly Lyon, 56
climbing boys. *See* chimney sweeps and apprentices (climbing boys)
clothing and construction of identity, 16, 18, 19, 132, 159n73; and the female body, 17, 23; gendered rites of passage, 17, 20; as metaphor, 16; power to contort and disfigure, 27; women in men's clothing, 7, 26, 30, 134, 156n9. *See also* breeches; Sterne, Laurence: *Tristram Shandy*
Collodi, Carlo, *Pinocchio*, 80–81
Corbould, Richard, and Samuel Springsguth, *Juvenile Philosophy*, 47, 121
Cox, James, 66, 68, 73, 169n3, 172n67
Cullingford, Benita, 86, 178n46
Cunningham, Hugh, 2, 86
Curious Facts and Anecdotes, 131
Curll, Edmund, 130, 137, 177n44, 192n69

Darnton, Robert, 129, 189nn11–12
Davies, Rebecca, 33, 47, 167n105, 168n124
Defoe, Daniel, 10, 108, 138; accounting for time, 50–51; *Colonel Jack*, 23; commerce and self-reliance, 10–11; *The Complete English Tradesman*, 126, 138, 182n14; independence and order, 50; *Robinson Crusoe*, 10–11, 50–51
Demers, Patricia, 34, 71
Descartes, René, 79
Dickens, Charles, 86, 108–109, 122, 130, 184n54
Diderot, Denis, 10, 129, 140
Douglas, Aileen, 68, 71, 75
Douthwaite, Julia, 73–74, 77
"Dreadful Life and Confessions of a Boy," 125; bad companions, 113; brought up to lie and steal, 105, 107; criminalized child's body, 115; death sentences (amended), 114, 115, 116, 118–119; desperate poverty, 108; ephemeral and disposable, 119, 124; and Hogarth, 112, 121; imprisonment and hard labor, 113; ingratitude and corruption, 109; judgment of malice, 114; juvenile crime as labor, 105; King, Thomas, 105–109, 116, 117–119; laboring children as threat to society, 119, 124; London as nursery of crime, 184n50; Mitchel, Thomas, 107; murder and execution as entertainment, 116; post-sentencing confession, 106, 114; public execution as terror, 115–116; transportation, 15, 113–114, 183n31, 184n54, 185n66; vagrancy, 110, 113; violence, 183n29; whipping, 118. *See also* boyhood and criminality
Dunton, John, 27, 159n66

Edgeworth, Maria, 35, 57
education: balancing sense of self and community, 41; as despotism, 42; domestic education, 47, 49, 54–55; educational amusements, 62–63; Enlightenment ideals about, 72; exclusion of girls from schools, 56; gendered differences in, 34, 35; the maternal educator, 33–34, 54–57, 59, 167n105; pedagogy, 4, 12, 70; reason replaces ignorance, 194n2; school as little world, 46–47; science and expanded curriculum, 62. *See also* boyhood and education; Fenn, Ellenor
Eisenstein, Elizabeth, 128, 137, 144–145, 189n5, 189n11, 192n56
Encyclopédie, l', 10, 129, 140
Enlightenment, the, 63, 146; and anatomy, 78; boyhood, 13–14, 72, 74, 146; and childhood, 3, 72, 155n1; and the *Encyclopédie*, 138; ideals about education, age, and gender, 71, 100, 155n1; literary and political publics, 69; mechanical arts, 11, 64, 65, 70, 129, 140; mechanical metaphors, 79, 100; and technology, 73, 74, 77–79, 138; and work, 51, 148. *See also* Diderot, Denis; Kant, Immanuel; Rousseau, Jean-Jacques
Equiano, Olaudah, 88, 97–99
Erickson, Robert A., 26, 28, 158n58

females and femininity: abuse of the female body, 5, 67; achieving adulthood, 23, 190n27; age of consent, 152n7; the Bluestockings, 57, 98; boys' escape from female domination, 49–50; and children's literature, 57, 59; clothing and, 24, 30; domesticity, 165n79; female authorship, 54, 55, 57, 59; female education, 47, 57, 161n27, 164n70, 171n39; female intellectual power, 49; feminine authority, 58; femininity constructed and performed, 5; feminization of boys, 5, 21, 48; feminized objects, objectified feminine, 67; and labor, 9, 47, 110; and the maternal as innate, 55; mercurial nature, 170n22; objectification of women, 9; response to patriarchy, 57; and reproduction, 60, 79; women aestheticized as ornamental, 8–9. *See also* girls
feminism, 5, 6, 148, 154n37; proto-feminists, 9
Fenn, Ellenor: *The Art of Teaching in Sport*, 56, 166n95; authorial personae, 38, 54–56, 59, 60, 61, 166n90; and Barbauld, Anna Laetitia, 33; *The Child's Grammar*, 53, 166n90; *Cobwebs to Catch Flies*, 34, 54; and the difficulty of learning, 40;

education and socialization, 12, 41, 42, 43; *The Female Guardian*, 55, 165n87; habits of learning, 40, 53; and Locke, John, 34, 40, 45, 61; *The Mother's Grammar*, 53; and Plutarch, 37–38, 41, 50, 52, 58–61; pseudonyms, 33, 59, 166n90; *The Rational Dame*, 55, 104; and the Rational Moralists, 34, 47; and Richardson, Samuel, 38, 49, 60, 132; role of maternal educator, 33–34, 54–57, 59, 167n105; *School Occurrences*, 35, 42, 59, 164n70; *Set of Toys*, 55, 166n95. *See also School Dialogues, for Boys* (Fenn)
Fielding, Henry: *Tom Jones*, 43; *Tom Thumb*, 76, 173n88; *Tragedy of Tragedies*, 76
Fielding, Sarah, 155n60, 167n105
Fielding, Sir John, 117, 119
Fletcher, Anthony, 2, 16, 25, 49
Flint, Christopher, 132, 137, 139, 192n56, 192n64
Foote, Samuel, *The Devil on Two Sticks*, 134–135
Foucault, Michel, 116–117, 167n110, 172n74
Foyster, Elizabeth E., 2, 4, 6, 147
Franklin, Benjamin, 135, 141
French, Henry, and Mark Rothery, 2, 35, 40–41, 69, 163n58, 190n22
French Revolution, 120, 123
Frere, William, 37, 161n25
Freud, Sigmund, 75, 173n82, 174n109. *See also* uncanny, the
Fulford, Tim, 88, 100

Gatrell, V.A.C., 107, 111, 113, 115, 116, 182n10, 185n65
Gee, Sophie, 87, 101, 136
gender, 9, 21, 24, 72; and the age of adulthood, 3, 21; ambiguity of conception, 19; biological gender, 16; constructed and performed, 5, 6, 16, 17, 26; criminality gendered as male, 112, 185n63; cross-dressing, 18, 26; division of labor, 147; "female" as whatever is needed, 8; Galenic single-body vs. essentialist two-body model, 6; gendered automata, 66–67; gendered discrepancy in punishment, 115; and gender identity, 5–6; and grammar and, 53; growing into, 17–22; homosociality, 13, 49, 57, 136; infants as gender neutral, 25, 158n47; male and female birth rates, 1; male privilege, 10; performance of, 5, 11, 17–18; and premature death, 1, 12; and violence, 185n61; women in breeches, 26, 30; young children as gender-neutral, 26
Gentleman's Magazine, 132, 135, 156n13, 190n23

INDEX

Gibbon, Edward, 38, 76
Gilbert, Sandra, 78
girls, 76; and abjection, 11; boarding school for girls, 35, 40, 42; clothing, 23, 24, 67, 157n37; criminality, 185n63; girls' schoolbooks, 161n27; limited access to education, 2, 56; literacy, 167n116; needlework and penmanship, 68, 171n39; supposedly weak, 21
Godwin, William, 43, 165n80
Gollapudi, Aparna, 10, 113–114, 184n51
grammar, 53, 131; books, 33, 52–53, 59, 69, 165n87, 166n95; and maternal educator, 52–55, 59, 166n90; metonymy of education, 53; and separation of the sexes, 53; social utility of, 53, 58–59; teaching and learning, 33, 39, 52–53, 58, 70, 165n86, 166n99; universal vs. vernacular, 53. *See also* boyhood and education, in schools: grammar (private) schools; Fenn, Ellenor
Greenwood, Emma L., 129, 131, 132, 141, 192n58, 192n73, 193n86
Grenby, Matthew, 2, 42, 120–121, 156n19, 187n98
Grub Street, 136, 137, 188n3, 191n48
Gubar, Susan, 78
Gutenberg, Johannes, 128, 138

Hanway, Jonas, 86, 118, 176n21, 186n88
Head, Francis Bond, *The Printer's Devil*, 128, 131, 133
Heidegger, Martin, 66, 79, 80
Hilton, Mary, 63, 75, 120, 167n107, 188n115
Hitchcock, Tim, 86, 108, 110, 111, 113
Hobbes, Thomas, 65
Hogarth, William, 112, 121, 164n69, 184n46, 185n64, 186n76, 187n104
Holcroft, Thomas, *The School for Arrogance*, 117, 133, 188nn2–3
Holland, John, 99, 109
Horne, Jackie, 2, 35, 167n116
Howard, John, 110
Hughes, Thomas, *Tom Brown's Schooldays*, 35, 162n38, 168n128
Humphries, Jane, 2, 176n16, 176n20, 193n76

Immel, Andrea, 33, 34, 166n95, 187n104

Janeway, James, 162n35, 168n127
Jaquet-Droz, Henri, 64, 78
Jaquet-Droz, Pierre, and his automata, 13, 78, 169n3, 169n12, 171n37, 171n54; *the Draughtsman*, 64, 67, 69, 73, 170n28; genius, mechanical, 65, 66, 76, 79; genius, natural vs. artificial, 71; inventor as father, 79; and luxury, 65, 72, 73; materialism and vitalism, 66, 77; mimetic mechanization, 65, 70–71, 73; miniaturization, 74, 76; the Musician, 64, 77, 78, 170n28; reception of, 169nn11–12; spatial liminality, 72; as spectacle, 66, 79, 82, 127, 169n11; and the uncanny, 66, 68, 74. *See also* automata
Jaquet-Droz, Pierre, the Writer *(L'écrivain)*, 13, 63–69, 73, 83, 124, 148; civilizing power of literacy, 71; embodiment of boyhood, 13, 63, 67, 70; imitation, 70–71; line between thing and life, 66; materialized memory, 169n5; penmanship, 68–70; performs gender, age, and social status, 65, 67, 68, 84; privileges class, education, gender, 67, 71, 73; reifies social order, 70; reverse engineers writing, 71; and temporality, 78; and the written word, 68–71, 75, 79
Jerrold, Douglas William, 129, 138, 189n10
Johnson, Samuel: Boswell's *Life of Johnson*, 32, 140, 163n56, 186n90; happiness as a schoolboy, 32, 163n56; on print and printers' devils, 128, 149, 189n6, 194n96; *The Rambler*, 128–129, 139; on reading novels, 133
Johnson, Samuel, *Dictionary of the English Language*, 17, 33, 53, 152n18, 177n40, 186n90; "boy," 3–5, 10, 22–23, 27, 163n46; "boyhood," 44, 144, 146; "breeches," 156n9; "devil," 189n6, 194n96; "tool," 63, 93

Kahn, Coppélia, 38, 161n28
Kang, Minsoo, 66, 77, 169n10, 174n102
Kant, Immanuel, 144, 149; on Enlightenment, 146–147; humans not means for others' ends, 7, 31, 100, 144–145; on relation to objects, 66; on women, 8, 195n5
Karras, Ruth Mazo, 2, 24
Kaufman-Osborn, Timothy, 67, 79
Kidd, Kenneth, 2
Kilner, Dorothy, 57, 79–80, 174n110
Kim, James, 6, 7, 157n45, 158n51
King, Peter, 109, 113, 119, 183n29, 185n63, 188n114
King, Thomas (boy criminal), 105–122; and apprenticeship, 105, 109, 111; as cautionary tale, 106, 112, 115–124; didactic deterrent, 117; fictional delinquent boy, 106, 116, 118, 119, 123; a fungible boy, 124; matter-of-fact tone vs. pathos, 106, 107, 109; severity of penalty, 113, 114
King, Thomas A., 61, 147
Kingsley, Charles, *The Water Babies*, 84, 184n60

labor, 3, 72, 97, 118, 127, 138, 172n74; damage and danger, 12, 14, 15, 85, 86, 96–98, 101, 104, 147, 179n70; and delinquency, 105, 110, 112; laboring classes, 10–11, 14, 73, 119, 133, 156n16; owning one's own labor, 10, 138; and schooling, 160n2; threat to propertied classes, 119; trade societies, 193n89; and violence, 14; wage labor, 141; and the workhouse, 113. *See also* apprenticeship; boyhood and labor; child labor

Lamb, Charles, 23; and chimney-sweepers, 83–84, 89, 98–100, 177n32; climbing boys compared to enslaved Africans, 89, 99; "The Praise of Chimney-Sweepers," 87, 98–99, 101

Lamb, Charles and Mary: "The Butterfly," 181n3; "Going into Breeches," 20–23, 28

Lamont, Claire, 88, 176n15

Lane, Joan, 86, 108, 149

Leschot, Jean-Frédéric, 64, 78

Lerer, Seth, 11, 68

Lillo, George, *The London Merchant*, 109

Linebaugh, Peter, 109, 112, 175n8

Locke, John, 34, 168n124; against corporal punishment, 45, 74; against crying, 161n19; against over-indulgence, 23, 45; and apprenticeship, 97, 108; children and military readiness, 22; children not learning machines, 171n44; *Essay on Human Understanding*, 4, 11, 23, 70; *Some Thoughts Concerning Education*, 4, 24, 34, 40, 45, 61, 71, 84, 156n19, 160n13, 161n19, 182n17; Sterne and, 24, 149; *Two Treatises of Government*, 10, 194n2

Lowman, Emma Battle, 115

Magubane, Zine, 97–99

Manutius, Aldus, 130

Marshall, John, 9, 161n21

masculinity, 17, 108, 147–148, 154n36, 161n28, 162n38; abject, 58, 93; anatomical masculinity, 19, 25, 75, 95, 148; anxiety of, 17, 19, 27; the male body, 19, 75, 95, 148, 153n32; the male body, damage and support, 148–149; masculinity studies, 2, 4–5; and the penis/phallus, 4, 16, 28, 75, 157n45, 158n59; the penis/phallus, damage to, 19, 148–149, 153n32; the penis/phallus, as the "tool," 12, 13, 16, 25; phallic symbolism of the pen, 57, 75, 78

masculinity and boyhood, 1, 6–7, 14, 44, 93, 148; boys usefully abject, 11, 89, 131, 139; innate masculinity, 146; privilege of maleness, 8, 10, 12, 23, 58, 105, 143, 146, 148; and Roman virtue, 38; and violence, 6, 44, 104, 183n29, 184n48, 185n61

mechanical philosophy: the clockwork universe, 79, 169n10; human body as machine, 11, 65, 100

mechanism, 65, 70, 148; enlightened mechanization, 73; in fiction and verse, 67; the guillotine, 73; the mechanical arts, 140–143; mechanistic language, 65; mechanization of boys, 8, 100, 133, 171n44; mechanization of labor, 73, 142, 143, 172n74. *See also* automata; Jaquet-Droz, Pierre, and his automata; tools

Meditation upon a Broomstick, A (Swift), 14, 85, 91–95, 100; a begrimed cleaning tool, 91; climbing boys and sweeps, 91, 93; destroyed by use, 91–92; human-object and human-human relations, 92; purification and its discontents, 92, 93

Mettrie, Julien Offray La, 65, 77

midwifery, 26, 158n58, 159n66

Milton, John, 78, 137, 162n31

miniaturization, 26, 75; automata, 13, 64, 74, 78; boy as miniature hero, 21, 26; Tom Thumb, 76; writing, 69

Montgomery, James, 88–89, 95, 98, 100, 101, 177n32, 179n70

More, Charles, 142, 193n86

More, Hannah, 57, 120, 133, 187n100

Moxon, Joseph, *Mechanick Exercises*, 11, 129, 189n9, 192n64

Müller, Anja, 2, 5, 89, 111, 112, 165n85, 184n46

Myers, Mitzi, 55, 57

Navest, Karlijn, 33, 165n87

Nelson, Victoria, 173n93, 174n109

Newbery, John, 40, 50, 76, 120; and Hogarth, 187n104; *Little Pretty Pocket-Book*, 40, 115; *The Newtonian System of Philosophy*, 75; *Tom Thumb's Exhibition*, 76

Newgate Prison, 14, 114, 116, 119, 135; the *Newgate Calendar*, 127, 184n57; "A Visit to Newgate," 121

Newton, Hannah, 3, 162n35

Nichols, John, 132, 190n23

Nicholson, George, 19–20, 24, 25, 149, 157n20

Nodelman, Perry, 57, 153n27

Norton, Brian Michael, 26, 27, 155n4

Nussbaum, Martha, 5, 153n20

object theory, 25–26, 66, 79–81, 91, 124; object (*It*) narratives, 170n20

Old Bailey, the, 105–107, 114, 118, 121, 135, 184n53; death sentences for children, 113, 114, 123, 187n91

O'Malley, Andrew, 2, 39, 50–51, 165n79, 185n64

INDEX

Park, Julie, 25–26, 59, 66–67, 70, 92, 169n14, 173n93

patriarchal culture, 2, 9, 147, 148; feminine writing responding to, 57; male monopoly of literary prestige, 56; male vs. female intellectual ability, 49; masculinity and class structure, 6; and representation of male bodies, 11, 148; woman signifier of male other, 9

Patterson, Craig, 109, 114

Paul, Lissa, 33–34

Payne, Dianne, 3, 13, 84, 152n7

Pepys, Samuel, 81, 85

Percy, Carol, 33, 48, 53, 56, 59, 166n95

Plumb, J. H., 39, 72

Plutarch, 37, 50, 161n26; exemplary and cautionary figures, 37, 41, 59, Fenn and, 37–38, 50, 58, 60, 61; *Lives*, 38, 50, 59, 161n26, 162nn30–31, 167n116; *Morals*, 38, 60, 168n125

Pointon, Marcia, 66–68, 73, 108, 158n47, 169nn3–4, 169n6, 170n32, 172n62, 174n104

Pope, Alexander, 46, 71, 136, 159n72, 192n69; *The Dunciad*, 58, 136, 137, 191n36, 191n52; "Epistle to Arbuthnot," 7, 135–136, 172n59, 192n63; *Essay on Criticism*, 143; *Essay on Man*, 42; feminized objects, objectified feminine, 67; "The Rape of the Lock", 9, 67; schoolboy as trope, 58; and the Scriblerians, 192n64; on women, 9, 181n101

Porter, Roy, 100, 148, 155n61

poverty: abject poor as Other, 90; Act of Settlement, 182n19; begging, 110, 119, 120, 186n90; climbing boys' destitution, 99; hunger, 1, 84, 101; impoverished boys and crime, 14, 105, 107, 118, 124, 147; and injustice, 97; and literacy, 120, 133; the "respectable poor," 86; starvation, 186n90. *See also* child labor; vagrancy

Powell, Manushag, 137–139

print: as a black art, 128; broadsides, 105, 107, 109, 114–116, 117, 119, 120, 121, 123, 124; compositors, 131, 189; Edwards, *On the Distressed State of the Printing Trade*, 142; an elite trade, 132, 190n26; irrevocability of print, 128–129; libel and sedition, 140, 190n31; presswork, vacuity, and error, 127, 171n40; the rise of, 130, 145, 189n5; the Stationer's Guild, 130, 132; tropes of the printing house, 129–130, 135, 139, 189n9; vehicle for noble and ignoble ideas, 133

printers' devil, 14, 129, 144–145; ambivalence about, 144–145; as apprentices, 127, 129–132, 134, 189n8; blackened by trade, 126, 129, 134; "black gentry," 137; communicating reproach to overdue authors, 139; as compositor, 189n11; as copy-lifter, 139; as drudge, 129, 131, 138; an error in print, 128, 143; as flies, 129–130, 135, 139, 192n64; intersection between art and trade, 127; learning advanced mechanical art, 140; lying, 135; as member of literary profession, 131, 132, 138; mischief, 189n6; mischief ensuing from reading, 133; in mobs, 133–134; other definitions of, 192n64, 193n75, 194n96; print and criminality, 136, 137; and secrecy, 134; as tool of the press, 126; upward mobility, 126, 131, 141; and vanity printing, 135–136; the youngest apprentice or subordinate worker, 129, 191n37

printers' devils, literary representations of, 133–135; Foote's *The Devil on Two Sticks*, 134–135, 139; Head's *The Printer's Devil*, 128, 131, 133; Holcroft's *The School for Arrogance*, 127, 133; Jerrold's "Sketches of the English," 129, 138; *Memoirs of a Printer's Devil*, 131, 133, 140; Stevens's *The Celebrated Lecture on Heads*, 134, 191n36

puppets, 59, 63, 81, 92; and androids and automata, 66, 172n74, 173n93. *See also* Fenn, Ellenor

racism: the Black body, 14, 85, 96, 97, 180n95; depictions of Others, 90, 177n40; justifications for slavery, 87, 97; pejorative term "boy," 22, 194n92; privilege vs. subalternity, 10, 105

racist stereotypes: Black proclivity for vice, 181n96; and apprentices, 85, 90, 130; tropes of servitude and suffering, 85; suffering inflicted on basis of, 96–97

reform: An Act for the Better Regulation of Chimney Sweepers and Their Apprentices, 86, 176n21; An Act for the Better Regulation of the Parish Poor Children, 190n27; appeals based on Christian charity, 100; campaign against cruelty to animals, 165n85, 181n3, 184n46; change effected slowly, 101; humans not means for others' ends, 7, 31, 100, 144–145; the legal-penal system, 110, 123; Society for Superseding the Necessity of Climbing Boys, 183n39; Society for the Improvement of Prison Discipline and for the Reformation of Juvenile Offenders, 188n114

Reilly, Kara, 65, 68, 73, 170n28

Reimer, Mavis, 46, 162n38

rhetoric, 11, 56, 57, 61, 85, 98, 108, 123, 126, 134; cautionary rhetoric, 38, 107, 115, 124; depreciative possibilities of, 58; and education, 36, 57, 104; maleness and efficacy, 27, 159n72; the play-mother, 55–56, 60; and the printing house, 126, 135, 139–140, 189n9; rhetorical questions, 55–56, 101. *See also* Fenn, Ellenor

rhetorical tropes and figures, 9, 13, 28, 55, 57–59, 63, 139; blackness, 85, 96, 99, 126; boy as tool, 10, 14, 18; as cheats, 58; the climbing boy, 85, 91, 98, 104; the climbing boy as slave, 99; the criminal boy, 104, 115, 124; the criminal corpse, 114–115; the fallen apprentice, 110; idleness, 187n103; infernal machinery, 133; the school as a little world, 46–47; the schoolboy, 13, 35, 58, 63, 92, 160n5; urban filth, 136; wasted paper and ink, 127, 188n3; women, 8, 9, 58, 167n118

Richardson, Samuel, 120, 132; *Apprentice's Vade Mecum*, 108, 132, 190n29, 190n29; *Clarissa*, 190n29; *Pamela*, 38, 59–60, 168n124; *Sir Charles Grandison*, 49, 164n72

Riskin, Jessica, 65, 151n1
Robinson, Mary, 134
Rogers, Pat, 136, 188n3, 191n36
Rorabaugh, W. J., 130, 142
Rothery, Mark. *See* French, Henry, and Mark Rothery
Rousseau, Jean-Jacques, 146, 160n1, 171n58; *Émile*, 4, 34, 51, 71, 72, 84, 114
Rowlandson, Thomas, *The Trades of London*, 89–91, 99, 102, 177n40
Ruwe, Donelle R., 20, 21, 24

Saint Paul, 4, 47
Schaffer, Simon, 66–67, 70, 71, 80, 169n5
School Dialogues, for Boys (Fenn): bad boys and moral contagion, 42, 48, 61; characters, cautionary (puppets), 13, 37, 38, 41–43, 46, 48, 51, 56, 58, 92, 120; characters, exemplary (phantoms), 13, 34, 37, 38, 40, 42, 43, 46, 51, 56, 58, 59; combatting vanity and pride, 40, 41; as conduct book, 34, 40; control of emotions and of the purse, 41; developing good character, 36, 40–43; dialogue form, 36–39; intended audience, 34, 36–37, 54, 164n68; rhetorically constructed schoolboys, 13, 36, 57–59, 63, 92; sententious good boys, 46–47; stoicism and self-mastery, 36; vice as weakness, 41

Segel, Elizabeth, 36, 49, 50, 164n73
Seidel, Michael, 92, 96

sentiment and sensibility, 52, 87, 89, 98, 100, 101, 182n10; and campaigns against injustice, 87, 98–99; feminized, 69; pathos and maternal sensibility, 106; sentimentalizing childhood, 112, 138; unsentimentality, 100, 111. *See also* Sterne, Laurence

servants, 10, 72, 139, 156n19, 172n67, 179n56; Black servants, 89, 90; "boy" pejorative term for, 4, 126, 132; depravity and laziness of, 108, 146; girls and women, 110; and literacy, 121, 133; as property, 61, 147; runaway, 187n95

sexuality and generation, 25, 53, 167n110, 179n70; ambivalence, 58; anxiety about, 77; asexuality, 58, 156n13; conception, gestation, childbirth, 6, 19, 26–28, 77, 78; heteronormativity, 6; homosexuality, 155n8, 168n128; masturbation, 20; sexual interference, 20, 168nn128–129; sexual maturity, 132; spermism, 156n18; transvestism, 156n13; women in breeches, 7, 26, 30, 156n9; women used for procreation, 9

Shaftesbury, Anthony Ashley Cooper, 7th Earl of, 100, 176n21
Shakespeare, William, 42, 55
Shelley, Mary, *Frankenstein*, 77, 78, 162n31, 174n102
Shepherd, Alexandra, 2, 5, 147
Shesgreen, Sean, 94
Shoemaker, Robert, 40, 183n29
Simonton, Deborah, 51, 108, 147, 176n17
slavery, 10, 42, 130, 187n95; abolition, 14, 57, 87–90, 96–97, 176n21; anti-slavery poetry, 57, 89; blackness fungible, 98; "boy" pejorative term for enslaved male, 4, 126; 152n16; compared with climbing boys and printers' devils, 88, 94, 98–99, 109, 131; compared with gender relations, 95; disposability, 11; enslaved people as tools of empire, 99; incomplete manhood, 10; persons as property, 61, 147; racialized justification for, 87, 97; satire and, 180n95; in Sparta, 37, 59–61; suffering as spectacle, 97, 99; transatlantic slave trade, 85, 87, 97, 98. *See also* Equiano, Olaudah

Smith, Chloe Wigston, 170n20
Sorenson, Janet, 53, 90
Southey, Robert, 24, 76
Spectator, The, 53, 80
Steele, Richard. *See Spectator, The*
Sterne, Laurence: body as soul's clothing, 26; breeches in, 13, 16–17, 26, 156n11, 158n49, 158n54, 159n73; and Burton's *Anatomy of Melancholy*, 28; and Dunton, 159n66; fear of Tristram looking like a

beast, 18–19, 25, 50, 84, 149, 156n16; and Locke, 23, 149; masculinity, 27; phallic authority vs. effeminacy, 157n45; the Phutatorius episode, 17, 27, 155n4, 191n53; and publishing, 16, 30, 135, 158n49, 158n49; *Sentimental Journey*, 67; *Tristram Shandy*, 13, 16–28, 155n4, 158n51; Tristram's penis damaged, 19, 28, 156n14; "True Shandeism," 25
Stevens, George Alexander, *The Celebrated Lecture on Heads*, 134, 191n36
Stewart, Susan, 72, 73
Stoker, David, 33, 161n25, 166n92
Strange, K. H., 97, 175n11
Straub, Kristina, 58
Swift, Jonathan, 9, 66, 85, 99; compassion and justice, 100; "A Description of a City Shower," 94; "A Description of the Morning," 92, 94; "An Essay on Modern Education," 44; *Gulliver's Travels*, 92, 94–97; "The Lady's Dressing Room," 92; "A Letter of Advice to a Young Poet," 94; *A Modest Proposal*, 96, 101, 123; *Remarks on a Letter to the Seven Lords*, 8, 93, 153n35; and the Scriblerians, 136, 192n64. See also *Meditation upon a Broomstick, A*

Tarlow, Sarah, 115
Tom Thumb: and anthropomorphic dildo poetry, 173n88; Fielding's *Tom Thumb* and *Tragedy of Tragedies*, 76; *Tom Thumb's Exhibition*, 76–77
tools, 8, 11, 94, 119, 122, 159n72; animals tools for humans, 156n16; automata, 80, 148; automata as tools of empire, 68, 69; the boy as tool, 7–14, 62, 63, 84, 85, 92, 100, 112, 124, 126, 129, 140; boy conflated with tools of his trade, 14; boy destroyed through use, 91–92; boy manipulated by others, 42, 84, 104, 124; enslaved people tools of empire, 99; objects without agency, 7, 9, 10, 12; the pen, 65, 69, 70, 80, 84; prosthetic, 148–149; strategies for survival, 50, 52; sweeps tools of domestic England, 99; tool, the male generative organ, 12, 13, 16, 20, 25, 27, 28; tool, a mechanical implement, 62, 84; tool, a pickpocket, 186n84; tool, an "unskilful or incompetent worker," 143; tool, a weapon, 104; tool, a wretch acting at another's command, 7, 84; tools of the state, 22; vs. instrument, 8
Tribunella, Eric, 4, 10, 22, 43, 105, 142, 143, 154n47, 175n117
Trimmer, Sarah, 57, 165n79
Tyburn, 109, 111, 112, 116, 121, 186n76

uncanny, the (*unheimlich*), 90, 173n83, 174n102, 174n110; and automata, 65, 67, 68, 75, 80, 174n109; and object narratives, 170n20

vagrancy, 110–111, 113, 116, 183n31
Vaucanson, Jacques de, 68, 77
vitalism, 25, 77
Voltaire, 117, 121
Voskuhl, Adelheid, 65, 67, 69, 169n11

Wall, Barbara, 37, 161n22
Walle, Taylor, 57, 166n99
Waller, John, 109, 188n106
Wall-Randell, Sarah, 128, 166n99
Watkins, Emma, 114, 185n66
Watts, Isaac, "Against Idleness and Mischief," 51, 110, 122
Wetmore, Alex, 65, 67
Wise, M. Norton, 67
Wollstonecraft, Mary, 9, 42–43, 57, 76
Wood, Marcus, 89, 180n95
Wordsworth, William, 143, 171n40

Zipes, Jack, 80, 161n22
Zwierlein, Anne-Julia, 87, 180n87

About the Author

Chantel Lavoie is a professor in the Department of English, Culture, and Communication at the Royal Military College of Canada. Her first monograph was *Collecting Women: Poetry and Lives, 1700–1770*. She has published widely on women writers, children's literature, and boyhood. She has also published three collections of verse, *Where the Terror Lies, Serve the Sorrowing World with Joy,* and *This Is about Angels, Women, and Men*. She lives in Kingston, Ontario.